chino and

the dance

of the

butterfly

Dana Tai Soon Burgess

CHINO
and the
DANCE
of the
BUTTERFLY
a memoir

University of New Mexico Press Albuquerque

ISBN 978-0-8263-6426-5 (paper)
ISBN 978-0-8263-6427-2 (electronic)

Library of Congress Control Number: 2022937719

Founded in 1889, the University of New Mexico sits on the
traditional homelands of the Pueblo of Sandia. The original
peoples of New Mexico—Pueblo, Navajo, and Apache—
since time immemorial have deep connections to the land
and have made significant contributions to the broader
community statewide. We honor the land itself and those
who remain stewards of this land throughout the generations
and also acknowledge our committed relationship to
Indigenous peoples. We gratefully recognize our history.

COVER ILLUSTRATION
Dancer Dana Tai Soon Burgess in Helix, 1998, Washington,
   DC photo by Mary Noble Ours
Wing Analisa Hegyesi | istockphoto.com

DESIGNED BY Mindy Basinger Hill

COMPOSED IN 11.35/14 pt Arno Pro

FOR JAMESON

CONTENTS

ACKNOWLEDGMENTS

I would like to acknowledge the generations of dancers, designers, artists, curators, historians, arts administrators, educators, and friends with whom I have had the pleasure of working and from whom I have learned so much.

Special thanks to the following individuals: Alicia Adams, Shahab Albahar, Nora Amin, Lily Arikawa, Deborah Hofmann-Asimov, Christin Arthur, Joan Ayap, Claire-Solène Bečka, Judith Bennahum, Kristina Berger, PhD, Mary Bisbee-Beek, Kaia Black, Jaya Bond, Richard Bott, Anna Kang Burgess, Ian Tai Kyung Burgess, Joseph James Burgess Jr., Marie Southwell Burgess, Patch Canada, Alan Cariaso, Johann Ibañez Casosul, Kay Casstevens, Josue Castilleja, Ian Ceccarelli, Helen Chason, Patty Chu, Polly Craft, Helen Craft, Sarah Craft, Jann Darsie, Bianca DeLille, Christine Doyle, John Dreyfus, Mary Eccles, Denise Edwards, Pamela Egnew, Jameson Freeman, Jefferson Freeman, Cary Frieze, Cary Fuller, Asher and Mati Gelman, Susie and Michael Gelman, Ailes Gilmore, Derek Gordon, Laurel Gray, Judy Greenberg, Carl Gudenius, Ken Hakuta, Sarah Halzack, Connie Lin Fink-Hammack, Eric Hampton, Sidney Hampton, Judy Hansen, Liz Harter, Amy Henderson, Dedi Liem Gunawan Hickory and Dr. Wayne Hickory, HIRO, Miya Hisaka, Richard Hoagland, Nicole Hollander, Terry Hong, Erick Hosaka, Bill and Jill Hudock, and Lester Hyman.

Also, George Jackson, Luke Jackson, Julie Jacobson, Sigrid Johannesdóttir, Michael Kaiser, Hio Voon Kang, Soon Kuen Kang, Joshua Kaufman, Sarah Kaufman, Sharon Khan, Michiko Kitsmiller, Bonnie Kogod, Alan M. Kriegsman, Ellen Kwatnoski, Berkley Lane, Valentina Lebret, Marcia Lim, Aaron Mancus, Laura McDonald, Elise McHugh, Patricia Michaels, Felipe Oyarzun Moltedo, John Neumeier, Isamu Noguchi, Fay Nguyen, Makio Nishida, Miyako Nitadori, Judith Viggers Nordin, Katia Norri, Mary Noble Ours, Eser Ozdeger, Alvaro Palau, Thomas Pallas, Timothy Parrott, Valerie Peña, Carol Penn, Carla Perlo,

Jennifer Predock-Linnell, Kristine Purrington, Jay Reilly, Sheri Rosenfeld, Kim Sajet, Deborah Sams, Ben Sanders, Pete Sanders, Daniel Schuman, Norma Schwartz, Sueraya Shaheen, Olga Shimazaki, Saturo Shimazaki, Aleny Serna, Anne Sidney, Leigh Slaughter, Steve Slaughter, Kelly Moss Southall, Anatol Steck, Jalal Shalahuddin, Toshiko Takaezu, George and Brad Takei, Jan Tievsky, Jennifer Tipton, Leonardo Giron Torres, Adolfo Matto Traverso, "Tati" Maria Del Carmen Valle-Riestra, Tim Wengerd, Maida Withers, Yang-Ro Yoon, Fernando Zamora, Steven Zatarga, Barbara Zelon, and Fengxue Zhang.

Many thanks also to the following: Arts Club of Washington, Bloomberg Philanthropies, Dallas Morse Coors Foundation, Dedi Liem Gunawan Hickory Legacy Fund, Dana Tai Soon Burgess Dance Company Board of Directors, Georgetown Day School, The George Washington University, JBG Smith, Microsoft, Morningstar Foundation, the National Portrait Gallery, Share Fund, US Department of State, and the University of New Mexico Dance Program.

preface SANTA FE, THE CITY DIFFERENT

I come from Santa Fe.

Known as "the City Different," Santa Fe was founded in 1610 as a Spanish colony. It has a long and complex history that remains visible and visceral today. Santa Fe is the oldest state capital in America and has a wealth of knowledge and traditions from several cultures. The art, the churn, and the identity tensions of Santa Fe in the 1970s and 1980s defined my youth. This was a time of new challenges between forces of history and gentrification. Ralph Lauren's Santa Fe Collection hit worldwide fashion runways during this era, shining a spotlight on a city that is more than four hundred years old.

As I reflect on my childhood years, what surfaces for me so powerfully are the historic adobes, the desert vistas, the vendors of native jewelry in front of the Palace of the Governors, and the lone flamenco dancer practicing footwork on a side street. In the midst of my own cultural and sexual confusion, and the experiences of day-to-day prejudice and poverty, there was also the rich leavening of paintings, and possibilities. My life was beautifully sculpted here in a confluence of dance and visual arts.

Santa Fe informed the start of my artistic journey, one that has taken me all over the world from my current home base of Washington, DC. I'll tell you all about it.

chino and
the dance
of the
butterfly

My Korean great-grandparents and grandmother arrived together at the Waialua Sugar Company plantation on Oahu, Hawaii, January 13, 1903, among the first Korean immigrants to what was then an American territory. They were fleeing starvation in Seoul, a city under a failing monarchy that seven years later would be annexed by Japan. The *RMS Gaelic*, owned by the Occidental and Oriental Shipping Company, carried 102 Koreans on that trip, all bound for Hawaiian plantations: fifty-six men, twenty-one women, and twenty-five children. Methodist missionaries acted as brokers—intermediaries between God and plantation—who promised safe passage to a new life. The indentured worker families signed contracts that bound most of them powerlessly to the owners of sugar and pineapple plantations of Hawaii for generations. These were much like miner contracts that tied workers to a controlled economy that made it virtually impossible to pay off debts, let alone save money. They and other workers picked sugar cane and pineapples, oversaw the counts of pineapple shipping crates sent to the mainland, cooked for fieldworkers, and did laundry.

My grandfather, Soon Kuen Kang, arrived in 1904 on the *SS Manchuria* when he was nine years old. He taught himself English, a skill that led to him being promoted to a coveted position as plantation foreman. He was granted the use of a brown horse and proudly rode through the fields checking on the crops and productivity. Only five of his seven children reached adulthood. Not having access to simple medical facilities, one died of appendicitis and another of influenza. My grandfather's ingenuity and thrift allowed him to fracture what seemed an unbreakable bondage. When he was fifty-eight and the plantation system was dismantled, he was able to purchase a home for his family on Royal Palm Drive. This road is part of the original winding driveway that once led to the Del Monte Plantation Estate. The house still stands, under the original towering palm trees, and my uncle Marvin lives there with his wife Joyce, a Japanese *Nisei* (a second-generation

Japanese American). In the backyard there stands a giant old lychee tree that my grandmother planted; it is surrounded by the remains of a lush lily garden from which she long ago nurtured and then sold two-foot stems each Easter and Memorial Day to augment the family income.

From the time I was a toddler to the age of thirteen when I attended my grandfather's funeral, I made a handful of summer visits to Hawaii. I loved to visit with my grandmother, Hio Voon Kang. I remember Grandma in her late seventies and early eighties. She was under five feet tall with muscular brown arms and legs leathered from a life spent under the unrelenting plantation sun, her face framed by thick tortoise shell glasses and haloed by short gray hair in a perm. I often studied her bow-legged arthritic steps as she descended the back stairs (backward, so as not to fall) to her garden where she would squat deeply down to tend lettuce and pull up turnips. She was blind in her right eye, and I learned that for me to be seen at all, I had to stand on the left side of her field of vision. As a three-year-old child on the *RMS Gaelic*, Grandma had been savagely attacked by a teenage boy; he hit her face with a metal tobacco pipe and severed the muscles in her eye. I felt that Grandma and I were connected by a mutual sense of traumatic displacement, each born into a harsh world of bullies in the midst of cultural calamity, one that made us rely on sensation over words for survival. But as much as that, I think, I was always closely noting the deliberate calibrations of her movement on those steps; the distinct gestures, slow and sure; the many coordinated steps that were unmistakably hers—a body language clearer than words. Hers were among the first steps that registered with me as the potential of what movement alone could signify. Grandma's dance.

Grandma didn't speak much, only Hawaiian pidgin: a mishmash of the languages that circulated among plantation workers—Hawaiian, English, Portuguese, Korean, Chinese, and Japanese. She called me Tai Soon, my given Korean name, which means "great serenity of the family." "Tai Soon, help Halmeoni [Grandma in Korean], chop da daikon [turnip in Japanese], make kimchi, mahwah [hot and spicy in Korean]." I enjoyed deciphering her words and swiftly learned her gestural language. A quick flutter of her fingertips pointing downward combined with an up and down head nod meant "come here for a hug." A gentle all-over caress of my head meant that she was intrigued by the shifting layers of color in my biracial hair with its deep red highlights that shone in the Hawaiian rays. A quick horizontal flash of her forefinger and thumb to the palm of the other hand meant she wanted me to thread a sewing needle so she could resume work on the finishing touches of one of her muumuus made from large tropical flower print yardages. Grandma's hugs held no pretense or hesitation, and they were often accompanied by a surprise gift that she would pull down from a shelf above her sewing machine: a green-eyed Korean dancing doll dressed in yellow silk, an Antonio y Cleopatra cigar box filled with hundreds of old buttons, a handmade pouch containing a *gogok* (a smooth Korean jade stone in the shape of an animal claw). From Grandma I learned that we all can translate the language of touch and gesture. Universal expressions of the body transcend spoken and written communication.

My mother, Anna Kang, attended a single room schoolhouse, barefoot, with twenty other children until she went to a high school outside of the plantation. She has told me that up to that time, the only child in shoes was the son of the Japanese schoolteacher because they lived in the paved city, Honolulu. Each Christmas, every plantation child-worker was given one gift, out of the "beneficence"—as they were reminded—of the plantation owners. Once Mom received a Shirley Temple doll—its painted eyes, golden ringlets, and cherub-cheeked waxen Caucasian features in the likeness of that Hollywood child movie star—and another year a little beaded purse that now, completely tattered, sits in her jewelry box as a memento of a past that she survived.

When Mom was eleven, she saw plumes of smoke rise from Pearl Harbor on December 7, 1941, and dodged the bullets of low-flying Japanese Zeros—the white planes of Kamikazes that wielded iconic insignias of the rising sun on their wings. After the bombing, Mom would live under martial law and carry a gas mask to school. In the evenings the family would close their black-out curtains and my mom and her sisters would pass their lockdown by playing a Korean card game called *Hwatu* or "battle of the flowers." In the fields from age thirteen to eighteen, Mom picked pineapples under the blinding sun and carried fifty-pound bags of the jagged-skin spiky fruits out of the fields on her back. Only her scarred, gnarled hands tell her distant past. Of her hands, she told me, "The leaves of pineapples are knives that can cut through a glove or blind the uncovered eye." To this day, Mom doesn't eat pineapple.

When not in the fields, she worked with her sisters, Alice and Annie, for their mother's laundry business. Mom stirred fabrics in giant vats of soapy water and then lifted and wrung out each water-heavy garment to dry. She then steamed, ironed, and starched them. She told me that once, she lost her balance and fell headfirst into a deep full vat. My auntie Annie pulled her out. Auntie Alice came running to assist and pounded her back, forcing water from her lungs until she could breathe again. She has never mentioned any regrets or remorse over a childhood subsumed by physical labor. The Kang sisters are themselves the remnants of a bygone era.

In high school, Mom revealed an inclination toward art, drawing island fauna and turning clay pots on a wheel. The ability to see and pursue beauty even in the midst of hardship defines her. Encouraged by a scholarship, she pursued a degree in art at the University of Hawaii. She was the first in the Kang family to receive a bachelor's degree, and then also a master's degree in studio art. In 1950, Mom became the first in her family to reach the American mainland because she was one of four Asian American women from Hawaii to attend the prestigious Cranbrook Academy of Art in Bloomfield Hills, Michigan. She submitted a simple portfolio, —photos of her ceramics, sketches, and paintings. Her sisters pooled their funds to pay for her graduate tuition and expenses because her father didn't believe that women needed a formal degree, let alone two. Cranbrook was then an anomaly, an experimental 319-acre incubator of midcentury modernism and American abstract expressionism. Founded in 1922, Cranbrook was the outgrowth of the curricular vision of Finnish architect Eliel Saarinen and his wife, textile designer Loja Saarinen. Cranbrook produced unencumbered designers with a craftsman's ability to create across media, from ceramics and painting to weaving and architecture. It begat an American art movement in which my mother was wholly immersed. The Hawaiian cadre included Anna Kang, Alice Kagawa, and Ernestine Murai, all textile designers, and ceramicist Toshiko Takaezu. Sadly, Ernestine passed away in her twenties from liver cancer.

Now ninety-two, Anna Kang Burgess is among the last survivors of the harsh Hawaiian corporate plantations. To this day, she maintains an upright figure of elegance and grace. I continue to emulate her posture and to consider it an inherited family trait. She also continues to make ink drawings and paper collages every day. She is deeply private in her creative process, obsessive, and often spends hours standing over her art table to piece together abstract forms that serve as anagrams to her interiority. I have inherited this genetic predisposition to obsessive creativity. She is my muse.

My father, Joseph James Burgess Jr., was the son of an Irish American father and German American mother, both from immigrant families who lived in Albany, New York. Their marriage ended in divorce within a year. In childhood, he flourished in painting classes. Dad received his undergraduate degree from Hamilton College in Clinton, New York, and then during WWII was trained by the Navy as an intelligence officer with a specialty in Chinese language. He attended the Military Language Intelligence Center in Colorado and was stationed in Washington, DC, during the war as one of a handful of officers able to translate messages from Chinese intelligence. This skill added to his portfolio of fluency in German, French, and English. Only after his death did I more fully understand the importance of his military assignments, the translation and decoding of secret Chinese messages for the United States.

After the war he attended Yale University on the GI Bill receiving a master's degree in what was then called Oriental Studies. There he was recruited to be a US intelligence agent. He told me that during that time he received a phone call from his former kindergarten teacher, quite out of the blue, to let him know several "G-Men" had visited her, in an exhaustive background check seeking to learn what sort of youngster he had been back then. Dad declined the invitation to join the clandestine ranks. He knew his life would never be his own if he accepted. Instead, he attended Pratt Institute of Design in Brooklyn, New York, earning credits that he transferred to Cranbrook Academy of Art for a second master's degree in studio art. There he met Mom. They married in 1959 in a Unitarian Church in Michigan that supported their interracial marriage. At the time he was director of the DeWaters Art Center in Flint, Michigan. My elder brother, Ian, was born in Flint in 1961.

My parents decided to explore the United States through their art, not worrying about long-term plans or settling down. They worked at the Cleveland Institute of Art for a year, then headed west. While teaching at Arizona State University, my father learned that academia and art making don't always mix. Academics often lock horns in dysfunctional turf wars in the pursuit of tenure. In his words, "Academia wages the biggest battles for the smallest fiefdoms." Soon enough, Mom and Dad left university teaching for good. When I asked Mom if moving so often in her life was a hardship, she said, "We were a team, so we would just pack up and go when he deeply felt it was time." Mom and Dad next exchanged landlocked academia for Carmel Valley, California, where they were entranced by the landscape and inspired to produce and sell their art at their own small gallery. They found a spot on Del Fino Place and opened their gallery, which they called Origins. They spent a lifelong journey of artmaking together until his death at the age of ninety in 2014.

two MONARCHS

I was born in Carmel, California, on February 26, 1968. The innocence of America was serially shredded that year with the assassinations of Dr. Martin Luther King Jr. and Senator Robert F. Kennedy, as well as the daily images on the evening news of the body bags being unloaded at airports, American soldiers killed in Vietnam. It was a time of sorrow and anger, protest and peace signs. But by Christmas Eve, NASA's Apollo 8, the first crewed spacecraft to orbit the moon, drew our collective thoughts beyond the gravity of troubles on Earth.

It is the often-repeated story that as a baby I cried inconsolably, as if I knew the world into which I had just been born held no security. Right before my *Baek-il*—a Korean celebration of an infant's one hundredth day of life—my exhausted mother took me to the doctor and insisted that I had colic. The Baek-il traditionally celebrates an infant's ability to overcome the earliest hurdles of sickness. But because I cried instead of slept and clung insatiably to her, she worried about how needful I was. In desperation for even a short break, she would resort to just placing me on the floor to fend for myself for brief intervals. I was too much for her then, and perhaps I sensed that and tested it. She was thirty-nine years old and faced the responsibilities of a surprise newborn who had arrived seven years after his brother. The pediatrician assured Mom that I didn't have colic, but that I was hungry and needed more breast-feeding and touch. So ever after she traced gentle strokes on my back with her fingers, as if it was a canvas, and rubbed my feet, as if I were her clay on the potter's wheel. She willed, molded, and coaxed me into an early independence. She had me crawling at five months, standing at eight months, and walking by my tenth, well ahead of the average child.

Mother would take me outside to the patio in front of their rented red wood cottage, unlatch me from her body, and have me hold onto the lip of a large circular planter abloom with wildflowers. In this way, I could do wobbly laps by myself until exhausted. When I at last wearily plopped to the ground, my mom would return from some-where beyond my line of sight and gently scoop me up and place me on the floor next to her weaving loom in her studio. Content, I would doze off to the rhythm of a shuttle and beater. Some infants had mobiles. My mother's six-foot loom towering over me was mine.

Although only five feet tall and ninety pounds, my mother's ability to throttle a rug into existence on that loom, before my eyes, was magical, powerful. Years later I came to think of her as the beautiful mythical Arachne, the spiderlike weaver with jet black hair in a bun, high cheekbones, cat glasses that accentuated her eye shape, and translucent pale skin. I can still remember how I longed for her attention, but I knew it would come and even when: at the point that she felt she had arrived at a creative stopping point. I took my toddler security from this, confident that her full attention would be mine soon. Mom, at her loom, and me, with her. This was my story. From lengths of yarn evolved full rugs and wall hangings that she would then adorn by hand with feathers and found objects, readying them for sale in the gallery. And those finished textiles did indeed sell, and the money was used to pay the rent.

My father, now a painter, was at their gallery during the day and my brother, Ian, was at school. My craving for movement and growing confidence and self-sufficiency, my appetites for attention and companionship and stimulation, so deeply sated in this one-on-one luxurious unique engagement with and witnessing of my mother, ultimately allowed me to sleep through the nights. My body grew stronger, and my unstable steps steadied.

My earliest memory of happiness is of an event that occurred when I was two years old. I had mastered doing my heel, toe, step, heel, toe, step toddle around the planter and could let go of its round rim to peer inside, with full focus on the wildflowers. My mother left me outside with the family rescue mongrel, Liliuokalani. Lili, as we called her, was a Border Collie mix who had but one family member—me—to herd. There at the planter, I spied a single monarch butterfly as it landed on a purple cone flower. This orange and black creature tentatively tip-toed, like me, stepping and then gliding over the petals, barely bouncing, wings softly waving up and down, nose probing, into each bloom. It appeared so fragile that I held my breath so as not to blow or startle this gentle—what was it?—this living silent other. I didn't even reach out to touch it. I just stared. I briefly looked up at the sky and was startled to see many more butterflies, just like this one, circling and hovering in the air, each floating on its flapping wings in an erratic path but not bumping into one another. They too descended upon the cosmos, daisies, and lavender, gently caressing them.

They were oblivious to enormous me. Much later I would learn that this was their coaxing of the nourishment they took from their sweet nectar. Our planter was a smorgasbord. The air filled with more monarchs, a dozen; a dozen became hundreds. I toppled over from the weight of my own head on my young neck, cocked back at the sky, —but I did not injure myself and I did not cry. Far from it. I righted myself and sat on the red bricks in the midst of the annual migration south of the monarch butterflies, in brilliant show, flashes of orange and black capes. Squinting upward, the sun was covered in moving silhouettes, and in my memory even now, decades later, I am able to see all this again, to feel the impact, as if it were yesterday, the small, winged creatures flashing mini eclipses against the sun. The sky filled with thousands of butterflies, fluttering valiantly, playfully, they surrounded me, dancing in the air, suspended and then landing on my hair, arms, and clothes like inquisitive fairies. They tickled and teased, clung to me, kissing me, exploring me as they had the flowers. I was rapturous in a pure infant's ecstasy. I propped myself up, came to standing, and tried to emulate the darting, the lifts, the gestures of flight by extending my arms and spreading my fingertips toward the sky and twirling my diapered toddler body through air. I wanted them to see that I was one of them, that I understood the invitation to play. Small wings tickled my face as I began to push off the surface of the patio pumping my legs and feet while desperately flapping my arms in vain. I jumped higher and higher until, breathless and exhausted, I crumpled to the ground. I lay my head back on the cool brick slabs and stared at the sky as the monarchs began a unified departure, continuing their journey without me. I laughed big peels of joy. They were my friends. When my mother returned and witnessed the very end of their visit, I remember her saying that they looked like orange and black snowflakes.

After their visit, when I spent time on the patio, I flapped my arms and leapt back and forth, wondering how the monarchs got up, up, up. And what was a snowflake? Both were great mysteries. What I did understand even at two years of age was that the monarchs were compelled to come here, that they would visit me, and then they had to go somewhere else. It wasn't a choice, it was a being called, a summoning, to each faraway place. My mom said, "All butterflies know when it's time to leave and where to go without thinking about it. A feeling in their heart guides them." I played with the idea that was "migration" for a long time.

Months later, now an avid walker and runner, I buttoned a windbreaker around my neck and charged across the open patio. Rounding past the planter, I would speed up and sense my fabric wings billowing. I would then return to the planter, clamber up its side, posing on the rim and jump off swinging my arms hard over and over. Another time, undaunted, I took my father's umbrella, opened it, and realized that if I did a deep squat before jumping off the planter, I could feel a fleeting moment of glorious air hang. Flight was so close, and yet . . . I had been left behind, by mistake, trapped in a corporal confusion without my own set of wings. This was perhaps some oversight of nature. Or more likely I had not yet sprouted my own pair. I was completely sure that I was something quite peculiar. I asked my mother where butterflies came from—she remembers this, too—and when she showed me a picture of a ravenous chunky green caterpillar on a spiky milk thistle plant, I understood that the awkward pudgy body I inhabited would transform just like that one did. And it did.

After a year, I still had no success with flight. But there was another migration in store for me. One day, my father announced, "Ian and Dana, we are all going to have a big adventure! We are moving to Santa Fe, New Mexico . . . in six months!" The looming family migration forced me to make a vow to myself. I would craft my own metamorphosis in time for my family's departure. As winter approached and rain and wind forced me into the house, I focused on exploring new personas that I could express through song and dance. I invented numbers and sets that I performed at the end of each day for my parents, brother, our dog, and two guinea pigs. Looking back, I identify this as a time when some deeply creative impulses were ignited in me, some synergy between my keen longing and this impatience at being defeated by gravity. Indoors, the neatly labeled cardboard moving boxes piled higher, and my determination intensified. I had made a creative connection between my own reality and how a caterpillar held within it the ultimate potential to appear one day as a magnificent butterfly.

All day, in my turns, my leaps, my struts, I planned my transformations from a pudgy knock-kneed kid to an entertainer extraordinaire. On our black-and-white TV with its wire coat-hanger antenna, I studied all those old Depression-era Busby Berkeley musicals—the ones with the big production numbers, dancers that kept on coming, with synchronized sashays and high kicks, high-heel tap shoes, platinum blondes and sparkling sequin-detailed dresses that floated like butterfly wings.

These—my earliest dances—I performed on an improvised set in our Carmel cottage. As ever, Mom was there to support my daring. Her best interior designs were born of economy. I remember sitting next to the pedal-pumped black Singer sewing machine as she turned an old Javanese Batik sarong into a curtain. She then meticulously suspended the curtain with large safety pins looped along a length of wire strung between two nails that she had hammered into the opposing upper frames of the doorsill. This curtain was now between the galley kitchen and the dining room: backstage and my audience. The kitchen was where I readied my props and costumes for the pre-dining performances.

The rhythmic rattle of the lid of mom's rice cooker as the rice came to its boil and the smell of garlic pork and bok choy stir-fry cued that it was the turning point for my entrance. I had little time to make maximum impact on my hungry, seated, dinner-theater audience. My debut show began. With a silk scarf from my mom wrapped around my neck and head and sporting my powder blue Winnie-the-Pooh onesie from Sears, I threw back the curtain to offer original extemporized songs about flowers and flight, quick footwork, and hops that ended dramatically with a slide into splits as I outstretched my arms to the ceiling. My parents and brother laughed and applauded in hearty approval as I ceremoniously rose to my feet and took deep bows. These were my first audience affirmations. This exuberant and spontaneous cheering came from parents who were typically reticent. In fact, they frowned upon giving and receiving compliments. Each felt that there was an unseemliness to praise. There was, too, a superstition: the craving of praise, the expectation of it, as a currency, and self-congratulation—hubris, vanity—would bring only bad fortune. But their delight had been genuine and overwhelming, for them and for me. I saw that dance had tremendous power to bring forth joy for others, too.

I was inspired to begin a nightly performance series. After breakfast, I scoured the house for bright clothing, pillaging my parents' closets, the coat closet, a storage nook, in search of plastic bangles and jewelry, hats and canes, all to raise my production value. And as I became overwhelmed by the strains of my Ziegfeld extravaganza and the churn of extra costumes and props, there appeared my imaginary collaborator, a backstage theatrical assistant that I named "Charlie" after a perfume I had seen advertised on television. Each day while my brother Ian was away at school, Charlie and I disappeared into our shared bedroom to discuss the dances. Charlie assisted me with costume decisions, oversaw my vocal repetitions, and critiqued rehearsals that took place in front of a small dressing mirror attached to the closet door. He even took the fall for me if I forgot a step or tune mid-rehearsal or performance. At a moment of blooper, I would scold Charlie for his incompetence—it had not been mine—and cry out in exasperation, "Take it from the top!" He always complied. And he had as much stamina as I did. Charlie supported my growing patience, and he taught me to be a prepared and infallible performer, to tenaciously continue until I was satisfied and the audience was won over. Charlie made my solo forays less solitary. Everyone should conjure a durable pal like Charlie.

Each evening that I threw open the sarong curtain, I filled the living room with song, hat-tipping, and leg kicks with my head held high.

Always a keen critic, my mother describes these performances as having included bent-knee cabrioles and exotic port de bras, accompanied by nonsensical off-key songs that at the moment of a potential rhyme always fell short. She recently told me that she had been worried by Charlie's abiding appearance, attributing his constancy to my loneliness at having no playmates. But she admitted that she sure cherished the free time that Charlie's companionship added for her weaving.

three MIGRATION

My father seemed to me to be a towering giant. He had dark hair with highlights of gray and white, thick black square oversized eyeglass frames, hip mutton-chop sideburns that cupped his face, and a moustache that was roof to his lips. He wore a blue painter's smock when he stood in front of his easel coaxing tubes of paint into dollops that he strategically brushed onto canvas. Abstract images emerged in crimson, cerulean, and lime, the forms always at odds with one another. Dad was experiencing what he called "a real creative block." Carmel Valley and family life—kids cost money, after all—had siphoned from them both energy, funds, and inspiration. Their original attraction to the beauty and affordability of Carmel Valley was overturned by rising prices and an impending recession economy. Every dime earned at *Origins* went back into art materials.

In 1972, my parents were searching for a new community and a landscape that could re-inspire my father's painting as well as sustain our daily needs. So, they packed up our 1961 turquoise, white-topped Volkswagen bus and drove us across the Mojave Desert in a reconnaissance mission to Santa Fe. We drove at night and slept during the day to avoid the worst of the broiling temperatures that radiated along the desert. In our cheap roadside motels, I reveled in the mechanical beds—like grown-up tin toys—that provided ten minutes of vibrating "massage" for every nickel you put in the slot. As my muscles shook on this makeshift carnival ride, I watched cloth streamers attached to the grease-blackened air-conditioner vents flap and snap convulsively in the air flow. These were quite the come down from the delicate fluttering of butterfly wings. Mom inspected all motel surfaces. She didn't allow any of us to walk barefoot on the filthy carpets. We had to wear our *seullipeo*—Korean house slippers. Nor did she permit us to sleep under the motel bed sheets and covers. She lay our own sheets over the comforters and pillows, closed the blinds to block out the midday light, and pushed a dresser against the front door to ensure our security.

We drove under a star-filled sky past twenty-four-hour gas stations set into the desert sand with green AstroTurf facsimiles of suburban lawns. The air was so dry I couldn't sweat. Instead, my skin turned red and hot to the touch and my feet and ankles swelled. I would lie back on the vinyl passenger seats, elevate my legs, and place my broad four-year-old bare feet on the van's window glass to cool them; I stared out the window imagining the twinkling stars as celestial fingers tickling my toes. My mother said I had rice paddy feet, strong and wide, good for keeping my balance in flooded fields.

With his index finger, my brother drew an imaginary border between us down the back seat. His space was twice as large as mine. My penalty for crossing over was hard pinches and punches to my thighs. He would use his flashlight to read aloud from one of his issues of *Fate* magazine. These focused on thrilling paranormal phenomena, stories that set our hearts racing with fear of Sasquatches, the Loch Ness Monster, alien abductions, and battlefield hauntings. I loved the outsized drama of Ian's reading, the entertainment of it all, in our edgy but cozy confinement. I was spellbound, too, fidgeting very little. Ian need not have feared my border trespasses. I was an audience who knew better than to do anything that might cause him to lose his place or prematurely end the show—a far more dreaded outcome than a pinch or shove.

Once we got to Santa Fe, we parked the van and took to exploring every narrow street, peering into trading posts filled with pawned jewelry and revolvers. And we poked around local art galleries, studied landscape paintings and portraits of cowboys and Indians, occasionally stopping so our parents could speak with artists in their studios. I was fascinated by the people who were blowing molten glass—how they pulled the glass from roaring fires to swiftly shape it into a vase or a dish before it cooled.

That day Dad allowed me to choose a tiny turquoise and silver ring with a stylized bear claw design, one I admired in a jewelry vendor's display along the Santa Fe River just off the plaza. He paid five dollars to the jeweler: four crisp one dollar bills and four quarters. The expense made my eyes widen. I stared at my ring constantly, the inset stone the color of the southwestern sky. The ring was a commemoration of a moment. That day we committed ourselves; we moved from being visitors to residents. Mom and Dad had decided to rent a house on the outskirts of the city and signed a month-to-month lease.

My favorite part of Santa Fe on this trip was its cathedrals, chapels, and *santuarios* (sanctuaries). I had never been in a church. I was crazy about the altars. They were like a stage. Crudely hand carved and painted, they wordlessly expressed the emotions of devotion through shape and hues. At the center of each was the magnificence of Jesus, represented as a nearly naked, vulnerable man nailed to a cross.

After a week exploring our new city, we drove back to Carmel Valley, held a garage sale, bid goodbye to neighbors, packed up our essentials, and left California for good. We piled into the VW bus for a one-way trip back across the desert. Lili and our guinea pigs, Alexandra and Wilbur, traveled on the floormat in front of me, the latter in a small smelly crate. I wondered if they would die in the car. Lili panted, suffering in the heat. Wilbur didn't make it past the second night. His desert funeral was delayed by my having to pour water on the crackled earth to soften it enough to make a small indentation into which I could ceremoniously place and then bury his little body. Would my brother and I survive this journey?

TORMENTO (TORMENT)

We moved into a small single-family adobe home on the outskirts of Santa Fe. The two-bedroom, two-bath home with a compact living room measured one thousand square feet. It was handcrafted and where the windowsills should have met the walls, there were holes where gentle breezes blew through. The landlord explained that after installing the new windows the young green wood had dried and shrunk, pulling away from the walls, but that these little holes would afford a young boy like me spy holes to see outside. Each afternoon a two-inch gap under the front door above the saddle let in a fine covering of sand to the foyer. The brick floor had been laid directly into the sand below; vacuuming was futile and would only suck more sand from the earth upward onto the bricks. My determined mother swept each evening only to be thwarted each next day.

The house suffered from assorted uninvited creatures. Bright orange and red centipedes, each six inches long, had their nests somewhere under those bricks, near the couch. Field mice casually dallied through, and furry brown and black bats flitted near the ceilings. Rattlesnakes and grasshoppers were frequent drop-ins. We shared the space with these original occupants of the house. It could be crowded. I was more curious than afraid, for the most part.

But those moths.

They were attracted to the light that emanated from our home on the dark edge of the city. At the peak of the moths' bombarding, between ten and eleven o'clock each night, my mom, dad, and brother performed a ritual. First, they extinguished all the lights. Then they would do their assigned tasks. My mother would grab my brother's flashlight, bring it into the middle of the living room, turn it on, and aim the beam up at the ceiling. Meanwhile, my father would arm himself with the long suction hose of the vacuum cleaner and stand next to her; positioned at the old metal vacuum canister, my brother switched the power to ON. The wings of thousands of moths collided in frenzied flight they made for the single elongated tower of light. Their bodies thudded loudly as they were drawn into the hose and into the chamber in which they would soon suffocate. The vacuum motor whined under the strain. Once the canister was full—you could hear that it was—we would stumble in the absolute dark to our beds, calling out "goodnights" as locators. I crawled under my sheets and covered my hands, toes, and hair so that any stray moths still in the house wouldn't take revenge on me in my sleep. The moths craved moisture and minerals. My brother said moths were dung eaters so they would especially be attracted to me. I believed him. These were not the monarch butterflies of my old home. These were dull pale indelicate night monsters that clung to every part of the human body, leaving a glassy gray film of dust from their wings that couldn't be brushed away. They were literally the monsters that go bump in the night.

I learned to navigate a land in which plagues swarmed in biblical proportions and sequence. When I turned five, the grasshoppers emerged in July and devoured every bit of green for miles. They jumped onto my clothes every time I stepped onto the open porch. I had to tear my pants off and shake them out to rid myself of them. They probed my skin with sharp feet. Grasshoppers have a dense body mass and when I pulled them, hard, off my skin, they resisted with tenacity far beyond their size. They were hideous creatures, muddy brown and puce, that angrily hummed by rubbing their angular legs together before hurling their bodies and latching on with a thump. They had the ability to jump great distances and fly with loud twitching wings. I would fight them off with sticks and stomp them under my sneakers. My brother occasionally joined my garrison. We were outnumbered and victory was hopeless. The grasshoppers were born starving in an environment that could not satiate them. As quickly as they had emerged, they disappeared back into the dry earth for another several years. The harsh desert delivered lessons.

Along with the steady flapping of moth wings and chewing clicks and predations of grasshoppers, I learned to interpret many other auditory and sensory events and movements of my fellow domestic inhabitants. The squeaking from a rusted bathroom exhaust fan meant that another field mouse had climbed the adobe walls and accidentally fell fatally into its churn. It would be trapped on a compulsory exercise wheel until Dad could come open the grate cover, holding a paper bag over the opening. Once the mouse was inside the sack, Dad released it outdoors. As cute as the field mice were, they were known to actually carry the bubonic plague, a threat that had somehow survived the Spanish Inquisition in New Mexico. True.

LA IGLESIA

The Santa Fe of my childhood was not yet the Hollywood branded version that it was to become. The year 1973 marked the beginning of a financial recession. It was eight years before Ralph Lauren would launch his Santa Fe Style fashion and home décor line, a decade before actor Val Kilmer would begin popping up at restaurants, and twenty years before actress and best-selling memoirist Shirley MacLaine felt the radiating crystal energy of the land and chronicled sightings of UFOs from her Santa Fe house on a hill. Santa Fe was a gritty Southwestern town that was more like a sprawling pueblo. For lack of upkeep, flat roofs sagged on adobe homes, low-rider cars prowled dirt roads that branched off main streets, and tumbleweeds blew and fastened onto barbed wire fences where they would dry to a crisp.

Santa Fe was a city with little economy and the pressures of three prominent cultures that were sometimes at odds: Indigenous, Hispanic, and Caucasian. Their relationships to the land were also varied. Although Santa Feans spoke with pride about the *tres visiónes*—the three visions—as a braided community, in fact the city was built on hundreds of years of conquest and conflict, land disputes, and clashes of religion.

On the main plaza, I sometimes saw children mock the glottal sounds of the Native people's language. I hid behind my mother when we walked downtown. I thought it better to not be seen, to be disregarded as interlopers until I understood this strange new terrain.

One early impression I had of the characters in my new hometown was that "The Church" was law in this Western outpost. The Catholic churches were packed each Sunday for mass with devout *señoras mayores*, old ladies dressed in black, wrinkled faces behind lace veils. They devoutly clutched Bibles and rosaries. These were the old crones who cast judgment on boisterous children, girls in miniskirts, women braless in low-cut blouses, and handsome dark men that leered and posed suggestively. The señoras mayores had no reservations about reprimanding strangers, a shaming as tough love that would ensure the streets remained safe and orderly.

When I turned six, I began attending Agua Fria Elementary, a bilingual Spanish and English public school. I jumped rope with the girls in complicated rhythmic sequences. We sang out in Spanish and our feet accented the downbeat in between swings of tattered ropes. "*Osito, osito, ¿puedes saltar? Ayúdame, ayúdame a contar uno, dos, tres, quatro . . .*" I excelled and soon was jumping between not one but two ropes. Daily the ropes were whipped around faster and faster, to push me further, until at recess an audience of older students formed a group to watch my mastery. My skills and joy were absolute. Students of all ages and teachers marveled at my timing, footwork, and endurance. Older students often assumed me to be a girl. After all, I was playing with the girls, wasn't I? Adding to their confusion were my gender-neutral name, my pageboy haircut, and a still high-pitched voice. What did I care? I was the main event. My skills were what mattered. I didn't care or even think about gender, mine or anyone else's. It was irrelevant.

Soon my performances would attract a new friend. A friend other than good old Charlie. A Spanish boy, Bobby Romero, with a lisp-like accent, sky blue eyes, and black hair resembling crow feathers was never far away, smiling any time I looked up, through lunch hour and at every recess. In class Bobby moved his large, red Big Chief tablet next to mine and gently bumped his knee against me as we practiced penmanship. We loved our writing pads, the covers with the illustrated profile of a Native American tribal chief in full headdress. Bobby and I believed it was Chief Iron Eyes Cody from the *Keep America Beautiful* antipollution campaign on TV. As an adult I would be disillusioned by both the discovery that the proud Indigenous face on the pad was unnamed, likely a generic rendering with no real model, and that the *Keep America Beautiful* "Chief" was actually an Italian American actor, Espera Oscar de Corti.

Bobby and all my classmates wore Roman Catholic scapulars around their necks: blessed small square images of Christ and the Virgin Mary. Not having a scapular drew a clear religious divide between a good Catholic child and me, a heretic with no formal religion.

But I did enjoy class field trips to the Santuario de Guadalupe and the San Miguel Chapel, the oldest church in America. Those held far more fascination and excitement among us impressionable children than our trips to the sterile and abstract Los Alamos Laboratories and the lifeless State Capitol Building. We wanted magic, animation, to hear of miracles, to light votive candles, and adorn the San Miguel Chapel bell with milagros: those tiny images of body parts and supplications pressed into alloy that were reminders to God of our prayers.

These field trips have provided endless material toward my dance vocabulary. I studied the postures and gestures of each retablo, bulto, and santo, special artforms in New Mexico that feature paintings and carvings of saints. Even then, I noticed the figurines' contrapposto—the "counterpoise"—that suggested weight borne on one leg, which caused a subtle curve of spine that ended in the slightly tilted head of St. Francis or Archangel Michael. I registered that this pose led me, as viewer, to perceive that they strained to hear my respectful salutations. The rigidity of Our Lady of Sorrows' black robes, and red bleeding heart with a silver dagger thrust into it, conveyed her eternal deep emotional agony. Her painted glass eyes, crystalline tears, and frown hinted at softness beneath. I copied the outstretched hands of Saint Joseph and mimicked the stances of multiple Virgins, seeking to unlock what each was saying with only their body language. There were stories within each pose that I yearned to understand, to mine, and to replicate.

On one field trip, while sitting in a pew holding hands with Bobby, it crossed my mind that a church was a monument to pain and suffering that in fact highlighted human sensuality and virility. Take Jesus on the crucifix. He was so handsome, with his flowing hair, defiant crown of thorns, and defined musculature. Although bloodied, Jesus's abdominal six-pack, his lengthened sinuous biceps and deltoids, pumped pectorals, strong and well-defined thighs, and luscious long legs were absolutely beautiful. They were intended to be so. And no one ever seemed to talk about that. Why not? His was the perfect male body. I wondered why he wore a low-slung tattered garment around his hips that just barely covered his penis; was this the shameful flaw of his body, Bobby's body, and mine as well? Jesus's image stirred me physically on a deep level, one for which I as yet lacked words. Surely I could not be the only person to perceive and to appreciate these things in his holy male form. I sat with Bobby in the front row staring at the altar for what must have been about forty-five minutes until my teacher, Mrs. Baca, pulled us away from there and from each other. I knew no terrors of religion, nor of the shame of sexuality, to stop me from being lost in the wonder of the candle-lit images that emerged from shadows as Bobby and I intertwined our hands. Up to this time I had only seen my father's stylized sketches of bodies and forms. This beatific experience, this potent blend of spiritual and physical arousal, was completely new and was my own. And had I known at age six what the tingling warmth was that I felt for Bobby, I would have called it puppy love. It was my first such attraction and it was to someone of my same gender.

My time at Agua Fria Elementary abruptly ended when my family had to relocate from rural Santa Fe to the Casa Solana neighborhood, just off West Alameda across from the Santa Fe River. We vacated the rental home on the outskirts of the city when the owner sold it to a family who bought it outright. On my last day at Agua Fria Elementary, I waited for my father to pick me up and take me home. Suddenly, Bobby approached. We looked at each other and he hugged me very tightly. I wordlessly reciprocated. Our embrace was abbreviated by the imminent departure of his school bus. We heard the engine turn over; Bobby whispered "goodbye" into my left ear, pulled away, bolted toward the impatient yellow bus, and clambered aboard and into the cacophony of our peers. The accordion door shut behind him, a suction seal capturing the belated passenger. I visually tracked Bobby through the windows as he made his way down its center aisle to a window seat in the back. I moved to a position in his sight lines. Once seated, Bobby searched for me, our eyes locked, we smiled wanly, and we waved at each other. As the bus began to pull away, I became acutely aware of a deep ache in my chest. I kept waving, trotting along just a few yards as well, until the bus was out of view, leaving only its tiny cloud of dirt and dust after a few stoplights beyond. For months afterward, I would think of Bobby. Always my heart ached. It does now, in fact. I have lost track of him all these decades later. Thank you, Bobby, wherever you are.

CLICKING HEELS

I tumbled into third grade at Gonzales Elementary School. Casa Solana was a new housing development, by Santa Fe standards, built in the 1950s directly over the Santa Fe Japanese Internment Camp of World War II. The school playground stood on the same land where from 1942–1945 a total 4,555 Japanese Americans had been incarcerated. When I found out at the age of seven that the Japanese had been interned here, I feared there was ignorance in the world that was so powerful and insidious that if I was not careful it would seek out my almond-shaped eyes and grab me and lock me away. It seemed to me that I was not wrong. Ignorance and hatred had fed the dirt and my classmates channeled its energy. This playground is where I experienced brutal and routine bullying. My peers nicknamed me "Chino"—a slur that meant Chinese or, really, of any indeterminate Asian heritage—and interchanged it with the feminine form "China" to further distinguish my effeminate soft nature.

I was no longer flying and diving like a monarch butterfly between jump ropes, but rather I was ever more clearly separate from other students by both my race and my emerging sexual preference. No one jumped rope at Gonzales Elementary. There were only hyper-masculine games of basketball played by boys on cement courts and rough football tossing and tackling in dirt fields. My father was never interested in sports and was older, already in his fifties, and so we never tossed a ball around in the way of so many fathers and sons. I knew none of the rules of sports. So, I did my best to make myself invisible and paced a small turf of schoolyard solo during recess.

But it was not in my nature to remain invisible for long.

Several weeks into the school year, I dressed up in all orange hand-me-downs from my cousin Norman: a pumpkin long-sleeved shirt with mother-of-pearl buttons and corduroy bell-bottom pants. Those pants were already so worn that they no longer made the scraping sound that corduroys make when thighs brush together. I also put on burgundy platform slip-on shoes.

I was a magnificent orange monarch.

That day in the schoolyard, I was targeted by a band of bullies who circled and taunted me, leaving no opening for escape. One asked why I was so dressed up for school. Another baited me, "Are you a niñita? Are you a little girl? Are you a "Chinita Niñita?" Then together they sang a chorus, "Chinese, Japanese, dirty knees, look at these." They animated their abuses, pulling back and upward the skin around their eyes to create a narrow slanted look. They tugged outward at their T-shirts indicating breasts. I was imprisoned by their jeers until the alarm bell signaled that it was time to return to class. Two boys pushed me into the dirt before they ran back to class. I got up, dusted off my pants and shirt with bittersweet attention, and walked slowly to class, inspecting the shredded threads over my scuffed knees. Confused and embarrassed, I said nothing to my teachers about the assault. I wanted to put the whole situation behind me. But the day's tribulations were not done. That evening at the dinner table my father said, "We were driving past your school today, and I recognized your orange clothes, I saw you on the playground with new friends." I was horrified by this convergence of events. There would be no Bobby Romero's smile and warm hand to be found here. I remained silent and eventually cleared my plate, retreating to my room to take stock of my colorful wardrobe. Pulling down each shirt and pant—blue, yellow, red, green, purple—I threw them into an old cardboard box and placed the carton on top of the waste-paper basket to be thrown out.

These bullies felt like those grasshoppers had felt in the old house, lurking and nipping. At the age of ten my classmates had morphed into swarms that could sense that something was different about me even beyond my unconventional name, my eyes, pudding-basin haircut, and effeminate gestures. Something to menace, to expel, to extinguish. A tightening seized my chest, like a flashback of being grabbed. I knew I had to come to terms with Gonzales Elementary as a place of danger for me.

In fourth grade both students and teachers spoke in "Spanglish," a combination of Spanish Santa Fe idioms and English. I was jouncing between misunderstanding words in both languages. For survival, I mastered the sing-song cadence of Santa Fe that rather resembles a convivial parakeet, with the occasional diphthong and drawn-out vowels. It's a unique accent that I have come to admire, and to this day I willingly, irresistibly fall back into whenever visiting my mom in Santa Fe. My parents were perplexed by my new pronunciation of words that accented the wrong "syl-lable." I pronounced B as V. Problem became provlem, number became numver. I added 'es' in front of words starting with S. Stop became es-top, stove became es-tove. I was soon dispatched to the school speech therapist, a further mortification that would pull me from class three times a week. In those sessions I would practice a slow-motion enunciation of lines from comic books. But I clung to this accent as a way to stave off bullies, as if to say, "listen, I'm one of you, we speak the same language."

That year I also became very self-aware. I realized that I ran with small steps with my arms down to my sides. And in all my conversational exchanges I held my head in the natural saintly head tilt, an affectation I emulated from church iconography and that feminized and softened my gaze and signified my vulnerability. In a world of budding masculinity and its aggressive postures, mannerisms and gestures, its looks, its growls, and its presumptions, I experienced myself in the antithesis of all that.

Determined to lessen the bullying, I sought to alter some of my mannerisms. I retrained my run and I practiced protruding my chin to appear defiant and tough. As part of my body retraining, I watched the popular teen dance show *American Bandstand* every Saturday morning and then locked myself in my room for hours to practice gyrating my hips to my vinyl best-selling 45-rpm single—"YMCA," a disco anthem performed by the Village People—which I played on a portable record player until the grooves literally melted away.

Unfortunately, my awkwardness reached an apex at the dance that marked the end of fourth grade. I went dressed in new skin-tight black polyester pants with big bell bottoms, a proud new purchase from Montgomery Ward. I had begged my parents for them. I wore a tight T-shirt with the image of the Village People's scantily clad Indian rock member. And I wore my signature platform heels. I took to the dance floor and showed off my best four-on-the-floor beat moves. I spun on my high heeled shoes and pointed my right index finger up and down in between circling my fists at the wrists à la John Travolta's signature move from *Saturday Night Fever*. I repeatedly slammed into the half-splits from which I pushed into righting myself—without the use of my hands—to full standing. But my dreams of sudden popularity quickly faded as I looked into the uneasy glares from teachers and students alike. In a world where people were taught to not stand out from the crowd, I realized that I was shining too brightly.

My hope for acceptance was extinguished by the increased ridicule that I could not ignore. Each day after school I was harassed all the way home. The long walk past the Piggly Wiggly, the drive-through liquor store, the S & H Green Stamp redemption store, and down six—I counted each one, SIX—intersecting residential blocks became a painful survival trial. "Why do you carry your books like a Chinita?" "Are you going to cry like a girl?" "Look, China is wearing heels like a puta, a whore!" I never spoke to my family about these taunts. Instead, I came up with a coping strategy. I found ways to delay departure. I volunteered to be the new Gonzales Elementary flag boy. I would stay after school and carefully lower the American flag. I drew it down ceremoniously through a sequence of synchronized arm-over-arm movements on an old squeaky rope pulley. I never let it touch the ground. As the flag got closer to me, I disconnected it and folded it neatly, deliberately, straightening any imagined wrinkle until it was a perfect taut triangle in my hands. I then delivered the flag to Principal Castillo's office, awaited his silent nodding approval of my new performance art, and then I walked safely home, unimpeded by tormentors. He likely suspected that the prolonged formal transaction after dismissal was in fact his gift to me.

In fifth grade my choir teacher asked me to join her Mexican folkloric and social dance club. It turned out that she had admired my talents at the school dance and knew that I was being bullied. For the next two years, after school and between classes, I had a safe place to be: the music room, where I would rehearse. The six of us, five girls of varying sizes ranging from stick thin to obese and now me (in midgrowth spurt) learned dance after dance. I was in heaven. We prepared these dances for holiday assemblies: La Cucaracha (the cockroach dance), salsa, cumbia, and merengue at fiestas celebrating Easter and Cinco de Mayo. Salsa's mathematical steps gloriously crystalized with the rhythmic cycle 1, 2, 3, pause, 5, 6, 7, pause. The Mexican Hat Dance became my favorite, clicking heels on 1, 2, 3, and double clapping hands on count four. My singular sombrero, assigned from the school repository of costumes, with silver sequins against black velvet, made the hat most spectacular. I loved to throw it to the ground in a flourish and performed alternating stomps as I circled it. I had rediscovered joy. Joy had rediscovered me. Later in life my bilingual schooling and this earliest global dancing sampler would be enormous assets of familiarity while living and touring in Latin and South America.

Being Asian in Santa Fe was to be an anomaly. My nickname "Chino" continued to dismay because I am Korean American; mine was an uphill battle trying to explain the geographical and racial differences of vast Asia. I would tell classmates and teachers that I was Korean, but this was in vain. All Asians were simply Chinos. Their assertion, based on ignorance and incuriosity, was enough for them to deem it a fact.

It took adulthood and some distance for me to understand that *Chino* can actually be a term of familiarity, acceptance, and endearment, not estrangement. A Peruvian boyfriend in Lima, whose nickname was also "Chino," would transform my association from hate to love. Chino is my nickname to this day among Spanish-speaking friends and feels now more comfortable from deliberate ownership than my given name. It encapsulates my unique journey and place in a Hispanic community. Dana, on the other hand, is a name that gave a kind of imposed shape to my sexual confusion for years. It is a name so unfamiliar to Santa Feans that my teachers often pronounced it Doña meaning "missus," eliciting giggles and sneers from my classmates. After several years, I simply gave up correcting people. That, too, was a relief. After all, I was not named after any ancestor. My folks had simply liked the name when they saw it in a movie credit for the actor Dana Andrews. That got tiresome to explain also, "It's Dana, DAY-nuh, you know, like the guy who plays a detective in black-and-white movies." But even that etymology drew blank stares. I was not the namesake of a family member; shedding it was not some familial betrayal. It was as natural to shrug off as a butterfly chrysalis.

When I was growing up there were fewer than two dozen Asian families in Santa Fe in a population of forty thousand. We were all aware of one another. There was the family who owned the Vietnamese restaurant. There was the woman, Mrs. Kim-Taylor, who owned the Korean take-out stand serving up *chop chae, bul-kogi,* and *kal-bi* topped with kimchi. She was partially deaf and yelled at the cook and customers alike and scared business away. Her "Korean Tiger" food stand limped along until it became a taco stand by 1976. There was a small community of Tibetans who relocated to Santa Fe aided by Project Tibet to escape political persecution by China. They lived in one building on Canyon Road and in another on the outskirts of town next to a traditional Tibetan stupa, Kagyu Shenpen Kuchab, founded by His Eminence Kalu Rinponche. And there was a smattering of Japanese: the Fukudas who owned Shohko Café, the Japanese restaurant and sushi bar, and my classmate Abel Ortega who was Spanish and Japanese. Makio Nishida, who owned the Japanese karate dojo, would become a powerful influence in my life, as would my mother's college friend Alice and their mutual friend, a half-Japanese woman, Ailes Gilmour. Ailes was Isamu Noguchi's half-sister. And there was my brother and me, offspring of a Korean mother and Caucasian father.

My mom had a personal Asian hierarchy that kept us further isolated, and although my father didn't agree, her manifesto controlled our interactions. She could be quite critical, her judgments nuanced, and conclusions calibrated. To her, the newly arrived Vietnamese immigrants didn't speak English well enough. At the same time, she had a deep empathy for their suffering, having to leave their own country during the Vietnam War. But she was sure that they suffered from post-traumatic stress disorder, so we were not allowed to socialize with their sons. We shared something too: a racial slur barked or hissed at us sometimes was "*gook*." This was big during and right after the Vietnam War, flung at us in undifferentiated contempt, to signify that we Pan-Asians were the enemy. *Gook* is a term that originated in the Korean War when American soldiers heard Koreans say *miguk* or, American, in Korean. The GIs interpreted this as the Koreans saying, "me gook." The term *gook* was picked up as a way for the US military to depersonalize and dehumanize Koreans, and when the war front shifted a generation later to Vietnam, it became a derogatory term for people of Vietnamese, Korean, and Filipino descent. We also spurned Mrs. Kim-Taylor and her food cart. This was because she had left Korea with her husband, a US Marine she had met in the Itaewon entertainment district of Seoul near the US military base. This meant that she was not of the correct social station. Mom said, "No good Korean woman should cavort with soldiers." There were exceptions and loopholes to this; being American and having met my father on the mainland after he had served in WWII earned her exemption from this category.

My mother had a frenemy relationship with people of Japanese descent because although the adults got along and I knew those few children from school, my mother seldom lost an opportunity to invoke endless references to Japanese treachery toward Koreans. Her examples started with General Hideyoshi attacking Korea in 1592 and continued through WWII, all offered as examples of their intractable imperialist nature. Stories of Koreans locked in churches and burned to death by the Japanese in the early 1900s always led to a description of her childhood Korean pastor scarred beyond recognition by Japanese soldiers who tortured him. She was a roiling repository of anti-Japanese resentment and questioned why America had bothered to rebuild the Japanese economy after WWII. She said, "Even though they have no weapons now, they have prejudice and economic power which is more of a threat than a Samurai sword." By contrast, the Tibetans were interesting to both my mother and father. Mom said that Koreans and Tibetans were related through a great Mongol bloodline. Dad found their meditation practices to occupy a higher order close to his interest in quantum physics. But the Tibetans cloistered and rarely spoke to outsiders.

Perhaps the oddest part of this hierarchy was that the outside world understood none of these perceptual distinctions and lumped all Asians together regardless of our own discrete identities, oblivious to our prideful prejudices against our Asian brothers and sisters. And as there were so few of us, looking back, perhaps it is understandable that the distinct countries of origin were, for the other residents of Santa Fe, simply beyond their exposure or distinction. The lumping of us all together felt dismissive, as if it hardly mattered or was worth their bothering to learn and remember. And it was awkward and impossible to constantly correct people, many of whom, while ignorant, had intended no harm. And if they could not pronounce Dana, you can imagine that to pronounce nonnative Anglo American names was utterly beyond doing. For the most part, the "Asian" people of Santa Fe adopted American or Spanish nicknames, to make things easier for Anglo and Hispanic customers and associates.

Still, the harm was real. When I was eight, I remember walking through the main plaza one afternoon with my mother when a man yelled, "Go home, Tokyo Rose!" He was invoking a reference given by Allied troops in the South Pacific during World War II to the all-female English-speaking Japanese propagandists who sought to systematically demoralize American troops across the Pacific. My mother was livid, glared at the ruddy drunk in disheveled clothes, and turned crimson with anger as she yelled, "Shut up, you old fool!" She was outraged to be called a war traitor and misidentified as Japanese, when in fact she was born in an American territory and held full citizenship. After that, my mother would admonish me to keep far away from the "drunk vet," but this was impossible. He kept a watch over the plaza from a seat beneath the Soldiers' Monument, an obelisk erected in 1867–1869, and he only left to restock on vodka. "Get out of here, li'l Jap!" he would holler at me as I ran past, swinging his half-empty liter in a slow, inebriated motion in my direction. Somehow injustice had found my mother and me and there was no telling us from any of the other Asian families from whom my mother had tried to quarantine us. I tried to be inconspicuous, but each day, my eyes welled up from his predictable slurs and ravings as I tried to outrace his voice. My mother finally reported the man to the police as a threat and he disappeared.

Everyone seemed to know one another and when I was questioned in Spanish by locals sitting on their porches or walking in the street, it was apparent that I was not from Santa Fe. In Spanglish they would yell out, "Why are you in the calle [street]?", "Quien es tu papa [Who is your dad]?" "Donde esta tu mama [Where is your mother]?" Their curiosity was genuine and unfiltered, meant to be familiar and inviting, but my own insecurities made me wary of speaking to strangers.

To avoid these conversations, I began at a very young age to fly across the dirt roads like a phantom, barely seen, leaving only a trail of dust in my wake. The hot air rushed past my face and tousled my hair as I zigzagged through the gravel past rickety porches on adobe homes and chicken-wire fences holding back barking dogs. There was an emerging freedom that I felt in my legs as I bounded through the streets. It radiated throughout my torso, expanded my ribcage, and ignited an endorphin euphoria. I was alight, aloft, free, and had escaped my interrogators. It seemed to me that I could even escape gravity.

I wasn't the only person in the family to experience bullying and isolation. Ian remembered California as his home, a place he still loved and that I was fast forgetting. Santa Fe was a disaster for him. With no aptitude for the Spanish language and faced with a completely different cultural landscape, he, too, suffered through middle school and high school. He was frustrated and angry. His unhappiness, easily ignited, amounted to a short fuse that destroyed any vestige of safety our home could have provided for me. He punched holes in the cheap drywall of his room. He was made to plaster and paint them over, only for him to punish them again during another bout of rage. One day his first girlfriend's father chased him away with a loaded shotgun. He often returned home from high school with a black eye or a bloody nose and torn knuckles.

Ian and I shared an unspoken consternation about the economic situation into which our parents had once again fallen, taking us with them. We felt kidnapped. This was exacerbated by our family dinners that now were spam stir-fry and powdered milk. Ian and I cringed alone in our separate rooms, ears pressed to the walls, to listen to our parents argue about unpaid electricity and water bills. Their evening conversation was combative, challenging, more martial arts than marital collaboration. This was the heated parry and thrust that emanated from the living room and lulled us to sleep each night: "How are we going to pay the rent?" "What do we do about getting Ian to college?" "Why can't you finish a piece of art to sell?" They, too, fell asleep from their own futile fatigue.

But Ian wasn't all hormonal anger and destruction. He discovered a talent for dismantling, re-envisioning, and rebuilding. And when Ian got his driver's license at age fifteen, he took a job at the Exxon gas station on St. Francis Drive. He learned to take apart and reassemble cars, one radiator, piston, and spark plug at a time. His aptitude for mechanics also afforded him a place to belong and a set of genuine friends, based on shared passion and skills, guys who tinkered on and souped-up classic power cars. Their V-6 and V-8 engines gave a power and prestige to their pubescent masculinity. From the time that he worked his first long shift at the station, he would be covered in thick grease. His navy-blue polyester pants and sky blue striped dress shirt with a machine-embroidered name patch were caked and covered in layers of paint and oil and smelled of gasoline. No amount of detergent could clean them. I stared in disgust at his permanently blackened, ragged fingernails. He used a cleaning product called Goop, supposedly formulated especially to remove mechanical soiling and gasoline and grease, but it never—or he never—completely cleaned his hands. Instead, the grime left an indelible ring of black and brown grease around the bathroom sink that could not be scrubbed off.

At eighteen, Ian found his independence from the family by refurbishing a 1969 Ford Mustang fastback with a V-8 engine. He drove at high speeds up and down dirt roads. Typically, he swerved out of control, skidded, and cat-tailed, a local "Evil Knievel" type stunt performer, leaving a twister of dust behind each maneuver. A few years later, Ian rode his white Mustang out of Santa Fe like a modern-day cowboy. He moved back to California and earned a degree in automotive design from the Art Center in Pasadena. His ingenuity, visual sensibilities, and intimate knowledge of what makes things work led him to launch a successful product design career. Today Ian is still obsessed with fast vintage cars and still stays at a distance. We rarely talk, but when we do it's on his mobile on speaker setting so that he can continue working on a chassis, the undercarriage of a car, or under a hood. He keeps his corral of vintage cars in fine tune. We were both obsessed in our youth with movement as means to self-realization and escape. His propulsion was within a car and mine the movement of my body. Recently, I asked Ian, "What is your notion of a home?" He answered, "A garage." "Mine," I told him, "is my body."

five INTRIGUE AT COURT

Despite the bullying, I wasn't entirely alone. I had one good childhood friend, Timmy Parrott, who lived on Canyon Road. He, too, had experienced loss and displacement at a young age. Timmy was Diné—the Navajo people traditionally call themselves this—meaning "The People." He was three years older than me, broad in the beam, with humped shoulders, a round face of tawny skin, framed by straight, thick long black hair that extended almost to his shoulders. Timmy and his brother, Ben, were adopted by Alice Kagawa Parrott and her husband, Allen. She was the artist friend of my parents from Cranbrook days. Timmy struggled too, having been discarded by his birth parents and then adopted by a Japanese American woman and her Caucasian husband. Neither of us was sure where we belonged. And we also shared secrets: we loved to play with dolls, we loved to dress up, and we were both beginning to be attracted to other boys. The prepubescent Hispanic boys our age seemed to be maturing more quickly than were we. The arms in their muscles rippled, and on hot days they flashed us their fully formed olive abdominals, carelessly fanning their shirts upward. We spoke tentatively at first, then more openly, together about homosexuals, wondering how men kissed each other.

In the seventies and early eighties, Canyon Road still had empty lots, wild dogs, and even a tame orphan burro who routinely wandered amidst uninhabited, desolate dirt patches foraging for a few blades of dry foliage. In this tableau of desertion, restlessness, and want, Timmy and I nourished each other's reciprocal trust and fertile imaginations. We saw each other once a month for sleepovers at the rambling adobe compound he called home. We created stories about characters in far away, dangerous locations. In his room, we had plenty of uninterrupted privacy, and we would dress up in capes and turbans fashioned impromptu of sheets and comforters, and when the sun went down, we would walk the length of Canyon Road, pretending to be Asian princes and princesses in search of a palace or the Taj Mahal. As night asserted itself with moon and stars we would run up and down Canyon Road hiding from plebeians and the headlights of an occasional passing car. On a typical night, we might run all the way down to Gormley's Family Market. We looked through the window at racks filled with brightly colored candies, and we wondered aloud what would happen if we were to hurl a rock through the window. We never did. Along dark Canyon Road we would dodge ghosts that locals said inhabited a dilapidated, boarded-up home. The site reminded us of how many generations had lived behind these high adobe walls.

One night while climbing up an old apricot tree, Timmy saw two of his young male neighbors holding hands and kissing. I was ten and he was thirteen, and we were Ninjas on a mission. This was different from plain old snooping. We climbed the eight-foot wall adjacent to their home. Gently dropping down, we tiptoed up their gravel driveway onto their back patio and peered through the curtained windows, hoping to catch a glimpse of their taboo relationship.

One night, Timmy finally swiped two *Advocate* magazines from their patio. From then on we would read the magazine over and over in order to experience gay culture. He hid them under his mattress until his mother found them and threw them away. When she never mentioned having found them, we naively assumed that she didn't know what they were about. Unfortunately, when Timmy entered high school and I started middle school our sleepover parties ended, and we drifted apart.

Both with and without Timmy, I found some peace wandering the landscape. Back then it was okay for a child to explore with no adult supervision. In the summer months I would roam the desert. We lived at the end of the street and the undeveloped land started within a hundred feet of our front door. I wandered for miles through nature each day. As long as I knew the direction of the house and could get back before sundown, I was fine.

I walked up and down the small rolling hills, between stunted piñon trees, past mesquite trees and Apache blooms. I studied how the wind moved the vegetation and swayed my body in the same way it moved the bluish-green branches on the chamisa bushes. I chased horny toads as they bolted out from under rocks and spit blood from behind their eyes. I studied the fire ants as they piled sand to cover their subterranean mazes. Sometimes the occasional escapees from a cattle crossing appeared with eyes like immense Apache Tears—the name for the smooth and shiny black volcanic glass pebbles of this region—reminding me how small I actually was in the midst of minotaurs.

The land was filled with unseen spirits that sailed on sunbaked zephyrs. I began to realize the relationship of movement and inhabited stillness; the sensation of fight or flight that I felt daily in Santa Fe amidst my schoolmates during the school year. There was a juxtaposition of environment mitigating the peacefulness, the unconditional untroubled setting of the land, and my home. This was my natural medium: the gentle layers of this, sometimes soft and undulating and other times cracked and dry flooring that was the desert, and where I would experience myself in sublime self-care and self-expression and invention in movement. This dichotomy holds the tempo to which I am still attracted to in choreographing for the stage. It is an expanse of movement that quiets to reveal detail, only to be swept into action again. The proscenium is my canvas, the dancers are brushstrokes along a complicated and layered dynamic, timeless landscape mural.

My sense of independence, of being able to wander uninhibitedly, changed when I was twelve. We received a call from the neighbor of my paternal grandmother, reporting that Grandma had been found crawling on her floor suffering from a broken hip. I had never met her before and now she was senile, at only seventy-two, and immobile. Dad hadn't seen her in decades. They were estranged. Dad needed to escape Grandma's controlling and overbearing nature in order to have an independent adult life. Dad flew out to Albany and brought her to Santa Fe to live with us. Thus, at the start of my seventh-grade year, this newcomer was installed in my room, and I was dispatched to the living room. Luckily my uncle Kupe, while on an earlier visit from Hawaii and staying in the living room, had built a Masonite wall. This feature now allotted me a seven-by-ten-foot enclosure where the dining table had been. My cell accommodated a folding cot; a tray table topped by a plastic lamp; and a cardboard box that held underwear, socks, three

T-shirts, and a pair of my jeans. Grandma's birdlike bones and starved flesh, thin white hair, and gray pasty skin made her appear to me like an ancient madwoman and hag—which arguably she had become. She woke nightly, shrieking, as both my parents led her, soiled, to the bathroom.

Ian and my parents were working, so I was caregiver from 3:30 p.m. to 6:00 p.m. each day. Grandma Burgess brought with her an eye-popping costume jewelry collection that she had amassed from Macy's, made from small biweekly purchases spread over fifty years from her meager secretarial paychecks. She also came with a well-worn fox fur collar, its dainty narrow mouth clamping its balding tail. I was smitten with her treasures. Absolutely enraptured.

She rarely woke during my afternoon shifts. She snored and I sparkled; her twinkling clip-on earrings pinched my ears lobes and her outsized garish holiday-themed brooches brightened and weighted down my T-shirts. An emerald-green, glass-encrusted Christmas tree, a sparkling black cat arching its back for Halloween, an Easter Bunny with zirconia eyes and nose were all mine to wear when she slumbered. Most of her jewels were still on their original paper backings; I would be the first wearer to bask in their splendor. Grandma slept soundly as I layered more and more riches on, strands of long plastic pearls, pale blue crystalline chokers, and cuffs inset with rows of sapphire- and ruby-tinted glass. I taught myself to walk regally adorned like the Qing Dynasty Empress Dowager T'zu Shi. With the fox fur on my head as a regal wig, I pranced through what had not long ago been my bedroom as if at the opulent Chinese court of the nineteenth century. From the edge of Grandma's bed, it took twelve steps to reach the full-length mirror hung on the closet door. Along this strip, I slowly walked in grandiose affectations toward a cavalcade of imaginary serfs who I would acknowledge with a curt nod and an assortment of grand waves and dignified slight bows that I developed and refined as I went along. This was a ramp toward dance, costume, and theatricality. My playful experiments were of necessity noiseless, slow physical expressions, walking, turning, pivots, and barely discernable nods of the head. Sleeping Grandma was a silent sidekick, like Charlie had been.

With no funds for an at-home aide, from 8:00 a.m. to 3:30 p.m., Grandma was on her own. One afternoon about three months after her arrival, I came home to discover her on the floor. She had slid out of bed and couldn't get up because her hip replacement hadn't yet healed enough to support her weight. I struggled to pick her up, but I didn't have the strength. She called me by my brother's name, not recognizing who I was. This made it somewhat easier to disassociate from her beckoning—"Ian? Ian?"—when I had no choice but to leave her where I found her for two and a half hours until my parents returned. Dad and I together then lifted her into the car. Mom and Dad drove her to the hospital. Grandma's hip replacement from months earlier had never healed properly and with complications from emphysema brought on by her chain smoking, she passed away two weeks later under an oxygen tent.

My parents sold Grandma's jewelry and little fox collar at a consignment store. These treasures that had afforded me royal privilege and regality, and had fueled my imagination, were now seized. Upon breaking open a small metal toy safe from the 1920s that she had kept under her pillow, we discovered a neatly folded piece of yellowed tissue paper in which was wrapped her small 10K wedding band. If there had ever been a stone in the empty setting, it must have been removed decades prior, maybe sold to make ends meet. And at the very bottom was a blue velvet box containing an art deco engagement ring from twenty years after her marriage to my grandfather, given to her by her previous fiancé, one who unfortunately died right before their marriage date. Her lock box of unrequited love had finally been pried open, exposed for all of us to ponder.

The time during which Grandma lived with us, and then the immediate months right after her death, were completely disorienting. I struggled to make my bedroom my own again. I didn't like sleeping in the bed my grandmother had slept in. I considered the possibilities for the bare walls of my reclaimed room. Could art exorcize spirits and bad memories? I combed the garage and Dad's paintings and chose a work he called *The Secret Garden*, a small abstract six inches by ten inches. I hung it on the wall that the side of my twin bed was pushed up against so that when I lay down, I could stare up at it. It had thick paint in a deep maroon with highlights of forest green and red. I imagined wandering in the painting and exploring its garden, walking along its thick oil paint ridges, and climbing thick tree branches. I explored ponds and knolls. It was the antithesis of the desert I lived in. It was my father's inner landscape.

On Cedar Street, my mother's loom sat in the living room while the kitchen and garage were converted to painting studios and artwork storage for my father: two easels; old coffee cans full of brushes; white tubes of acrylic paint in a myriad of colors; canvases square, rectangular, and even circular, each one gessoed white in preparation to receive his inspiration. Underneath all of this, the artist's preferred carpet covered the cement floor: a canvas tarp stained with dried spills and splotches of his paints.

At this time, my dad primarily managed Blair Galleries where he also sold his paintings. It was owned by Don Blair, a Standard Oil Company man turned photojournalist who documented midcentury images of the Navajo Nation. He had a keen curatorial eye. The gallery was next to the Compound Restaurant on Canyon Road in the hub of the art gallery sector, just a few blocks away from Timmy's house.

Dad struggled to sustain acquaintanceships. He was not interested in small talk or niceties. He favored conversations about surrealism, fauvism, and expressionism: "isms." He became close to Don Blair and his wife, Bettina Steinke, a portrait artist, because of their intellects and talents. They were his surrogate parents. They could speak the artist's mother tongue of techniques. Bettina would critique dad's portrait studies, encouraging him to go deeper with his shading and highlights. He respected what she had to say. Don and Bettina occasionally let me sit with my father in their gallery. The three of them spoke about the canvases hanging on the cream-colored stucco walls. They noted the brilliance of color when an artist had not over- or under-worked the paints and applauded a well-rendered hand, noting it was one of the most difficult parts of the body to capture. High caliber shoptalk. These are the fondest memories I have of my father, the passionate intellect and artist, in his zone. Work at Blair Galleries inspired him to paint a series of works he then sold there. Some of my favorites were impressionistic, like the one of a red-cloaked Spanish woman with a tortoise *piñeta,* or ornamental comb, anchoring her coiffed hair, and a landscape near the sacred Santuario de Chimayó. There was also a Taos feast-day dancer in full pow-wow regalia and one of a New Mexico sky at dawn dappled with cumulus clouds. Some kids may have been able to boast of a dad's collection of say, firearms, or taxidermy, dead animal head wall-mounted hunting trophies. I had no envy of them. By contrast, my dad's trophies were life affirming and vibrant and created from his talent and imagination, conjured from thin air. His work fascinated me. His abilities to observe, to record telling details of his subjects, to convey time and place, these were gifts I felt surely that I had incorporated within myself as well. His braiding of art with drama and tableau was part of my own budding identification.

During this era, Dad used two names when signing his paintings to differentiate his works: Schick, one of his German family names, was for his portraits and landscapes, and Burgess for his abstract expressionist works. The use of both names reminds me that he never healed from a broken family. His painting styles seemed to honor two distinct family perspectives, each developed independently, from his childhood.

Dad struggled with recurring creative blocks throughout his life. At these times, his gentle soft badger and horsehair brushes and painstaking paint strokes rarely brought a canvas to fruition. His blocks even led to his packing away his easel for months, sometimes even years. His melancholy could be crippling. My father grew up during the Great Depression and this often put him at odds with materialism and in collusion with romanticism. In his late twenties, his career trajectory was bright. He was adjudicated into a group exhibition at the Museum of Modern Art (MoMA) in the early 1950s and was seen as an aspiring new voice in the visual arts. But for all his brilliance, he harbored a debilitating sense of abandonment and self-doubt. With the responsibilities of a marriage and family his creativity waned. As a child, I dreaded his bouts of depression that started with the packing away of his brushes and paint and other tools and supplies. Having witnessed his frightening shift from creative productivity to the inability to create, in fact, drives me to never stop making art. To have artist's block, to diminish in the process of making art, to be depressed—these are my greatest fears. I consciously separate the obsession I have to make art from the disposition to depression I may from time to time also harbor below the surface. I am driven to engage in—and with—art every day, whether in the form of rehearsing a dance, researching a subject, or listening to the musical scores I am using for my dance projects over and over again.

I always sensed that my soft-spoken father was . . . unusual. He cherished beauty, and deplored formal religion and right-wing politics. He had a rich internal world of memories that he refused to share. When I saw photos of his teenage years and youth, he gave short responses. No anecdotes, no stories. A glimmer of information came one day while we were watching the movie, *Willy Wonka and the Chocolate Factory.* He said that Willy's living situation was like his childhood in the 1930s, when he and seven relatives lived in a two-bedroom house. Dad was a Renaissance man born into the wrong era and socioeconomic class. He spoke with discernment and knowledge about every subject that might arise, ranging, say from the Mongol Empire to the depths and horrors of the Holocaust.

Over time his candor, and his choices about what he might care to share, evolved, as had my own. Our relationship deepened when at nineteen I told him I was gay. He said, "Don't tell your mother, I had relations with men when I was young. Exploration is normal. Perhaps this is a phase, perhaps not. Take your time." I asked what he meant, and he said, "Love comes in many forms and society accepts some forms more than others so be sure what you can withstand." His reaction was prophetic and it was caring . . . and it was knowing. We never again spoke of his history with men. Dad was gentle, veered from things aggressively male, including sports, and had the ability to cry when touched by a movie or poetry. I believe that when he got too close to expressing his inner emotions through his painting, he stopped. His canvases revealed a generationally unacceptable societal male tenderness that today is accepted, lush with colors and confused forms that seemed to push and pull against one another, a tension that conveyed a deep emotional realm. My parents shared a loving relationship.

Years after his death, my mom called one day in 2018 to say that she had found letters that my father had written back and forth with a male friend during the early 1940s. She said, "You will understand what I am telling you and for me it's okay." I didn't tell her that I knew. It was the rare secret that I had kept from her. I feel as though I am living the unrequited dream of my father, to inhabit a world that is accepting of experimentation and love in all its forms, of working surrounded by art in a museum, and married to a man.

six EARLIEST INFLUENCERS, EARLY MENTORS

Despite our financial struggles, I was extremely lucky to have parents with such an assortment of artistic friends, like Don Blair and Bettina Steinke, and I count many of these people as my earliest mentors. Ceramicist Toshiko Takaezu, Mom and Dad's classmate at Cranbrook, was an unassuming person who adored my parents. When I was twelve, my parents drove us from Santa Fe to Taos with Toshiko to take in the scenery. She spoke with a local Hawaiian accent and was dressed in a tie-dyed denim blouse and skirt, topped with a straw sunhat. She spoke to Dad about her new clay slip colors, and in particular how much she loved her indigo blue. Upon seeing an especially beautiful vista, Dad stopped the car, and we piled out to admire the pinkish sand and green polka dots formed by juniper trees framed by a cerulean clear sky. Here their friend began scouring the ground for rocks and dried sticks. I asked her if she needed help and she laughed and said, "I am choosing inspirations for pottery." I obviously looked perplexed, so she nodded cheerily, urging, "Yes. You can help me. You see how this rock has a subtle hue of grey and white and brown and how this one is smoother and pink? I can make vases to look like these. See this stick? What if it were four feet tall and made out of clay? Now, young friend, can you find me a special rock?" I hadn't thought about how a small stone could inspire a vase, or how a stick could be studied for its form and imagined in another size and material. I searched the ground but instead chased a lizard that had been basking in sun. What was so clear to me, just by that exchange, was that Toshiko saw form in nature. Form that was hers to adapt and conjure in her own art. But I looked around me and noticed something else: movement. And that was a crucial artistic epiphany for me.

Throughout the 1970s, my parents took me with them to small dinner parties. I was an engaged listener. When one person spoke, I moved my complete attention to them and when another answered I refocused accordingly. I remained quiet; adults spoke freely in front of me, not editing their words. It was at one of these dinner parties at Alice Kagawa Parrott's home in 1975 that I first met the late legendary sculptor, landscape architect, and performance-set designer Isamu Noguchi for the first time. I was seated at the dinner table directly across from Isamu, sandwiched between Timmy and Isamu's sister, Ailes. He was the first half-Asian adult man I had ever met. His slight frame and aquiline face seemed familiar. His wide Eurasian eyes sagged at the corners and deep-set lines channeled vertically down his brow and cheeks—nearly sculptural features—that conveyed gravitas. Wisps of gray and white hair on the sides of his remarkable cranium outlined a tan scalp. At age seventy-one, his Zen-like appearance made him seem much younger than his actual age. He possessed a defiance and self-confidence that commanded the study of his every elegant move. He ate sparingly, alert like a hawk, his focus never diverted from the conversation around him. His chiseled face, always in intelligent control of his features, and his upright posture together accented his acerbic stories of someone who vexed him named "Martha." Everyone at those dinners seemed to know to whom he referred. In college I would understand that this "Martha" was American modern-dance pioneer Martha Graham. But for now she was just "Martha" to me. He complained that Martha didn't take enough time with her dancers to explore his sculptures. And, he went on, she put him on ridiculous completion timelines for the building of stage sets. He still resented not having been chosen by the Japanese government to design the Hiroshima Memorial. He explained his design, mapping it out on the tablecloth with strong thick fingers, his hands disproportionately large on such a thin torso. Indomitable. When he spoke about being half Japanese, he paused and studied my face with his unusual steel-gray eyes until I shyly looked down at my plate. And then—I will never forget it—he said that all Amerasians are outsiders everywhere, not quite Asian or white enough, but that alienation allowed one to focus on art. He too was stuck between worlds, and I felt a deep empathy from and affinity with Isamu. This great man had the vision to witness me, a young, quiet, and attentive boy—one who sought to absorb and to lean into the world around himself—and to see inside me, too, without my having needed to tell him a thing. This feeling of reciprocal connection and identification from that time extended to a peculiar childhood crush on him that has never gone away and an admiration that has ever deepened. A photo of Isamu as a young sculptor in the 1920s sits on my office desk, and my many dance collaborations with sculptors over the years are testaments to the artistic and personal spell this magnificent artist and intriguing man has cast over me since childhood.

I was lucky to have ongoing exposure to him in my formative years. Isamu's half-sister, Ailes Gilmore, admired and commissioned my mother's clothing designs. To pay the bills, Mom often made special custom dresses for the elite of Santa Fe. She sketched and designed, chose raw silks, individualized patterns, and then sewed her creations. With no babysitter, Mom took me along for fittings at Ailes's home. Mom admonished me not to talk, not to touch, and not to move from wherever I would be seated. That would prove to be just fine for me: I remember being glued to a brick step in Ailes's living room and conversing with Isamu's stone and bronze sculptures. Her home was like an art gallery. Each piece was honored with space for proper viewing in uncluttered sophistication. It seemed that Ailes's elegant home held sacred lessons. I wondered if Noguchi paper lanterns and abstract sculptures had at one point been people who had been frozen, transformed into odd formations for some past wrongdoing, as in the biblical story of Sodom and Gomorrah. It was a dwelling without evidence of children except for a small bronze sculpture of a fat little boy she called *Kintaro*, the Golden Boy in Japanese. *Kintaro* refers to a folktale about a little boy of superhuman strength, raised by an old mountain witch. He could communicate with animals and excelled in martial arts. I loved sitting next to Kintaro; this silent little boy was like me, round in shape and perched alone on the edge of a step waiting to be spoken to, and I was only too eager to speak and listen and reply.

Ailes had been a modern dancer. Now in her sixties, she had performed with the Martha Graham Dance Company in 1932 at the opening of the Radio City Music Hall. She wore floor-length dresses; her feet were not visible, and thus her smooth glide gave the impression that she was floating across the floor. She was medium height, round, with freckled tan skin, and she wore her white hair in a tidy bob that went just below her ears. I found her swollen hands and lymphedema-loaded wrists and arms fascinating. When exposed to view, her limbs were like articulated water blisters. She spoke with a righteous clarity, enunciating each syllable, squeezing meaning out of each one.

At the end of one fitting, Ailes acknowledged me as I crouched on her living room step, staring at Kintaro, and copying his upheld arms. My arm movements must have reminded her of her bygone years. She glided silently toward me. At first it was a revelation to be noticed by her at all, and in retrospect, I can say now that it felt portentous, like I had made a deliberate pilgrimage to an ancient oracle. Alert and receptive, I waited for her to speak about my future. She said, "Now look at you, you are a dancer with the strength of Kintaro." I mustered the nerve to say, "I don't think I am a dancer. How do I become one?" She said, "Watch the world around you, listen to stories, take dance classes like any artist takes classes. Train your body and mind. A dancer is made of hard work and desire. You already have desire." Sensing how overwhelmed I was by her attention, she broke the tension with a grin and warm laugh. Mom came in, having finished packing up her tape measure and garment bag, ending my dialectic with this exotic fortune-teller and muse, and reached her hand out to assist me in standing up. Ailes floated past and opened the door for us to depart.

On our car ride home, a hole that had rusted through the floor of Mom's 1965 faded burgundy Falcon allowed me to stare at the asphalt whizzing between my feet. I pondered if Ailes had really foreseen my future. This conversation, and her movements, the way she inhabited her space as a stage, held gifts that would surface in my regular thoughts, my ways of looking at art and dance for years to come. It would spur questions about the journey of an artist whose body is their medium, whose art is dance, whose language is gesture and movement in air and space. To be the sculpted as well as the sensual sculptor seemed a riddle, a paradox beyond me then, but a riddle that would thrill and engage me always. Many years later, I had indeed become the modern dancer that Ailes had foreseen and anointed that day. By the early 1990s, in fact, I would come to legitimately own my art, living life fully integrated, as art, able to make further connections to the events of my synchronistic childhood.

At the beginning of the summer when I was eleven years old, I decided that I would be a pianist and entertainer like Liberace. I had come to this decision after watching Liberace's 1979 television special filmed in Las Vegas. He paraded across stage in his long fur coats and crystal encrusted pants suits, his beaming smile a bridge spanning his entire face, telling impromptu jokes and playing the piano while dazzling the camera with his bejeweled fingers. I identified with him. Liberace was "different" and he knew it. He made no attempt at concealment or toning down his personality; rather he flaunted it, and people adored him for it. Audiences loved how he dressed and moved and spoke with a high nasal voice. He was invincible in an armor of sable and rhinestones. He was spectacular—deliberately—self-referential and commercial. His persona struck a chord that resonated with his audiences of all ages and backgrounds. He loved being Liberace. He reminded me of how I felt when I wore my grandmother's finery. He loved being him.

I announced my need for a piano, lessons, and new clothes. Of course, Mom and Dad were not in a position to afford any of these things, so they just didn't respond. Instead, they talked about the national news as if I hadn't said a word. They hadn't said No—that had to be a good thing, I thought—but they hadn't said Yes. So to close this deal I said, "I really think I could be Liberace." My mother responded, "He's garish and panders to old ladies." I didn't bring up the subject again directly. Instead, I relied on the power of suggestion, making them stakeholders in my dream. I began humming and singing the Liberace standard, his sign-off, "I'll Be Seeing You," around the house as a subliminal reminder to them of my entertainment potential.

My campaign seemed to bear results after a couple of weeks. One day my dad said, "Your mom and I have thought about what you can do this summer. Let's take a drive." I got in the car thrilled, thinking that I was going to my very first piano lesson. We drove to Canyon

Road, turned off onto a narrow dirt road, and stopped in front of a large, unmarked complex.

What cruel trick had my parents played on me? Under false pretenses I was here, walking through the main doors of a newly opened karate dojo. The sensei, Makio Nishida, greeted me, "I've been expecting you!" I was too polite, too embarrassed to leave, so I stayed and took my first karate class. And what do you know? I absolutely loved it! Oh my goodness, this was thrilling.

My parents had privately agreed that physicality and discipline would be better for me than piano lessons. After interviewing Makio, they thought he might make a great mentor. They were right. That crucial decision allowed my body to truly become my instrument. Years later, when I saw the movie *The Karate Kid* for the first time, it felt like my story. Sensei Makio was a real-life Mr. Miyagi, straight out of Hollywood central casting. He was wise, patient, and no-nonsense with zest and joie de vivre in proportions that I had not experienced in any single adult before. He was an Asian male role model when I was struggling so terribly to locate my own sense of identity and to bring shape and form to my own story.

That summer, karate became my all-consuming focus, obsession, and sanctuary. It was a sport, one that originated in Asia. It was culturally mine and a space in which being Asian was a *good* thing, the *best* thing. An *enviable* thing. The dojo became the place where my mind-body connections and deeper awareness and integration were foremost and were to be cherished and formed, refined, shared, and celebrated.

Each evening I took two group karate classes with Makio that consisted of vigorous warm-up exercises, repetitive punches, kicks, unified strategic guttural cries, sparring, and the memorization of *katas*—long movement phrases that posed the student against hypothetical, imagined attackers—in a kind of purposeful combat dance. I had lived with so many fears for so long that I fought my visible and invisible attackers with pent-up gusto. My body felt completely enlivened with movement. We ended each class with a meditation session that calmed our minds and allowed us to methodically and deliberately check back in with the parts of our bodies that together served us in this art.

Over that summer I had a growth spurt, too. As I entered puberty my body, in its vulnerable pupa stage, was being sculpted by repetitions of arm and leg extensions, facial expressions, and kicks and punches, formed by the cohesive discipline of karate. My body thinned, became muscular, and I felt more confident about my appearance, my capacities, and about my identity. I began to believe—to actually see—this transformation and that I could rely upon my body and trust it to serve me. And that my body could trust my judgment, too. The pudgy green caterpillar was maturing. I knew the butterfly's name for this. Metamorphosis.

Six days a week, my father happily drove me to the dojo, which was located in the Project Tibet building, an unusual five-sided structure with an open courtyard in the middle. Each night he waited in the car for me, reading a book with a pocket light, so that I, his son, would have this place, this privacy, this exploration, and to be myself. The years I practiced karate were a breakthrough period for me. I belonged. And movement was celebrated, expressed extravagantly, and spent here, in endorphins, elation, exhaustion, and collegial exaltation.

Instead of Liberace sequins, I wore a simple unadorned *gi*, the traditional white tightly woven cotton canvas uniform of the martial artists with a patch that said *Genji Kai* in *Kanji*, Japanese calligraphy. Drawstring pants were worn under a kimono-style jacket held closed by a white belt—the white signifying my beginner rank. "Genji Kai" referenced the literary character associated with flawless courtesy and aesthetic genius as shown by the character in the Japanese classic *The Tale of Genji* by noble lady Murasaki Shikibu in the eleventh century.

My only day of rest from the dojo was Sunday. I sat glued to my family's black-and-white Zenith television watching *Just for Kicks*, a weekly two-and-a-half-hour program that included one Charlie Chan film followed by a Hong Kong martial arts flick. Chan was an astute fictional detective of the 1930s and '40s who globetrotted from Egypt to Hawaii to Mexico. A spotless white suit and Panama hat were his sartorial signature. He was an outsider, alone able to decipher clues to mysteries. At that time in my life, I didn't mind the yellow makeup that altered the face of Swedish actor Warner Oland or of Sidney Todler as long as "Number One Son," Keye Luke, or "Number Two Son," Victor Sen Yung, made their appearances. Scores of these movies were made between 1938 and 1946. American and European actors would adapt a pastiche of exaggerated Chinese accents and features. It was almost impossible to see Asian American male actors on television at all. These Anglo guys in cartoonish disguise, pretending to be Asian, were all Hollywood and television had to offer me. Perhaps the Chans could solve the greatest mysteries I now faced—who to love and how to find the strength to accept and to express, what was increasingly clear to me, as my sexual preference.

During this karate immersive era, in 1980, I began to attend Alameda Junior High. I walked to school each day across an *arroyo*, a steep-sided gully with fast flowing water, the ravine of the Santa Fe River. We were all warned not to walk through the arroyo due to the flash floods that would tear through the arroyo when rainstorms in the mountains unleashed torrents that simply could not be absorbed by the desert sand. Still, we took the risk to shave ten minutes off our commute. Like jaywalking or darting across a busy intersection, this was a bit of a juvenile thrill.

We were wary, however, of *La Llorona*. In the Mexican folklore that was the fare of this state, the ghostly apparition of a weeping woman who locals alleged haunted the arroyo. In her frantic search for her own drowned children, she snatched boys and girls. During one full moon, an old Hispanic man who lived next to the river claimed he had actually seen La Llorona. Although the story of La Llorona could not keep us tardy children out of the river in the light of each morning as we ran to class, she did keep us safely on the banks when the sun waned. We kids whispered to one another in a thrill of adrenalized fear about the white specter as we scrambled over the riverbanks before sunset.

At this age many of my peers were torn between continuing to believe in a magical reality or to step into an adulthood that meant leaving magic behind. For many, La Llorona faded away that year. I refused to let go of the mysteries and folktales of Santa Fe. Artists often live in multiple realities, best described by the beloved authors of magical realism, Gabriel Garcia Márquez, Jorge Luis Borges, and

Isabel Allende. We see inspirations for art all around us, in the swaying of branches of a tree, the ripple of water in a ravine. I saw nature as animation—movement. I find great solace in artmaking where multiple simultaneous realities coexist and remain permeable.

To my dismay, my nickname, Chino, followed me to junior high and nothing much changed. Well...a few things. One pair of straight-legged pegged stonewashed jeans supplanted my bell-bottom corduroys. Every Thursday I would yank them fresh from the washing machine and hang them on the clothesline. Within ten minutes the hot desert air made them ready to wear. With only one pair of jeans to my name, this was an important ritual.

I keenly noted the changes in the bodies of the male students. Occasionally a pubescent boy would make overtures toward me that I didn't entirely understand. There was sexual experimentation and also rumors about which kids were gay. By this time, my classmates clearly assumed I was gay—they never asked me which girls turned me on, for one thing—and boys flirted discreetly, and some daringly, baiting me to see if they could get me to admit my longing. I fought that stigma, ignoring any teasing or overture, and focused on my studies and my martial arts classes.

I excelled in the katas and suppressed my sexual desires. Over the next four years my skills would increase, and the color of my belt moved from white, to blue, to yellow, to green, and then to brown. The time came when Makio decided to put his two best students, me and Ayame Fukuda, the daughter of the family owners of the Japanese restaurant in town, on a competition circuit throughout the Southwest. Ayame was three years older than me. She was short and muscular with a round face, opalescent skin, and wavy, tousled black hair. At almost eighteen, she already exhibited a tough sophistication and skills—unflappable concentration, some enviable pivots, balance, and coordination and elbow control—which had clearly grown out of years of waiting tables, crammed with demanding diners at her family's restaurant. Makio, Ayame, and I would pile into sensei's dark chocolate–colored Lincoln Continental and drive for hours to get to karate tournaments in Albuquerque, El Paso, Dallas, Flagstaff, and Las Cruces. These tournaments gave me audiences before whom I could demonstrate my movement skills by performing a kata, a standardized sequence that Makio had taught me, one that had been handed down through the centuries from sensei to student and which the judges were familiar. I would be called to my age bracket and belt rank where I would wait kneeling on the floor until it was my turn to perform my kata. I would rise, bow deeply to the judges, and approach the floor—a measured square defined by tape on the ground—and when I felt it was time to begin, I would fight off imaginary attackers. I felt these attackers as real; I could sense them. I believe this is what made me successful in winning at these competitions. This repeated immersion into another unsafe world—one that I was successfully able to fight my way out of and with a warrior's dignity and seasoned technique—raised my self-esteem and further fueled my training efforts.

With master judges and sports fans watching, being alone on the martial arts competition floor is the closest thing to performing a solo dance I have experienced outside of a formal stage. On the competition circuit you would often come up against the same competitors. At fourteen, I saw one Hispanic boy from a dojo in Alamogordo over and over. I became intrigued with him, enamored of his auburn hair and peach fuzz of a moustache. The opening of the fold of his karate gi revealed his sternum. An odd sensation of deep physical attraction surfaced during my teen years and became stronger as I turned fifteen and sixteen, one that I suppressed. I understood it by then to be more than physical admiration. It was sexual arousal. I tried to allot myself no time to think about my sexuality; instead, I excelled in my course work and exhausted myself through karate classes.

My sexuality and karate came in conflict when I turned sixteen. By this time, I had spent almost six years at this dojo, a safe place, filled with adventure, where I had stretched my mind and lengthened my body. But I turned down my natural next rank increase from brown belt to black belt and instead quit altogether. It was a tough decision. However, I knew that my next immediate explorations had to be about clarifying my sexual confusion, and this was not going to happen when I was spending so much of my life at the dojo and in a single community.

My gi had been my butterfly chrysalis, ready to crack open and move me closer to being a monarch.

My sophomore year in high school—the year I quit karate classes—I admitted aloud to Norma Ortega, a proud lesbian with a dyed red flat top, oversized shoulder pads, and pegged pants, that I thought I was gay. There it was. The words were now in the air. She looked at me and said, "Well, of course you are, you always have been. And now you know it." I realized I was only fighting myself and needed at some point to give in to the flirtations from other boys. I wasn't quite ready yet to do so.

eight TAKING CHARGE (SORT OF)

It was an odd time to come of age in Santa Fe. In the summer of 1981, Santa Fe burst upon the global fashion pages, and this city would never be the same. When Ralph Lauren launched his Santa Fe Collection, the city became an immediate international style and arts destination. At the same time, the tres visiónes community felt the exclusionary pains of a rapidly exploding tourist economy, a real estate boom that left them out, and the gentrification and commercialization of Santa Fe. The place in which I had grown up morphed into what locals dubbed "Fanta-say." Rising costs of real estate alienated longtime Santa Feans as gallery after gallery popped up to sell local facsimiles of artifacts as well as authentic art. The prices of everything—gasoline, groceries, essentials—climbed. Rents for low rises rose sky high, and the lucrative demand displaced longtime neighborhoods and families.

At ages sixteen and seventeen, I listened to gender-bending bands that helped me to feel more comfortable with what was still my undeclared gay sexuality. On the local radio station, Duran Duran, Brian Ferry, Flock of Seagulls, Frankie Goes to Hollywood, and Soft Cell were juxtaposed to salsa and mariachi music. In a time before the Internet, smartphones, and social media platforms, music on the radio and music videos on the cable station MTV gave us alternative views of life outside of Santa Fe and glimpses into liberal lifestyles being pursued in such trend-setting hubs as New York City, London, and Berlin. I bleached streaks of yellow into my dark brown hair and scoured thrift stores for clothes that I could wear to emulate pop bands. I practiced MTV video dance routines in front of that mirror on my bedroom door and knew the words to every Top 40 chart hit.

The public Santa Fe High School had almost three thousand students then. A dreary campus on a hill. Like prisoner transport, a bus arrived at dawn each morning at the corner of Alameda Street and Camino Alire to collect the bed-head-crowned teens of Casa Solana and deposit us at the base of the campus. The school was a haphazard

layout of mobile classrooms, corrugated steel Quonset huts, and dilapidated buildings of various vintage. Getting to any next class on time
was almost impossible. Each part of campus was a turf for a specific
clique; the Hispanic gangs stood at the top of the parking lot stairs,
the popular students and jocks positioned themselves on benches in
front of the library, and drama and art nerds sat at the very base of the
main school steps near the theater entrance.

During my junior year the two Vietnamese brothers from the family
that owned the Vietnamese restaurant were mercilessly teased for the
vowel-filled sounds of the mother tongue they spoke together. This
teasing finally exploded as a fight at the top of the stairs to the parking
lot. The brothers were jumped by a group of *Cholos*—Mexican American street gang members—in white "wife-beater" shirts and hairnets,
in the style of the larger Los Angeles gangs. The brothers wielded *nun-
chucks*—fighting sticks appropriated from martial arts weaponry—and
knives in a valiant display of Bruce Lee tactics. But they were soon
overwhelmed by sheer numbers as the fights rolled in a mix of ad hoc
punches and kicks, the air pierced by threats and agonized screams.
The terror I felt from witnessing their "othering" made me back away
from the crowd and search for a place to hide.

I focused on my classes and excelled in anthropology and sociology. Mr. Zinn, a handsome tan hippie, made these subjects riveting,
ranging from the story of the discovery of "Lucy," the little Australo-
pithecus in Tanzania, to the evolution of the human opposable thumb.
Ms. Jolie, the sociology teacher, was in her fifties and always wore a
bright flower in her hair. She knew my name and greeted me each
morning in class by saying, "I like your style!" She would be referring
to any of my assorted PayLess brand dress shoes, cargo pants, and thrift
store blazers and tuxedo shirts. Ms. Jolie taught a progressive unit called
Tolerance and Human Nature. The units of two days were dedicated
to the discussion of homosexuals, where she asserted forcefully that
"people are all people" and that in some societies at different times in
history—such as ancient Greece—homosexuality was the norm. I
was transfixed by her lectures and deeply empowered by the fact that
a teacher would speak openly about sexual preference. Mr. Baca taught

accounting and was rumored to be gay. His comb-over alone made him a topic of conversation. All this made me wonder how, why, and by whom the rumors were started and propagated.

During my junior year of high school, I became friends with Patricia Michaels. She left her home, Taos Pueblo, and moved to Santa Fe, where she enrolled in classes at Santa Fe High School. Her flowing long black hair, doe eyes, and perfectly proportioned lean body lent her an air that made her seem older than the rest of us. She was sophisticated, often wearing all black, typically a fringe leather jacket with Native hand beadwork, chic boots, and tight jeans. As her friend, I knew firsthand that she was often bullied. She and I found refuge sitting on the bottom cement steps outside the school's theater entrance. Here we plotted escapes from this Alcatraz where we were both cultural outsiders and easy prey. She talked about her love of the fashion houses of Paris and Milan while I showed her the latest popular dance moves. Patricia showed me sketches of her designs and styles in an oversized notebook. This fed conversations about how she could shape the body with cloth, how the right cut could elongate the look of the length of the legs, how shoulder pads and a wide belt could accentuate a V-shape of the torso and hide pounds, and even how fringe could add motion to a dancer. Years later, her fringed tunics—inspired by traditional Native costumes and iconography and to which she gave a contemporary haute couture edginess and cachet—would premiere at New York Fashion Week shows and around the world. Patricia was first runner-up on *Project Runway* in the 2012 season. Her work continues to be featured on runway shows in Santa Fe, New York, and Paris. Recently, I choreographed a dance for the advanced dance students of the National Dance Institute in Santa Fe and Patricia generously designed the costumes.

Patricia and I got out of many dangerous situations through combined quick wits. When outside my own neighborhood, I realized that anticipating danger was my best defense. Karate taught me how to protect myself if and when I might need to do so. I earned major street cred after an incident in which I knocked out the neighborhood bully. The bully was behind me as we prepared to exit the bus. Suddenly he pushed me down the steps and yelled, "Maricon" (faggot). In reflex, I spun around and slammed him in the jaw, and he fell down the steps instead and crumpled to the ground. Kids roared with laughter. He never bothered me again. Instead, when he saw me, he made it a point to always shake my hand, a ritual and respectful three-step greeting— palm-to-palm, finger-to-finger, and then knuckle punch finale. I later learned that he took care of his father, a blind and house-bound veteran, and that, in fact, he was a very kind person.

I had done odd jobs since I was thirteen. At sixteen I landed my first real job, as a part-time retailer in the gift shop at the Museum of International Folk Art shop. There I spent hours exploring all the exhibitions. This is where I met the multifaceted Alexander Girard, or "Sandro," as he was affectionately called. He was an architect as well as an interior, textile, and furniture designer. Alexander placed his massive collection of folk art into meticulously conceived anthropomorphic menageries that could have been straight out of a child's imagination. His displays were arranged in such a way that each artifact, each toy, is displayed so as to look frozen in midmovement: busy market scenes with fruits, vegetables, and chickens being bought and sold to crowds; Day of the Dead scenes depicting families picnicking in cemeteries amidst tiny paper flowers and surrounded by mini skulls made of sugar. I still wander the Alexander Girard Collection several times a year and study the miniature toy theaters built from cardboard that show both the backstage as well as the front of the house and displays of milagros from Mexico to Morocco that remind me of the beauty of serendipity.

After working at the Museum of International Folk Art for a year, I took a job at Packard's on the Plaza, a trading post on the main square of the Santa Fe Plaza just across from the La Fonda Hotel. I was drawn to being in the busy and stimulating heart of Santa Fe. Here, I sold high-end Navajo jewelry and Southwestern rugs and pottery by day, and by night, I assisted local interior designer and retail window dresser Glynn Gomez as he created displays that showcased Santa Fe Style as art. He would strategically place a giant pueblo pot next to cowboy boots and drape antique Navajo rugs and silver turquoise and coral Concho belts over pedestals, to heighten dimension and clarify perspective. He instructed me how to paint stylized forms with a roller brush that, when placed in the window, created a desert filled with cacti highlighting a lone coyote howling at a paper moon. When Christmas approached, he had me spread faux snow around hand-carved *Nacimientos* (nativity scenes) and climb up ladders to adjust spotlights onto the baby Jesus and hang twenty tiny clay angels from Cochiti Pueblo and a gilded two-foot-long plywood star above. Glynn wore eye shadow in shades of plum and painted his black eyebrows in a theatrical style typical of a Japanese Kabuki actor. He had foot-long curly black hair that he dyed a deep purple. He went to the gym daily, following a regimen that gave him an oversized chest encased in tight shirts and muscle-engorged arms in relation to his spindly legs that were displayed every day, under the hem of short culottes. I admired his fashion fearlessness. He draped himself in long rows of *heishe*, handmade shell beads that he bought from the Kewa Pueblo. Glynn was Hispanic and had grown up in Santa Fe. He had molded himself into a fascinating androgynous creature that was beyond ridicule, and instead he was sought out for his sage advice and wisdom, a sacred Phrygian, Cybele. His cool practiced voice made pronouncements, what he called "laws to live by." He stated, "Dating men is like dating women, as long as they have a clear head and aren't conflicted, that's when they act like idiots," and "Go for the handsome ones, but make sure they have a brain, too." I took note. One day I would use this counsel. Although I had not formally "come out" as of yet I knew Glynn was gay, and he could tell I was gay. Glynn was the first openly gay man I knew, and I relished his dating stories, from hearing about Iggy, his personal trainer, to the ones about the man who worked behind the counter at the Galisteo Street Deli making sandwiches. Glynn had been able to cultivate an aura and lifestyle that was far beyond the city and its oppressive beliefs about homosexuality. He was more than a survivor. He was a mentor, inspiration, and role model for me as an emerging gay man. My apprenticeship as a store window display designer—tailoring my work to attract and hold the attention of passersby, as still-life art and tableau, all toward providing the best representation of the culture and goods of the area and this focused retailer—also introduced me to the theatrical elements of light, color, and perspective. These tools I would come to understand in all their limits and ranges, diverse applications, and efficacy, and that I would use later as a choreographer. Watching Glynn create window displays gave me an understanding of how audiences perceive scale, light, and shadow, and even how they perceive dramatic tension due to the thoughtful placement of figures in space.

Summer in Santa Fe features breezy restless desert nights. In 1985 I began sneaking into the outdoor Santa Fe Opera. I saw *The Marriage of Figaro, Orpheus in the Underworld*, and *The English Cat*, sitting on the ground under the stars. I would jump the fence and settle behind a bar lined with vodka, gin, and scotch—the perfect cover for a grand view of the stage. The bartender was a friend of my older brother, and he kindly turned a blind eye on this ardent intruder, as long as I was quiet.

I was fascinated by the staging, costumes, lighting, and deft set changes. The unique and breathtaking singularity of the Santa Fe Opera is its inherent relationship to nature. Because there is so little light pollution in Santa Fe—no urban high-rise towers, for example—the stars and the moon spectacularly frame the stage. The sky is the infinite luminous backdrop. Only rain could interfere—rare in the desert— but, still, it happened. At those rare times of a sudden downpour, the audience was forced into large movement improvisations. Not all the seats were sheltered by a roof; most were under the open sky. An evening thunderstorm would force people to frantically seek cover. I keenly studied how the large group scenes on stage also moved to the orchestra and voice. The performers never faced upstage, which would have of course garbled the singing. And although sung in Italian, French, and German—none of which I spoke—I could understand complicated stories through vocal intention and pantomime. This, too, was crucial training for me as a budding choreographer.

That winter I saw live concert dancing for the first time, at the little stage at the New Mexico School for the Deaf. My friends Jody and Salome performed in a show for their dance studio, which had rented the space. Shortly after, they invited me to class, and I took my first dance class at the Prince Ballet studio. I then took a handful of dance classes. One of those was in modern dance improvisation from an instructor who wore a tie-dyed tutu and accompanied himself on a tambourine. His garb was so over-the-top that the outrageously odd class seemed tame by comparison. The four dollars a class was more than worth the novel entertainment I garnered from the two dozen classes I attended.

I dropped out of Santa Fe High School at the end of my junior year and completed my high school credits through the Santa Fe Community College. During that last summer in 1986, I immersed in the open-minded community of dance and searched out like-minded young men. My dance classes and extra time lingering on the plaza gave me entre to a secret group of friends who also were starting to identify as gay, bisexual, or were gay friendly. "Mariposas" (butterflies) was the nickname for young promiscuous gays who figuratively flaunted their colorful wings and flew from man to man, or fragrant flower to flower. We fluttered about on the plaza. My outrageous Mariposa friend Michael Ortega emulated the legendary performer and pop idol Prince, dressed in purple and lace and high-heeled platform boots. He was often in the company of our new friend Sharon Khan, who dressed like Tina Turner in little black dresses, stiletto heels, and big backcombed hair. She had moved to Santa Fe from New York City. She was Trinidadian with an island accent infused with a forward-thrusting New York toughness. We called her Chaka Khan after the rock star, and she fed us stories about the neighborhoods of Jamaica Queens and Harlem.

That summer I kept seeing a handsome man with blonde hair around the main plaza. I asked here and there and learned that he was from Germany and named Thor. Young men and women alike talked about him. He was a novel figure with his spiky bleached hair, all pastel designer outfits, and the scent of his cologne wafting as he chatted in an exotic English. At the Häagen-Dazs shop, the forum of teen information, I asked where Thor worked, where he lived. He was rumored to be bisexual, and stories of both his male and female partners were shared. One night while I walked up San Francisco Street to the plaza, Thor, in hues of lavender and light blue, suddenly appeared next to me in canary yellow head to toe. "Hallo. You're Dana, ja?" "Ya," I said. We lingered in conversation and the divine smell of Lagerfeld cologne filled my nostrils. Thor circled me slowly, his hands boyishly thrust in his pants pockets, asking questions about how old I was and what ethnicity I was until he said, "I hear you have been asking about me, too, ja?" It was a flirtation of such skill that I was mesmerized. We went to a restaurant and talked for hours and then he asked me to go home with him.

It was the night I truly realized I was gay and that this fact was a passionate reality. I would emerge from my chrysalis closet. He drove us to Eldorado, where he lived in his mother's guest house. Under moonlight my eyes and hands explored his physique like it was the Michelangelo statue of David. My body quivered at his every kiss and touch. He kept asking if I was okay and I said "ja." He had obviously honed his skills with other men and knew how to caress and kiss and please. That night I was reborn. The next day I felt liberated. I truly could be with a man, not as a hypothetical but in physical reality. And it could be joyous and I was no longer an outsider in my own life.

For a time, Thor and I were inseparable, having grown-up dinners at high-end restaurants and evenings filled with intellectual discussions that always ended in his bed in his arms. The power of our physical attraction combined with the newness of gay sex led me to fall deeply in love—or perhaps infatuation—with Thor. All I could do was think about him until I could be with him again. To my dismay and confusion though, after four passionate weeks, Thor fluttered away to other flowers, leaving me quite heartbroken. No explanation. I stalked him for weeks after our breakup, calling him, stopping by his home until it became evident that he had begun seeing a girl as well as another man.

I wanted to participate in a gay community, to see gay couples interact, to understand how people disconnect and have casual sex, and to really know that I was no longer alone with these clear attractions. My young gay friends and I had heard about the *Cactus Club*, a gay bar on the edge of town, with dancing and a drag show. Each of us came up with plans to acquire a fake ID. I drove to the little city of Espanola and used my brother's birth certificate to acquire one at the DMV. The next Saturday night, we dressed up and met at the *Cactus Club*, a tiny bar hidden behind an old Travelodge on Cerrillos Road. The doorman turned out to be good old Mr. Baca. He obviously recognized us all. We still nervously flashed our IDs at the door, and he waved us in, tipping his cowboy hat and winking. Inside I saw several classmates from Santa Fe High, a football player, a basketball player, and two theater students, the sources of the mysterious rumors about Mr. Baca.

I became a regular on the disco dance floor. If I met a man and was attracted, we kissed, surrounded by other gay men moving in abandon and in kaleidoscopic simpatico and unison. Unlike several of my friends who still felt a Catholic guilt about being gay and said a hundred Hail Marys for each of their perceived sins, I felt absolutely none. No shame, no guilt, no beseeching of forgiveness from my Maker. I came into my own identity as a proud gay man that summer. Flashing lights and glittering drag shows came to a close when a voice over the sound system announced, "Last call for alcohol." At this point we dashed home in time to sneak quietly back into our bedrooms.

I had found the monarch wildflower fields at last. I was finally completely free.

Within three months, I would leave Santa Fe to attend the University of New Mexico in Albuquerque and immerse myself in a whole new world of formalized, rigorous dance studies and ever deepening and crucial lifelong lessons, about myself, and about my art.

Albuquerque is the largest city in New Mexico. Its heart is the University of New Mexico (UNM), a sprawling six-hundred-acre campus. In 1986 this center of literati had twenty-five thousand undergraduate and graduate students. Santa Fe's total population was less than double UNM's student enrollment.

Santa Fe had given me an ethereal, spiritual understanding of the world, a vision of the ineffable and unseen, mystical and inchoate. Albuquerque would give me the sinews, bones, and guts to move through it. The key to New Mexico is to develop the self-possession and endurance of a viscous succulent, to earn and to occupy the hot and dry landscape as one of its idiosyncratic tough-skinned, spiny, and indomitable beings, gradually earning and achieving a kind of rugged beauty, of belonging and respect that comes from hard-won survival. Like the cactus, I was determined to thrive.

While some freshmen have educational travel experiences within the United States and beyond—school trips, camps, and exchange and study-abroad programs—I had not. Moving to Albuquerque for college was my first learning, liberating, and overwhelming adventure away from home. By now in Santa Fe, I had found a community of gay friends; in Albuquerque I would have to start again to establish that camaraderie.

At eighteen, I weighed 120 pounds and was a gangly five feet, ten inches tall. I dyed my hair burgundy, combed it up in a three-inch high flat-top crown, and anchored it with Aqua Net. I had decided to jump into my new life with a stand-out look. I didn't want to conform or be invisible; I wanted a look that was unique and untamed. My two 1970s Samsonite hard-shell suitcases were filled with thrift shop finds and my signature ankle boots. I loaded them into my four-door, secondhand light blue 1981 Mazda 323 that I had saved so long to buy, and I headed one hour south to Albuquerque.

I arrived at the maze of the UNM campus. I circled, lost in the array of massive adobe stucco buildings, finally parking a block from the registration building. I took my place with other new students to be signed into classes, hand over tuition payment, get a student ID, and keys to an assigned dorm room. Mine was a two hundred-square-foot shared room on the third floor of dilapidated Hokona Hall. The floor had been designated for the swim team plus a few academically inclined nerds. I was obviously the latter. My roommate was to be Larry Brown, a physics major with a quantum theory bent. Larry arrived wearing glasses with thick lenses, and his girlfriend Lynda had nearly matching eyewear. They were easy going and while unpacking, shared that Lynda had been joking, "What are the odds that you'll be assigned a room with a gay guy?" Lynda assumed I was gay by my appearance and soft-spoken manner. Lynda's best friend was gay, she said. Furthermore, she said, Larry's mom's best friend was gay, and so forth. I unpacked brightly colored shirts in primary colors, many with shoulder pads I had sewn in by hand and three pairs of black ankle boots, each with three-inch heels. Larry unpacked flannel shirts, faded jeans, and worn Docksiders. We had two twin beds pushed against opposite walls, two small desks and a mini fridge. We easily made a pact: no dirty clothes on the floor, no open food in the trash, and we would coordinate date calendars to give the other the room. He would go home, or I would go to Santa Fe on those appointed weekends.

The swim team, half-naked Neptunians, walked the hall shirtless and in boxer briefs. Like puffed up ticks, full of their meal, their long spindle legs were a reminder that land was not their natural element. And me, I was a Santa Fe desert lizard in reaction, my head jerking, eyes darting and blinking. I studied the carpet, to suggest that I was consumed with the weave, oblivious to their skin. Unlike Larry, who was at ease with his sexuality and had no problem with me being gay, the swimmers did all they could to establish that they were straight, making gay jokes and talking loudly about their female conquests.

Monday of the first week of the semester, I woke to an alarm I had set the night before to sound early, to give myself time to prepare to make my debut entrance. It is what I do. As I approached the giant bathroom at the end of the hall, I was reminded of my painful body shaming incidents in high school PE class. At fourteen, I had been the only one without armpit hair or a muscular body. I was still thin, and in the midst of these swimmers, many of whom were upperclassmen, I again felt my relative corporal deficiencies. In my pajamas, I made way to the communal shower, towel and soap in hand. I undressed in a corner, entered the shower in flip-flops and faced a tile wall for further anonymity. In contrast, the team yelled good-naturedly at one another, not an ounce of flab or shyness. In water—apparently any water—they most came to life, a pod of dolphins. I showered hastily and scurried back to my room where I donned black skinny jeans, a blousy white pirate tunic with a plunging neckline trimmed with ruffles, and my black pointed ankle boots of faux python. I would make the entrance to my first business course, but it would be in the spirit of punk rocker Adam Ant. I had absolutely no intention of getting a degree in the Arts. I had lived through my parents' financial struggles as artists. I had grown up in three dilapidated rentals and attended some of what were literally the worst public schools in the country. I thought that the lifestyle I craved would be conscientiously built through the financial success of a business degree that would land me a nine-to-five job with nice pay and the means to buy things brand new. I willed it: "I will be an accountant." I would model myself on Japanese businessman Yoshiaki Tsutsumi. In 1986, *Forbes Magazine* said he was the richest man in the world. If my mental posture in this businessman mindset was a karate kata, my invisible foes were named dance and art gallery. I would vanquish them.

I strutted into classes taught in this foreign language of debits, credits, spreadsheets, and income statements. But within two weeks I found I was now to be bullied and baited by balance sheets. I could never get my practice cash flow charts to add up. My expense and revenue columns always projected a bottom line in the red. Was this, then, a family curse, the inability to get along with money? After my Introduction to

Business Accounting class, I sought out the professor for guidance. He took a long hard look at my finished homework. Puzzled, he asked me what I saw. He sought to compare my answer with what he saw within the narrow lines of rows and boxes. He quickly surmised that I seemed to have a moderate case of dyscalculia, a difficulty in comprehension and manipulation of numerical calculations. Who knew? It is not the same as math dyslexia, but it is related. All the numbers in my charts were jumbled, no matter my tortured efforts. And it was not my fault. A relief. Many things now at last made sense: why I couldn't write phone numbers correctly on the first, second, or even third try; why it took hours longer for me to do math homework than any other subject; and why I had to drop out of algebra in high school. I was absolved: the blame was impairment, not indolence.

In despair, I started skipping my business classes, undecided about what classes to switch out or drop. I rose late now and wandered campus during my accounting classes—much the way I had wandered alone in the desert as a child. Roaming eased my stress as I searched for a new direction. I spoke to Larry who was excelling in his physics classes. "I would ditch, too, if I was studying what I wasn't capable of doing," he said. "I always loved physics in high school. Had you always liked accounting?" No. I adored the undulations of the desert dunes, the set designs of retail windows, and uninhibited dancing in discos. But those inclinations were not an accredited curriculum.

I took daily walks along the UNM duck pond all the way to Central Avenue. Then I would head into the Frontier Restaurant and sit for hours. Established in 1971, Frontier Restaurant is a greasy spoon incubator for heartburn and front seat for people-watching. I learned right away that everyone went here for green chili-pepper hash browns. New Mexican chili dates back to the original Pueblo and Hispano communities. It would be hundreds of years before Japanese American Roy Nakayama, a horticulturist, would develop New Mexico's chili plants, making them marketable and profitable. Chili is still a primary crop for New Mexican farmers. Chili season is August through September, and New Mexico air fills will the rich smell of smoky red and green chili peppers roasting.

Walls at the Frontier are decorated with paintings of New Mexico, a mash-up of Southwestern images. It is a kitsch-fest of skewed scale and perspectives. One painting depicted a hand-carved Kachina doll, a figure meant to honor the deities of the Hopi people who live in Arizona. It was poised atop a huge wooden table in front of a colorful basket filled with red, blue, and yellow Indian corn cobs, a symbol of the fall harvest season. Another painting depicted a *caballero*—a horseman—wearing a ridiculous outsized sombrero and standing next to his palomino, surrounded by desert agave plants. In another painting of a caballero, the subject bore a likeness to actor John Wayne, in his "Duke" Hollywood cowboy movie era, complete with giant boots. These paintings and others of local iconography and nature, with their almost absurdist conflated beauty, always amused me. One element they shared held my interest. Their perspectives were completely wrong. The background agave plants dwarfed the caballero's stallion in the foreground, and his sombrero looked like it was intended to be four feet in circumference. The Duke's cowboy boots were not smaller than a size twenty. Only a minimally able amateur could have painted these. In their absurdity lay their charm.

The tabletops and pleather booth seats were sticky with spills and old grease, and the insides of the self-serve coffee pots allowing for free refills were stained with heavy mineral deposits. The clientele seemed to consist of the entire social strata of Albuquerque, from the very wealthy to former and current UNM students, to tattoo-covered bikers, punks, goths, and wanderers. Its pace was much faster than at any cheap eatery in Santa Fe. People breezed in and out for quick bites. I loitered here undisturbed for hours—this was my classroom—observing each patron's' movements—until I couldn't drink another refill. I listened to the conversations of all its diverse denizens to learn if there were people like me, in 1986, looking for a place to belong. The Frontier means something to a lot of people, by the way; it is still open for business and is as popular as ever.

During one of my daily walks back to campus from the Frontier, the third week of classes, I wandered into Carlisle Gymnasium, home of the UNM Dance Program. As I meandered adjacent to its pueblo revival–style architecture—adobe stucco walls with windowsills outlined in turquoise—I heard pop music blaring from open first floor windows. I entered the building and slipped into the darkness of the upper bleachers. The 1920s-era gym had been converted into a voluminous dance studio. The original wooden basketball court was now a dance floor though you could still see the boundary, midcourt, and foul lines. The soaring white ceiling was like the one to be found within an airplane hangar, with metal beams that supported the weight of the roof. From the privacy of the shadows, I stuck around and watched a jazz dance class.

A university offered dance classes? This emancipating sight, of lines of bodies moving in sinuous, sweaty exuberant unity was so different from the restrictions of accounting columns, arrayed and confining like a holding pen or prison bars. I sat hypnotized by the undulations, contractions, and kicks. The students wore bright shades of spandex tights and leotards, leg warmers, and the occasional oversized T-shirt with the neckline cut out to hang off one shoulder. These were mainly female dancers, but there were three male dancers, too. I brightened at that. There might be a place for me here.

I will never forget the routine that I watched that day. Each dancer shimmied their hands, whirled their arms like windmill blades, popped their shoulders up and down, and whipped their heads around before freezing in a pose. These dancers worked hard to perfect the synchronized snappy routine through exhaustive repetitions. I realized that this is the work that goes into the TV shows that were America's and my own favorites. Shows like *Solid Gold* and *Dance Fever* and the cult dance movies *Flashdance* and *Footloose*. The gym pounded with staccato moves and with attitudes. The teacher signaled the students to perform the combination one last time. The class surged forward, and on the count aloud, "5 . . . 6 . . . 7 . . . 8," they became a dramatic moving mass of confident self-possession. In unison, they performed a high leg kick, turned twice in a row, contracted their torsos while spinning their arms, looked side then front as they strutted forward with shoulder rolls and a series of full-body gyrations that ended in a perfect wide-stance, hands at their hips. This pose they sustained in the mirror until the teacher dismissed them. This level of training far exceeded the quirky little dance studio in Santa Fe with which I was familiar. These were not messy, improvisational exercises done to the beat of a tambourine. This was a group of cohesive dancers whose legs and feet had been lengthened and strengthened by the fine repetitions of strategic exercises and stretches, dancers taught to condition and contour their torsos and isolate their shoulders. My meandering had delivered me my destiny, a secular temple where dancers were tempered into competitive, professional-level performers.

The class adjourned and the space cleared for a modern dance class, students clad in T-shirts and sweatpants. Wordlessly, they warmed up—rolled on the ground like newborns making breathy waking sounds as they readied their bodies. The teacher, a Latina woman in her late twenties, walked to the front. Her carriage exuded energy and self-assurance. At the side of class, an accompanist with a long white beard and ponytail pulled percussion instruments from protective bags and containers—large and small drums, a cowbell, and a xylophone set—which he set around his folding chair. She called out his name, a greeting and cue, "Jack!" She led students through a unified warm-up, slowly rolling down the spine to touch the toes in eight counts and rebounding back to standing with an audible breath in four counts. The students stretched their toes and legs on and off the floor in tendus and dégagés and extended alternating legs to waist height in swings. They then glided across the floor in a movement pattern that folded and unfolded their limbs: lunge, tip toe, tip toe, lunge, crease at the hips to roll to the ground, and return to standing in order to brush a leg off the ground, while balancing on one foot before repeating the phrase. Complicated stuff. Dancers rolled to the floor gently with an ease and grace different from the aggressive steps of karate. They changed their facings, driven by their core, as Jack banged rhythms on his drums and sharply clanged other metal instruments. Jack eventually pulled out a Güiro, a hollow gourd with grooves, across which he rhythmically rubbed a stick. This instrument added a sound not at all unfamiliar to me—one made by locusts when they rub their hind legs together.

This drone added to the music of multiple percussive instruments that accentuated every move. He was a busker, old Jack, and boy did he have old-school chops. The sounds were mated not only to the combination's appropriate counts, but also to the steps of each dancer, their shifts of weight, balances, and even gestures. Jack was actually creating music that mimicked the dancers' movements. A lunge was a deep drumbeat, tip toe steps high pitched xylophone keys, a brush of the leg off the floor, the brush of a stick across the Güiro. I was in absolute awe and bliss.

This magical realism, merging images both real and suggested, coalescing dance and music, and felt in my veins and sinews viscerally, was soon to be expanded. Just then, a group of female flamenco dancers entered, and they moved past the edge of the modern dance class. The sound of *pasos*—stomped steps—like those of the flamenco dancers I had seen on the Santa Fe Plaza, signaled the entrances of several more flamenco dancers who dragged behind them bright red, yellow, and orange *batas de cola*, colorful long ruffled skirt trains. Their polka-dot skirts looked like a field of flowers had snapped free from their stems in animated search of an *ofrenda*, a Day of the Dead altar. The dancers were like the marigolds with which family members cover their altars to guide the spirits home on October thirty-first through November second: nights that the spirits rush back to the world of the living, to be honored by family members. The dozen Spanish dancers stomped past with crisp elegance and disappeared into a studio down the hall oblivious to the modern dance class. Ten minutes later, the modern dancers went into gentle cool-down by folding over their legs and placing their hands on the floor to loosen their lumbar muscles and hamstrings. As Jack's accompaniment grew soft, I could hear flamenco dancers in their distant dance studio in the vast building, the sound of *palmas*—syncopated clapping—and the strum of a live guitar against a rush of pounding heels.

When the modern dance class was dismissed, as the gymnasium emptied, I at last looked at my watch and couldn't believe that three-and-a-half hours had passed. I descended the bleachers and went laughing, leaping, jumping, and skipping, out of the building, as if trying to catch a thousand butterflies whirling around me. I hadn't felt such elation since I was a child and first spied a monarch on a coneflower.

That night, I couldn't sleep. Restless and excited, I considered what truly made me happy: dance. Dance. DANCE. I considered how to reconcile a business class schedule when juxtaposed with the exhilaration I felt from watching the dance classes. In one world I was bankrupt and paralyzed, while in Carlisle Gym I was rich with inspiration and a natural path forward, with at least hope for a happy future. I realized that my parent's financial struggles had scared me away from being an artist and that, in reality, the joy that dancing brought me was my wealth.

The next morning, I returned to my hidden perch at Carlisle: a hive of organized dance activity that ran seamlessly in one and a half hour increments with fifteen minutes between each class. Dance students studied their craft every day and went from morning to late afternoon, including advanced, intermediate, and beginning technique sections in modern dance, ballet, and jazz. In the lobby, I scoured the posted class schedule and read about how one went about earning a degree majoring in dance at the university. There were even classes in dance history, kinesiology, and choreography.

By day three of my intelligence gathering, the pursuit of dance officially asserted itself as imperative. I woke early, dressed in white sweatpants, a black graphic T-shirt emblazoned Duran Duran, and a black headband. I infiltrated the back of the beginning modern dance class. I followed each warm-up combination, preparing my muscles and joints, and allowed my body to soar in the final across-the-floor combination of extended leg leaps: kicking into the splits while airborne. My surreptitious presence was spotted. Professor Licia Perea, a beautiful Latina woman with a long black ponytail, approached, "You are doing great! Who are you?" Flushed, I thanked her. "My name is Dana. I'm from Santa Fe. I've taken a few dance classes there, but nothing as good as your class." She grinned and said, "You did great, but if you want to come back, as I hope you will, you need to enroll. I can help with that if you don't know how to do so." She looked at me with kind dark eyes, understanding everything, and waited patiently for my response. I blurted, "I'm a business major but I'm not happy in the business school." She said, "Be a dance major. Judging by how quickly you picked up my class, you could be a successful professional dancer. You can do this. *Do it*." I was overjoyed. "I'll go and register right now!" Professor Perea—Licia, as we would come to call her—smiled and said, "Perfect, hasta la próxima clasé!" This was the universe's signal for which I had been waiting. That afternoon I dropped my business classes, signed up for all dance classes, declared a change of my major to Dance, and moved from being an observer to being a participant in UNM's dance community. I mark that as the moment I also moved from being an observer to a participant in my own professional life as well, much as I had already done with my sexual life.

Modern dance training shares key elements with karate training. Dance and karate warm-ups include regimented exercises that warm the muscles and prepare the body, mind, and spirit to move as one. Movement gave me physical challenges and a pride in mastery of new steps and combinations. Dance endorphins carried me from depression to brightness and lightness. Dance built my self-reliance. Me, the guy who once could not do math sequences in school, the algebra dropout with "dyscalculia"—that guy—was now suddenly counting and long streams of numbers and intricate intervals, juggling simultaneous counterpoints. They posed no obstacle. Numbers welcomed me, came toward me, and moved through me like water. They now met me on my own turf, in my own element. We were friends, not opponents. I began to be able to recall long combinations and sequences, able to count and stay in sync with the music. I was absorbing formal techniques, foundations, such as how to gradate my physical energy in a class. In karate everything was centered on how to knock out an opponent; in dance the goal was to engage, involve, invite, to communicate through movement with others, in unison. I worked on aligning my sway back, extending my limbs, and pointing my feet: daily multifaceted exhilarating physical challenges.

The spring semester of freshman year I added ballet to my schedule. My professor for ballet was Judith Bennahum, a strawberry blonde with a PhD in dance history who had studied with George Balanchine at the New York City Ballet and had been invited to dance with the company in the early 1960s. It was a daunting honor to study under a professor who had reached the astronomically top echelon of the field.

She terrified students with Socratic one-liners. If a student arrived late and disheveled, she serenely proclaimed, "The ballet dancer you will become is clear from the moment you step into the studio." Should a prideful dancer become complacent with their leg exercises at barre, in a stage whisper she would say to that student, "The art of ballet isn't just about leg extensions ... it is so much more. Think about art, Dear. Now work harder." She did not waste opportunities to instruct, when she could use individual lapses as teaching moments for us all, always related directly to dance itself, not to individual flaws, but to move us closer to being the best dancers we could be. She nailed every bad habit, from tardiness to gluttony, with truthful advice that set students to soul searching, not shame. That said, she tore down in order to build up, so that each of us would know ourselves to be strong enough to survive both the emotional as well as the physical rigors of a professional dance company. Graceful Professor Bennahum demanded that each student honor the legacy of ballet as art. In her fifties, she still danced circles around us, was beautiful, wise, and willing to wage war against our lesser inclinations and lapses.

Ballet was difficult. I was unfamiliar with the form. I had only watched the *Nutcracker* televised on PBS—three times—and had attended exactly one live ballet recital, at age sixteen, performed by my dance friends in Santa Fe. So, I lacked even a complete picture of what ballet could look like.

This beginning-intermediate class had students of widely varying skill—even advanced dancers who had been training for more than a dozen years. I lacked any of the exacting training and sculpting, the muscle development that some students had built over years of immersive practice. Ballet features a unique specificity of outward turned muscle groups that are engaged for each exercise. It is a highly stylized art form, refined over five hundred years in the courts of Europe. In France, Louis IVX's noblemen had to be skilled in the art of fencing as well as the art of dance. Ballet had absorbed complicated court dance steps that then evolved into stage dance. The fundamentals of ballet today owe a lineage reaching directly back to the royal courts of the sixteenth and seventeenth centuries.

The "royale step" is a little beat of the feet in a jump that starts front and lands back. It was created and named for the King Louis IVX. The quick triple step, or *pas de bourré*, has its roots in court fêtes and references the steps of tipsy partygoers because of the way it sways side-to-side in a seemly off-balance kilter. In 1661, Louis XIV created the first state-run professional school for ballet, the Académie Royale de Danse. To learn ballet is to express history as told through the body. Each exercise that the ballet dancer executes, poised and one hand maintaining balance at the barre, builds length, grace, and stamina. These perfected exercises ready the performance of balletic choreography.

Each class, I worked my feet, pointed them. I strengthened my calves by rising onto the balls of my feet in relevés and by executing small jumps over and over. I built my hamstrings and quadriceps by jumping high into the air. Ballet literally transforms the musculature and ultimately even the bones of the body. As the muscular attachments grow strong the insertions of those muscles require thicker bones to hold onto, the muscles feed the bones accordingly, supplying richer blood and nourishment. Ballet was health.

Each exercise was a new road hewn to my hips and legs. Parallel karate leg stances had to be replaced by outwardly facing limbs. My struggles were made more so, ironically, by the years of rigorous karate training. The years of inwardly rotated and parallel stances and flexed feet of karate had to now be reversed, unfurled, and dissolved through a constant engagement to build new neurological pathways over and around old ones. Now my heels touched, and my toes on each foot turned away from each other as if in feud—oh, but it was a glorious opposition. Bedtime sore muscles, sometimes agonizing, heckled me throughout my legs and lower back. But I thrived upon exactly these exertions and recoveries as evidence of my emerging dancer's body, and I awakened eager to return to this grueling course every day. Ballet was the bully I could love.

The old inhibitions, from being bullied and displaced—all that isolation that I had withstood on a daily basis as a child and teen in Santa Fe—were being overwritten when I danced. I became an exhibitionist, harking back to my innocent dining room recitals in Carmel Valley. Dance exposed a creative tension, a duality in me; in speaking with many professional dancers, this seems not uncommon. The introvert drawn to the discipline of dance, one accustomed to solitude and sacrifice, becomes a showman in class and on the stage.

Spread across a section of the shiny gymnasium floor was a sheet of gray vinyl, called a "Marley dance floor." It allowed us just enough traction to not skid unintentionally in our ballet slippers, with enough smoothness to execute complex moves without inviting injuries. Pirouettes, or turns on one leg, for example, could be done without twisting an ankle.

In class, I was often counts behind because I didn't use the plié or knee bend preparation properly, meaning I was late to bend my knees to pump me back into the air. The skilled dancers, the ones with years of training, skimmed across the Marley surface like dragonflies on a pond. When my feet were on the floor, the class was off the ground and vice versa. This lone water beetle loped across a puddle to stay afloat.

Instead of surrendering to fear of failure, I pressed onward. I would arrive an hour early to class each day in order to better warm up my legs and my back. I would place a foot on the ballet barre, lengthening my knee, and grab onto my foot as I folded over until my back and hamstrings finally loosened. Then I would repeat this on the other leg. I massaged my feet and calves, increasing the articulation of the muscles. I focused on my flat medial arches and slowly coaxed them to lift, as my ankle joints opened revealing a pointed foot. After class I routinely stayed late to practice my leg extensions and my jumps. Not once as I struggled did Professor Bennahum tell me I did not belong. I dreaded banishment, but such an excision never came, and I slowly began to relax and be better able to execute the steps.

left Hio Voon Kang, Oahu, HI, 1920c. Dana Tai Soon Burgess Photographs, Archives Center, National Museum of American History, Smithsonian Institution.

below Soon Kuen Kang, Oahu, HI, 1926c. Dana Tai Soon Burgess Photographs, Archives Center, National Museum of American History, Smithsonian Institution.

Anna Kang Burgess, Oahu, HI, 1932.
Dana Tai Soon Burgess Photographs,
Archives Center, National Museum
of American History, Smithsonian
Institution.

Marie Southwell Burgess,
Joseph James Burgess Jr.,
Albany, NY, 1940. Private
Collection of Dana Tai
Soon Burgess.

Joseph James Burgess Jr.,
1942. Private Collection
of Dana Tai Soon Burgess.

Anna Kang Burgess
weaving at her loom,
Santa Fe, NM, 1974.
Private collection of
the Burgess Family.

Joseph James Burgess Jr.,
Dana Tai Soon Burgess,
Carmel, CA, 1968.
Private Collection of
Dana Tai Soon Burgess.

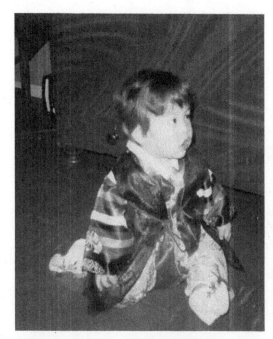

Dana Tai Soon Burgess, first birthday celebration, Carmel, CA, 1969. Dana Tai Soon Burgess Photographs, Archives Center, National Museum of American History, Smithsonian Institution.

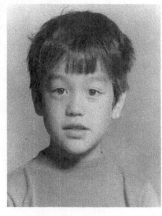

above Dana Tai Soon Burgess, class photo, Carmel, CA, 1972. Dana Tai Soon Burgess Photographs, Archives Center, National Museum of American History, Smithsonian Institution.

left Ian Tai Kyung Burgess, Dana Tai Soon Burgess, CA, 1973. Dana Tai Soon Burgess Photographs, Archives Center, National Museum of American History, Smithsonian Institution.

Makio Nishida, Dana Tai Soon Burgess, Flagstaff, AZ, 1979. Dana Tai Soon
Burgess Photographs, Archives Center, National Museum of American History,
Smithsonian Institution.

ten THE MONARCH FINDS

HIS FLIGHT PATTERN

It took three years to reshape my legs and feet. While moving back and forth between modern and ballet classes I had a crucial and sustaining insight for the long-term: a professional modern dancer's ability to move from vertical positions to curvilinear forms of the body with ease came from cross-training in both styles. This full body knowledge gives the dancer a three-dimensional range of movement.

To this day I only hire dancers skilled in both idioms. The ability of a dancer to execute modern, ballet, and even one or (preferably) more than one culturally specific dance form, is something I seek out when auditioning dancers for my company. The synergy of line and fluidity that comes from being proficient in multiple techniques creates a world-class dancer.

At the same time I was studying modern and ballet, I took classes in art history, Asian history, and dance history. This combination brought to surface how the human body has been celebrated in art since even before the illustrious *Venus of Willendorf*, a stone-age depiction of figurative art dating from 30,000 BCE. Art directly reflects the socio-political context in which it is formed. My history courses clarified the confluence of visual and performing arts in relation to the stories of human evolution. Great choreography mirrors golden ages, and disastrous regimes create dissident art. This was a revelation that I would import to the dance studio years later.

I studied the relationship of traditional South Asian dance, Bharatanatyam, to the interpretation of stories from *The Mahabharata*, a Sanskrit epic from ancient India. I learned about the great Silk Road at its height in the T'ang Dynasty of 618–907 CE and how this trade route carried not only material items but also religions, dances, and philosophies between the East and West along winding routes from Chang An, the old imperial capital of China, to Persia, India, Indonesia,

Korea, Japan, many other Central Asian and Middle Eastern cities, and Venice, Italy. I studied the writings of Lao Tzu and learned how the *I Ching* was actually used by Merce Cunningham to create "chance dance," a theory of combining random dance phrases and stage elements to create postmodern dances. My history and dance classes were intersecting, and this was a tremendous and crucial look into dance as a fundamental form of communication across the globe and time. My mind and body were becoming emblems of an ever-expanding universe of influences and ideas and inspirations that took residence inside me. It was absolutely thrilling.

When I was a sophomore in 1987, Professor Bennahum asked me to call upon dance icon Eleanor King, unaccompanied. She asked because not only was I a dance student but also because I am Korean American. Professor Bennahum told me that Ms. King was eighty-one years old and trying to organize her life's work into a professional archive. Ms. King was one of the pioneers of modern dance who, as a young woman in 1928, danced for the original Humphrey-Weidman Dance Company in New York City and was a principal of the modern dance scene. Her 1978 book, *Transformations: The Humphrey Weidman Era, A Memoir,* published by Dance Horizons, chronicles her early career, which started on the East Coast and went West in the late 1930s to Seattle, Washington, where she founded and choreographed for her own company. In 1952, she accepted the offer of a teaching job at the University of Arkansas, and she stayed there until 1971 after which time she retired to Santa Fe. She had tackled Noh Theater in Kyoto at age fifty-four and studied Tai Chi two years later (seeing the relationship between martial arts and dance). Then, at age seventy, she began studying classical and shamanistic Korean dance in Seoul. The shamanistic traditions of Korea date back five thousand years and are steeped in beliefs of magic and ritual as a means to contact the spirit realm. That in turn inspired her to create and perform a series she called *East–West Dances.*

At the Kimo Theatre—a Southwest deco-style architectural gem in downtown Albuquerque—I had seen a performance of two inspiring reconstructions of her early solos: *Mother of Tears* (1935) and *To the West* (1943). *Mother of Tears* especially resonated with my early introduction to images of the Virgin Mary—Our Lady of Sorrows—seen so many times in Santa Fe churches. This simple solo exemplified the strength that can be conveyed through the clear performance of detailed gestures and small movements. The female dancer, dressed in a black religious habit from head to toe, appeared trapped under her tunic, symbolic of heavy sorrow. The dancer moved her feet in small twitching motions, exemplifying her inability to advance across the floor. Instead, she was stuck in a six-by-six-foot box of light where she responded to a repeating ultimate maternal tragedy, one that implored her to gesture the wiping away of tears and the clutching of her heart.

Professor Bennahum hoped that I could help Ms. King sift through her dance programs and choreographic notes toward curating an ordered archive. But on another level, she was setting up a cultural learning opportunity for me to engage with a dance legend who held Korea close to her heart. I enthusiastically agreed to meet with Ms. King at her home in Santa Fe. And what a dual purpose: I would be going back to my own hometown. That itself was a form of putting into order my own earliest memories and archives.

In Santa Fe, I knocked on the door of a dilapidated adobe hovel, once white but now a dull gray from wind and desert and neglect. When within a few minutes no one answered, I gingerly peered in through long grimy front windows. In the living room cardboard boxes towered next to piles of loose papers. I rapped on the glass. Ms. King walked toward the front door and opened it; I beheld a tiny old woman with skin like crackled parchment, dressed in a white cotton *jeogori*, a traditional crisscrossed Korean garment, and *paji*, traditional billowing pants. Her top had a perfectly tied *goreum*, or closing ribbon. Her outfit was a Korean man's outfit like the one my grandfather wore as a young man in photos from the 1920s. She wore her long white hair in a *sangtu*, a man's style top-knot—a man bun nowadays—tied in place with a wide white ribbon. Her slight frame and aquiline features made me think how beautiful she must have been as a young woman and how bizarre it was to see an elderly Caucasian woman in traditional Korean man's clothing from sixty years earlier. Modern Korean men no longer dressed like a *Yangban*, or a gentrified Confucian scholar.

After I introduced myself as Professor Bennahum's student, Ms. King bade me come in and we sat on cushions around a traditional low, square Korean-style table—one covered in film of white cat hair and flaky dander. Her white cat coordinated with her own garb. It wandered, wound and slunk about ... everywhere. She told me that Professor Bennahum, or "Gigi," had told her that she would be meeting me, who had described me as "a Korean—and aspiring modern dancer." Ms. King shared her fervor for Korean culture and that she had boxes of Korean primary research materials from her time there that needed to be organized. After our cups of *Nokcha*, a Korean green tea blended with roasted brown rice, she asked me to begin opening those boxes. Ms. King's materials revealed the study of *mudangchum*, a shamanistic trance dance that purportedly moves the performer between the physical and spiritual realms, often performed in exorcisms. The skill to release the veil between these two dimensions moves the dancer to a trance state for days and even weeks, a performance during which the audiences come and go. Holding a rattle—small bells strung together on a handle—in the left hand and a large fan in the right, the mudang dancer circles the space while flicking their fan and bells, sometimes against each other, accompanied by musicians who play a cacophony of horns and cymbals. Their steps speed as euphoric left-turning circles whirl faster and faster, arm movements outstretching, at the approach of the spirit realm. Audiences are riveted by the shaman's journey.

During my second visit, as we rummaged together, Ms. King said, "Consider the role of the dancer and the audience in relation to internal and external performance foci." I asked, "What is 'foci?'" She answered, "A fancy word, plural for multiple focus." Could the performer actually hypnotize the audience? Entrance them by using their own invested performance state?

It fascinated me that Ms. King, who was not Korean, would be so invested in the dance traditions of Korea and that she would know so much more about my mother culture, half of my identity, than I did. I asked more about the role of the shaman as dancer in Korean society. "The shaman learns to cast a spell over the audience." "What exactly do you mean?" I asked. She responded, "A dancer is like a shaman who invests deeply, believes completely in their performance, and is able to transport the audience to another world." Ms. King believed that the audience acknowledges this deep, altered state and is compelled to leave their reality and move their consciousness to another dimension of time and space. The role of the dancer as shaman is to reintroduce the overall emotional capacities to feel, from which the audience has become too long disconnected.

Ms. King's philosophy was informed by decades of study and contemplation. I was a callow but earnest nineteen-year-old, and our questions and answers as we sorted those boxes still resonate like unanswered *Koan*, or paradoxical Zen riddles, more than thirty years later.

Our dozen three-hour work sessions—a semester that I dared to hope was as priceless for her as it was for me—were now complete. Ms. King's oral archives, at least, had been transferred, absorbed by me. For the record, I had barely organized any part of Ms. King's massive archive. We never seemed to move past our philosophical conversations over Nokcha. It is likely that the oral history, the passing of knowledge and nuance from old to young, the bonding, and my own enlightenment about my culture, especially as it related to dance, had been the real point after all. Ms. King exemplified indelibly for me how fulfillment in a lifelong journey in dance can deepen, unbounded by age, even as the body deteriorates.

Cue the entrance now of that eternal dancer, Serendipity.

The next and final time I would ever see Ms. King was in 1990, in Washington, DC, just months before her death. She was sitting on a park bench three blocks from the White House. She stood out in her white Korean chogori and paji, quite alone. I could barely believe this . . . conjuring. She was the beatific image of *Gwan-eum*, the beneficent Korean goddess of compassion, surrounded by a swirling DC rush hour. I approached and I reminded her who I was, "I'm Dana," as I had that first time two-and-half years ago, and asked if I could join her. She made room for me on the bench. Although initially confused to see me out of context, but still vaguely remembering me, we had an elegiac conversation about dance. It was, though, with that same hospitality I had enjoyed in her home during my undergraduate years. "What are you doing here, Ms. King?" She answered that she was setting an old choreography for a dance company in the area and was awaiting the director. She spoke to me about a handheld Korean drum, a *sogo*, that she was considering for a new choreography. Although her mind was slipping, she was still a generous and creative genius. A giant, even then, really. In 1991, I read that Eleanor King had passed away on February 27 at the Actor's Home in Haddonfield, New Jersey. I was deeply saddened that she had died away from her beloved Santa Fe. But I was so happy to have had one last dialogue with her that way.

How appropriate that I should have come upon her in my new home city—exactly as if she were offering me her beloved mudang dance—and that bustling audience, coming and going at that raucous thoroughfare. For this final dance, onlookers in their honking and spinning cars would supply her with the horns, the clashing cymbals, the swirling lively cacophony, as she migrated now from this physical world to the spirit world, leaving this audience member with eternal fondness and gratitude that she brought me toward her one last time.

Her influence was manifest in a signature work of mine, *Tracings*, which I choreographed in 2003 as part of the Korean American Centennial Celebration at the Kennedy Center. *Tracings* is a danced prayer to my own ancestors. It is based on my family's history—our ancestral move to Hawaii from Korea in 1903. The main dancer dons a traditional hanbok dress and a white cloth which she manipulates like the shaman, inviting the chorus dancers to symbolically come to life and dance with her. It is akin to a séance. The dancers also wear white, the original color worn by Koreans in mourning—the opposite of westerners in grief, who wear black. Traditionally, a shaman takes a long white cloth and, with a dagger, rents it in half, a representation of breaking the wall between the physical and spiritual. I assume that she sees me, and this dance, wherever she is.

Also starting in my sophomore year, I trained three days a week for two years in intermediate modern dance with Professor Jennifer Predock-Linnell. Jennifer was in her late forties. She was—still is—a powerhouse. Each sinuous muscle she has formed from decades of excellent ballet and modern dance training and aerobic exercise.

Jennifer attended Julliard in the sixties where she worked with the choreographer Anthony Tudor. Tudor was acclaimed for his "psychological ballets" of the 1930s and 1940s. He pushed the ballet dancer to explore depths of emotional turmoil. In *Jardin aux Lilas* (*Lilac Garden*), a woman must choose between an unfeeling fiancé and her former lover, and in *Pillar of Fire* three sisters subtly and painfully fight over their romantic interests.

Jennifer taught a Humphrey-based class, focused on gentle swings of the torso and legs while staying tuned with the body's natural inhalations and exhalations, to keep muscles released and responsive. A swing of the torso and arms meant that one exhaled on the descent and inhaled on the recovery. This created a full-body integration of release and rebound, over which she layered ballet exercises to extend lines of the legs and feet. A lifelong learner, Jennifer was also at this time in the midst of her doctoral degree in psychology, uncovering connections between the emotions and body movement. Jennifer had a tough New York façade and nasal accent that gave her a semblance of armor, although in reality she was and is extremely kind and empathic and maintained an open-door policy for her students. She had been raised in New Mexico and her father is the well-known architect Antoine Predock. This patrilineage must have aided her in conceiving a structured approach to teaching a dance technique toward building an optimal dancer. Jennifer nourished me with support and helped me receive a dance scholarship, which also empowered me to believe that dance had value at the college level and beyond.

As the dancer builds muscles through rigorous exercise, he or she is also filtering through memories and their meanings, identifying and purging the emotional residue trapped in muscles. Memories of trauma are triggered when the dancer strives to let go of old postural holding patterns. For example, a recessed sternum and sloping shoulders can be the sign of years of feeling downtrodden and a prolonged depressed state. A dancer coaxed out of this holding posture can release pent up fear and anxiety. To thrust the chest forward and roll the shoulders back in self-assuredness pushes the dancer to have a proactive bearing, a more assertive relationship with others. In order to move from a disempowered stooped posture to an upright one, an elevated attitude toward life has to emerge. Not an easy emotional process. A realignment of the cranium, on top of the spine, may release emotional pain held there for many years. The dancer thrust into a rehearsal regimen they can't stand may soon manifest injury in an ankle or foot. This is the mind-body connection many dancers explore.

In Jennifer's classes and in our talks during office hours, I began to shed the difficulties of my childhood and to integrate physically and emotionally. We would cathartically discuss so much that came up for me—a breakup with a boyfriend, fear of failure after a poor rehearsal showing, and, along the way, a physical manifestation in, say, my obstinate swayback posture. Tapping into her insights on the impact of the emotional interior life on the physical instrument, I learned to listen to my emotions toward optimizing my body alignment, pain elimination, and my dance communication.

Young dancers spend all day in front of a mirror picking apart their movements. Obsession with body perfection asserts itself especially in the teenage years. I was no exception. I demanded symmetry of a body that was not symmetrical. Whose is? I couldn't reconcile my left arch being less supple than the right and often placed my extended left foot under benches, couches, and table legs in hopes of stretching it. Although my posture was upright, I wanted my legs to be more flexible and streamlined. For a year, I struggled from a preoccupation with my body image. In class I wondered why my arabesque—the position of the leg when held to the back—was not as high as another student, why my triple turns were not always perfect, why a balance on my right foot was steadier than my left. I wanted a larger chest and a thinner waist. Distorted self-perception and demands, micro-focused assessments, led me to overwork the body, not eat properly, and not sleep enough. Jennifer helped me navigate this brief transitory passage. She spoke to me about balance and the fact that to dance is a life journey; it is important to be forgiving and accept the body, as opposed to doing harm to its natural integrity. Dance rigor can create obsessions that lead young artists to pride and denial, alienating themselves from others, too. Instead of trusting dance friends, who are natural and necessary allies, they become one another's competitors, real and imagined. Such a world, especially as a dancer ages, can be a very lonely and isolating one.

Jennifer Predock-Linnell's expertise in drawing me out, with unconditional care and empathy, was crucial to my evolution as a person and dancer. Decades later, as a mentor and dance company director, I seek to emulate her.

Today when I meet with my company dancers, crew, and artistic team, I address the unique emotional demands of this art form in which the body is both art and the instrument. I emphasize the need to have trusted friends and professionals with whom, if need be, they can speak or work with therapeutically, well before any crises may arise—a social worker, a therapist, or even a holistic body worker—when anxieties or muscular issues intrude upon wellbeing and peace of mind. It is inevitable that the performer will, at some point, have to confront self-doubt. Having a support system in place ensures mind and body integration and keeps the dancer on a healthy track. I strongly believe the audience is drawn to the artistry presented by an integrated body and mind versus the one assembled piecemeal, from the dancer's starved bits and pieces. The audience relishes the unique quirky qualities of the individual, not robotic conformity and homogeneity—health exudes an irresistible allure.

No doubt my two most precious gifts as a young dancer were my enthusiasm and an unquenchable drive to explore the diverse choreographic opportunities presented to me. These qualities allowed me to catch up in technique, stamina, and accomplishment with dancers who had typically trained formally in a more streamlined and linear manner, and more conventionally for many more years than I had. A dancer's willingness to delve into a piece of choreography, to authentically explore all its potential and emotional range, time, space, and rhythm can outweigh another's years of technical training. This is especially true for dancers in their late teens and early twenties. The ability to invite and sustain, to nurture and cherish this fully enthused state is powerful and can manifest as a captivating stage presence. Thus, as some students burned out from years of dutiful but perhaps joyless practice, without that context or sense of wonder, I was just getting started on my life-long journey. It is enthusiasm that I instill front and center in my dancers today. This is the magnet to which audiences are drawn and are held.

In the spring of that sophomore year, a buzz went through Carlisle Gym. Albuquerque's prodigal son of modern dance, the famous Tim Wengerd, would return soon to Albuquerque from New York City, to open a studio and start a dance company. Tim had been the lauded soloist for the Martha Graham Dance Company during the 1970s heyday, was a founding member of the Repertory Dance Theatre in Salt Lake City, Utah, and in 1982 was assistant director to the Paris Opera modern dance troupe. Tim was forty-two years old, six feet tall with light brown hair, a chiseled All-American jock physique, and matinee idol facial features. But he was so much more than an anatomical Adonis. He was known for thoughtful performances and characterizations. Before his stage debut in 1974 as the Minotaur figure in *Errand into the Maze*, the classic 1947 Graham study of sexual fear and anxiety, he analyzed the role for weeks and studied historical images of the Minotaur in order to design his makeup.

This celebrated native son of New Mexico was ours and he was coming home to us. Rumors held that Tim had hired Gloria Fokine, the illustrious ballerina who married Leon Fokine, the nephew of Ballets Russes choreographer Mikhail Fokine. She had moved to Albuquerque from New York to teach in Tim's school.

Two years into my serious studies, after class one day I overheard two MFA candidates talk about auditioning for spots in the newly formed Tim Wengerd & Co. I asked if I might tag along. I was still green to dance and didn't then understand the scope of Tim's career or even how an audition functioned. I had never auditioned for anything myself or accompanied anyone to theirs. The only auditions I had seen were those portrayed in the 1985 Hollywood movie of the 1975 Tony Award–winning Broadway musical, *A Chorus Line*. My relative ignorance kept me from being nervous. On arrival, we filled out the boilerplate form, name and address, and then all thirty of us were ushered into a studio. We spaced ourselves and took a Graham-technique class, led by Tim. Sweat-drenched, we then continued to learn phrases—unfamiliar ones—involving contractions of the torso and geometric body angles. We twisted our legs and torsos down to pretzels, seated on the floor, and wrung ourselves out to standing, in order to run and leap in unison across the studio length.

Then, said Tim, we were to now move as if we were . . . wait for it . . . desert animals.

This can't be, I thought. This I could do flawlessly: reenact every day of my Santa Fe childhood! Many of those eager dancers were stumped by the instructions and just stood still or did classroom exercises, essentially dropping out. Meanwhile I crawled on all fours, sporadically stopping and starting like a lizard. I darted my focus like a warbler, and I zipped across the floor like a roadrunner. I extended my arms with noble eagle wings, my head a feathered crest, my eyes alert, neck turning left, then right, noting every movement far below that might be my meal, nostrils flared and mouth sharpened as a beak, my feet imagined as talons tucked for takeoff, then wings extended in mighty slow, elegant gliding, swooping down, dipping and dodging dancers, each imagined as a cactus, a bush, a dune, and then, finding rare updraft, soaring up, up, up and over their heads, chest wide, so wide open, taking in the air and my dominion, weaving my flight path through the room, at last landing, talons spread, motionless and noble, nearly a statue again. By the end of a grueling three-hour audition, Tim, a jury of one, had chosen his eight new company members. I was one of them. I was both thrilled and shocked to be among the anointed eight. Only one of the two girls with whom I had come, Cary, was offered a spot. Cary had danced with the Stuttgart Ballet for years. My relative detachment was surely the key to that success. I had no nerves to shred because I held no expectations. I was free to fail—so I didn't. From this point onward, my daily schedule doubled. I focused on my UNM dance studies by day and rehearsed performances late into the night with Tim's dance company.

Tim was hard-working, inspiring, hilarious, and self-deprecating. He had a rounded, exaggerated way of enunciating, like an opera singer poised to break into an aria. He was supportive and complimentary—

"Isn't that WON-der-ful?"—exalted by how hard we worked. On alternate days Tim taught either a Graham or Merce Cunningham class that he accompanied with a set of rosewood claves. He could perform a perfect side tilt with his legs pulled apart in two different directions, as if standing in the splits, and then fold into an angular form on the floor without missing a beat of his clave sticks. The way he used the contraction and release had such clarity. He used his breath to create an ease that I rarely see any longer in the Martha Graham Dance Company. Now Graham dancers seem to focus on shapes rather than a more nuanced setting in motion, the latter derived from natural internal pulses that then initiate the actual flow between movements and thus create sculptural forms.

Tim knew the importance of ensemble morale. One day he paused during an extremely taxing rehearsal, swung open the emergency exit door that led to the parking lot, tires and hoods caked with dust, on pitted and pocked asphalt. He beckoned, "Come outside. Isn't this GLOW-rius? Hmmm, YES." And then, "LOOOOK at that sunset!! Hmmmm, YES!" Often I return to such moments, summoned by his contagious enthusiasm—his distinguishing inclination—to take in the beauty in every environment. Tim taught me that an artistic director's first responsibility is to lift the whole company's awareness by celebrating and developing the gift of basic perception, which is at the heart of the creative process itself. Through this shared knowledge, a dance company reaches its highest artistic standard—and its crucial member unity and harmony and zest.

Months of rehearsals with Tim Wengerd & Co. culminated with two performances at the Kimo Theatre. I wore a turquoise unitard and orange cummerbund and too much makeup. I was terrified as the curtain went up. I went blank for a moment before I realized that the dance, *Blue Mesa*, was over. It was a hit. From the wings I then watched Tim perform a solo he had choreographed, *Journey to the Mouth of the River*. It was autobiographical. Tim had returned to Albuquerque from New York City because he had contracted AIDS. One day, when he was ready, he told us that the solo was about his own impending death. It was accompanied by an electronic track of ambient sounds of animals and flowing water. In this solo, Tim returned over and over to a metaphorical riverbank. On each repetition, he put on a different Mexican animal mask and drank from this river of life, until at last, he assumed the mask of a human skull: Death had arrived for him.

Back then, this gentle man was often confronted by the ignorance, fear, and stigma around AIDS. Most painful for him, no doubt, this distancing included those among us who were his most devoted students. One night a fluorescent bulb fell from the studio ceiling lighting fixture and shattered. As Tim picked up a few shards, he got the tiniest cut on his finger. Gasps. Silence. We took steps back, instead of forward. We froze. In dignity he quietly continued his choreography. No one helped him or offered him a bandage or so much as a paper towel. Not our finest hour. But it was among his.

It all sounds so hideous, so unfeeling, and ridiculous now. But in the 1980s, the fear of contracting AIDS was itself epidemic and the little understood disease was claiming a mortal swath on the dance community. News headlines about AIDS were often sensationalized and only intermittent. Was the virus airborne, the moment a cut occurred? Was it in droplets of sweat, of saliva? We knew nothing. There was no social media, no viral information chains or 24-hour cable news cycles, unlike the Coronavirus pandemic of 2020–2021. Tim had spent his life creating a healthy physical instrument, a body that was lauded by critics, students, and audiences, but now was only to be ostracized, punished, ruined, and shunned. Tim and I spoke on the phone several times before he died; he didn't want visitors because he was so gravely ill. The disease was ruthless in its decimation. And he had his pride. We talked about his mask collection in his home studio. It was, he said, as if those eternal fixed gazes were in a big gathering and speaking with one another, and with him, companionably. They were his witnesses, support team, and his social life—a balm for isolation.

At the end of our last phone call, he signed off with, "I have a mask for you, it's to be yours, YES." But I wouldn't see Tim alive again. This mask was never to materialize. More significant is the metaphorical and durable mask of a dancer that I wear, in tribute. It was a privilege that for a time I got to be among his dancers. Tim passed away at home on September 12, 1989, at forty-four years of age.

Years later, upon learning that I had worked closely with Tim, one of the board members of my own dance company, Daniel Schuman, a former US cultural attaché, told me that through the US State Department he had once invited Tim to Tanzania. He shared how Tim had accepted and did a fabulous residency there, inspiring the whole community to dance. Now the story had come full circle, like a completed dance cycle. I think of Tim driving through the open desert of New Mexico in his Jeep, in search of serenity, and I hear his voice, "Isn't that WON-der-ful, YES!" His work ethic, gusto, his capacity for creating art even of his own death, has ever been a model for how I direct my own company. I have tried to absorb and reflect all the illumination he left here. A 1976 photo of Tim captured in mid-leap while performing in Martha Graham's *Diversion of Angels* has been on my desk for decades. Tim was Wonderful. Yes.

Growing up gay in New Mexico was difficult because sexual experimentation everywhere in the 1980s—in particular, casual, bisexual, or gay sex—was considered risky, often unsafe, because of this merciless disease. Gay people carried a stigma, and the "free love" of the sixties and seventies had given way to a more restrictive ideology. Students would occasionally catcall "Maricon!" while I walked to Carlisle Gym. The gay bars had extra bouncers, as it was dangerous to walk through their parking lots. Gay bashing was on the rise due to fundamentalist Christian views about the evils of "alternative" lifestyles. These exacerbated the antipathies, gave some license to the bullying of men even suspected of being gay. Daytime threats signaled nighttime assaults. On Saturday nights I often went out with my three gay friends from the UNM dance department. We piled into Roman's sky blue 1978 Pinto and drove to clubs, parked, and ran to the front doors, quickly ducking inside because hoodlums with baseball bats and fists lurked in the shadows of every parking lot. Unlike Santa Fe, Albuquerque had a seedy hub of gay culture back then. We frequented clubs with names like Foxes, Booze 'N Cruz, and the Albuquerque Mining Company, all located near sex shops, surrounded by hookers, call boys, and their johns. These holdovers from the late 1970s were a nearly anonymous approach to sex.

We danced through the flashing lights, across the open floors to the blaring sounds of Stacey Q, Prince, Janet Jackson, and Madonna, our fingers popping and arms locking. Our own sexual encounters were complicatedly closeted courtships, awkward open dating, and coupling with other gay, bisexual, or curious dance or theater students. Secretly, I dated both the leading actor of the theater department and a fellow dancer, both highly conflicted about their sexual orientations. There were potential repercussions from straight peers. To avoid discovery, our dinner dates had to be far away from the university. Liaisons were timed for when our roommates were away. We arrived and departed each other's dorms under cover of darkness. Because of these reflexive habits of a long era, one that fell backward one step for every two forward, it took me until a couple of years ago to feel comfortable to hold my now-husband's hand in public, and to say clearly to new acquaintances that I am married to a man. American society is marching forward with increasing tolerance for the broader fluid spectrum of nonheterosexual and nonbinary sexual expression and identity for genders and preferences. Dance can be a powerful positive vehicle within this movement.

In 1988, internationally renowned ballet dancer Rudolf Nureyev came to Albuquerque with his troupe *Nureyev and Friends* to perform at a fundraising event for AIDS research. I mentioned Nureyev's upcoming appearance to my father. Unbeknownst to me, Dad had sketched a series of portraits of Nureyev, years prior when he was working on male figure studies. He pulled one of the sketches from the garage and donated it to the auction, with the understanding that his son would be permitted to work backstage for Nureyev and to attend the performance as well as the VIP reception where conversation would be possible. Nicely negotiated, Dad. It was a loving gesture of support. And the sketch was absolutely wonderful. It captured beautiful Nureyev at his prime. (I was gratified and proud that my father's drawing of Nureyev sold handsomely at that benefit for AIDS research.)

The day of the show I arrived early to work at UNM's Popejoy Hall and introduced myself to an officious man with salt-and-pepper hair. He handed me an envelope. I opened it to find cash and a shopping list for essentials that Maestro Nureyev needed for his dressing room suite. These were all alcohol: miniature bottles of Chambord, Kahlua, and Grand Marnier Liqueurs, Bombay Sapphire Gin, Absolut Vodka, Bacardi Rum, Jose Cuervo Tequila, Jameson Irish Whiskey, and other common labels. I was to purchase two miniatures of each and place them on the left-hand side of Nureyev's dressing table with all the labels alphabetized and clearly visible. A pair of each suggested to me that he feared the stigma of being seen as drinking alone.

I didn't have my fake ID on me, so I quickly found someone over twenty-one to ride with me to a liquor store and help me assemble the complicated list. Two and a half hours and three liquor stores later, I returned to the theater with brown paper bags filled with the boozy loot. I knocked gently on Nureyev's dressing room door and his dresser bade me enter.

There was Rudolf Nureyev, the greatest male ballet dancer of his generation—among a handful of the greatest of all time—the one who brought ballet to living rooms in the television era. Here before me was the spectacularly handsome and dazzlingly gifted man, one who was not only a famous Soviet defector during the Cold War but that rarity, a world-famous elite choreographer who was a household name in America—as if a friend or neighbor—nearly unrecognizable now, dressed in a pink cashmere warm-up outfit, pancake foundation, false eyelashes, mascara, and thick rouge, with a mere tuft of dyed, thinning hair. I hoped to cover my absolute horror—it returns to me now, just in the recollection—with a polite hoarsely whispered, (I had not even saliva, I was that shocked), "Sir, I have your beverages." He motioned to the table with a hand that looked younger and softer than his fifty years of age. With shaking clammy hands, I took the bottles out of the bag and alphabetized the Noah's Ark disembarkation, two by two. At first by type of liquor, then out of nervousness I re-alphabetized them by brand name: ten minutes that felt like hours. That task completed, I fidgeted with the paper sacks; in that silent tense room their crumpling was loud. With his dress rehearsal time slot approaching, Nureyev looked at me, squinted his eyes, and posed a one-word question. *"Vear?"*

It took a moment to realize that he wanted to know "where" the stage was. I quickly showed him to the side of the stage, to a ballet barre. There I watched Nureyev do several contorted leg bends. It's hard to even call them pliés because his knees were so twisted, so torqued out of alignment that his feet, ankles, and knees didn't come close to lining up. His lower legs and knees were completely shrouded in athletic tape under his tights in order to support his shin splints. He did just a few more warm-up exercises, continuing to torque his legs and feet into submission. Nureyev then marched out onto stage to rehearse the evening's performance.

Charles Jude made an illustrious appearance. He was a striking Eurasian dancer with a Vietnamese mother and French father. At the Paris Opera Ballet, he had reached the highest rank, a *sujet étoile*, officially a star. Charles Jude walked by and said hello to me; I was star-struck and blushed. As an Asian male, his ascent to such heights in Europe was all the more impressive. He built a career working against prejudices in ballet, ones that deemed the Asian male as too effeminate to take on virile, strong leading or romantic hero roles.

I then set glasses and pitchers of water in the wings and in his dressing room and went into the house to take my seat. Charles Jude bounced onto the stage with Nureyev, and they ran through a duet, *Songs of a Wayfarer* choreographed by Maurice Bejart in 1971. The duet exposed every diminishment of Nureyev. He adopted a slightly insane exaggerated expression, projecting himself as still in his twenties on a grand Russian stage. It had been twenty years since Nureyev's prime. He was now reduced to this curiosity circuit. A couple of hours later the theater filled with the murmur of an excited audience here to take in the actual performance. The house lights dimmed; the curtain rose. When the lights came up again, the dances received polite applause, but no more than that. No ovations. No curtain calls. No tossed roses. I went backstage. He was displeased to see only me. "Vear?" That is, where was the long line of autograph and photo seekers that he presumed me to be holding at bay? To his vexed question, I could only shrug and shake my head, as if to suggest that I, too, was mystified. I smiled and offered him my program and a pen and asked him if he would kindly autograph it. He scrawled a dismissive signature across the cover.

Nureyev's best dance of the evening occurred later at that VIP reception which followed the staged event. This was the very first VIP reception I had ever attended. I closely studied the artist in his beret, glossy patent leather boots, black-and-white polka dot silk ascot. I was painfully aware of my hand-me-down blazer and scuffed suede Hush Puppies with worn-down heels. Nureyev went stalking, a practiced feline, moving in slow motion across the room, making himself available for their petting and praise. And with the praise, he settled in as might a pampered house cat might. Then he would tiptoe to the next outreached hand and await more strokes of his ego. They always came.

Encounters with great performers can go a few memorable ways. An artist might read those as opportunities for them to demonstrate generosity—however brief—to offer encouragement, mentorship, an indelible imprint of their role modeling. Or an artist might find even a brief exchange to be a chore and imposition. In fairness, many fall somewhere on the spectrum between those points. The worn idol Nureyev I met in 1988 appeared to have been quite entirely spent. He had been cosseted for so long, and his temperament, with age, likely had moved as out of alignment as his overworked and badly maintained body. He had lost dimension and capacities in body and soul. He had been by this time, I suggest, perverted by adulation and entitlement. No dancer is immune to aging and it was a pity, truly, to see him this way.

So that was one unexpected lesson for this dancer. Something else had happened, though, that was to be the real gift of this experience. Charles Jude and I had several delightful conversations that day, cobbled from broken French and English. He made me believe that there was a place for a dancer that looked like me in the professional world of dance, on the stage. With true grace he made time, on his performance day, that I might really share with him all I wished to express with my body as instrument, and a growing choreographic vision. Our contact did not go beyond that transformative day—nor did it have to. It was complete and stirring. The affirming and rousing message and impression—that I was someone to be nurtured as a peer, a colleague—sustains me regularly to this day. Today he directs the Ballet of the Opera National de Bordeaux. And I seek to emulate his lesson of giving time—even on a performance day—and an eager ear always. In those moments, I think especially of him, with gratitude.

After these encounters, I thought about all the elements of a life in dance that excited me, and I realized it was how choreography is made that fascinated me most. Great choreography moves dance into a rightful occupancy of true art versus a spectacle of physical feats or athletic prowess. I began to take choreographic composition classes my junior year. These were my favorite and most challenging classes. Questions that arose in each class stretched my mental bandwidth thrillingly: how to portray through set moment, subject matter, story line, and dramatic intention. I played with techniques such as theme and variation by manipulating dance phrases so that they were not identical but were identifiably related, so that the phrases interacted as if in dialogue. I set movement to musical scores by mimicking tempos and themes I heard with complex movement phrases. I made abstract dances, scores for the body based on a series of isolated moving body parts; I instructed dancers to move across the floor initiating from the elbow, then the knee, then the neck and shoulder. The classroom became a study in the limitless manipulation of movement and the setting of these explorations into repeatable dances.

I also realized that choreography is extremely complicated, that the process cannot be rushed, but must be learned and nurtured over time. Through trial and error, it gets richer as the choreographer experiences life and has more to ask in life, and of life, and to share. For the novice student, the body freezes, phrases imagined can turn inert, and spatial patterns dissolve like table salt. What is anticipated to be electrifying or dynamic in class or in theory or on paper can in performance actually be leaden.

That year I assembled a cast of two novice classmates in modern dance, good intermediate-level dancers, one woman and one man, and created a modern five-minute trio dance that we auditioned for the student showcase. We were thrilled to be chosen to perform. I costumed the two backup dancers in nude spandex unitards and myself, the soloist, in a purple spandex unitard. As a result of this awful dance—it was godawful, really—I confess, to this day spandex triggers a cringe. The dance communicated angst through chest-beating fists, then some rolling and writhing on the floor, followed by more angst—thrusting fists, a jump kick, the leg splits, and dramatic silent movie facial expressions—and mated with dance phrases performed in canon and unison. I now know that emotional agony is a common theme for young choreographers.

After the showcase, my cast and I went out to greet the audience of friends and family. My mom was utterly speechless . . . because the dance was just that unutterably bad. My father's review of this, my first choreography, was as follows, "Well, you are no Baryshnikov. . ." End of review. Silence. I took this in stride and turned it into a challenge. My resolve was sharpened to continue to experiment with choreographic structures. Onward.

Unfortunately, along with my packed dance schedule came tendinitis, an inflammation of tendons causing pain and swelling. My tendinitis was in my ankles, each step excruciating. I had overworked my body by dancing at school and professionally outside of the university. It also related to my emotional stresses now being made manifest in physical pain, a growing realization that the dance world was so much larger than Carlisle Gymnasium.

When to rest and when to work through the pain of an injury is a difficult equipoise, especially for a young dancer with no experience in injury avoidance, rehabilitation, rest, and recovery. And there is the mind-body connection that dancers feel so strongly. I wondered what was so terrifying and painful that I could not move forward and to where I couldn't stand it any longer? My daily regimen of rest, Ibuprofen, alternating ice bag and heating pad was dismal and ineffective.

The tendinitis came to me with a chaperone via a recurrent premonitory dream: The phone would ring, and my Auntie Alice would say, "Let me talk to your mom, Grandma Kang is dying." I would wake to find myself sitting up in bed, quite fearful of the presentiment of death. Worried, I finally called my parents to mention the dream. They assured me that she was fine. But within three weeks my intuition became a reality, at 3:00 a.m., Grandma's spirit came to me, perched beside me on my bed. As always, wordlessly she beckoned me to sit up, to lean in for one of our long hugs. Moments after, a shadow flew past my dorm window and brightened the moonlight; she was gone. I wept. It was just that real.

By 6 a.m. my parents were calling to let me know what I already knew. Up until this moment I had felt—and had literally been—quite immobilized. Grandmother's pre-dawn visit and passing through me was an epiphany. The timing of this was to be her final and greatest gift to me. Change is the natural course of life, and it is to be welcomed, desired. To struggle against this truth, to work against it, is to invite agony, distortion, and futility. I thought about my Korean grandmother's courageous migration and all we had in common, yearning for the next iteration of ourselves.

And with that, rather miraculously, my tendinitis began to heal. Three years at the university had passed and I needed to push on. It was comparable to my departure from Santa Fe—at the cusp of earning my black belt in karate. It was not impulse, but instinct, restless within a sheltering exoskeleton suit that had served me wonderfully but that I had outgrown. It was a summoning forward, for me to push and stretch for freedom in a newly formed body, to emerge from my chrysalis and to stretch my wings. There was nothing keeping me at UNM any longer. I had excelled in all my classes, had no love interest or deep friendships. I wanted to get into a modern dance company on the East Coast.

I began attending a series of modern dance performances at the Kimo Theatre. These hinted irresistibly at the dance world that lay on the East Coast. Without the Internet, smart phones, or other forms of technology, the only way to understand what this dance field was—that I was training so hard to be part of—came in sporadic glimpses: one-night concerts of companies that moved through Albuquerque on the way to larger West Coast bookings. In retrospect, it is quite amazing to think that I was so dedicated to an artform that I knew so little about.

These companies would usually do one or two master classes at UNM or at Tim's studio and move on immediately after their performance. I saw Nikolais Dance Theatre, Bill T. Jones/Arnie Zane Company, David Gordon/Pick Up Performance Co., and Laura Dean Dancers, among others. I took classes with them all. Nikolais's dancers were striking. Classes were taught by Tito del Saz, a mysterious dark-haired Spanish man. He had us roll up and down on our backs into the splits on the floor; once we were all standing, he taught us how to glide across the floor with minced steps like modern-day robots. The Nikolais Company showed us how improvisation and props could be used. Tito's workshops culminated with a performance by the company that included bright kaleidoscopic lighting, projections, costumes that extended the form of the body into cone shapes, and even used giant rubber bands that stretched across stage and were manipulated by the dancers. It was a visual extravaganza. In contrast, Laura Dean placed tape on the gym floor and made us spin from one X to the next until we were quite dizzy. Her performance was an aerobic feat of interlacing floor designs made out of traveling turns that were sustained for more than one hour. The dancers didn't even seem human. How could they possibly turn for that long?

But one such class would set the course for my East Coast destination. I took two classes with the Liz Lehrman Dance Exchange, a DC-based dance company that focused on social justice and that mixed young and old dancers on stage. I had never heard of them before, but my teachers had. The founding director, Liz Lehrman, gave me her card after I took her dance improvisation class. She was interested in hiring me and asked for an audition tape. On it I was to tell a personal story while dancing. I spoke about my family's history on the plantations of Hawaii, while dancing a modern phrase out of doors in jeans and a T-shirt. I sent her my VHS tape and after two weeks Liz called with an offer of a one-way airplane ticket to Washington, DC, a working contract for the upcoming season upon my arrival that would have me working for not one, but three, dance companies—Sharon Wyrrick's Full Circle Dance, Carol Penn's Penn Visions, and her own company, an affordable, temporary housing set-up, and the promise for a ride from the airport, all these things guaranteed upon arrival.

Without a second thought, I sold my car for $1,000 to start a new life in DC. I hadn't finished school; at age twenty, I had given up my university dance scholarship, and I was going against my parents' wishes. I bought a duffle and tossed in clothes. I bade farewell to my parents, thanked all my teachers, and gave my roommate Larry and his girlfriend, Lynda, my few belongings. Adios, Amigos.

And with that I abruptly left the desert oasis of my beloved UNM dance program. I buckled my seatbelt as the airlock sealed decisively and my plane lifted off from the Albuquerque International Sunport. Nauseous, adrenalized, and for the second time in my young life— since that first solo migration from Santa Fe to Albuquerque—I had decided to go it alone. I peered down at the diminishing city below.

The monarch was in flight.

On descent I peered out the window over green Virginia and the Potomac River and soon our wheels scraped the landing strip at National Airport. I grabbed my duffle and stepped off the plane, into a maze of departure and arrival gates, kiosks, and signs toward exits and options. I headed to glass sliding doors that opened into DC summer air, thick, wet, and heavy. It soon soaked my hair and clothes. I used the sleeve of my burgundy dress shirt to mop my face.

I scanned the long line of cars. Drivers jumped out and assisted people with luggage. I considered contrasts: this city, built over a swamp—and so humid that I was wet as if emerging from a hot bath—and my landlocked home, an arid desert, parched and dusty, scorched. After twenty minutes, a green Subaru appeared, and the driver rolled down the passenger window. It was Sharon Wyrick, one of the dance company directors. "Dana?" "Yes, yes, I'm Dana!" I called out, placing my bag in the backseat, and climbing into her air-conditioned car.

Sharon wore her blonde hair short, was slight, austere in a white blouse and black skirt. She had a bulbous mole on her cheek. Robotically, she asked, "How was the plane ride?" "Did you eat on the plane?" "Was it hot in Albuquerque today?" I complied with her clear preference, one-word answers. I craned my neck to the Lincoln Memorial, Washington Monument, and Jefferson Memorial. The towering white marble edifices were so different from the low-rise pink adobe rows of New Mexico.

The traffic patterns made no sense. The occasional fork in the road led to a circular roundabout. Instead of lines and grids, roads spun in circles. Green freeway signs—like a giant had shuffled a colossal deck of playing cards—replaced scenic landscapes. We drove for thirty minutes before the parkway merged into a rundown neighborhood of red brick, two-story homes and six-story apartment buildings and a large sign: "Welcome to Maryland." We passed a Metro entrance surrounded by rows of parked blue-and-white buses with lines of waiting passengers.

I had never ridden a bus or a Metro. Ever. But I would soon master both to get to rehearsals.

Ten minutes passed and we turned onto a side street of small 1940s brick houses in Wheaton, Maryland. This, my new street, would turn out to be a fifteen-minute bus ride to the Metro and a thirty-five-minute Metro ride to Metro Center, and that was in turn a fifteen-minute walk to the rehearsal space. With wait times, my daily commute to rehearsals in downtown DC would be ninety minutes each way.

Sharon said, "We're here," stopped the car but kept it running, in front of an overgrown yard and a small brick house. I would inhabit this rental now shared by a dancer in her company, Valerie, and her boyfriend. I got out, removed my bag, and walked through foot-high weeds up to the battered and peeling red front door. Sharon rolled down the window and called, "OK, I have a shift bartending that starts in an hour. See you at rehearsal on Monday." "Thank you!" I waved to a blur.

Now, why would a well-known Washington, DC, choreographer have to also be a bartender?

I would learn.

I knocked on the door and a tall black woman opened it and in a deep voice she introduced herself as Valerie Hollis. Long ringlets surrounded her broad face. She projected a soothing maternal energy. As we sat over coffee and a sandwich, Valerie told me that she had graduated from Oberlin and was a singer as well as a dancer. She had recently moved back to the states from Germany, only too happy for an extra roommate to share the rent. Her boyfriend, Frank, introduced himself in candid self-deprecation as a recovering alcoholic who attends daily AA meetings but falls off the wagon every now and then. Frank had worked at several sandwich shops in downtown Bethesda, Maryland, over the year, always fired for his "anger issues." Over time, he told stories about "Juvie Hall" that terrified me—felons being shanked for giving a fellow inmate a bad look, beating people to pulp for boosting a pack of cigarettes, and so forth—but which entertained Valerie. My horror doubled their entertainment. I would come to enjoy her infectious, bawdy baritone laugh. But I would also dread their fights, which after a few months became frequent, long, and loud.

Valerie told me that the neighborhood was built when returning WWII soldiers flooded in, lured by the promise of new cheap housing, mass produced two-bedroom homes with partially finished basements. This house had been minimally furnished for us renters, with, a large 1970s faux leather couch, glass coffee table, and a television. The original 1940s kitchen had worn white metal cabinets, rusting white and chrome appliances, a small table, and two folding chairs.

Valerie showed me to a door in the kitchen that led to the unfinished basement where I would live. My bed was a very old mattress that lay directly on the burgundy-and-black linoleum floor tiles and a bathroom with a swinging door—like in an old frontier saloon—a small shower, toilet, and sink. A washer and dryer were next to the bathroom. I thanked Valerie and settled into my new reality.

I hung my six shirts and three pair of pants on wire hangers on a clothesline over the washer and placed my sneakers, two pair of black boots, and my worn pair of ballet slippers on the floor near the bed. I folded my dance clothes, socks, and underwear and placed them in a discarded cardboard box in the room. I unpacked a top sheet and draped it on the mattress and installed my toiletries and towel. A wooden crate was now a nightstand. I ventured out the basement door to the backyard—a junkyard—and scavenged broken chairs that once upon a time had a gilded finish. I took the seat and legs of one and made of it a golden altar for a small metal Buddha, a gift from my father on my thirteenth birthday. This Buddha always offered me solace, inspiration, and connectivity to my Asian-ness. My father had years before told me that this Buddha was very old and that its *mudra* or hand position, was called *varada mudra*, one hand palm up in the lap with the other on a knee facing downward touching the earth. It references when the meditating Buddha was frightened by demonic visions; to calm himself he reached down and touched the earth. From this came his insight that demons exist only in the mind. This Buddha was my friend, one who had followed me from Santa Fe to Albuquerque and now to DC, witness, and simpatico ally in this dank, wet place. I had no telephone, no radio. The décor was minimum-security carceral.

On Monday morning Valerie and I commuted to downtown DC

together, to a white church with a red steeple. Sharon's rehearsals took place in a small gymnasium in the church. While the other dancers warmed up, I asked Sharon to speak with me about my contract. I knew nothing about artist contracts. She explained that my $700 a month was to be paid by a loose braid of three choreographers, each with her own company, Sharon, Carol Penn, and Liz Lehrman.

Sharon was to pay $250 per month and I would personally collect the rest from the other choreographers. Her company of four women and two men was a modern dance and performance art company; Carol's was an education-focused ensemble comprised of twelve visually impaired teens and three professional modern dancers, two men and one woman; and Liz's company was a mix of amateur seniors and modern dancers. A motley cast of characters that by no means conformed to my expectations of being a professional dancer in a major East Coast city. I was confused, deflated, and heartbroken.

Cost-sharing can be a good thing, but after two months, Liz's company—which at the time was the most established and had been the one to invite me to DC—delayed any communication with me. Today we would say she ghosted me. She still had not produced the written performance contract initially promised. Carol and Sharon did produce contracts, a fact I appreciated, but the contracts suggested a stability they did not possess; neither was in any financial position to sustain a full-time dancer.

So, each paycheck fell short and shorter. One month I made $400, the next only $250. Their one perfected dance move was mutual finger-pointing with synchronized swivels pointed at Liz. I would run between rehearsals, three days a week on Sharon's project, two days a week on Carol's. I was a cat batting a mobile but getting clocked on the head by each soft deflection.

Sharon's work included vocalization and text. It was difficult for me having not been trained in acting or voice. Hers was a tedious work process and she had a penchant for tantrums. For six weeks, twelve hours a week, we developed her dance in which walking, lying down, and standing up alternated with piling toy wooden blocks into towers, as we took turns reciting scripts to the audience about the perils of urban sprawl. Having lured them with art, we were now essentially going to deliver polemics, harangue and browbeat them. As we worked, it was easy to imagine an audience desperately crawling out to the exits. Hell, we would have joined them. This boy, this desert-dancing iguana, knew nothing about urban sprawl. The dance made no sense. We six built miniature cityscapes as Sharon yelled her only directions: "NO, that's NOT it!" Each four-hour rehearsal was over when Sharon kicked our deficient skyscrapers to the ground.

After two months of pistol-whipping, Sharon announced that ready or not, we were going to tour this thing to Bogota and Medellin, Colombia, at an annual international dance festival. A week later, a series of drug cartel–related bombings hit the airports and major cities of Colombia. Drug lord Pablo Escobar was exercising his own reign of terror. The US State Department warned of threats to traveling Americans. Sharon called off the tour. Three dancers quit and within six months her company toppled, just as had our block towers.

I also worked with visually impaired and physically disabled youth of color through Carol's Penn Visions. I was one of three professionals who danced with these kids, whose ages ranged from twelve to eighteen. This was my first exposure to visually impaired youngsters. Carol told me that each student had to be guided safely and coached to understand where he or she was in the space, to walk through dance phrases without becoming disoriented, and to do gestural phrases in unison by recognizing musical cues. Carol had trained at the Alvin Ailey School. I gently led them through lateral leg tilts and upper body phrases of extended arms in the Alvin Ailey style.

The students were excited to be together doing something performative in this accepting atmosphere. Beautiful shaping impulses informed their movements. Often, they spoke about the feeling of air on their skin, or of how the music made them want to move. I enjoyed having them take my arm as I led him or her through the space while I described our surroundings, how many steps to take to the front, right, and left. One day, the youngest, twelve-year-old Tanya, squeezed my arm and asked, "Are you a boy or a girl?" I said, "A boy." She frowned, hesitated, and said, "Maybe that's not the right question...." I said, "I like boys," and she relaxed her grip, "Got it! That makes sense." Tanya wasn't judgmental in her question or assessment. She sensed that my energy felt different and had been searching to articulate this. Emboldened, Tanya asked, "May I touch your face?" and I said, "Sure." She felt my cheeks and nose and I closed my eyes as her hands carefully, deliberately sought to scan their shape. Upon opening my eyes, I saw my reflection in the glasses she always wore, with dark, mirrored wide-angle lenses. She asked, "And *what* are you?" I responded, "Korean." She said, "Wow! I haven't met anyone Korean before." Her fingers had read the landscape of my features. She smiled and said, "I like your eyes." I said with a smile—one that I strove to make clear in my voice, "Thanks, Tanya!" In that exchange, her unfiltered questions and my matter-of-fact answers, received with matter-of-fact acceptance, we were mutual mentors. Now she was able to welcome me and give me her trust.

Tanya and the other students relished jumping and leaping, taking risks, and moving with freedom. When someone fell, I helped him or her up and they just continued on. Falling instilled no fear or shame. How could I not thrive as well? Creatively the students interpreted verbal movement instructions. They were unencumbered by judging themselves in a mirror or making competitive comparisons by looking at their classmates. When I asked them to, say, wave their arms above their head or to articulate gestures with their hands, they innovated responses that sighted dancers would not have. Their waving arms took on unusual sculptural shapes that flashed in a multitude of speeds.

Carol's dance program was intended as student therapy. But it was therapeutic for me, too—a departure from the technical dancing in which I had trained—and, wow, it expanded my grasp of movement as means to sense and better interact with others, one's environment, and the interplay of the dancer and sound. Being young myself, twenty, and displaced, here in DC, this experience drew me to consider what binds us together. Carol's program was way ahead of the trends. Today there are many companies and dance programs that work with what were then called "disability communities," but in the late 1980s this was brand new ground. Carol's program survived and slowly gained funding. A natural healer, Carol became a successful medical doctor.

After two-and-a-half months, Liz Lehrman still had not produced either a contract or a rehearsal schedule. I at last received a reply from a guy named Bob, who was her company manager. "Unfortunately, we did not receive a grant we were counting on to make good on your contract, so we won't be adding you to the schedule after all. You can dance for free for us if you want."

Liz had recruited me. Couldn't she have picked up the phone herself to break this news? I was in shock that an established national company, one based on "community" and "social justice" work, would treat a young employee this way. I had no source of income, no savings left from the sale of my car in Albuquerque. I called Bob back, and he told me further that Liz's rehearsal space was now in an old amusement park in Glen Echo, Maryland, which had no Metro service. It was three bus rides from Wheaton and would take over two hours each way. "Bob," I said, "I don't have the money to buy peanut butter and crackers, much less the time and fare to rehearse for free," and he said, "I get it, that's tough, good luck," and hung up.

Back then, there was no Internet to check on the reputation of a company, no digital hive or crowd sourcing or social media. Valerie informed me that they were notorious for not making good on their promises to wide-eyed dancers they had lured with the same bait-and-switch. There was no time for heartbreak. I had made a huge cross-country move to be a professional dancer without a backup plan for another source of income or even a way back to New Mexico. I was down to $100 and I had three weeks left until the rent was due again. I needed to get a job fast.

I went through the City Paper employment ads. Without a college degree, realistically all I could seek were restaurant or retail jobs. I came across a sales-clerk gig at an Asian antique store, *Arise*, in Takoma Park, Maryland. *Arise* was one bus ride and three Metro stops from the house. I called the number in the listing and got an interview with the owners Paul and Cheryl. The mammoth antique store occupied eleven thousand square feet in an old paper warehouse. As I walked in, I knew I could do this job. The store was packed with hundreds of antique Buddhas from Thailand and Cambodia, vintage kimonos from Japan, furniture from Indonesia, Korea, and Japan. Paul and Cheryl seemed skeptical of my claims of knowledge. I explained that I had taken many courses in Asian history and had worked in Santa Fe at the gift shop at the Museum of International Folk Art. I turned up my performance dial, as far as it would go, to "stage charm." I commented on the beauty of a traditional Korean blanket chest, properly referring to it as a *bandaji*, noting correctly the provenance. I noted the serenity of a standing Thai gilded Buddha, "Look at its hands, facing forward, the gesture for Calming the Seas," I said with a sentimental smile, a theatrical move meant to suggest a kind of nostalgic reverie, recalling good times. I then complimented their taste in the array of Japanese garments, naming them, from the *hakama* (traditional men's pants), to the *haori* (short jacket), and then, demonstrating my sensitivity to the way their inventory should be handled and shown to customers, I gasped in retail-mode delight at the long elaborate *uchikake*, or wedding kimono. I had danced, whether I meant to do so or not. This was my "Hire me" improvisation, an audition, and I was officially booked.

I worked there fifty hours a week at minimum wage for several months to pay my rent and save some money so that I might resume dance classes. I used my day off, Sunday, to explore DC and especially Chinatown. I walked past century-old rowhouses with gold lettering in Chinese calligraphy indicating that they had formerly been a Tong House or society for newly arrived immigrants that had financed Chinese businesses. I wandered stores that sold traditional blue-and-white porcelain soup bowls, spoons, and teacups, and also smoked Peking Ducks hanging appetizingly in the windows. Small grocery stores, abuzz with Cantonese, displayed clusters of mushrooms, fruits with reptilian skin, bins of aromatic cooking and medicinal spices, from turmeric to lemongrass, and exotic liniments, and pickled snakes and toads. Tony Cheng's Dim Sum House hummed with people who looked like me, devouring dumplings of all kinds and sizes, at round communal dining tables that each sat a dozen eaters and where I would now take my own regular and grateful place. The dumplings were wheeled on a cart, tantalizing and steamy, and I would point—I always thought of my grandma in those moments, and her pointing instead of speaking—and select two *cha shu boa*, large pork-filled steamed buns, for two dollars and guzzled complimentary refills of dark tea. In Chinatown I felt comfortable. More than that, I was profoundly aware that for the first time in a long time, I felt . . . safe.

I meandered a lot in those days. A dancer loves to stretch and walk. One Sunday I ventured up the steps of the National Portrait Gallery. With no entrance fee, I would be permitted to spend entire days taking in portraits. I studied the faces of George Caitlin's 1830s-era portraits of Native American chiefs and photos of Harriet Tubman and Frederick Douglass. I studied the muscular body of Thomas Hart Benton's 1924 *Self Portrait with Rita*, Martha Graham's defiantly upright posture in Paul Meltsner's 1938 portrait, Ralph Barton's 1925 gaunt self-portrait, and the 1946 portrait by Betsy Graves Reyneau of Joe Louis at the height of his professional boxing career. Like Tim's walls of curated masks, these faces in portraiture were my new companions. They did not need to speak words to be heard.

But the painting that stopped me in my tracks was the Winold Reiss 1929 portrait of Isamu Noguchi at age twenty-four. Isamu is shown in a black suit, with a background of blue geometric shapes. His clear gray eyes and tousled hair were captured in all his intense creative energy. Noguchi was only four years older than I was now when this was painted. I visited this portrait on many Sundays. It was as if I were calling upon an Asian American friend, receiving welcome, affirmation, and taking away with me well-wishes, resolve, and positive energy each time. The Gallery held constancy, fellowship. Many of my peers made pals by being a welcome denizen at a watering hole, like the fictional pub in that 1980s show *Cheers*, "where everybody knows your name. And they're always glad you came." The Portrait Gallery was my equivalent.

I look back today on those whose spirits I called upon in pilgrimage and entreaty in that Gallery. That unmoored young dancer with not a dime to spare beyond bus fare, and no map for the future . . . how could he ever have dreamed that, decades later, a portrait of him by Mary Noble Ours, in 1998, and another, by CYJO, a Korean American artist, in 2007, would be added to the National Portrait Gallery collection?

One Sunday while getting off the Metro at the Chinatown/National

Portrait Gallery stop, I made eye contact with a handsome man in his early thirties. The mutual attraction was undeniable. We smiled flirtatiously and he introduced himself as Jonathan Katz, a Smithsonian art history fellow doing PhD research at the National Portrait Gallery. We took up a convivial stride together into the Gallery. He offered to show me around the collection and said that he was interested in the intersection of gay studies and art history. He pointed out the undeniably wanton gazes of two men in a painting and the musculature of the male torso in another, interpreting paintings themselves as forms of seduction.

Jonathan had a physique like a Greek statue, muscular chest with a trim waist. He was ten years older, worldly, informed about art and the gay lifestyles of artists. We embarked on a love affair, satisfying as much for our passionate common interests as for our physical sparks. He told me about Robert Rauschenberg, married in 1950 and siring a child before he divorced three years later, realizing that he was gay. We spoke about the love Merce Cunningham and composer John Cage shared physically and as expressed in their dance and music collaborations.

In 1989, Jonathan took me to my first performance at the Kennedy Center, the Joffrey Ballet reconstruction of Vaslav Nijinsky's 1913 masterpiece *The Rite of Spring*. From my red velvet chair, I stared up at the crystal chandeliers and down to the stage and vowed, "One day, I will be on that stage. *I will.*"

After a few months, a winter when Jonathan's fellowship was winding down, he planned to return to his home in San Francisco. He sought someone to take over his lease in the gay neighborhood of Dupont Circle. "Would you like to take over the efficiency? I know how inconvenient your housing location is," he offered.

I didn't realize that one needed to have a bank account and credit history to rent an apartment in a city, plus both the first and last month rent upfront. I had none of these. Jonathan called up his landlord—a gay Chinese American—and advocated that his friend was gay and Korean American as well as an aspiring artist. The landlord liked the chance to help a young Asian American and let me rent the apartment.

A miracle. Two weeks later Jonathan gathered my few belongings and me in his rental moving van and established me in the apartment the same day he moved out. What a seismic psychological shift for me. I was now at the epicenter of the chic, arts-enriched "gayborhood." No longer an other or outsider, I had moved to a real community, one where I felt seen, serene, and stimulated. Furthermore, here was a Metro, a good dance studio, an LGBTQ bookstore, and several nice and openly gay bars. In 2010, Jonathan would co-curate the ground-breaking exhibition, *Hide/Seek: Difference and Desire in American Art*, highlighting how modern art was influenced by social marginalization and of artists' explorations of fluidity of gender and sexuality.

Now on Sunday mornings I began to take dance classes again, back-to-back, two jazz classes and a modern class, getting back in shape. After some months I ventured to a ballet studio. In my threadbare black leggings, leotard, and well-worn slippers, I arrived early to stretch at the barre. Another dancer entered and said that I was in his spot. I vacated the spot obligingly. "Are those your only ballet slippers?" he asked. I thought perhaps he needed to borrow a pair, but when I looked, I saw he was already wearing enviable new shoes. "Your shoes are so old. I just worry I might slip on the floor where yours go," he said, in a cruel attempt at intimidation. Looking up then, he drew his shiv of a tongue back in his mouth, a sheath that now bore a sly smirk.

Just then the teacher, Eric Hampton, arrived. He was a petit man in his early fifties with a kind smile. He had joined the Dance Theatre of the Netherlands in 1969 and returned to Washington in 1978 to become a soloist and resident choreographer for the Washington Ballet. I was prepared to have more unconstructive shade thrown my way. Eric jovially smiled, "Welcome! I haven't seen you before. I'm Eric. And who are you?"

"I'm Dana. I am just back to ballet from a hiatus," I said, to lower his expectations. His class was quick, combinations that were syncopated. The stretch of the foot along the floor, a tendu, would sometimes have a musical accent out and at other times in, all within one combination. He had a quirky whimsical way, the carriage of the arms, the port de bras lilted, and the tilt of the head referred to a European style of

Romantic ballet from the mid-1800s. He joked with several students; the jokes were corrective tweaks. I'd encountered this pedagogical style back at UNM in Albuquerque with Judith Bennahum. Maybe this was typical of ballet pedagogy, this banter to leaven the formality. I felt right at home.

When a student arrived late, Eric would say, "I'm glad you made it, despite your alarm not going off." When a student faltered, he asked, "Do we have bugs in here? Are you sure you have stomped them to death?" causing laughter. After class Eric approached me again and said that he liked how I nuanced his phrases and picked up the small details. I was so gratified to hear this from him because his class had many talented and longtime professionals. In fact, several women took the whole class in pointe shoes and two men added beats of the feet and legs between every jump, which surpassed the level of the class. He saw something in me that he could work with, he said. Might I be interested in dancing for his company? He had a show coming up. Eric Hampton Dance was the premiere neoclassical company in DC. This was the professional dance opportunity I had been seeking. I eagerly accepted.

After several rehearsals with Eric, I learned that he had attended the Julliard School with my former teacher Jennifer Predock-Linnell and had also worked with the famous psychological ballet choreographer, Anthony Tudor. I loved Eric's musicality and his focus on detail. His phrasing, much like Tudor's, pushed the dancer to reach almost impossibly through to the next downbeat. This approach to music, lagging through the "one-e-and-a" before the two arrives, creates an inherent emotional tension, sensed by the audience. He preferred three counts over even four counts, explaining that a four count makes an audience comfortable, but a three count creates emotional tension. Eric's steps were small and fast, and he focused on little quirky gestures which he layered over petit allegro, quick footwork topped by a peculiar epaulement, or placement of the head and neck. He often chose a cocked head tilt, coquettish and impish.

I learned to identify archetypes among dancers in a company—for example, the dancer who is an egotist, obsessed with his image in the mirror; the know-it-all, who, although not asked to do so, announces an opinion on how others could improve their dancing; the chronically late dancer who is naturally tremendously talented; the jester who interrupts a tense rehearsal with a joke that unites the group with shared laughter; the hard worker; the aging dancer who is bitter and in chronic back pain; and the ingénue, the starlet who poses a threat to senior female company members. The dynamics of this array often led to tense rehearsals, and that had never been an aspect of Tim Wengerd's rehearsals. Tim and Eric had very different beliefs about the curation of talent and of the creative process. Tim saw the potential of each dancer and developed each through positive coaching. Tim tried many different movement phrases and improvisations before setting his choreography, to ensure that each dancer's strengths shined. Eric, on the other hand, coming from a ballet background rather than a modern background, assumed that everyone came to him with the same movement vocabulary from their ballet training, so he set choreography with much less experimentation. He often demonstrated a series of steps to music, and we would learn them verbatim. In retrospect now, I believe that experimentation best galvanizes a company and ultimately broadens and deepens the artistry of its repertoire. There is skill in curating not just a group of technical dancers but also to developing camaraderie without competition.

I considered group dynamics a lot now during classes, how to best relate to others in order to give my own best rehearsals and performances and that would hopefully encourage the same in others. I studied the neuroses and temperaments of the team. I wanted to keep a positive mindset, one that helped my peers and me to feel safe and creatively vulnerable—as we needed to be—to open ourselves to new choreography. Dancers have to stay in a sanguine frame of mind in order to move with complete mind-body freedom. Worry and stress about the next gig, romance, aches, and aging, any of life's buffetings, must be left outside the studio so that a choreographic vision can gel.

Although I was now under a professional dance contract, Washington, DC, is expensive and to buy a pantry of crackers, bread, and macaroni—and cover rent—was still not easy. I needed more money.

A customer I met at *Arise,* Monique, offered me a position with the Nina Ricci perfume company as her part-time assistant. I was to accompany her to various perfume counters in the region as she made presentations to customers, designed to increase Nina Ricci product sales. That job would easily pay four times what I was making an hour at *Arise* and I could work three nights a week and be able to dance all day. I accepted. Monique said that my wardrobe would never do. She bought me a conservative blue double-breasted suit and black leather loafers. She administered her crash course on how to be her assistant: never interrupt, never stray from the script she used on customers, and always say "Merci!" after a sale. Attitude and comportment were as essential here as they were to dance. This was theater. We had roles to play. My official title was "fragrance model" for Nina Ricci's signature floral label, *L'Air du Temps.* I would stand next to Monique, the "French fragrance layering specialist just in from Paris, France." She wore a navy-blue Chanel pantsuit, and on the lapel, she pinned a yellow enamel and rhinestone broach, a stylized lily. She put on a show for every customer, as if she were a French doyenne. She fluttered her false eyelashes, smiled with serene grace, and made feminine gestures that gave full fanlike show of her red manicured nails and faux yellow diamond cocktail ring. Monique was a distillation of the character I explored when I walked from the edge of my grandmother's bed to the closet door mirror, a royal at court. As customers descended the escalators toward the cosmetics department, I would ask if I might to spray a whiff of Eau de Toilette on them. This would slow them down just enough for Monique to engage them in conversation that would optimally lead to a sale. As I spritzed a customer's wrist with *L'Air du Temps,* Monique would prattle about the long, very exclusive history of the couture house of Nina Ricci and that if the prospective customer bought a bottle of perfume at this time only, she would receive a collectible limited edition miniature bottle—called a *flacon,* in French—of *L'Air du Temps.* I would then pull out the sample gift from behind the fragrance counter, hold it just out of the customer's reach—that was important—a one-ounce round flacon with two plastic doves on top. This was a well-practiced ballet routine, with steps and hand-offs.

Monique and I were essentially a touring duet on a grand regional circuit that spanned from Woodward & Lothrop in downtown DC, to the behemoth Nordstrom's in Pentagon City, Virginia, to the Macy's in White Flint, Maryland, and beyond. As the customer stared longingly at the gift, so near and yet so far, I would elegantly say, "The crystal flacon was designed by the famous Marc Lalique himself." Monique would then swoop in, take hold of the customer's hand, and firmly, then suggestively, tenderly massage it with *L'Air du Temps* lotion. A literal deal clincher. She would not let go until she had then sprayed fragrance on the well-oiled hand and powdered it down with *L'Air du Temps* body powder. A boneless pink chicken cutlet could not have been more oiled, tenderized, and finally breaded. She told the hapless and by now hypnotized subject that this process was "fragrance layering" and described how Marie Antoinette had repeated the same regimen right up until her untimely departure from Versailles. Even Scheherazade could have taken storytelling lessons from Monique.

In actuality, Monique (I never learned her real name) lived in an old apartment building in Arlington, Virginia, and had moved to America in the early 1970s. Her accent thickened at the sight of potential customers, identifiable, she said, by their designer handbag. She had a running list of their prices memorized: Gucci, Chanel, Prada, and Dior. Monique also had hundreds of little bottles of *L'Air du Temps*, "limited offer gifts" in the trunk of her car, that she would leverage to make sales. Monique's theatricality and hand gestures were themselves lessons in movement. Although she was overweight and at least sixty years old with badly damaged bleached hair, she could sell anyone a bottle of fragrance, a moisturizing lotion, and dusting powder. At the end of each sale she would slump, completely spent, like a psychic medium after a séance.

I studied the way she inhabited her character, right down to the eyebrow raise. For a year I took note of how customers, like butterflies, were attracted with fragrance, and Monique's repertoire of regal hand and wrist flicks, as if she were a bloom, brought them to land and settle a while. I learned to flutter and fascinate spectators and create diversion and detour. Our intimate duet, powers of persuasion and illusion, helped make her a top regional representative for *L'Air du Temps* in 1990. Together, we stuck our landings.

By spring of 1991 I had acquired enough dance work to make my living entirely from the artform and I was able to resign from the fragrance gig. I now taught two weekly modern dance classes at a local studio and had a growing student base. This allowed me time to meet friends and date. I met Josue, a flamenco student my age. He was studying graphic design by day at the Corcoran School of Art, and by night he was taking class at the studio next door to the one at which I taught. That is how I first ran into him. Josue is originally from San Antonio, Texas, and our Southwest backgrounds made us quick friends. Tuesdays and Thursdays, we would synchronize our exits. He was outspoken and loud with a Texas twang. "Out East here, people have no idea about Hispano culture. They all assume when I open my mouth in class that I'm going to talk like a cholo. I like shocking the hell out of all of them," he told me at our first meeting.

On Saturday nights we went to *Escandalo* (Scandal in Spanish), a gay salsa club. We flirted and danced with men all night under flashing disco lights to tunes sung by Selena and Celia Cruz. The scene was bilingual, familiar, and inviting. Josue and I were both on tight budgets and because he lived only five blocks from me, we shared cheap eats several nights a week to save money for our rents. I supplied the hamburger and Josue supplied the Hamburger Helper box mix and together we cooked and talked. From his balcony overlooking P Street, the gay heart of Dupont Circle, he practiced his flamenco castanets as we watched gay peacocks parading in tight tank tops and worn jeans. He'd comment on the passersby, "That one's too old, that one's obviously easy, that one looks like he cheats. That one is HOT! And THAT one is older and more parched than an adobe brick in the noon sun!" He made me laugh and our easy bilingual conversation felt like I was back in New Mexico.

When we weren't appraising men, we discussed our futures. At nineteen he wanted to be an award-winning designer and at twenty-two I wanted to be an acclaimed choreographer. I'm happy to say that Josue is now the Smithsonian Folklife Festival's graphic designer. Today his giant banners and event advertisement posters line the National Mall each year. We remain wonderful pals.

I also made a Filipino American friend. I met Alan at a costume dance-party for SMYAL (Supporting and Mentoring Youth Advocates and Leaders). We were the only Asian Americans among more than one hundred attendees. Neither of us wore costumes, so we waved at each other and made our ways across the dance floor for our introductions. Alan had recently moved to DC from Queens, New York, to work at the US Patent Agency. He was 5 foot 5 inches with a tough New York accent and a husky laugh. We walked together to the center of the dance floor where a woman wildly thrashed to the beats in an octopus costume made from stuffed legs of panty hose. Alan and I each grabbed hold of several of her legs and danced in circles and were soon dizzy with laughter. Alan had recently joined several social groups for gay Asian American men, and I started to tag along to potluck dinners and socials where I made many gay acquaintances—Thai, Korean, Chinese, Japanese, Indonesian, and Filipino.

Josue, Alan, and I shared the fact of our hyphenated ethnic identities and hyphenated regional identities as well. Josue was Hispano Texan, Alan was Filipino New Yorker, and I was the Korean New Mexican. We were each openly gay, and we were all building careers in this, our new city. I was building a community of easy camaraderie.

I didn't make friends among my Eric Hampton colleagues, though. There was an inherent cultural and socioeconomic divide between them and me. By and large those dancers had grown up attending traditional ballet academies on the East Coast. This pedigree demands a high level of financial wherewithal to cover all the necessities: wardrobe; transportation back and forth between home, school, and studios for what are often daily rehearsal and class sequences; performances; special summer programs and private coaching; and recitals and receptions. Many had corporate sponsors, grants, or other family or private funding.

At twenty-two, I felt a deepening sense of artistic autonomy. I may have been poor and unsponsored, but that also freed me from any bonds of obligation or indebtedness. I auditioned for pick-up projects in order to learn more about varying choreographer's creative processes. I discovered that the DC Contemporary Dance Company was directed by a Japanese American woman from California. Miya Hisaka had a culturally diverse casting policy. Her dancers were black, Latino, and Asian American. I auditioned and was hired. I learned works by such artists as Kevin Jeff, who has set works on the Alvin Ailey Dance Ensemble, Dallas Black Dance Theater, and the Cleo Parker Robinson Dance Ensemble. I was partnered with Sandra Park, a young Korean American dancer with whom I found working to be an absolutely silken simpatico. We worked cordially for hours to perfect difficult lifts. She shared her lunch with me that typically included an array of Korean food from kimchi to *bibimbap* (mixed rice, meat, an egg, and vegetables).

This was also the first time I was introduced to the African American diaspora and its extraordinary dance repertoire that reflected a rich cultural legacy. Increasingly I began to wonder about the potential of my own Asian American background as a source for dance material. I was absolutely confounded, too: how was it possible that the DC metropolis—a major urban region with a high Asian population—did not have a modern dance company with an Asian American repertoire focus or troupe?

At night in my apartment, I was aware of an internal shift. I was content, sustained in every way now because I was making a living working in my passion. A dignified life, lean means, to be sure, but not demeaning, not desperate, neither craven nor so hardscrabble that earning my way here had chipped away at further dreams. It was the opposite. I had come to a landing place where I could afford to entertain some next dreams and convert them to goals.

I lay on my futon and summoned the many stories told by my family. Questions poured forth, unstoppable, and I craved answers. How might I bring these stories to life, to experience them myself in the language of movement alone, to share their voices, in the voice of dance? How had choreographers' works been informed by their cultural and personal histories through the ages? I decided to get a library card at the Martin Luther King Jr. Memorial Public Library in Chinatown. This alone was a consequential coming-of-age milestone for me. A membership card in the world of further belonging, scholarship, and research that would be both passport and fare to my future as well as my heritage and past. The name of the library itself that housed the collection, writ large above the entrance . . . I entered this new portal in awe. I shall never forget this event and the relationship I began to build with this public library, another community for my cultural explorations.

Once I had started on this path, I began to check out as many biographies, memoirs, and autobiographies of artists of color as my library card would allow each time. I would take a pile of books and walk across the street to the National Portrait Gallery. There I would go to the second floor and sit on a chair and read. On Sundays I would spend the entire day there. I read about how José Limon's Mexican heritage inspired his first major dance in 1938, *Danzas Mexicanas*. I read about Alvin Ailey's critically acclaimed *Revelations* and how it was inspired from "blood memories" of his youth in segregated Texas in the 1930s, surrounded by a black community, the church, spirituals, and the blues. I read about Katherine Dunham's interest in anthropology and how she had received a fellowship to study Caribbean dance traditions, and how that ultimately informed her modern dance technique.

And what about historical representations of American dance history in visual art, in paintings and sculpture? Was dance represented here? One day, I set aside my pile of books and began studying the art collections specifically for dance images. I studied Paul Colin's prints from his 1927 *Le Tumulte Noire* that highlighted the energy of black dancers like Josephine Baker. I studied Alfred J. Freeh's 1924 prints of Michio Itō in angular dance poses, with his chiseled facial features. I stared into the proud eyes of Philip Grausman's 1969 bronze bust of José Limon. Here were dancers, their energy captured for all time.

I bought a sketchbook and a colored pencil set at the museum bookstore and next turned my studies to figuring out how to interpret movement in paintings. My intention was to sketch impressions of the movement I perceived in paintings and sculptures so that I could later refer to them, to piece them together in the dance studio and start to create original choreography.

One day, I began my next extended migration. I was migrating from movement to representational art, and then, collecting the images there, importing them, transforming them back into actual movement, in the finished art of dance. My intent was of a migration in which I would cross-pollinate two arts, two different vernaculars, visual art and dance.

I walked to the Smithsonian American Art Museum from the National Portrait Gallery. I perused the exhibitions, sketched, and wrote copious notes, ideas that I could later develop into dances. I would squint my eyes to better see the trajectory of brush strokes on a canvas. I drew lines with arrows to indicate the direction of movements and wrote down which part of the body I thought should initiate each phrase. Thus, an abstract sculpture like Louise Bourgeois' 1978 *Maquette for Facets to the Sun* became a series of random spoking and flicking arm phrases. Jackson Pollock's *Miners* (ca. 1934–1938) became a series of bent over curves and lunges. Yasuo Kunioshi's 1920 *Landscape* became a series of waving arms and off-balance steps pushed along by a tropical storm. I was in a dynamic communication with these portraits.

As soon as I had a free moment to myself in a dance studio, I would lay out the pages of my journal on the floor to mimic the posture and lines of each image, randomly. This approach forced me to solve the problem of linking all the movements together seamlessly into repeatable phrases. Each sketch led to a novel new dance phrase. Limitless possibilities emerged because of the interplay of the energy captured from the visual art and migrated into and through dance.

This process expanded and I began creating gestural and postural phrases from traditional realistic portraiture that became short choreographic studies. The Presidential Portraits at the National Portrait Gallery produced a series of gestures. Douglas Granville Chandor's 1931 portrait of Herbert Hoover inspired me to create a series of hand gestures that mimicked a right hand clasping the arm of a chair while the left rummaged through a pile of paper notes. Chandor's 1945 study for a portrait of Franklin Delano Roosevelt, *The Big Three at Yalta*, depicts a series of hand studies. They appeared to me as the potential of gestural phrases. The subject, President Roosevelt, holding eyeglasses, a cigarette, a pen, melded perfectly into a repeatable hand phrase that I then placed atop a larger dance phrase when I began working in the studio. Dance was everywhere, and the ease by which I could look at art and be inspired to create movement was a revelation. The two most influential elements of my life began to merge, in my two laboratories, the studio and the museum.

I craved more choreographic training and formal studies to better realize my concepts. This was a quandary now. I had quit college and didn't know how to access more intellectual training toward this fusion of dance and visual art. I wanted to grow as an artist and to make a mark on the field of dance by expressing my cultural and personal background and what I perceived as the associations among choreography, painting, photography, and sculpture.

I had always been fascinated by hands. I sought an exquisite gesture, sublime and knowing, that expressed in its open palm, its relaxed extended fingers, reaching toward me, beckoning in invitation to walk together, toward a solution. Whenever I closed my eyes, the hand that reached out to me, again and again, belonged to my beloved guardian and hero, Serendipity.

On a November evening in 1990, while dancing for DC Contemporary Dance Company, I waited backstage to make my entrance. The company was performing in a dance festival at Dance Place, a small black box theater in northeast Washington. While in the wings, I watched other groups, one after another, perform postmodern dances. There was one in which five dancers walked the stage as if it were divided into a grid. They fell in and out of their walking patterns interrupting them with what appeared to be random individual improvisations. Each member of the cast chose when to leave or return to their walking grid. Another troupe interacted with images of outdoor landscapes shuffled from six projectors placed on the front of the stage, focused in pairs on the cyclorama, left and right walls, and the ceiling of the theater. The projector carousels were packed with hundreds of slides of mountain streams, rolling hills, and forests. Three dancers mimicked rolling down grassy knolls and diving into water.

A middle-aged woman scheduled to perform her work in the showcase saw me watching from the wings. She came over and introduced herself as Maida Withers, a professor of dance at George Washington

University. "What do you see out there?" I stalled for diplomatic neutrality. "Oh . . . well . . . I may not have the words." Her manner at once became more direct. "I saw you dance during dress rehearsal. I've been watching you. You have talent, real talent." She jerked her head in a motion toward the stage. "Do NOT waste that talent on choreography that looks like it should be on a cruise ship." I was shocked and relieved by her bluntness and, true, the dance in which I was cast did look to be headed for the *MS Pacific Princess*, destination Gilligan's Island. She said, "You're young. . . . I imagine that you don't yet have a graduate degree, right?" I confessed that I didn't have even an undergraduate degree yet from UNM. She brightened. "Albuquerque? Did you ever meet my friend Tim Wengerd?"

Invoking Tim's name was like flashing a No Expiration Date, Get Out of Jail card. "Yes, yes, I danced for Tim." She told me that they had the shared common soil: they had both danced in Salt Lake City when they were young. I spoke about my time with Tim a bit more and she nodded enthusiastically. She said, "OK, great! Listen, just go back and complete that bachelor's degree, and I will get you a fellowship to learn the art of real professional choreography. You really have to have that, to do your next big things. You know that, too." After the show, Maida tracked me down a final time and commanded, "Call me!" She handed me her home phone number scrawled on a scrap paper and jaunted out of the theater wearing only a leotard.

I thought about Maida for several days. She seemed to have an earnest trajectory in mind for me, perhaps even channeling our Tim? I had already danced for two well-known companies in Washington, DC, and was urgently now in need of steeping in how to choreograph. Tim Wengerd had clearly sent her to me . . . this . . . odd unlikely messenger, one urging yet another leap of faith.

So, one morning I uncrumpled Maida's mash note and called her.

Serendipity had indeed arrived, in the thorny form of Maida, with an eagle-sharp face, a laugh that shredded the air like pinking shears, and a manic, scary no-nonsense, tick-tock, hop-to-it-what-are-you-waiting-for-manner. This Serendipity didn't seduce or ingratiate. She heckled and she brayed. Maida answered on the first ring and filled me in on her background. She had studied with Mary Wigman, the pioneer of German expressionist dance; Merce Cunningham, the American pioneer of abstract modern dance; and Anna Halprin, the postmodern dance pioneer who investigated modalities of healing through movement. In 1975, she founded Maida Withers and the Dance Construction Company, through which she explored her own choreographic interests.

We spoke for two hours about the graduate program she had started. "You will learn to choreograph, you'll have a cast of undergraduate students, a studio and a theater as laboratories, learn to teach, study lighting design and costumes, and, most of all, you will use your creative as well as technical brain." A fellowship included free tuition and the chance to earn a teaching stipend. "Call UNM, get that degree, and be back here by the end of August."

I transcribed ten pages of notes from that conversation. It seemed that there was no other way to achieve my goals except to commit to the intensive creative studies in a graduate degree program. I placed a rental ad in the classified pages of a gay-oriented newspaper, the *Washington Blade*, and signed the apartment over to a young Chinese American gay man. I gave notice to the dance companies that I would be departing at the end of their respective spring seasons. In this way I did not renew contracts to start late summer rehearsals for the start of their fall seasons, so those partings were very amicable. No bridges burned.

I called Jennifer Predock-Linnell and returned to Albuquerque to complete one last semester at UNM in order to earn a bachelor's degree. As my academic advisor, Jennifer assisted by counting my professional experience toward graduation. My parents were now thrilled with me: I would have not one, but two university degrees. I lived off-campus in a furnished efficiency, in a brutalist-style cinderblock apartment complex. I craved to return to DC with its large arts scene and an exciting graduate program. I turned in my paperwork to GWU and quickly received my acceptance, inclusive of a letter from Maida outlining my fellowship and the starting date of class. Within five months, I had finished up that undergraduate degree, I bade farewell to Carlisle Gym, thanked Jennifer and Judith for their support, packed, and boomeranged back to DC.

I crashed at Josue's apartment in DC for a week until I found the cheapest efficiency in the Foggy Bottom neighborhood, just a block from the university. The building was next to a branch of the public library on Twenty-fourth and M Streets. The homeless converged to sleep here by 9 p.m. each night. My view from my second-floor studio was of the long corridors of rooms of the Columbia Hospital for Women, on Twenty-fourth and L Streets, off Washington Circle. Patients in white gowns, hooked up to IVs, shuffled down the hall. The apartment building reeked of the stewing vapors of broccoli and cabbage coming from the kitchen of an elderly woman who lived on the first floor. She had two wooden legs jointed at the knees and swung herself along with crutches. Even she proved to be a sort of inspiration, for her resourcefully achieved mobility born of desperation. Her colorful floral outfits were complemented by her extreme eye shadow and rouge. She lurked in the doorway for most of every day waiting for neighbors, at whom she would fling her wild and improvised tirade, a verbal stew boiling over with conflated obscenities. I soon learned that she had Tourette's Syndrome. As I hastened to escape her each time, I was reminded of the veteran in Santa Fe, at the plaza, who would lob ethnic slurs at my mother and me.

On the first day of class I walked excitedly to GWU's main campus. I arrived outside of Building J, the dance headquarters, half an hour early for my first class, Performance Trends, an overview of performance art from the late 1800s to the present, which Maida was teaching. I entered the lobby—a musty ten-by-twelve-foot area with two green faux leather faded chairs from the 1950s, the feet of which had worn holes through the brown linoleum floor.

There was a sixty-by-one-hundred-foot studio on the first floor and one half the size on the second floor. The Marley dance floor of the main studio was gray, and the ceiling foam tiles were yellow with water damage. Leakage from the radiator pipes that ran along the sides had stained the long-ago white walls with swatches of rusty-brown streaks. The men's restroom and changing room were outside the building, accessed by a key on a metal loop that hung on the plywood wall between the lobby and main studio. Built-in ballet barres and a wall of mirrors completed the fixtures. A door interrupted the mirrors, through which the women's bathroom and dressing room were accessed.

In retrospect the condition of the building can be attributed to two things. First, the university did not believe in the arts enough to fix the building, and second, Building J was considered to be among the most historic buildings on the GWU campus. It was originally the atelier and home of architect John Joseph Earley. He was an innovator of colorful mosaic cement used throughout Washington, DC, and inventor of the prefabricated concrete homes built throughout the region. This designation protected the dance program's home. The university had determined that the upgrades needed in order to use it for any other academic program would be cost-ineffective. This 1907 building, still used to this day, finally had a partial face-lift in 2022 due to hazardous materials and mold found throughout. Setting aside its decrepitude, Building J exudes the genuine and abiding feeling that thousands of dancers have come through here. I have come to see that it is the architectural embodiment of what happens to a dancer's body, the physical scaffolding and infrastructure, if it is not supported or taken care of during a career of overwork and neglect. The inescapable cautionary visual messaging of Building J was, and is, in its own way, a gift to dancers.

Three more students arrived for Maida's class. Lara was a tall, leggy Southern belle; Vincent was an earthy hippie with black ringlets that he constantly pushed out of his eyes; and Stacy, a thin Olive Oyl look-alike in a red miniskirt and thick patent leather Mary Janes. Maida entered ten minutes after the hour, arms filled with papers. "Welcome! Let's all introduce ourselves." Lara had gone to undergraduate school in North Carolina and wanted to teach high school dance; Vincent had attended Virginia Commonwealth University and planned to dance in Europe; and Stacy had already been in the GWU graduate program for five years and didn't feel moved to end it.

Maida said, "Today we tackle Dada and the theater of the absurd. Dadaism was an avant-garde movement of the artistic intelligentsia that began in Europe around WWI that rejected capitalism. We will be writing and performing personal manifestos based on the concept of the absurd today." She fumbled through her paper jumble and gave us each a copy of the 1896 play, *Ubu Roi*, by Alfred Jarry, and assigned each of us a part to recite while interpretively dancing. *Ubu Roi* was the precursor to Dada and theater of the macabre, a satire about a corrupt, greedy king and a complacent middle class, so I marched around the room with a cardboard box on my head reciting the absurdist lines of King Ubu as he announces that he will overtax the poor. Lara, cast as my wife, egged me on as she performed a high-kicking French Moulin Rouge can-can. Stacy and Vince pretended to be the bourgeoise who complacently sit back, look away, and ignore society as it crumbles under the dictator. When we finished, Maida abruptly and wordlessly—and in keeping with the day's theme—absurdly left Building J, leaving us to discuss whether she had lost her mind or was a mad genius. Each of Maida's classes pushed our comfort zones and forced us to plunder the stacks of the library to unearth clues to the underlying intention for us in her lectures and assignments.

Throughout the semester Maida's classes challenged superficial or habitual movements to which a dancer too often clings for comfort. They were anchors, she said, ones that kept us stuck. In another class Maida said, "Today you each make an expressionist solo, only movement from pure emotion. I don't want to see one recognizable dance move." For a trained dancer this felt truly impossible. I began. While beating rhythm with a handheld drum, she yelled at me, "Why, oh why, are you pointing your foot like a ballet dancer? I don't believe a thing you are doing, stop being pretty, try being grotesque instead!" In that moment she reminded me of my frothing screaming neighbor. I struggled to remove my personal movement decision making derived from dance training in order to discover what she said was the authentic ways of moving. Her classes were psychological torture, and in keeping with that, they did draw out twisted contortions and exaggerated hand gestures that I had not suspected possible, much less within my circumscribed—trained—imagination and capacity. How many different ways were there to express pleading, using outspread fingers? There were far more than I had heretofore imagined. She dismantled us, our conventions and habits, in order to rebuild us, or rather, to invest us in reinventing ourselves.

All of her courses were challenging. In one class she talked about the 1960s Judson Dance Theatre in downtown New York City and bade us make entire dances built from pedestrian jogging and game playing. Students each had to compose simple movement scores. One score went like this: jog for two minutes, play hopscotch for forty feet, fall ten times, and yell at the top of your lungs. Simple scores would produce four completely different outcomes from each of us four students. We performed these as ensembles: I jogged in circles, Vince jogged back and forth, Vince threw himself to the ground violently while I gently folded. Another day, Maida brought a hat to class filled with strips of paper that corresponded to four musical scores she kept ready to play on the stereo system. "Today we 'Chance Dance,'" she announced. She taught us Merce Cunningham's technique of associating random dance phrases with seemingly unrelated musical scores. We drew a score name from her hat and she blasted it on the stereo. Then we struggled to create a logic between our dance phrases and the music. Picture a ballet phrase created to Bach, but forced to be performed to acid rock, or a modern dance phrase choreographed to synthesized music, but instead now set against a recording of Marlene Dietrich playing the sexually taunting and flaunting cabaret singer Lola in the 1930 German film, *The Blue Angel*. Maida made me realize that while dancers spend most of their lives learning how to perfect known, codified vocabularies, it is the choreographer's challenge and creative obligation to help dancers unlearn them—and then to innovate new ones.

My choreography teacher, Tish Carter, introduced me to theatricality, character development, and the manipulation of stage props. Tish was a performance artist who had, through her Ford Foundation grant, studied both visual arts and the dances of choreographers Lar Lubovitch, Pina Bausch, and Merce Cunningham. Tish was a neurotic genius who played with perspective and scale toward creating psychological symbolism on stage. In one assignment, Tish had me study Alfred Hitchcock's 1960 film *Psycho*. She developed a solo dance role of Norman Bates, the titular wacko with mother issues, through studies in his postures, gestures, and facial expressions. She handed me a one-foot-high replica prop of Norman's iconic "house on the hill" and had me slowly lower it to the stage floor with fishing wire. This set the reference place for the audience before I performed the solo to the audio accompaniment of the screeching violin score, the same one that was played in the film as Norman repeatedly stabbed his motel's only overnight guest. The largest symbol in the movie, Norman's house, became the tiniest object on stage, but it was absolutely recognizable and signified perfectly the same looming contextual message.

One day I asked for her thoughts about Hollywood's systemic use of "yellowface"—its portrayal of and treatment of Asians in the black-and-white movies of the 1930s and 1940s. The topic invited exploration, she said, and encouraged me to do an independent study investigating Asian American identities, US norms in casting, and Asian American choreographers.

There was virtually nothing in the GWU library about Asian American modern dance. However, my friend San San Wong, an arts administrator and Asian American arts advocate, knew of three Asian American choreographers in New York City to whom I could write: H. T. Chen, Michael Mao, and Ping Chong. I wrote to each, and they all said I could call them. I spoke briefly with each of them by phone. Collectively they talked about a lack of representation of Asian Americans. In a time when multiculturalism in American dance was receiving a wave of interest, the focus was on African American and Latino American perspectives.

And the crucial discovery I made? There was no dance company in the nation's capital that performed Asian American stories, none that illuminated Asian American histories or the Asian diaspora. My graduate degree was paying off in so many ways.

In the fall of 1993, for my Master of Fine Arts (MFA) in dance thesis project, I proposed to choreograph an evening about the Asian diaspora. I would need a cast of Asian and Asian American dancers. I dropped by the undergraduate technique classes and asked seven dancers if they would be willing to commit to rehearsals for my thesis concert, to be performed in December: Junie and Christina were Korean American, Miho and Miyuki were Japanese, Dawn and Nicole were half-Chinese, and Cathy was half-Japanese. I added three professional dancers to the cast: Veronique Dang Tran (we called her "Nica"), a Vietnamese dancer recently arrived in DC from Italy; Isabel Hon, a Chinese Costa Rican modern dancer from Maryland; and Li Chiao-Ping, a Chinese American dancer who taught at the University of Wisconsin. Chiao-Ping agreed to come to Washington for three weeks to develop a duet with me. In addition, Isabel and I worked on a duet separately. The rest of the dancers and I met three nights a week for three hours for three months to put together an hour and a half show of five dances.

The final concert premiered in December 1993. It consisted of two solos, two duets, and a group work for seven. Each dance was designed to highlight a cultural myth or family story pertaining to our dancers. Nica chose a Vietnamese myth about a woman, ThoThi, who waits for her husband to return by sea; she waits so long on the shore, her heart broken, that she turns to stone. I designed *Seeds of Toil* to reflect this tale. Nica, her body powdered in white clay, crawls among a pile of white rocks to an electronic sound score of the ocean, until she slowly rises and finally freezes in an upright pose, staring out to sea.

I created *Solitude*, a solo dance that represented my search for my own family tree. A strong backlight accentuated the outline of my body as I traveled along a diagonal, twisting across from upstage right to downstage left where there stood a clump of large willow branches. Clothed in billowing silk pants in autumnal colors and covered in stylized leaves, I moved through a mix of martial arts kicks and leaps and high ballet leg extensions, and turns with sequencing arms and torso, until at last I arrived at the branches, where I mimicked their shape with my body and limbs, gently swaying as if moved by a gentle Hawaiian breeze, in proximity to my own ancestry, the tree.

For the duet *Phoenix*, a superb Japanese American visual artist, HIRO, painted the backdrop that we hung from the top of the proscenium onto the stage floor: a thirty-foot black ink calligraphy on canvas of a flying phoenix. HIRO had a personal stake in so generously supporting this dance. She was an Asian American activist who believed in art as social change. The dance referenced the Pan-Asian myth of an immortal creature whose body symbolizes the cosmos: its head is the sky, its eyes the sun, its back is the moon, its wings the wind, its feet the earth, and its tail the planets. Chinese storyteller Linda Fang told the myth of the Phoenix, reciting lines that alternated in English and Mandarin. Li Chiao-Ping and I emerged from under the backdrop and improvised an athletic phrase of rolls and tumbles, kicks, and arm swirls—movements that expressed feeling the earth under our feet, our arms like wings, and our backs as crescent shapes waxing and waning like the cycles of the moon—advancing toward the audience until we moved off the stage and were among them.

Then Isabel and I danced *Plantation Hawaii*, based on my family history there, accompanied by a recorded interview done with my mother about picking pineapples. Isabel and I mimicked picking pineapples among imaginary rows and slicing the fruits from stalks.

Dreaming of Fox, the Temple, and Betrayal, the single group dance of the evening, was based on the Japanese tales of the Kyubi, trickster foxes, who can shape shift to appear as beautiful women. The cast was dressed all in white cotton tunics and one dancer wore a traditional Japanese white papier-mâché fox mask on the top of her head, so that when she looked down, the mask was then surrounded by her long black hair, a sudden transformation from that of female to fox. The dance was ritualistic and built in energy to a score by Lou Harrison and his American Gamelan Orchestra. As the clanging sounds gained volume, the cast surrounded the masked fox kicking and contracting like crazed bacchants under a full moon.

This was my first attempt at a full evening program of my own choreography and by the time we got close to performance weekend, I was exhausted by rehearsals. I was also worried that there would be no audience. This was well before the era of instant social media saturation. The student dancers and I hung flyers from Dupont Circle to Foggy Bottom in windows of local businesses. We also contacted aligned networks, local Asian student organizations, and Asian American community groups. The word was out: A young group of Asian and Asian Americans was premiering a new modern dance program. Up until this time DC had only had local companies that performed the *wǔ long*, or the Chinese dragon dance, and the *wūshí*, or Chinese lion dance, at New Year's celebrations, and an assortment of Japanese traditional dances at the Cherry Blossom Festival—all of which were annual and extremely well attended. This, though, was something altogether different.

On opening night, we (backstage) and an audience of two hundred listened to Kathleen Homm, the director of the Mayor's Office on Asian Pacific American Affairs, read words of congratulations from Mayor Sharon Pratt Dixon: "Congratulations to the dancers of Moving Forward: Contemporary Asian American Dance Company for this evening's launch. The Mayor wishes you luck and success with this new endeavor." We dancers held hands in a circle and wished one another luck. We were called to our places in the wings and the curtain rose.

The show went beautifully, and our hundreds of hours of hard collaborative work paid off. The crowd clapped loudly and appreciatively as we took a group bow at the end of the show. As I bent deeply and appreciatively, I took in the reality that had once been only a dream: I had a dance company, we had the beginnings of an audience base, and we had arguably begun to make a positive change in the cultural landscape of DC through the language of dance. We took another group bow, savoring the experience of our first ovation. My heart overflowed.

We even received a review in the *Washington Post*. That such a thing might happen had been way beyond our imagining. The generous review mentioned both the artists and the choreography and described each work. Critic George Jackson wrote that among notable works and performances were "*Seeds of Toil*, with its strong spatial design and quietly intense performance by Veronique Dang-Tran. She positioned her body in three circles of light. The first she shared with small, chalky stones. One was left with a Nietzschean sense of the heaviness of life. Another solo, *Solitude*, nullified the feeling from which it emanated— adventure. Burgess used his own long, smoothly muscled frame to meld angular stances, torques and pulses for the torso, plus extensions as linear as columns."

His review signaled that the dance and dancers had most assuredly communicated their stories, and this affirmation mattered. It meant that we were on the right path toward building awareness of diasporic and Asian American experiences through movement. This "overnight success" had only taken twenty years. I had come a long way from pirouettes in Pampers, from my Carmel Valley dinner cabaret for family. I had moved beyond that five-minute homage to misery and angst I choreographed for the junior year student showcase at UNM—the one that left my cheerleading parents struggling to find a kind word to say afterward and me with those episodes of wicked tendonitis.

And then on December 26, 1993, in his "Year in Review" column for the *Washington Post* Pulitzer Prize–winning dance critic Alan Kriegsman included me as a dancer to keep an eye on. I was overjoyed to open the paper and see this mention. I was deeply honored to be noted among such talented dancers from large established companies, and especially so because this praise gave special mention of my company. I had a company. I let it sink in. Mr. Kriegsman was a gifted dance scholar who, in 1976, had won the Pulitzer Prize, the first one ever awarded for dance criticism. His reach went well beyond dance trade magazines. He gave dance an enormous platform, a legitimate written voice in a major national newspaper that reached millions of global readers. Because of his support, other dance writers and curators, such as Alicia Adams and Derek Gordon of the Kennedy Center and Sarah Kaufman of the *Washington Post*, began to take note of my work. Ms. Kaufman would win a Pulitzer Prize in 2010 for criticism.

These early accolades from those with prominent and penetrative general standing were timely encouragement because my financial reality was grim. I had put all my money into meeting expenses for Moving Forward. To support it further, in 1994, I took a job teaching dance at an English as a Second Language (ESL) high school. The main populations were Latino and Vietnamese immigrants and their ages ranged from fourteen to twenty. The school was located in DC's Mount Pleasant neighborhood. At the time, Mount Pleasant was far from pleasant. It was rough and under pressure from the gentrification that was driving rents and prices up. It was also in the midst of a turf war between the resident Salvadoran and Vietnamese communities. Police clashes with the Salvadoran community had led to parked police cars being overturned and set on fire, left to char, and storefronts boarded up after demonstrations.

While teaching at the school, I was vividly reminded of my own experiences in bilingual schools as a child and between going to the school and the dance studio I realized how far I had come from my life in New Mexico. I straddled an expanding career and was also in the midst of a very familiar cultural landscape from my not-so-distant past. It was intriguing—transformative and healing—to live the future and the past at the same time. When other teachers at the school didn't want students with "behavioral issues" in their classes, they simply kicked them out and the students would wander the hallways. Many roamed to the cafeteria, and that was where my dance classes took place. Lured by the sound of salsa and Vietnamese music, they would lurk in the open doorway and watch the dancing, much the way I had spied on dance classes at Carlisle Gymnasium at UNM. I always invited the kids in. Additionally, an overzealous counselor who wanted to keep "hooligans" from wandering the halls solved her problem by assigning dozens of extra students into my classes each semester—that was their punishment and my boon—making my average class size thirty students, half girls and half boys. What a favor she had done me, without intending to do so. These "hooligans" were my dream come true, and I hoped to become theirs. In my class, students could excel through the universal language of dance. They were not frustrated by a lack of verbal skills or cultural barriers. I spent three hours every other morning in the cafeteria teaching three forty-five-minute classes in a row, with fifteen-minute breaks in between each, before the cafeteria workers arrived and began rolling out long folding tables, readying them for lunch.

The students were all quite brilliant, creative problem solvers who excelled in their spirited collaborations for group dances. They had become hooligans out of boredom, otherism, and frustration. The tensions among students melted when they performed hip-hop, modern dance phrases, and salsa to popular Latino and Vietnamese music that I played on an old boom box. I assigned them to partner with one another. Each pair then had to take turns, lifting each other into the air and gently lowering each other back to the ground.

I set boundaries. No one could make fun of another's language skills. In this class, the only language was movement, dance. And everyone had to support any dance partner and see to that person's safety, no matter what. Trust quickly took root when peers took responsibility for the physical wellbeing of one another. The students improvised together. In one class, I assigned them to partner with someone. The assignment was to stand back-to-back, press their bodies together, and with no hands, lower themselves to the ground and sit. Then, without losing contact with the other's back, and without using hands to assist, they had to come back to standing. They had to work together, feel each other's weight, and to be a unit, two moving as one in order to accomplish the assignment. In another exercise, I asked each student to gently lift and carry a fellow student in his or her arms and hands. Next, I then said, do so while walking, skipping, or jumping across the floor. The dance exercise reminded me of my martial arts friend who had sharpened her competition skills as a waitress carrying and juggling heavy platters without spilling or dropping them.

All the exercises were based on developing trust, friendship, and empathy—qualities particularly crucial in a student population that too often reflexively adopts defensive, confrontational, or combative tacks. Dance acts as a bridge over barriers of language, culture, appearance, and age. We all inherently understand the language of the body. Rhythm is our first experience of being alive, in heartbeats, in chewing, swallowing, in taking our first regular steps, one after the other. At this school I was reminded of what a literal obstacle course and walking on eggshells the immigration and relocation process is and how traumatizing building a home in a strange new land can be. Fundamentally, everyone wants a place to call home, to be heard, and to be treated with respect. I was teaching them dance but ultimately, together, we solidified lessons of building a community from diverse individuals. And I applied those lessons ever after as my dance company grew.

After one intense year juggling my own dance studies, rehearsals, and performances in the evenings and weekends, and teaching, I simply had to leave the ESL school. I hated to do so, but I was running ragged. For years afterwards while walking in my neighborhood, I would hear, "Señor Chino!" I would look up and wave at a former student on a bike, zipping by on the way to Mount Pleasant. I will never forget these fine student dancers. After all, they were the ones who had taught me.

thirteen BRINGING ASIAN
AMERICAN EXPERIENCES TO THE
FOREFRONT IN DANCE

The question for me in 1995 at the age of twenty-seven was this: what technical base for dance should I be teaching that directly relates to an Asian American modern dance diaspora? Michio Itō was in my thoughts again. He is considered to be the first Asian American modern dancer and choreographer. A pioneer. Itō was born in in Tokyo circa 1892, studied dance and music visualizations from 1912 to 1914 at the Dalcroze Institute outside Dresden, Germany, and escaped WWI by moving to America. He had a successful career in New York City and eventually opened a dance studio in Los Angeles where he choreographed for motion pictures. He also created spectacular dance events that were performed at the Rose Bowl with full orchestras and choirs. As a young man in the 1920s his dancing talent, dashing jet-black hair in a bob and gender-bending looks, secured his celebrity on stages around the country. He was Lester Horton's mentor. The Horton technique is what the Alvin Ailey American Dance Theater still trains.

His fame and adulation notwithstanding, one day after the bombing of Pearl Harbor, Itō would be rounded up, incarcerated, and charged as an alien enemy. On February 19, 1942, Executive Order 9066 was signed, which allowed for the incarceration of more than 100,000 people of Japanese ancestry living on the West Coast without due process. Itō was charged wrongfully and was repatriated to Japan in 1943. He never returned to the United States. His school and legacy were dismantled, and his repertoire, venerable reputation, and comprehensive foundational technique were obliged to be preserved and broadly disseminated and passed down through a mere handful of select dancers.

That year he became my mentor. If I did not study Itō, how was I to understand or ever lay claim to being part of the modern Asian American dance community? Through conversations with visual artist

HIRO, I was able to be introduced to both first- and second-generation Itō dancers: Mitchiko Kitsmiller, Lily Arikawa, and Saturo Shimazaki. They all spoke fondly of this gentle, supportive man whose career had been a pendulum between the colonialist concept of the "Exotic Oriental" and "The Yellow Peril," as coined in 1897 by Russian sociologist Jacques Novikow in his essay "Le Péril Jaune."

Mitchiko and Lily were in their late sixties and early seventies, and Saturo was in his fifties, and each still embodied Ito's dance genius, carrying forward their knowledge of his life's work in the form of personal stories and dances. Lily, talented in Japanese dancing, was his muse in California before WWII. Mitchiko worked with him in Japan after WWII, and Saturo had studied with his protégé, Ryuko Maki, when he returned to Japan. They were part of Itō's surviving legacy and a living archive. Saturo taught me Itō's basic technique and several of his earliest dances.

Itō's technique is based on what he called "ten male and ten female arm gestures." These sculptural gestures could be interchanged, manipulated musically or with breath, and placed atop rhythmic walks and lunges to form choreography. From Saturo I first learned *Pizzicati*, Itō's 1919 signature solo, set to the music of French ballet and opera composer, Léo Delibes. It depicts a music conductor madly commanding an orchestra and is lit with a single spotlight set on the floor in front of the dancer, casting a giant shadow on the back of the stage. I loved the costume, an art deco Japanese-style top, harem pants, and a wide red cummerbund, all of which sparkled with silver threads. The dancer is in place with legs far apart and the upper body moves in sync with the music. Each gesture commands another part of the orchestra to play out with martial arts accuracy. Saturo had me waving my arms like propellers for hours until I couldn't lift my arms and had bruises and scrapes under my biceps where they hit my chest. This dance—a mere two minutes of performance duration—took me days of rehearsal before I at last gained his approval.

Ave Maria, composed by Itō as his graduation dance in 1913 from the Dalcroze Institute, holds a unique value for me, for several reasons. For one, in this dance he took on the form of a statue of the Virgin Mary.

This of course spoke directly to my earliest and enduring attachments to the shapes and gestures of religious statuary of the Virgin Mother. I was learning the arm gestures and legwork for *Ave Maria* when Lily mentioned that Itō was close friends with Isamu Noguchi. They had moved in the same intellectual and artistic circles and avidly supported and identified with each other's work. Michio opened opportunities for Isamu in the social sets of arts aficionados, impresarios, and the literary intelligentsia.

I also found out that Michio and I shared more than dance and our friendship with Isamu. We had both at different times lived in the same neighborhood in Santa Fe, but under very different circumstances. Itō had been imprisoned in the Japanese Internment Camp in 1942 where the neighborhood of Casa Solana now stood. He would be repatriated from the Santa Fe camp in 1943. For me this archaeological fact made me wonder if, as a child, I had perhaps absorbed his lingering emotional presence in the land. After all, Santa Fe was a hub of magical realism and spirituality. The soul took different means of commuting between the living and the dead. I recalled the many poignant artifacts that my brother and I found while digging fortresses in our backyard. We found trowels, hoes, and other gardening tools by the dozens. One of the neighborhood kids found a cache of old metal springs from beds that no doubt had been dumped in a landfill and plowed over when the camp was closed at the end of WWII. To contemplate such a brilliant artist imprisoned on the same ground where I too had felt confined, physically and emotionally, my cries muffled and my creative urges either suppressed or disposed, fills me with awe and artistic debt. In our admittedly very different contexts, one in a real prison, and the other, decades later, in a psychological prison, we shared dreams of escape and flight. Our dreams were what made our escapes possible. Dance permitted us to be each other's eternal family.

This new knowledge of legacy would help me continue to evolve as an artist and allow me to train young dancers. A month later I was contacted by a man who identified himself on the phone as a representative of the DC Commission on the Arts and Humanities. He asked me to perform *Solitude* at the upcoming Mayor's Arts Award

Ceremony. I didn't even know that the office of the mayor had such an annual event and I was thrilled to have my solo seen by the DC arts community. There would certainly be many influential Washington individuals in that crowd, and that would be a tremendous exposure for the underrepresented Asian American arts. The event took place in Lisner Auditorium, a 1,200-seat theater on the GWU campus. *Solitude* went over wonderfully in this big venue. I was so deeply satisfied.

Back in my dressing room, there came a knock on my open door, just as I was readying to leave. A striking African American man in a suit and tie appeared. I greeted him, he complimented my work, and he hastily said, in his own rush to get to other appointments, "I am going to get you into the Kennedy Center." With that, he handed me his business card and vanished.

I had no idea who this man was, or how he got backstage, or why he was not out there schmoozing and congratulating the mayor and glad-handing all those influential people. His business card identified him as Derek Gordon, the senior vice president at the John F. Kennedy Center for the Performing Arts. I called him first thing Monday morning. He asked, "Can you meet me at the Center? I have an idea for you." I thought to myself, "Oh, hell yes, you had better believe I can. Are you kidding me? Am I dreaming? If I have to walk on my hands, I will. And . . . um . . . did I hear you correctly?" But what I actually said was, "Sure thing. What time?"

The following week I put on my only blue suit and my leather loafers and walked for forty-five minutes to get to the Kennedy Center so that I might avoid the cost of a taxi fare. Derek Gordon's office in the heart of the Kennedy Center was on the third floor. It was filled with performance memorabilia, posters of stars from Alvin Ailey American Dance Theater, photos of him next to presidents and prima ballerinas. I was utterly overcome with my setting, overwhelmed to be sitting there, and I thanked him profusely for his time. He said, "So, let me tell you why I asked you here. I have an idea. I want to design a summer dance program, one that will empower Asian American youth and which in turn will naturally also propagate Asian American attendance at the Center. Do you think you would be interested in doing this, Dana?" I couldn't believe my ears when he followed that with, "We can design it around you, how you want to train young dancers and help them express their stories and cultures." I eagerly said, "Yes, yes, I am all in!"

Several meetings with Derek led to a residency for three consecutive summers that allowed me to work with my company as well as Asian American youth from throughout the region, headquartered within the prestigious hive of the Kennedy Center. Derek walked me through a crash course in planning and budgeting. I turned in a workplan that included how many participants we would have, guest teachers, my salary, costumes, set and lighting designers, our press and PR needs, and even dancer stipends for performances. How well I knew firsthand how crucial to survival were those stipends to struggling dancers.

By June 15, 1994, we launched the Asian American Modern Dance Summer Youth Program at the Kennedy Center. Derek walked me to my assigned dance studio in the Center, which was located directly across from the rehearsal studio of American dance legend Twyla Tharp. It was not a time for introductions. She was at work on a new choreography and was in residence at the Kennedy Center at the time. But I did watch her a bit that day in her studio—dressed in white from head to toe, with an impeccable gray bobbed haircut—rehearsing with her awestruck acolytes.

It is difficult to even express the measure of my daily awe each time I entered the Kennedy Center. At age twenty-six, I had a dance company and a summer youth program based at the nation's premiere performing arts center. My program now had twenty-four Asian American participants ranging from fourteen to nineteen, with cultural backgrounds that included Thai, Filipino, Japanese, Korean, Vietnamese, and Chinese. They were first- and second-generation Americans who shared the common fact of being perceived as outsiders in American culture. But together, we would overcome that. The nation was going to welcome us inside and ask us to stay.

We worked five days a week for five hours a day. Our schedule was packed. Each day I taught a class in modern dance that included parts of the Itō technique. This was followed by a group discussion centered on what it was to be Asian American. The discussions were moderated by guest cultural scholars, who bridged conversations around such topics as "Yellow-face casting" and the casting of *Ballet blanc,* or white ballet. While officially the term "white ballet" historically refers to the all-white wardrobe that is customary for dancers of romantic ballets, there is historically a far more insidious, coded meaning to the phrase, all too well recognized by today's dancers. It refers to a conspiratorial discrimination practice that excludes dancers of color in the casting of romantic leads. Rarely were black, Asian, or Latino dancers cast as leads in the romantic ballets by major US companies until the late 1980s. The individual firsthand experiences of exclusion that these youth shared were poignant and for them indelible memories, ones that this program, I hoped, would help them to change in the world and restore their own cultural confidence. No question or sharing was off-limits in these discussions and participation was lively.

We then would have lunch in the cafeteria where the kids met cast members from touring shows that were currently performing at the Center. The cast of *The Phantom of the Opera* gave the dance students a backstage tour of the wardrobe and elaborate sets. The dancers from the Houston Ballet informally shared lunch with the kids, happily answering questions about what it is like to be a professional dancer on tour. These encounters were more or less organic, spontaneous, and joyful for all as impromptu mentorship opportunities.

After lunch the kids took a master class with a special Asian American guest teacher. I brought in teachers that included Japanese American soloist Janet Shibata from the Washington Ballet and Filipina American dancer Elizabeth Rojas from the Alvin Ailey American Dance Theater, among others. After the master class, I set choreography so that by the end of the summer we had a performative outcome, a whole show that was presented in the Center's black box theater.

The first summer I created a work titled *Red Cans, Blue and White Bowls.* The red cans referred to American Coca-Cola cans and the blue-and-white bowls referred to traditional porcelain noodle and rice bowls. The work was about the hyphenated daily realities lived by young Asian Americans. The dance told a story of a Chinese American teen, who while working in her family's grocery store in Washington's

Chinatown, is transported by the Chinese deity Guan Yu to a dream world where she meets her ancestors. She tells them how it feels to be stuck between two worlds. Her ancestors help her to embrace tradition, while also being a hip teen in urban America.

For this show we decided to expand the program to include twenty additional Chinese American kids, ones who studied Beijing Opera at a traditional local school run by Chu Shan Zhu who had served in China as the director of the Shanghai Beijing Opera Theatre in the 1970s and '80s. These kids danced the ancestor dream sequences in full Beijing Opera costumes and traditional face paints while the modern dance students performed sequences that were taking place in the lead character's waking reality, working in her parents' store. More than forty—forty!—youth performed to live Beijing opera music with a modern keyboardist and singer. The hour-long performance sold out, received an eruptive and long, standing ovation, and a full-color spread in *the Washington Post Magazine*. It was absolutely a dream come true—not just for me, but for all involved. This artistic and cultural phenomenon had never been attempted, much less realized, in such a magnificent, original, multifaceted way in DC prior to this, all in the language of dance.

At the end of this first summer, the Kennedy Center, in collaboration with the Korea Society, featured my solo and new trio titled *The Ebb* at *the Terrace Theater* in an Asian American showcase called *Asia in Washington*. I shared the bill with two traditional dance performers from the region. Performance offers accelerated after this. A US State Department official who had attended the showcase got my number from the Kennedy Center and called to say he loved the performance and was intrigued by my bio in the program booklet. His office sought an artist with Spanish language skills to do a project in Panama. My years in bilingual schools and streets of Santa Fe paid off. I was offered an arts residency in Panama as a US cultural envoy. The Envoy Program sent American artists to other countries where they created and presented their work over a period of several weeks.

So that fall in 1995, I headed for Panama City and the University of Panama. I was to organize and oversee an integrated evening of multimedia art-based events around a theme, drawing in artists from the area. I met with dancers, faculty, and community artists. We agreed that the theme would be "dreaming about the body." I choreographed a full evening of works under an umbrella title, *Sueños* (dreams). *Sueños* was an immersive community event not only of dance but also theater, poetry, music, and visual art. I staged the performance in the university gymnasium, a space reminiscent of Carlisle Gym. I taught classes in modern dance during the day. In the evenings I choreographed, coordinated, and directed the cornucopia of offerings of a whole community that came forth when the call for submissions went out. I accepted any and all artists that wanted to be involved. We mapped out a performance score and instructions for each artist, with cues for when their performance would take place. A group of poets wrote and recited original text about corporal and spiritual connections of the body; three visual artists cut out life-size paper forms of the body from tracing paper that they hung on a clothesline and animated with oscillating floor fans. Drummers, guitarists, and singers worked together to create an improvisation that accompanied fifteen modern dancers in a choreography I set based on sleepwalking and dreaming. The dancers gently supported the weight of one another as they moved across the gymnasium from supine to standing positions. Dancers assisted each other up and down from the floor until the whole group collectively lifted one person and then another and another high above their heads in waves. They leaned in and on one another, cradled torsos and heads in their arms, carrying each other for a few feet before gently touching down to a horizontal position again. The effect was hypnotic. The message was of trust.

Two weeks after I returned to Washington, I received a call from a curator who was putting together an Asian American modern dance festival at the historic LaMaMa Theater in the East Village of New York City. LaMaMa, established in 1961, is a huge black box theater that serves as both incubator and hive for performance art, music, dance, and theater. It supported the early careers of composer Phillip Glass, singer Bette Midler, director Robert Wilson, and had even presented butoh dancer Kazuo Ohno. I had always hoped that New York City would be a stop for me as I built a career. Being asked to perform *Solitude* at LaMaMa afforded me this opportunity. On the same billing was Japanese modern dance choreographer Kei Takei, whose signature work *Light*, composed of more than thirty parts and spanning thirty years to produce, had registered as singular in the annals of dance history. Kei's dances drew from both Western dance traditions as well as Japanese dance, martial arts, and ritual.

I rode the bus from DC to New York City and made my way via taxi to the theater from Grand Central Station. LaMaMa occupied an old four-story, turn-of-the-century brick apartment building with big red doors. I walked into a cavernous maze of lobbies, studios, and offices, until at last, I found the huge black box theater: the stage looked out on wooden bleachers, flanked by high catwalks on all four sides and a lighting grid attached to the two-story high ceiling. I waited in the dark to rehearse my solo with lights, watching Kei Takei go through her dress rehearsal with sixteen dancers in front of a ceiling-to-floor backdrop of faux ivy. When their drumming score began, the cast began to violently push and shove one another. They tore at each other's costumes until the fabric came apart in tatters, leaving the dancers bare and vulnerable. The dance was an evocation of humans' destructive treatment of the earth and ultimately of one another.

At 8:30 p.m. I performed to a small crowd of keen modern dance aficionados. I enjoyed their eagerness and appreciation. After the show I was thrilled to meet dance writer Marcia Seigel. It gave me a chance to express my admiration in person: her reviews and her descriptions of performances she had attended of dance in New York, when taken together, create a historic cohesive archive.

I also met an Italian man, roughly in his thirties, tall, dark hair and eyes, dressed in an expensive black suit of light wool with a punctuation pairing of a pale green Hermès pocket square and silk tie. And a rolling accent. I would have to listen carefully to decipher what he was there to say. He told me his name—Carlo something—and then, "I attended the event here this evening in order to recruit talent for a performance I am organizing for the United Nations Fiftieth Anniversary celebration [1945–1995]. I see from the program that you live in

Washington, DC. I would like to bring you back to New York in a week to dance at the United Nations Headquarters for this. I have lined up three opera singers from the Metropolitan Opera to perform as well, as a chamber group. It will be *favoloso*, fabulous!" He rattled off the singers' names and they flew over my head because I had been staring at his lips, focused on catching them there. I chuckled inside, imagining that anyone might think I needed any such additional incentive. On the spot, I agreed to return, and he handed me his contact information, scrawled on the torn edge of his program. I reciprocated as he handed off his sleek black Montblanc pen and his program. He nodded, said, "*Arrivederci*," pivoted, and elegantly exited. I scrambled to the curb, hailed a cab to the Greyhound Station and boarded my bus back to DC.

Carlo phoned on Monday to go over details. The organization would pay me $800 immediately after I performed on Thursday of the following week. I would have to purchase my own round-trip train ticket, but I would be met at Grand Central Station by a limousine that would take me directly to the UN. This program would be in the afternoon, not evening. When I asked about the timing for a technical rehearsal in the space, the conditions of the stage floor, lighting, and other technical preparations, he trilled, "Dana, *andrà tutto bene, Io prometto! Non preoccuparti!* [It will be alright, I promise. Do not worry.]" I thanked him and said that I would see him at noon the following Thursday. He assured me that he would give me plenty of time for acclimation and preparation. "Ciao, Dana!"

Lacking answers to my questions, I harbored concerns. A dancer must be a logician before they can be a magician. Come on, Dana, I replied to my inner nag—he was so charming, he must know what he is doing, right? He sought a racial and international diversity of performers to underscore the mission of the United Nations. And he sought a mix of performance media. There was no theme, but the goal was to create an atmosphere of uniqueness and to leave a spectacular impact. And besides, this is a supreme honor and unique venue and nice bucks. I had never been to the United Nations before. What could go wrong?

I traveled on a commuter train for the first time to New York City early on Thursday morning: luxurious legroom, dining car, and multiple bathrooms. I stared out my window and studied run-down neighborhoods near Philadelphia and soot-covered apartment windows directly in view of the train tracks in Trenton, New Jersey. As we neared Manhattan, train platforms were papered in posters for Broadway shows, like *Miss Saigon* and *Sunset Boulevard*.

At Penn Station, I found the exit where cars waited for travelers and I waited. I looked for any driver holding a sign with my name. None. I called the phone number that was on my torn piece of paper. No one answered. After thirty minutes I panicked because it was almost noon and I was due to arrive at the UN. I made uneasy peace with the now emergency expense, got into a cab, and we crawled through lunch-hour business traffic to the Turtle Bay neighborhood of Manhattan, East Midtown.

I arrived at the United Nations Headquarters at 12:30 p.m. and ran to the security line where two guards were checking IDs before allowing entrance. In line I stared up at the flags from around the world. A guard asked my name, looked at my ID, and then to a list of names on his clipboard. He checked me off and ushered me through. He pointed to two large double doors. Before I could get to them, I turned to my left and there was Carlo. He said, "There you are, Dana, the car was *bene* [good]?" and kissed my left and then my right cheek. "Not so bene. There was no car at the station; I'm late because I took a cab here." He replied, "What? No black Jaguar? I sent a Jaguar. You should have called me on my cellular." He held up a cellular phone that had a large external antenna. I told him I *didn't* have his cell number—he had never supplied it, I reminded him—and that I *did* call his landline from Penn Station but no one had answered. He draped an arm over my shoulder, his mouth close to my left ear and whispered unctuously, "Dana, rilassati, divertiti, relax, enjoy." We walked to the grand General Assembly Hall.

It was six stories high, from the green carpeting under my feet to the domed ceiling. In front of me was a malachite façade where the president of the UN sat and above that the golden emblem of the United Nations. "Impressive, sì?" I replied, "Sì," and scanned the room looking for the stage. There was none. . . . He purred, "*Ascolta*, listen, Dana, I need you to dance from the top of the façade down to the floor." I stared up at the secretary general's platform, two stories up. Was he crazy? No stage, no plan, and seemingly no technical rehearsal. He said, "When the three sopranos sing, you will just appear at the top and dance down to them." In front of the façade were three imposing women with garment bags that I assumed held their formal performance gowns. I was here, steadying my nerves with a palliative mantra: "This is a once in a lifetime opportunity, adjust expectation, and adapt to situation." If "There's no place like home" worked to transport Dorothy to Kansas, surely my incantation would carry me up and back safely on this wall.

I considered how a dancer must always be prepared to be flexible, limber in body and also in attitude, whether at LaMaMa with its funky wooden benches, but with a nice performer-centric stage, or in the swank formality of the United Nations, with no stage whatsoever: two dramatically different settings for my solo.

I changed into my own "formal" performance wardrobe: a black leotard with attached short pants (essentially a wrestler's uniform). I was barefoot and ready to climb. The problem here was the audience sight line. Carlo had a vision of me dancing on the secretary's desk. I would have to stand on desks that were each at platform level to be seen, otherwise I was hidden behind the tables and their chairs. Although that sounds simple, it was daunting, because the dark wood desktops were highly polished, perilously slippery. And the desks clearly lacked railings. I started up, slowly, toes spread for grip like mountain goat hooves. I was my own stunt double.

On the floor below me, already in formal silk gowns, the three opera sopranos warmed up. Apparently, this was our only rehearsal. Then, looking down again, I gasped: audience members were beginning to file in and take seats. Oh. Dear. God. This had been scheduled so tightly, this "rehearsal" was now the actual performance. I was stuck on the top of the façade, and I would have to improvise a dance that went from desktop to desktop until I could get down to the main floor. My delay in getting here had erased what tiny slice had been allotted for my dry run.

I hid behind the UN secretary's desk. The sopranos down below began to trill in harmony, and I remembered that this was my cue to start dancing. Absolutely terrified now, I climbed carefully as if in slow motion, up onto the secretary's desk, outstretched my arms, and slowly flapped them while balancing on one leg. I held my opposing leg with a bent knee against my standing leg. I flapped my arms downward and lengthened my supporting leg. Then I flapped my arms upward and bent my supporting leg, giving the overall illusion of gaining lift from the airflow under my arms. I did small circle eights of my torso . . . a bird gliding on updraft . . . then with straightened arms mimicking soaring in the wind as if catching unseen air currents. I was again that Santa Fe desert eagle from the audition with Tim Wengerd in Albuquerque. I extended my bent leg and spun in place. I took a few steps and jumped to the next desktop and continued mimicking a bird in flight. I did pirouettes and took small steps so as not to slip or lose my balance before jumping down to land on another desk. It took me six or seven minutes to make my way down the stone façade. This was a solitary journey, being watched by several hundred people. I had to stay completely focused on my footing. I finally took my last three-foot leap to the carpeted ground and did lateral extended leg turns, right next to the opera trio, that eventually settled into one last one-legged balance. I landed safely.

I watched the remaining performances, collected my pay, and prepared to beat it back to the Penn Station before surge pricing would kick in for my five-hour return trip. No lingering or networking. I communed with myself, briefly. I was so relieved to have made it out alive with my skin, ego, and leotard intact. I was awash in sweat from fear, adrenaline, and physical exhaustion. Before I left, I leaned on a wall in the lobby and absorbed the day. I experienced a deep sense of personal and professional landing, like that eagle. The event—the impossibility of traditional preparation, the demand that creative improvisational impulses guide me, my years of solid athletic preparation—to be able to execute it all was profoundly transformative. A gift of temperament that kept me calm and that did not succumb to negativity or futile anger at the impresario, Carlo, this too, had been in my toolkit. For hundreds of people that afternoon, I became the incarnation of the American eagle that aligned with our country's role as a leader of the United Nations.

I took a cab back to the bus station and was home in DC by 8 p.m., back in my tiny efficiency. I lay in bed feeling restored from that performance. Today had deepened my awareness of the value of the work I was doing in Washington, and the depth of gratification it gave me for the career and reputation I was building.

In the summer of 1996, my Asian American youth dance program at the Kennedy Center resumed with the same format of classes, discussions, and choreographing as the previous year. And there was an exciting new challenge. Derek was interested in seeing if I could develop a work that he could tour across the country. He suggested that I workshop the idea on this incoming group of kids. He asked me to somehow base it on *The Nightingale*, by Hans Christian Andersen, the tale of a Chinese emperor who prefers the bejeweled song of a mechanical Nightingale to that of a real bird. On his deathbed the emperor is saved by the song of a real Nightingale who chases death from his bed chamber. I decided to focus the story on love, nature, and preserving the earth and natural habitats. I had long conversations about environmental activism with the twenty youth whose backgrounds this summer were Chinese, Korean, Vietnamese, Thai, and Filipino and came from a variety of socioeconomic situations.

But how to uncouple the inherent exoticism that is built into *The Nightingale* story in order to focus on the theme of conserving the earth? The kids and I discussed historic Western "Orientalist"—ugh—perspectives of the Middle East and Asia that were inherently patronizing and obviously colonialist. We excised any reference that made the Emperor or his court seem ignorant or arrogant and in need of Western colonizers to develop Chinese society. In our version of *The Nightingale*, the Emperor and his courtiers were actually technologically very advanced, thus they had built a robotic Nightingale, but in so building it they had ignored the environmental effects of their technologic development. In our story, there was toxic factory run-off that was polluting waterways and nonrecyclable garbage from building machinery. The production had large dance numbers in which the students performed robotic dance phrases blending modern dance, hip hop, and martial arts, juxtaposed to the natural flowing movements of the real Nightingale. The students surrounded the Emperor as he celebrated the mechanical bird, which locked and popped—a dancer performing isolations of her hands, arms, and shoulders. These choreographed movements were much like the hip-hop style of "Tutting," a dance phrasing named after the ancient King Tutankhamun because the movements of the body resemble the hieroglyphic flatness and linear lines of two-dimensional artwork on a temple wall. Conversely, the real Nightingale flapped her arms like real animated wings, perched and skidded across stage before taking flight in graceful organic flesh-and-blood leaps. There was not the same amount of spectacle as the previous summer but there was a more sophisticated message.

Derek loved the show, not just because it was inclusive of kids of all technical dance abilities—that was the most important goal—but also because he liked the timely contemporary spin on the story. He was also happy to see how this summer's program rallied the Asian American students' interests around three major issues: how the West has historically viewed the East and how that permeated art, in this case literature, and how important it is to be cognizant of and sensitive to the natural environment. The work was sophisticated; my ability to choreograph was deepening. After the show Derek commissioned a version of *The Nightingale* for the Center's touring Families & Young Audiences Series. This arm of the Kennedy Center developed works for toddlers to adult family members around the themes of classic and contemporary literature. Unlike the youth program, these shows are cast with all professional dancers, actors, and singers so that they can tour contractually and for extended periods of time.

Derek's assistant, Kim Peter Kovak, wanted a team he had worked with before to take over the show. He assigned a writer-director, a musical composer, as well as set, props, and costume designers to the project and I was, of course, the choreographer. In retrospect, he took these steps so that he could maintain quality control of the production; he had never worked with me before and considered me too young to work alone. To be fair, to him, I was an unknown. So, unlike the youth program, all budgeting, contracting, and final decisions would fall to Kim. For the next three months we reformulated the show, cast it with all professional dancers and actors—several of whom were my own professional dancers. I work shopped the Emperor's role on a talented teen dancer, Rasta Thomas. Rasta had recently won the annual USA International Ballet Competition in Jackson, Mississippi (also known as "the Jackson Ballet Competition"), a very prestigious accolade, and would go on to found the Bad Boys of Dance Project, an all-male company that debuted in 2007 and toured the next decade. Rasta had a martial arts background as well as ballet training that made it easy to develop the choreography with him. I added a martial arts *bo*—a traditional wooden fighting staff—to the role that he, as Emperor, could use to cartwheel off of and to assist in acrobatic aerial kicks. Once the choreography was set, Rasta announced that he couldn't commit to a month of performances because he had other opportunities. However, he said, his good friend, Won Chol Lee, a Korean classmate of his from the Kirov Academy of Dance, would be tremendous. Rasta was right. Won Chol was actually better in the Emperor role. He, too, was dynamic in his movement, but he had a larger emotional performance range and could project a unique vulnerability on stage. Perhaps because he had only recently moved to America and he didn't speak much English, his struggles with the language and assimilation forced upon him a heightened emotional communication and lexicon through the body.

The set consisted of a fourteen-foot round Chinese moon gate, a golden throne, and an elaborate bird perch. In Chinese culture, a moon gate is a large round aperture through which a beautiful garden is accessed. The costumes accentuated each character's attributes; the hooped skirts of the obsequious courtiers swung back and forth like bells as they walked and served the Emperor's whims. The Emperor wore a black spandex unitard with a golden dragon stitched embellishment that snaked up his leg, around his waist, and up his arm, and a snake headband as a crown. The character of Death wore a hideous mask on the top of her head and transformed from a beautiful woman to a hag when she strategically flicked her head down. It was the same technique that revealed the shape-shifting trickster in my work *Dreaming of the Fox, the Temple, and Betrayal* a few years prior. Kristina Berger, now a teacher of the Horton Technique and member of the Erick Hawkins Dance Company, danced the role of Death. She rode in on the backs of two dancers so that, standing ten feet tall, she towered over the Emperor. She would jump to the floor and fight with a long twelve-foot staff, the two dancers she rode in on assisted her with smaller wooden staffs as she attacked the Emperor and the Nightingale.

There were several changes to this production that varied from my original. The performance became a traditional interpretation of the Andersen tale, meaning that a focus on the environment was downplayed and dated cliché representations of China, ones long abandoned and recognized as neither accurate nor quaint or charming, crept back in. Second, an actress was added as a narrator and singer. She would stop the action and narrate the story. I didn't agree that the dance needed literal lines to convey the story and thought that young people should have more of a choice to interpret the meaning of the show. My resistance on these issues were to no avail because contractually I had no control over the shape and flow of the touring show. I was to only focus on the choreography. I couldn't change the mind of the director when it came to images that I pointed out as bordering on stereotyping or colonialism. I fought with the director and musical composer—neither were Asian—about why they wanted the Chinese courtiers to appear as bumbling characters. This portrayal contained obvious racial bias. The music sounded like a Western, Orientalist approach to Chinese music as well. It was inauthentic when it so easily did not need to be so. That was a deliberate aesthetic decision that was not in the spirit of the tour. It is so important to be meticulous in the development of a production to avoid committing acts of cultural appropriation or perpetuate tropes, or caricatures, such as of "the bumbling Chinaman." Often these things are not quite so overtly racist templates, of course; most are less obvious, insidious, and based on intractable unconscious biases that are ingrained in society and perpetuate aggressions.

The experience diluted my artistic sovereignty and artistic free hand to execute a pure vision. For example, the performance was visually pretty, but just as the dancing was building in its phrasing it would be interrupted by the narrator with explanations of what the audience "should" be seeing. I found this stop-and-go quite jarring. It took one out of the mood. What mattered was the potent messaging of the bodily movements and gestures, the phrasing—and this, of course had been the whole point of the dance. In my work with children, I came to strongly believe that a young audience possesses the innate ability to interpret movement as language—a human being's first language—and after all, they were less removed from that than we older adults. They could naturally translate the dance movements, to feel the intrinsic deeper messaging of the stories, without the pass-through filter imposed by spoken words. They could experience and think within the language of their own bodies, functioning on a higher level of understanding and deeper absorption than the spoken script. Narration effectively dumbed down each scene.

It is so important to give the audience credit and to build their appetite for dance as a language that uniquely conveys meaning and emotion. Audiences need and crave art that they can move toward and into, that does not force itself upon them. Audiences long to stretch and grow through performances that are not spoon-fed—those are not fulfilling and will not ultimately sustain subscriptions and ticket sales. Humans love that which beckons and leaves room for discovery and laying claim to that discovery individually.

This was the first time that I was not contractually the lead voice and ultimate decision maker on a project that had originated with my creative concept. This was a huge lesson for me, a mistake I would not repeat. The touring show was highly successful, but it could have been so much more consequential. After this experience I decided that I would not tackle another collaborative project unless I had total control of the artistic team.

The one enormous, lasting satisfaction from having produced this touring adaptation: having Won Chol dance the lead. No shows in the Center's repertory of touring shows in the Families & Young Audiences Series touring shows had heretofore featured an Asian American dance lead. As you might well imagine, it was a deeply emotional experience to coach a Korean American teenager in this demanding lead role. I was his mentor with the responsibility of building the confidence and technique and opportunities for a young artist with whom I shared a cultural lineage. This was a deeply joyful milestone for me.

The Nightingale toured to more than 120 American cities on its first tour and went on two more such penetrative and lucrative tours over the years. Its metrics—attendance and number of venues booked and cities visited—made it the Kennedy Center's best-selling Families & Young Audiences Series show at that time. The cast traveled the United States in a van and via short airplane trips cross-country, and a semi-truck with the technical crew met the cast at each new venue with the set, props, costumes, and lights.

While sitting in the audience, kids covered their faces when Death arrived on stage, bravely peeking through splayed fingers to cheer the Emperor and the Nightingale onward in battle to their victory. By the end of the show, the kids would cheer boisterously when the Emperor realized that he should not cage the Nightingale, rather he should let it remain free and to keep it close enduringly only in his heart.

Over five years, *The Nightingale* would be performed in more than 250 American cities, large and small venues ranging from the Muny theatre in St. Louis, Missouri, to the Majestic Theatre in San Antonio, Texas, to the Poway Center for the Performing Arts in Poway, California, and always—always—with the inclusion of Asian Americans in the cast. Kids across the country adored the energy of the show; they were in awe at the acrobatic dancing. And for many of the audience it was introduction to Asian Americans. I have no doubt that many children went on to take dance classes of their own, signed up by eager parents.

The Nightingale's premiere season at the Kennedy Center closed at the end of 1997, and in 1998, my own personal dance of love and flight would unfold. I met Fernando, an Argentinean man, at a salsa club. While I was taking a break from dancing, a Korean Argentine woman came up and said in a thick Argentine accent, "My friend likes how you dance and wants to meet you." She was an opulent self-invention, batting long false eyelashes and pout-smiling in silver lipstick, decked out in a tight-fitting silver cocktail dress and towering in five-inch heels. "Tell him to come over and introduce himself," I said. Fernando appeared out of the crowd, jet black hair, huge deep-set eyes, and a Rudolf Valentino swagger. Fernando confessed that he was wandering the world to escape a crashing Argentine economy that offered little hope for his future. He had only recently arrived in DC and didn't speak any English. His accent combined with his fast talking made it impossible to understand everything he said. So, we danced. What else did we need? That was my native tongue and clearly one in which he was fluent.

I fell in love. Fer, as I would come to call him, was a terrific salsa dancer. Our habit was to dance all night and go to dinner at 2 a.m. at a twenty-four-hour Salvadoran, restaurant, El Tamarindo, that filled with gay nightclubbers and drag queens after the area clubs shut down. Fer was complicated, hot to temper and easy to cool. We fought over his chronic lateness and my punctuality and how far down the road ahead we cared to consider: he lived for today and I lived in the future. After several months of worry about his tourist visa, set to expire, his uncle got him an interview for a chauffeur job at the Embassy of Argentina. If he got the job, he could have a work visa covered by the embassy and extend his stay. Fer didn't get the job, though. Within days, he left DC suddenly and continued his global travels to South Africa, then to Bilbao, Spain, and ultimately settled in Santorini, Greece. Fifteen years later, we would rekindle our warm relationship, super-heated on a dance floor, naturally, in Santorini. By then he had built a dinner theater there, and I had a well-established dance company and audience following in DC, and so we were not meant to be. But I think about this sustained connection and durable friendship as exemplifying how dance really is a universal language that breaks down barriers of spoken words between strangers and bridges their temperaments. We danced, we loved, he had to fly away, and we understood each other. Such is the nature of migration of monarchs everywhere.

fourteen COLLABORATION COMES CALLING

In October 1997 I received a call from Samuel "Sammy" Hoi, then dean of the Corcoran School of Art. He was to host a conference in mid-November to train executive leaders in creative problem-solving skills. Sammy knew me from my Asian American youth program. I had received terrific support from him back then; he had assigned one of his teachers to help us build our theatrical sets. Sammy asked me if I would consider teaching a one-day-only basic movement class to nondancers at this conference as a means for the participants to team build. I was delighted by the invitation to lead a workshop to these twenty participants, from thirty-five to sixty-five years of age. I shared Sammy's enthusiasm for the potential of such an exposure, for them and for me.

Sammy and his attendees and I met in the main lobby of the Corcoran Gallery of Art. The Gallery faces the White House and is the oldest private institution of culture in Washington, DC. From there we walked together to a grand foyer; the class would take place here. We formed a circle and sat down in chairs provided especially for us. I decided to break the ice with an exercise that I often use with my kids. Sammy introduced me, and I handed each participant a traditional Chinese blue-and-white porcelain bowl, the size one might receive for an individual serving of rice or soup. I asked attendees to individually introduce themselves by saying their first name and then to simultaneously make a hand gesture. The gesture could be a finger snap, a fist, a finger point, anything. After each introduction and gesture, we would, as a group, repeat that person's first name, their gesture, and then pass our bowls once to the right. With each introduction of a new name and gesture, we would repeat all the previous names and gestures, thus creating one long phrase. This process created a repeatable movement, name, and gesture phrase; this exercise not only allowed us all to memorize one another's names but to also learn a "word" from each person's gestural language. This exercise sharpens not only memory habits but also heightens everyone's awareness of the human connection among the members of the entire group. It calms everyone, forces them to breathe, align internal tempos, listen, and trust one another. We start as strangers, but soon enough we come to recognize one another, invest in and share a new shared movement language.

We discussed their experiences of having to decide how the rhythms of the bowl passing and gestures created a group effort, and how now they all knew everyone's names! They had created associations, unique proprietary hand signatures. When I completed the hour and said goodbye, one student stayed back. He lingered, trying to catch my eye. He loudly proclaimed, "I've been looking for you, Dana!" Yikes. Was this to be an awkward situation? My mind raced. I did not recognize this participant who claimed he has been looking for me. "My name is John Dreyfuss, I want to collaborate with you. I'm a sculptor—in addition to being an executive—and I'm interested in a dialogue like the one between Martha Graham and Isamu Noguchi." The reference to Isamu piqued my interest and took me back to my childhood dinners with Isamu and my parents in Santa Fe. And I knew of his work, the fact that his sculptures were in major public spaces and collections throughout Washington. In fact, while I was in graduate school, I had walked past his imposing bronze sculpture of two fourteen-foot-tall femur-like forms called *Solomon's Gate* that is installed in the Foggy Bottom neighborhood on the corner of Twentieth and I (Eye) Streets, Northwest. He was famous. And had been looking for me? John said, "Please stop by my studio—tomorrow, perhaps? Can you?—to see my work." Sure, I would.

I have always admired the creative processes of sculpting but had not spent time in an actual atelier. The next day, I walked up to an imposing five-story Federalist-style building on the corner of Prospect Street and Thirty-fourth Street in Georgetown. Corner, did I say? In fact, it took up the entire block. A brass plaque identified it as Halcyon House. It was so grand, I decided against ringing the front door and instead proceeded around the corner to ring at the servant's entrance—after all, I thought, an artist's studio must be tucked away out back. A voice sounded over the camera-intercom, "Go to the front door!" So, I walked back around the block to that huge black double door with its imposing brass knocker. I banged on the door that in response made an automated clicking sound and dramatically creaked open with no one in sight. I stepped inside, just as a woman entered the foyer dressed in a coral color wool pants suit with a deep red silk scarf around her neck. She introduced herself as Wendy, John's assistant. Wendy guided me to a leviathan staircase lined by three-foot bronze creatures on pedestals that led to a cavernous subterranean studio. There John Dreyfuss stood working on a wax mock-up of a life-sized lion surrounded by colossi monoliths in the shape of giant arrowheads. These oversized arrowheads were twelve to fifteen feet tall and made out of a matrix of brown wax pressed over wooden skeletons. The skeletons thus had an organic look that was reminiscent of Isamu's work and loomed on the scale of works by Henry Moore. John was the image of Phidias sculpting the statue of Zeus at Olympia. Being able to make this connection was kind of a terrific little bonus for all my hundreds of hours in museum pilgrimages and all those trips to the Martin Luther King Public Library, checking out and devouring all those piles of art history books.

John's studio was far more familiar than it was startling to me. I actually had a sense of recognition the moment I walked into it due to a recurring dream I'd been having for the past several months. In this dream I would descend a towering staircase lined by Mesozoic creatures. The staircase led to a huge room that housed prehistoric animals in a giant glass aquarium that, somehow, I knew was clearly from the turn of the last century. As I approached, a Plesiosaurus and a Spinosaurus violently pressed against the glass held together at its four corners by a thin antique molding. They slammed against the glass trying to break free as water splashed over the enormous brim. I would awake from this dream in a cold sweat. I did not understand its message. But when I walked down the stairs at Halcyon House that first time, I recognized that this was the place in my dreams. I had arrived at a time to let go of old extinct ideas and to break my mold and venture into new artistic future. I have always believed in the power of dreams to guide my waking life. I had already worked the concept of dreams into so many of my choreographic works. I keep a dream journal next to the bed and it is filled with my best choreographic images, ones that always seem to surface at three in the morning.

I yodeled a little whispered, "Excuse me, hell-ooo," but he was so intent on his work that he didn't hear me. I cautiously walked around him, into view, and waved when Wendy comfortably blurted out "John! Dana's here!" in a musical Jamaican accent. She departed and he placed his sculpting knife down. That done, he immediately started talking about his Cycladic-inspired arrowhead works and a series of stylized Greco bronze harps. It was as if his internal monologue had suddenly gone off a default mute setting and moved straight to broadcast. John, then in his late forties, with thick, topsy-turvy gray hair looked very much like Kirk Douglas. John said he needed to communicate and collaborate with other artists, or he would go insane. His personality was intense, his habitual lining up of tiny sculpting tools as he talked, obsessive compulsive. We soon understood each other's idiosyncratic urges toward art as statement. We both wanted to push our art to the next level and have a deeper dialogue, a breakthrough cross-pollination. We excitedly spoke about the sculptors Constantin Brâncuşi, August Rodin, Alberto Giacometti and choreographers Martha Graham, José Limón, and Alvin Ailey. After speaking nonstop for three hours, we agreed to collaborate on a sculpture and dance project. A project that I would have a clear say in, could mold, and ultimately be a decision maker in its manifestation. This collaboration would not be based on a children's fairytale like *The Nightingale*. This was a whole new level of adult conversation focused on the actualization of artists' dreams.

Before I left, John said, "Choose a maquette and I'll make it full-size for stage. You may do anything you want with the work, with my blessing." It all seemed oddly simple on some level. I walked through the studio and zeroed in on a ten-inch plaster maquette that resembled half of a human pelvis. It was related abstractly to the core of the body, to the bones and sinew that combine allowing for locomotion. He handed it to me and urged me to take it home.

I visited John's studio weekly to talk about dimensions for stage, the fabrication, and mechanization of the sculpture. Each week he had made progress in resolving questions we had discussed about the optimal scale and weight. Within a mere four weeks the small plaster maquette had been realized in wax and now stood three feet tall. Three months later it was thirteen feet tall made of white plaster. The plaster form was top heavy and had to be anchored to the ceiling. Now what remained to be figured out: how to make the sculpture lightweight and at the same time substantial and durable enough to bear additional weight or stress if my choreography required that.

John researched a new process of enlarging sculptures in fiberglass by using military laser-tracking technology to plot points of the sculpture in space. This process involved scanning the full-size plaster sculpture and inputting its data points into a computer that communicated exact dimensions to a giant 3D printer that, in turn, fabricated the full-size sculpture in fiberglass. In order to produce the sculpture in fiberglass, John brought in a brilliant collaborative team of engineers including Richard Bott and Steve Slaughter from the military subcontracting company Lockheed Martin Skunk Works. Over two weeks, the team created a mapping of the sculpture; it was then fabricated in pieces at the California headquarters of Skunk Works and shipped back to DC, where it was assembled and quality inspections were completed. The sculpture—my new dance partner—was now full-sized, light weight enough to be able to turn on its axis when I pushed it and also perfectly balanced so that it wouldn't topple when I climbed it. It had come to life in an almost Baron von Frankenstein process. I became engrossed in how best to interpret and work with this abstract form. But first things first: I named it *Helix*, a universal symbol of building and resilience.

John always envisioned things in a big way and enjoyed gambling on his own ideas. He asked, "With whom would you wish to collaborate for light design?" I froze, silent. He said, "Remember, think as big as you can because we all might die tomorrow!" I blurted out, "Jennifer Tipton." She had worked with Mikhail Baryshnikov, Jerome Robbins, Twyla Tharp, and Paul Taylor, among so many others. "Now you're talking!" he said. For costumes, we agreed upon Han Feng, a fashion designer who would soon go on to design costumes for *Madame*

Butterfly at the Metropolitan Opera. Within a month our dream team had signed on. Everything was as elevated as our spirits, including our ever-refining thought processes and artistic conversations. We spoke about the philosophic convergence of form and points in space for stage. We talked about Martha Graham's collaboration with fashion designer Halston and about Isamu Noguchi's mammoth sets for the Martha Graham Dance Company. We talked about what the future would bring from this new team of collaborators.

John let me rehearse at his studio. It was inspiring to be in a grand space with almost thirty-foot ceilings filled with art, shadow, and mystery. I learned that his home, the 21,000-square-foot Halcyon House, was built in 1787 by the first secretary of the navy, Benjamin Stoddert. The house had also been part of the intricate network of the Underground Railroad in the mid-1800s. Halcyon House is also known to be one of the most haunted homes in Washington; it is apparently on the list of "most spook" destinations in ghost-fan world. Among its purported ghosts are unfortunates who died in the basement moving through the Underground Railroad, as well as the nephew of Mark Twain, Albert Clemens, who had once owned the house. Clemens believed he was cursed and would die if he stopped building within its walls. He literally built intricate hallways to nowhere and tiny rooms that could fit but a single chair—all of which John had to make sense of through a renovation that took him two decades to complete. Albert Clemens and John Dreyfuss: now there's a far-fetched and enduring collaboration.

I often danced late into the night in the underground studio, surrounded by John's towering specters. I witnessed flickering lights to which John would command, "Not tonight! Leave us alone!" and the lights would respond by suddenly restoring themselves. When the spirits were active, I heard mysterious whispers and moans without a source. Doors would either slam or gently pull shut when I would reach for their knobs. When I was finally allowed to open a door that had heretofore been firmly held closed fast against me . . . no one would be in sight. The spirits were playful when bored, and I made for quite an amusing toy. They choreographed their own dances, and apparently, I was their human maquette.

One late afternoon I witnessed a repairman driven out by terror. I was beginning to rehearse in the studio while the repairman replaced part of a wooden step on the main staircase. The man suddenly stood up and slowly descended the stairs looking over his shoulder nervously. He interrupted my rehearsal and quivered, "Some-thing...just whispered my name and tapped me on the shoulder." He asked if the place was haunted. My eyes didn't lie as I stared at a ripple of energy behind him, like a mirage in the desert. Before I could respond, he turned, saw the spirit, and ran up the massive two-story staircase and out the front door, not delaying to shut it behind him.

I never felt threatened by the mysterious goings on at the house. Rather, I felt it was a magical place where my dreams unfolded, at the meeting place of physical and magical realities. Why not? How was this any different from the magical realism of my own New Mexico? I relished exploring my relationship with *Helix*. I climbed up the sculpture, huddled in it like it was a womb, and my first home from which I would be born. The vocabulary was completely unique from anything I had previously choreographed. It felt like an actual rebirth.

Christopher Nichols, a young pianist and composer with a passion for electronic music, created a musical score for us, incorporating primordial whale sounds and ambient bird calls. John, Christopher, and I had many conversations about movement, sculpture, and sound. When Jennifer Tipton visited from New York City, the conversation multiplied to include light. Jennifer is a regal woman with a philosopher's refined diction. I would show her a dance phrase and she would remind us that light is another entity on stage that is always animated. She said, "If a spotlight shines on the floor behind you, take the time to sense its presence. The audience will understand that light is another being on stage, with energy and lending intention, and that it demands as much attention as the dancer." These and many other gifts of her singular artistry have informed my understanding of theatrical lighting ever since and made my own choreography and staging the better for it.

After twelve weeks of choreographic exploration, I got a call from a representative of the Korea Society of Washington, DC. I accepted an invitation to present *Helix* on May 8, 1998, at the Kennedy Center's Terrace Theater. *Helix* was placed on a split program with a dance by Peggy Choy, a Korean American choreographer. I would get the chance to share and explore *Helix* in a formal stage setting. Although technically I was performing as a soloist, I was not going to be alone on stage. I felt relaxed and confident in performing *Helix* because the sculpture had become a friend. All those spectral spirits of Halcyon House, my gang of invisible conspirators, would certainly be there in the audience as well, to accept the credit and congratulate one another on this premiere.

I was pleased with the audience and critical response, including a wonderful review by Nora FitzGerald in *the Washington Post*. But as I studied the performance video, I realized that this organic, evolutionary tale lent itself naturally to a dance rendering of the Adam and Eve myth: this primordial journey would be wonderfully adaptable as a duet. I began to study its many facings. Some facings were more curvilinear than others. Curves implied a female form and linear facings the male form. The enigmatic and androgynous *Helix* sculpture would be the perfect incubator for an Adam and Eve creation and evolution story. I began to sketch ideas for this second version of *Helix*.

After weeks of choreographic exploration, I brought in my dance partner and *Helix* secret weapon, Sarah Craft. She danced with my company and had trained with me since she was fifteen and was now twenty years old. She had a pixie haircut, pale skin, and hazel eyes like a cat, and had an ineffable dance quality as a partner. She moved seamlessly as if underwater, with a flow and flexibility that I had not seen before. We moved together in perfect unison and complemented each other's energy. In rehearsals with Sarah, I realized that *Helix* demanded that our movements stay within certain unseen parameters, confined and defined by its form. I learned that if we moved too far away from it, our relationship deadened. The sculpture seemed to want us close. I set choreography of unusual forms and movements of the body that referenced the evolution of life from sea creatures to amphibians to avian gliders that finally landed and arrived at upright locomotion.

Sarah and I learned to physically push the sculpture on its axis to reveal its multiple facings. All our movements had to be framed by the extension of the sculpture's lines through space. It was a unique learning experience in how the audience and the performer perceive spatial tension. My night vigils with Sarah reminded me of working with Glynn Gomez on window designs in Santa Fe. Glynn's talks about the relationship between foreground, background, and light in a retail window for dramatic intent went through my mind in this serene rehearsal context. But in this new scenario the scale had grown to a large theatrical stage.

After months of rehearsals, Sarah and I were ready to show the dance. We premiered the duet version of *Helix in November 2000* to a mostly full 624-seat capacity Sylvia and Danny Kaye Theater of Hunter College, in New York City. Dressed in sculptural rust-colored silk costumes by Han Feng, we emerged from the base of the sculpture, mimicking protozoan forms, sea creatures evolving, using our arms, hands, and legs as tentacles, then transforming our movements to that of a lizard, to flying creatures, to apes moving then from all fours to standing erect. At the point of standing and locomotion as Homo sapiens we acknowledged each other, each finally climbing into the *Helix*, seeking and reaching and at last caressing each other. We received excellent audience responses. A post-performance question-and-answer session was lively; the mostly young crowd was eager and inquisitive about this unique collaboration. And John, who shied away from stage bows and public talks, learned how to travel the sculpture between his studio and new venues. A flatbed truck and a team of five men moved the sculpture long distances and installed it at each location. And happily, there would be many locations.

At the beginning of 1999, Alicia Adams, the dance curator for the Kennedy Center, approached me about choreographing and producing a complete trilogy. Alicia's idea was that the duet version of *Helix* would be performed (it had not yet been performed at the Kennedy Center for Washington audiences; only the solo version had been shown at that time), along with two new dances that I would create inspired by and in dialogue with John's sculptures. She proposed that *Trilogy* would open the Kennedy Center dance season in 2001, giving me more than two years to research, experiment, and put the works together.

John chose to create two entirely new sculptures for *Trilogy*. They were *Alexander's Lure*, a giant hanging orb, and *Vertebrae*, a twenty-two-foot cervical bone shape that could spin and go from horizontal to vertical through a hydrolyzed robotics system. As with *Helix*, John worked with Skunk Works on the mechanization of *Vertebrae*. It took at least nine months to complete the new sculptures, so I began choreographing without the full-size sculptures and then finished the choreography when they were complete.

For these two works, I decided to use larger casts of dancers, four for *Vertebrae* and eight for *Alexander's Lure*; I also decided that I wanted new musical scores that were rhythmically driving versus ambient. Alicia suggested Jon Jang, a West Coast Chinese American composer. Jon agreed to create two new scores for the dances. When he was ready to record his musical compositions, I flew to Oakland to sit in on the recordings to make sure the tempi would match my choreography. Jon had recently received a Meet the Composer Grant to create new compositions and graciously used part of the grant to fund excellent live musicians to record his scores. The recordings included singers from the San Francisco–based all male professional chorus Chanticleer, a male counter tenor, a classical Indian singer, tabla players, and a chamber orchestra. The score for *Vertebrae* was for a dance I called *Mandala*, and it was propulsive, nonstop drumming, and haunting vocalizations. The score for *Alexander's Lure* was for a dance I called *Silk Roads* and that was more varied rhythmically, with allegro and adagio movements accented by vocals, violin, and cello.

It took John and me two full years of preparation to coordinate the dances and the sculptures. I continued to work in his studio to workshop how the dancers interacted with the sculptures, moved with them, and climbed them. Safety was always an issue because dancers were being asked at certain points to climb very high. *Vertebrae* was twenty-two feet in length and twelve feet across at the widest, one foot across at the narrowest part of the taper. *Alexander's Lure* was six feet by six feet, a round sort of wrecking ball shape.

Trilogy premiered in December 2001 at the Kennedy Center's Eisenhower Theatre, a 1,100-seat venue with a fifty-foot stage. More than 1,000 patrons attended opening night. And *Trilogy* occupied the entire evening's program, a full eighty minutes, with two fifteen-minute intermissions. The curtain opened on *Helix* as a duet. Next was *Silk Roads*, a dance for eight (six women and two men, including me). High above the stage hung *Alexander's Lure*. The stage was made to look like a desert landscape with a full moon hanging in a deep blue sky. The dance phrasing was sustained and flowing, and accordingly we dancers were in flowing silk trousers and tunics of muted gold, blue, and charcoal, moving iridescently across the stage—as if possessed by the haunting choral voices of Jon Jang's score.

Sequential rolls to the floor were juxtaposed to sweeping unison movement phrases that filled the stage with curvilinear contractions of the torso and gentle shapings of the arms and hands in the air. The dance phrases moved between unison and trio and duet phrasings, but all the movement was sustained—danced in a conjuring of the chamisa plants of New Mexico, bobbing in a gentle breeze. As we danced, the lights shifted color from deep blue to subtler hues to evoke a desert vista, orange, pink, and purple. This was an homage to the Santa Fe desert—my home—and that Jennifer Tipton's lighting design made possible. The scenes were reminiscent, too, of a surreal Georgia O'Keeffe canvas, a giant organic skull or bone floating in the sky. Finally, one by one, we released into the floor, leaving only one dancer standing. *Alexander's Lure* slowly began to lower to the stage, directly overhead of the solo dancers who, in turn, longingly reached upward, as if calling the moon down from the heavens to earth so she could cradle it.

The last dance on the evening's program was *Mandala*, stark and void of color, four dancers costumed in white silk pants and hooded jackets lit with white spotlights that heightened the drama. Dwarfed from the size of the white vertebrae sculpture they surrounded, they looked like the offspring of the sculpture. The dancers knelt on the floor and began a slow gestural phrase in unison. This image they created was shamanistic, as if they were casting spells. Jon Jang's tabla instrumentation and Indian vocal score accentuated this mood of mystery. Quick angulations of the hands and arms escalate to full body contractions, gyrations, and acrobatic leg kicks and jumps, as if possessed by unseen spirits. The unison phrases finally break apart into complicated duets that circle the stage as the *Vertebrae* sculpture suddenly does the same. The sculpture turns, looking like it was sweeping the dancers across the stage. The twenty-five-minute dance never rests; the dancers appear to be trapped in their ritual, leaping higher and running faster, expanding out into space. *Mandala* reaches a conclusion when a dancer climbs onto *Vertebrae* and is elevated twelve feet above the other dancers. *Vertebrae* stops with the chosen, the anointed dancer, atop as the remaining three dancers on the stage below slowly surround the sculpture as if it is a temple meant for prayer.

The audience rose to their feet clapping and whistling, stomping their feet deafeningly. We received three curtain calls this evening. Three. I was aware even as it was happening that this unrestrained audience reception was astounding in a culture capital like Washington, DC, and this fact, too, was recognized and reported in *the Washington Post* by chief dance critic Sarah Kaufman.

We had successfully—more than successfully—brought three massive sculptures to virtual life through dance, light, original new music, and costume. John Dreyfuss's vision of so many years before had been actualized. And so was my own. In creative union, we accomplished something extraordinary. It took three years to complete and premiere *Trilogy*. These years informed and deepened my understanding of the collaborative process.

Trilogy solidified my dedication to working with the visual arts, a passion with which I had grown up from earliest childhood. The collaboration further defined my aesthetic and clarified how I would incubate dances in a studio and a museum setting. It allowed me to see that visual and performing arts audiences could be successfully—thrillingly—cross-germinated. The merging did not dilute either of the two arts, nor did one attempt to explain the meaning of the other. Neither was subsumed, dominated, or appropriated by its mate. Rather the union of arts heightened the potentials of both and gave birth to another entity—a third form of art—that derived its power from both.

In fact, one might say that *Trilogy*—more than just referencing a suite of three different dances—stood for this concept of a third sovereign art. *Trilogy* set a new bar for me and let me see what long-term projects were possible with the right team in place, and when I had real authority over the final product. John always graciously deferred to my artistic decisions, and we respected each other deeply. It was this respect and our deep dedication to a creative goal larger than each of us that made the project soar.

In retrospect, *Trilogy* was a watershed moment in another way: I was moved to own that commitment by formally changing the name of my company. In 2001, I changed the name of the company from Moving Forward to include my own name and ultimately the company was rebranded to Dana Tai Soon Burgess Dance Company (DTSBDC). With the building of these mammoth works also came the parallel building of a business structure that could support my artistic endeavors and a savvy board of directors who re-envisioned the company and prepared to propel it through the 2000s. The board of directors and I felt that the brand of the company—the sorts of projects that we did, and the top quality of it—was baked into my name. I was so proud of the work I was creating with this team and happy to permanently move my own name front and center. With pride came accountability, and I wanted the world to know that I stood for the mission and the work of this ensemble. The 2000s were a prolific time of dancemaking for me, leaving little time for anything else. One after another, I created dances that related to or were inspired by visual art.

fifteen MY CALL TO DANCE DIPLOMACY

When I was ten years old, my father took me for the first of many times to a place he tantalizingly called "a curiosity shop." This shop was just off the Santa Fe Plaza on San Francisco Street, two doors down from the F.W. Woolworth "five-and-dime," next to the Häagen-Dazs Ice Cream shop. The place we were going, he said, was called the Gamut. As we walked, Dad explained that *gamut* means a realm of possibilities—of things, of places, of experiences and feelings. The word, he said, suggests an invitation to be thrilled by a wide scope of discoveries, a spectrum. With that, I kind of wondered if this place maybe sold . . . kaleidoscopes? I was psyched. If not, well, Woolworth sure did. I hoped we could go there afterward and get one. And after **that**, next door for a waffle cone filled with Rocky Road ice cream.

But the Gamut did not disappoint that day, or on any other of the excursions to it that we would make thereafter. We entered. Wow. **Wow.** Every aisle was crammed with tall exhibit cases, shelves buckling top to bottom. The owner, an old man with tufts of stringy white hair, told us that he got inventory from places like Tibet, Mongolia, Afghanistan, the Congo, and "everywhere on the world map." Gadgets, taxidermy, medical instruments, dioramas, figurines and dolls, tokens and dubious talismans, Native artifacts, tins, and antique medicinal bottles, all crammed together on shelves. The best finds were usually safely behind glass—but not always. Some you could actually touch. The effect of the overall array itself was hypnotic, part cluttered closet and part museum, a mad inventor's laboratory. It was anthropology as 3D comic book, wizardry, and wonder of other times and unpronounceable places. If it were an ice cream flavor, it could have been named "Curio and Kitsch"; I immediately loved my generous scoop.

Dad held my hand as we entered one aisle, took a step or two, our gazes respectively held enthralled by some next and nether object of fascination; we stopped, dropped hands, and pivoted right and left in each cramped aisle, often summoning each other to "Come look at this!" Dad seemed to know the origins of all the items, to which he attached stories steeped in the histories of the Mughal Empire, the Sokoto Caliphate, the Khmer Empire, and more. I was pretty sure Aladdin's magic oil lamp was inside one of those cabinets. Ancient instruments of medicine, fortune telling, mind reading and sorcery—all rolled into a single bizarre multipurpose artifact—were on display and alleged to be authentic.

I peered at something labeled "Ceremonial Cup, Origin Lhasa": an upside-down human skull, eye sockets, and nasal cavities sealed with turquoise and coral. I stared at a canoe paddle hand-carved of wood, attributed to a tribe along the Sepik River of New Guinea. I froze before a set of decorated "Canopic Jars, containing preserved viscera; Origin—Valley of the Kings, Egypt." These were real mummy guts that they were taking with them to the eternal afterlife. I didn't blink or breathe for five minutes in awe. I pressed my face to an étagère filled with wooden and bronze idols of gods of all cultures, and "Opium Pipes, Opium War era, China," and "Women's Ornate Hair Combs, 1870s, China," the latter encrusted with delicate sterling silver flowers and painted with the vibrant metallic blue feathers of Kingfisher birds. The contents of the case quivered with the vibration caused by my footfalls. In an adjacent case I spied a two-inch high bronze dog, a thick mane framing its face: "Lion Dog, Opium Weight, 1880s, Burma." The dog sat upright on a pagoda-shaped pedestal, one paw holding down a little metal toy ball as if he was at play. I recognized it as a shih tzu, "Look, the same as our dog!" I said to Dad.

My father bought that "Lion Dog" for me that day. When we returned home, I placed it on my nightstand. I studied its face and alert upright torso. Who had made it? I grabbed my world atlas, spread it open on the bed, and located Burma. My finger traced the line from Rangoon to Santa Fe. How had this treasure made it all the way across the world to my bed stand? And if it could travel this far . . . how far might I be able to travel?

From that day with my dad at the Gamut, I invited the world toward me. The great beyond and I were now pals, utterly carefree of distance and time. What was time, after all, at age ten, but the evening streetlight signaling me to come home? What now was distance, but merely my fingers stretched across the map? If that antique little dog could journey, so would I. As a child I had dreamed about flying to faraway places where I might be accepted into a culture that celebrated me, that recognized me and treated my arrival as a return, as a warm homecoming. I longed for a place where I felt comfortable to openly express all the aspects of myself. I began to place offerings under the little weight—pictures I cut out from *National Geographic* magazines. My offerings included pictures of the Great Sphinx of Giza, the stone sculpture of the emaciated fasting Shakyamuni Buddha of Pakistan, of Machu Picchu, Angkor Wat, and the Great Wall of China . . . all far away from the reality of our dilapidated rental home in Santa Fe. With a light touch, at the Gamut my dad had managed to teach me, his impressionable young son, the correct pronunciations of faraway places and about distinct cultures. He opened my mind and heart as he opened my world. He introduced me to the tandem concepts of tolerance and respect for the beliefs and practices of all human beings. I was being schooled in humanity without even realizing it. I just called it fun.

The power of a child's dreams to become reality in the world cannot be underestimated. Throughout the decades ahead, as a dancer and choreographer, I would indeed explore many of these destinations and scores of others. I began touring my company in 1994, with the support of the US State Department, the Fulbright Program, and foreign governments. At times my role was that of observing as a student, at others as an active cultural ambassador. Throughout all these experiences my goal was to build positive diplomatic relations for the United States in communities across the globe through arts programming. Since 1994 I have toured dozens of times, often several times a year, either solo or with some or all the dancers in my company. These international tours have included every region of the world from Asia to Africa, from Europe to the Americas. I've learned crucial lessons about dance from my access and exposure to exceptional local artists. These experiences have fed my artistic appreciation of our universal human experiences, and they have made me even more aware of the stories that we share and the ones we have not yet heard or told. These journeys have informed my own artistry and individuation immeasurably. Each country in which I have studied, performed, and taught has been a mirror onto the self—reflecting to me my feelings of acceptance, of difference, of exclusion and inclusion—and each has helped me to witness and understand each face of my layered identity. Touring has answered my questions: What is artistic freedom in America? What is it to be nonconforming? What is it to be Korean American? What is the outcome of growing up in New Mexico in a Hispanic community? What is it to experience oneself as an outsider, as singular? What is it to be gay, a gay artist, a gay man? And it is my hope that I have left behind some impressions of dance as storytelling and of American dance arts that were valuable in those communities as well. The rich and varied interactions to diverse ways of thinking have led me to refine how deeply I want to live and to give back, as a citizen of the world and of the United States.

There are three early and seminal touring experiences that stand out for me, especially for the ways they challenged and expanded my understanding of my own art form. These were my trips to Pakistan in 1999, to Korea in 2000, and to Peru in 2003.

sixteen PAKISTAN FLASHLIGHTS, FLASHPOINTS, FOOTWORK, AND FIRESTORMS

While working on my commissioned Kennedy Center dance *Silk Roads* in the spring of 1999, I had the opportunity to travel to Pakistan—Islamabad, Lahore, Taxila, and the Swat Valley—as well as to the tribal lands along the Afghani border. I needed to visit the Khyber Pass, the historic mountain passageway that connected the East and the West, to infuse this dance with sights and movements of this singular place, to incorporate its tumultuous energies, its historic evolution in the region—from moving merchandise to militia—and its marketplace colors and sounds.

With my dear friend Sueraya Shaheen, now a photographer for *Vogue Arabia* and cofounder of *Tribe Photo Magazine*, I set about outlining a two-week trip to Pakistan. She was building her portfolio of photographs of daily life in far-flung destinations. Sueraya and I first met in May 1998 at Govinda Gallery, which was across the street from John Dreyfuss's home in Georgetown. I was going there with my sketchpad nearly every day. At that time Sueraya was an intern at the gallery. We struck up a conversation. I told her I was a dancer, but that I go to galleries much as a dowser might seek to divine the locations of precious water or ore. That is, I was tapping art for its buried gems, noting in my pad the movements, the expressions, and gestures—to which I would then apply the alchemy of choreography.

We hit it off immediately. At Govinda we would visit to laugh about our day's artistic triumphs and failures, share recollections of our displaced childhoods, and map out our future careers. Sueraya is Syrian Christian. Her family immigrated to America during her childhood. She was born in Beirut, Lebanon, and has spent her life on the move. Her keen eye for detail captures candid soulful portraits, revealing the vagabond in the dilettante and regality in the pauper. I was thrilled by her portfolio; her focus complemented my own creative agenda. Our artistic visions dovetailed wonderfully; ours was a two-pronged dowsing rod. We would each surface our "Eureka!"

Together we approached both the Pakistani Cultural Council and the US State Department with our outline of a collaborative artistic research trip that would culminate in a performance of new original choreography at the Kennedy Center and her photo exhibit in the Terrace Theater lobby. Both governments saw this as a tremendous opportunity to build a friendship through art in the midst of rising political tensions brought on by an insurgent group called the Taliban.

In 1999, the Taliban was virtually unheard of outside of Pakistan except among people high up in international governments who were beginning to take notice. Art would be the medium of communication. Both governments collaborated financially to support our trip—airfare, hotel, meals, local ground transportation in Pakistan—and in the coordination of an armed guard and tour guides to assure our safety. While we were indeed there in a nonpolitical context, we would still need protection.

The Khyber Pass is a narrow strip of land that connects Central and South Asia and has historically been and continues to be a key to mercantilism and military stability. Whoever controls the Khyber Pass controls the region. My central intention was to research the first images of the Buddha, which were created in the ancient Gandhara region of Northern Pakistan along the borderlands of Afghanistan. I wanted to infuse my choreography with postures and gestures drawn from the ancient artwork of the area. Sueraya sought to photograph ancient sculptures and depict them in parallel to portraits of the region's modern inhabitants. My desire to trace the origins of an East-West visual arts aesthetic—an art movement connected to the Greek and Macedonian artisans who traveled with Alexander the Great on his crusade to conquer the Persian Empire—came from my childhood. My father had shown me pictures of the Gandhara Buddhas, and by age eleven I had already formed a deep affinity for this faraway place. It was a place where angular, almond-shaped eyes were the norm and not the anomaly. Greek and Macedonian artisans who specialized in working with stone, clay, and painting, stayed in the Gandhara region. Their artistic influences gave birth to the first images of the Buddha. Used to depicting the Greek pantheon, these artisans applied their Western aesthetic outlook to shaping the physical form of the Buddha, which had up until this point only been depicted through symbols, such as two footprints, an empty space under a parasol, and an empty throne. Here Buddha's corporal form took shape draped in Greek-style chitons, with Eurasian eyes, and bodies and stances resembling those of Apollo and Zeus: the conjoined aesthetics of the East and West.

Upon landing at the Islamabad International Airport, Sueraya and I were met by our US Embassy hosts who expedited us through the visa entry line and escorted us to a white unmarked van. Sueraya and I were introduced to our driver, tour guide, and security guard Arif, an imposing man more than six feet tall, assigned by our embassy to assist us in every way on this journey. As Arif helped us load up our baggage for the harrowing ride to the Swat Valley, we noticed two holsters strapped to his hip: one held a revolver and the other a new accessory back then, a flip cell phone. Nothing on this trip—absolutely nothing—would be what it at first appeared to be. The trip would sharpen all my skills of observation. We said goodbye to the embassy staff and got on the road.

With its lush orchards of persimmon, apple, and peach trees, the Swat Valley is the fragrant fertile center of Pakistan's agriculture. Arif drove for three hours down two-lane highways, dirt roads, past ox carts, stray dogs, and pedestrians, past herds of goats tended by men in traditional wool hats and long white tunics. We stopped on the side of the road to eat a prepacked meal that had been sent along for us by the embassy. As we fell upon our delicious picnic, I watched children playing at the hooves of a water buffalo that stood in a large murky puddle.

I quickly realized the children had adapted garbage—disposed glass medical syringes—as toy squirt guns. And the mud puddle? It was, in fact, human waste slurry, the sewage runoff from a community outhouse on a small hill just above them. The poverty in rural Pakistan was like none I had seen before. I felt guilty relief when we got back on the road, but I would carry the juxtaposed image of innocent play and its dystopian context permanently in my mind, heart, and ultimately in my art.

After two more hours we finally arrived at the edge of the Swat Valley. This could have been a scene out of John Hilton's novel *Lost Horizon*. We began our descent into the viridescent Swat Valley passing irrigated terraces of vegetables. Arif warned, "It is so beautiful here, yes, the land shimmers green in the sun, but when you get out, you must believe me and watch for snakes, many snakes—poisonous snakes." Sure enough, the sparkling landscape was practically writhing with these poisonous snakes. I could not help but to recall my house in Santa Fe, with its plagues of locusts and invasive moths. But that was nothing like this.

We pulled over to stretch our limbs at the bottom of the valley. Sueraya and I jumped out of the van and were immediately greeted by an exuberant group of boys. At first, I thought a couple of them were carrying a big stick with a shiny green branch. As they moved closer, I realized that, in fact, they were brandishing a six-foot iridescent emerald-skin snake. In my mind I heard the words of Indiana Jones, "Snakes. Why did it have to be snakes?" Its green faceted scales shimmered with fresh red blood; the snake was still twisting, writhing belligerently with all the remnant reflexes of its ending life. I wincingly acknowledged their prize, overtly forcing a ghoulish smile that was more like a grimace and waving, all while trying to keep my horror inside.

We got back into our secure van, and I exhaled an audible gasp. I don't think it was the sudden close-up sight of an enormous and once powerful snake that shocked me as much as it was witnessing its last heartbeat of futile valiance. I had been audience, close up, to a mighty animal in its unique solo, coiling death dance. It was at this moment I also realized that I was, in fact, somewhat of a trespasser in this area and this country and that I needed to be especially mindful of that tenuous status on this trip.

Arif steered our van up a long drive and stopped in front of a two-story museum—more like a stone mausoleum—with large wooden doors. These were covered by an additional set of security doors formidably chained by an old-fashioned eight-inch iron padlock. We were informed that the museum was closed to the public because the Taliban had recently attacked the museum. They had vandalized and looted the exhibition halls because the site contained ancient images of the Buddha. The fundamentalist phalanx of the Taliban, we were told, considered these antiquities to be "sacrilegious idols." Arif stood by with our governmental paperwork that gave us access to cultural sites throughout the region. Posted on the front steps were two military guards in sharp, smartly creased tan uniforms, carrying rifles. Arif had a long conversation with them as they inspected our paperwork. One guard finally nodded and withdrew a large skeleton key that hung from his neck under his uniform. The guards unwound the thick chain, pulled the cage open, and ceremoniously pushed wide the twelve-foot-tall wooden doors. These doors had been shut for weeks, perhaps months, and creaked loudly at their hinges—an almost human vocalization of protest and violation.

Sueraya and I quickly entered. The imposing doors swung closed behind us, leaving us in total darkness. The guards turned on their handheld flashlights, revealing a large exhibit hall with a forty-foot-tall ceiling. Dark wood and glass display cases lined the walls, and I felt like a child again with Dad at the Gamut. The curators had not yet reentered the museum to assess the damage or fix the cases out of fear for their lives. Inside the cases were row upon row of carved Buddhas and friezes, in poses rendered in stone two thousand years ago. With a sense of urgency, in the available light, I sketched in my journal—images of the body from the time of Alexander—as Sueraya took myriad photos.

Here were stone carvings of faces and bodies of those who had once moved through this valley from the Middle East to India to China. The stonework and sculptures depicted praying, conversing, riding elephants, feeding peacocks, and harvesting crops. Some told stories of the Buddha's life: elaborate scenes of the Brahmin caste prince enjoying performances of dancers in his garden; a depiction of the Buddha as a skeletal ascetic starved to near death; the enlightened Buddha meditating under a Bodhi Tree with gentle hand positions. These postures and poses became actual moving positions of the torsos, feet, legs, and hands of my dancers for years to come. The strobe effect of Sueraya's flash camera going off in rapid succession in the hall gave our own motions a choppy mechanical quality. From the display cases, in positions supine, seated, and standing, hewn of gray schist or shale, clay, and stucco, the serene Eurasian eyes of carved Buddhas stared back at my Amerasian eyes. Many—far too many—still lay fallen and broken from the recent looting.

We spent two hours in the museum and were then ushered back into the van. We drove through the narrow valley of Marghuzar, staying the night at the White Palace, a 1940s-era formerly private villa, next to a stream. It had been built of the same white marble from the quarry that supplied stone used to construct the Taj Mahal. I stood on the lush front lawn trying to sort out an optical illusion: how many white pillars support this wrap around porch... twelve... eighteen... twenty-four? I gave up as a bellhop greeted us and took our bags inside. We entered its musty lobby filled with chipped and broken antique furniture of inlaid stone and marble. We approached the front desk for check-in, walking and turning pinwheels to take in our setting. As the sun set, the buzz of the generator that supplied electricity to old ceiling fans and light fixtures began to hiccup, and lights flickered, sputtering on and off. The effect on our gestures was a bit psychedelic, akin to what Sueraya's strobe had been in the museum.

My room was simple except for an opulent faded red embroidered bedcover. It faced the back gardens that—from what I could tell from my window—must have at one time had a complex logic, before the flora reclaimed its walkways and stone seating. The garden had fallen into semi-wild disarray, another clue to the overall economic decline of the whole region.

Sueraya and I went to the restaurant for dinner. A local official greeted us in English and invited himself to join us and share the history of the now run-down hotel. Guests had included Queen Elizabeth II and Prince Philip in 1961. It seemed a strange thing for him to bring up—strategic, in the manner of brand marketing. It led me to wonder how Sueraya and I were perceived in this meeting place of East and West. Did Sueraya and I look to be American outsiders, more Caucasian than Asian? And how was this perception different than when I was in America? Out of the blue, he asked if I wanted to study Buddhist art versus the much superior Islamic Art, and at another point he blurted a bizarre non sequitur, "Alexander the Great was a disgraceful homosexual." This signified to me that intel about our visit and about us had been moving across the valley. I responded noncommittally to all his queries and statements. Frustrated with my flat responses, he poked at Sueraya, expressing his views on the "proper" place of women in Pakistani society. He asked her, "As a woman who is not married, why would you be traveling and working as a photographer?" Sueraya took the bait and said, "Women can be independent and have careers." At that very second, the electrical generator gave way and the whole hotel went black. Given what we had been hearing about the Taliban and the recent attack on the museum, we thought the hotel was under attack. Sueraya gasped. I ducked below the table. After a few chaotic minutes, waiters illuminated the room with candles; I pretended I had dropped my napkin and had to pick it up from under the table and sat back in my chair. The generator never came back on. Sueraya and I excused ourselves to review the events of the day before turning in.

I was relieved to be getting back on the road early the next morning because our presence in the Swat Valley was being questioned and I simply didn't feel safe. To ignore these concerns any longer would tempt peril. That feeling was an old one, but once roused, it assumed its occupancy. We packed up the van and ascended out of the verdant landscape. Fertile land became arid, and our wheels kicked up dust that coated the windshield. Four hours or so from Swat, we at last reached the Khyber Pass, a treacherously steep twisting one-lane road reaching to an elevation of about 3,500 feet. Trucks and cars were forced to stop to allow one another to nudge past in single file. With each passing, shards of shale and limestone broke away, tumbling down steep drops. We were trapped in this hair-raising intertwining for two hours. Out the window, I beheld the wreckage of autos that had slipped over the edge. I leaned my weight away from the passenger's side of the road each time we were near the edge, but if a few rocks were to give way, no amount of shifting would have steadied the van. We made no conversation; it seemed to us any vibrations of even our vocal cords, any sound could have tipped our balance fatally. When Arif finally got the van to the top of the Pass, my T-shirt was soaked with fear.

We pressed on along dust-covered streets lined by crude adobe fortresses three stories high. The occasional shape of women disappeared from the streets, replaced by long black burkas, with netting where eyes and a face should be, scurrying furtively from doorway to doorway with small children clinging. Despite my discomfort at seeing these women so obviously in fear, I still took choreographic note of their movements; these would be powerful fodder for future dance motifs. Men in beige *shalwar kameez*, loose pants and long tunics, walked slowly along the side of the road. It was as if the industrial era had never happened here. It looked and felt as if we had driven hundreds of years back in time.

With the backdrop of tribal compounds, men casually held hands, walked arm-in-arm, or with an arm draped around another's shoulder. The fixed fundamentalist Islamic moral standards condemned homosexuality and gay men. And yet the body language here strongly demonstrated that there were other sexual and physical interactions and communications condoned and even strongly supported between men that the West did not even express. In fact, there seemed to be conspicuous evidence all around us that there was a far larger and more nuanced spectrum in this culture of how men could openly interact with one another compared to the West, especially in the freighted strictures of the absolute separation of the sexes.

In ugly contrast, I stared at a woman running down the road away from a man chasing her, brandishing a stick. Arif said, "Here women need to be off the streets, be quick about it, or the religious police will punish them." The Islamic fundamentalists of the region were oppressing the minds, hearts, and bodies of the people of this region. I wondered how these women expressed themselves from under the burka, this garment designed to mask any recognizable body language and facial expressions that suggest emotions, engagement. They were branded mute by a garment.

This area was controlled by violent tribal factions. I could tell that we had entered a zone where human rights were at great risk. As a gay man, I would be treated as a heretic; I was nauseous with stress about this. I slumped down into my seat and didn't sit upright again until the adobe fortresses yielded to an expansive arid landscape that looked so much like my homeland, New Mexico.

In Mardan we drove up a steep mountain on which stood the Indo-Parthian ruins of Takht-i-Bahi, a Buddhist monastery built in the first century CE and used well into the seventh century. A sun-leathered guard in an oversized faded green uniform tried to sell us stucco figurines that had been ripped from the walls of the site. We declined, instead having Arif press for our exploration of the well-preserved monastic rooms and courtyards. We were led to the base of a huge stupa, a dome-shaped Buddhist shrine. At the small stone entrance, our guide handed us large tattered black umbrellas. This perplexed us—there wasn't a cloud in the sky.

Taking the steward's lead, we opened our umbrellas and entered the chamber where ancient sculptured Buddhas once stood. The guard flipped on a flashlight revealing a cavernous space with an exit on the other side about two hundred feet away. As we walked, it began to rain on our umbrellas, large heavy splats. I assumed that plaster from an often-patched ceiling was crumbling down. I asked our guide to shine his light on the ceiling. The ceiling was a shuddering mass: thousands of bats clinging and dangling upside down, wriggling and displacing one another, sometimes resulting in falls. The dislodged sleeping creatures pelted our umbrellas. Sueraya and I screamed and bolted. We made tracks to the other end of the stupa where seeping sunlight led us out, via a small four-foot exit. We pushed our way through, momentarily sun blinded. We could hear the guard still inside, his laughter reverberating in the cave. This was his payback to us, for our not having purchased a stucco figurine.

Back in the van, our nerves settled. We had only one more stop before reaching the city of Lahore. The Pakistani National Council of the Arts had arranged for me to visit a very important Kathak dancer. Kathak is a classical South Asian dance form that originated in North India and dates to about 400 BCE. The Kathak dancer expresses stories from the Vedic Sanskrit epics of the Indian Puranas; these are the stories, ideas, and virtues of Hindu deities and rulers told through the language of gesture, postures, theatrical expression, rhythmic footwork, and upright quick turns. With roots in ancient storytelling, Kathak is defined by an incredibly fast pace yet is graceful with spins and intricate footwork. It is an example of transnationalism, of the cultural exchange of peoples along the Silk Road that blended Northern Indian, Persian, and Central Asian themes and inflections. Kathak was at this time discouraged, as it was at odds with the provincial government and Islamic religious factions that saw it as lewd and un-Islamic to dance and to express Hindu stories. Some dancers in the region—those with family ties or other connections—still performed publicly with little fear of imprisonment, assault, threats, or ostracism. As we discovered, though, others were not so lucky.

After four hours in our headquarters-on-wheels, Sueraya and I at last arrived at a home tucked away on a hill amid trees and boulders. It was not large, it looked fairly Western and modern, with rectangular shapes and large picture windows that appeared to be inspired by the architectural aesthetics of Frank Lloyd Wright. I walked up to the door and even before I could knock, it was opened by a woman in her late thirties with a long black braid. She introduced herself as Aisha. Her long indigo tunic was detailed with intricate vibrant floral embroidery. Her matching pants narrowed at the ankles with cuffs of embroidered flowers. Aisha was clearly a dancer and our hostess.

She ushered us in, and we politely removed our shoes and sat at a low table for tea where Sueraya and I formally introduced ourselves. Sueraya asked Aisha if she might take photos. Our hostess declined. If photos of her dancing were to circulate, she explained with evident nervousness, it might bring danger. We all spoke about our work as artists, our creative assumptions and aesthetics. I shared how I created modern dance choreographies and she was especially interested in the freedom of the form. Aisha spoke about her interest in rhythmic cycles and then, losing none of the short time we had together, she ushered us toward her dance studio, a small sitting room with a wooden floor and no mirrors, so she might better demonstrate.

She tied *ghungroos*, small metallic bells strung together, on her ankles and began to stomp a rhythmic cycle at terrific speed with her bare feet, turning in place, rapid cycles repeated over and over. The little bells, anywhere between fifty to two hundred knotted together, accentuate the dance rhythms and permit complex footwork to be heard by listeners. She held her hands and arms at her sternum and extended them outward as arrows in front of her as she turned. I listened intently to her complex rhythms, counting out the musical cycle in my head. Her statement was accented—threes to fours in a twelve-count repeating phrase—1, 2, **3**, 4, 5, **6**, 7, **8**, 9, 10, 11, **12**. The cycles were undeniably reminiscent of flamenco and exemplified how the rhythms and footwork of Kathak had migrated from Northern India to Spain and elsewhere in Europe over a span of five hundred years, along with the people who became the Romani, the Gitano, the cultural keepers of flamenco.

Aisha invited me to join her. We started off with arm and hand positions that circled on diagonals from back to front. I learned the neutral position of the arms, palms facing down at the sternum with elbows positioned perpendicular to the floor at 90 degrees. Our arms sped up and we sliced through diagonals, high, middle, and low like knives as we began to turn underneath ourselves. I copied her quick turns and arm movements; I experienced this in a kind of euphoria, spinning faster and faster as we danced for some time. Kathak's inherent power, the ability to express an emotional narrative like a body levitation must have indeed been a radical trigger for fundamentalists who sought to control the whole region. And that this magic would be controlled by and conjured by a woman . . . yes, she understood the potential dangers of her dance virtuosity.

After a long period of dance, a slight man in his twenties entered. He was drawn by the rhythmic music of her bells and our pounding feet. Our dizzying duet came to an abrupt halt. He was dressed in a thin white hospital gown, conspicuous bandages on his chest and left temple. He wheeled an intravenous drip bottle on a rolling rack. His gait had an alarming weightlessness about it. I felt as though if he were to release this tether to his rolling IV pole he might float upward and away.

The young man gingerly sat and began to speak softly and deliberately. Aisha translated his Urdu to English. He told us that he had been attacked and shot by fundamentalists for his crime, they told him, of public dancing. Three men had hunted him down after an outdoor performance. They violently beat him, breaking his lower left leg. As he crawled away, they shot him, once in the chest and once on the side of his head and left him for dead. He remembered nothing more until he awoke three days later in a hospital bed. Having recently been released, he was now in hiding in this home, afraid for his life. It was unclear whether he would ever be physically able to dance again. Had he been mistaken for someone associated with the *bachas*, dancing boys? This term in Afghanistan refers to a custom associated with male child prostitution in the highly gendered Islamic world of the Middle East and Central Asia, where females are prohibited to appear and perform in public. For hundreds of years the role of entertainer was filled by young boys who wore makeup and dressed as girls. Some gained great popularity but were vulnerable to abuse by powerful men and warlords. Under the Taliban, being a bacha carried the death penalty. Sueraya and I were horrified. His performances of the Kathak dances—which nearly cost him his life in this society—would never have been seen as life threatening in the United States.

His story also heightened my own awareness that dance is, in fact, a powerful language all its own, one that can be subject to censorship and retribution. This was eye-opening for me, even as a seasoned dancer. Depending on the setting, the use of the language of dance itself can be controversial and even dangerous. Dance is a unique barometer by which we may measure societal freedoms within any given country. It ought not to be overlooked as such. If dance and free creative thought are celebrated, then that society is in an essential way thriving; if dance is suppressed it signals that dangerous extremist conservative and intolerant ideologies are on the rise. Dance is resilient, a durable artform of physical self-expression—for all living creatures it is one as old as time. Our tour of Pakistan deepened my awareness that dance is a language that must be protected the same way those of us living in a free and democratic society protect our First Amendment guarantees of freedom of speech. I felt sudden gratitude for being an artist in America and for a civil right I take for granted.

With sunset approaching, Arif entered and urged Sueraya and me to return to our van. Upon seeing the injured male dancer, his anxiety about the time was heightened. He worried about the potential for another attack on this dancer after sundown. We bade farewell and good luck to our new dance friends, who had shared so much on this visit, and for whom we had ever greater respect and appreciation, and we hastened to the van as daylight dimmed.

I share this young man's story often. To this day I don't know if he ever danced again, if he ever safely reentered society. I received no updates in any of my ongoing inquiries to Aisha.

We drove for three hours in darkness. There were no electrical lights along the dirt roads. We would not have any illumination until we reached the outskirts of Lahore. Once in Lahore, streets bustled with pedestrians, many exploring open food stalls and restaurants. Multi-floor dwellings with ornate, arched wooden window frames, typically covered by lattice work, rose above storefronts.

We arrived at our hotel, a gated compound of a dozen units. We checked in, took our keys, and continued to our assigned bungalow, the word itself derives from a Hindi word that means "house in the Bengali style" and that came into English during the British administration of India. It was one level and had two apartments, one for Sueraya and one for me. The walls were a dirty beige; the bed covers and the few pieces of bare wooden furniture were identical in both units and depressing. Even the one decorative mass-produced piece of artwork was the same in each room: a framed quote from the Koran. Sueraya translated it: "You prefer the life of this world where the hereafter is better and more lasting." Yikes. We read these words more as threat than a welcome. Arif retired to the van and parked just outside the bungalow to stand guard. Sueraya and I were exhausted and debriefed about the long day. We were finally able to speak in private about the young dancer we had met. Even with government support, we both felt isolated and increasingly anxious about our safety.

Suraya has an expansive social network of artists and arts patrons around the world. Her network included Jalal Salahuddin, an LGBTQ supporter whose grandfather was the late Muhammad Iqbal, one of the founders of Pakistan and now called *Mufakkir-e-Pakistan*, the Thinker of Pakistan. We decided to reach out. Sueraya called Jalal and within twenty minutes he was knocking at our front door. This striking Pakistani man in his twenties, dressed in designer Western clothing walked into our bungalow and called out, "Sueraya!" They greeted warmly and she introduced me to him. His English was polished. He said, "I was so bored this week! How great you are here; you must know the sights of Lahore. Come, let's go." Suddenly, Arif rushed through our door and demanded to know who Jalal was. In heated Urdu, Jalal announced himself and Arif froze upon hearing his pedigree. Arif backed up, bowed, and said, "Pardon me, thank you, and please take care of my friends."

We walked to Jalal's brand-new white Cadillac Escalade SUV. His own driver jumped out, opened the door, and we climbed in. Jalal said, "Shahi Qila!" and with that we were off to the historic Lahore Fortress. His driver drove wildly, speeding, honking, barely dodging pedestrians and motorbikes. We rounded the high pink walls of the Lahore Fortress and careened into a small lower attached gate leading into his family's historic compound. The driver jumped out and banged on the two-story wooden gates until an attendant opened them, at which point he jumped back in and sped into the compound, screeching to a halt in front of the grand manor.

In a matter of heart-stopping minutes, Jalal had transported us to an alternate reality. This ornate compound with immaculate flowering gardens accentuated the socioeconomic divide of the Pakistani people. Outside these walls people struggled and starved. All here was lavish, opulent. The manor had been built in the 1600s at the height of the Mughal Empire style, with curved windows and door archways with finials. It had a vaulted ceiling entry way, faceted chandeliers, wooden furnishings with detailed shell and bone inlay and deep curvaceous Victorian couches and tufted chairs.

Jalal walked us quickly through to his favorite room, the music room, and ordered a servant to bring refreshments: fruit, cookies, tea, soda water, and gin. The large room had slightly outward-bulging walls and a domed ceiling completely covered in small round mosaic mirrors, each about three inches in diameter, and each slightly curved like the eyes of a fish. The floor was covered in Persian and Pakistani hand-woven scatter carpets, predominantly in rich blues and reds. Sumptuous floor cushions were tossed around a central silver-topped tray table. Jalal called out and a young man entered with a *Rubab*, the traditional lute from the region. Here dancers and musicians had performed for hundreds of years, as they had throughout the region. But now dance was scarce and in great danger of extinction. The musician played as the room shifted in the flickering light, giving us the sense that the walls were pulsing to the music.

After an hour, Jalal led us up a staircase deeper into the Lahore Fortress for a private moonlit tour. He showed us the remains of elaborate gardens and fountains, and scalloped archways and windows. Four-hundred-year-old towering "picture walls" were embellished with glazed tile; faience mosaics; and frescoes depicting royal hunts, mythical creatures, and dancers. Looking at the 240-foot frescos and mosaics Jalal woefully said, "Where has all the dance gone? Muslim culture cherished it once. . . . Dire times."

We stayed at Lahore Fortress all night. As the sun came up over the pink walls of the citadel, Jalal dropped us off at our hotel. We quickly packed so we could depart to Islamabad. Jalal returned an hour later and insisted that he drive us. We rode in his Escalade and Arif followed behind in our white van. During the ride we spoke at length about the power and importance of dance and of celebration. Today, Jalal and his company, JS Events, is the primary event and promotional planning company for all of Pakistan. Perhaps the exuberance of the dances of the Mughal Empire now resides in Jalal's prolific public and private parties.

After four hours in the air conditioning of Jalal's Escalade, we arrived at a security checkpoint in front of the American Embassy in Islamabad. A minute later Arif drove up. Five minutes after that, an old military truck with a green canvas tarp pulled up. A dozen armed men assigned by the Pakistani government spilled out of the truck. Sueraya and I stared incredulously. I recognized one man from our time in the

Swat Valley and realized that they had been following us the entire trip. Were they following us for our safety? Or were they keeping tabs on us to make sure we weren't doing some sort of cunning intelligence work? We never found out. That night we stayed in the US diplomatic compound and the next day ventured out to museums, artisan markets, and more landmarks.

On our last night in Islamabad, we were hosted by Richard Hoagland, a public diplomacy officer at the US Embassy, a gay man in his fifties who had a Russian boyfriend living abroad. Hoagland had a prestigious career that eventually would include being the US ambassador to Kazakhstan and Tajikistan. Over dinner we discussed the state of Pakistan with several guests including Pakistan-born Ahmed Rashid, a prominent international journalist and television commentator, and at the time the foremost expert on the Taliban. He was working on a book that in 2000 would become a *New York Times* hardcover nonfiction best seller, *The Taliban: Militant Islam, Oil and Fundamentalism in Central Asia*, eventually translated into twenty-two languages.

After dinner, Jalal picked us up and whisked us off to a private party at the mammoth home of a young senator, Abbas Khan. Abbas was educated in England and bore a likeness to Keanu Reeves whose career had just hit international fame. An enviably stocked bar and private disco dominated his first floor. Under pulsating lights, the young VIPs and elites of the city, clad in Versace and Armani, moved to the rhythms of top ten dance tunes of America and England. Abbas was open-minded and charming. He could tell that I was gay and said, rather like a politician making a statement for the record: "We must respect and support the rights and viewpoints of everyone. I have so many gay friends and I believe it is a basic human right for everyone to be treated equally." It was so apparent that this society was in turmoil, deeply divided about modern viewpoints and modern mores. But we had no way of knowing what was to come. Within six months of our return to America, in the fall of 1999, Pakistan would undergo a military coup d'état led by General Pervez Musharraf. He walked a tightrope between supporting the military and averting and waging a war on the Taliban and Al-Qaeda.

I returned to DC overwhelmed by our experience in Pakistan. The artistic takeaways from this trip exceeded all my expectations. The immersion fed my choreography with both historic and contemporary images from the Silk Road, and it roused a heightened awareness of human freedom with dance as a lens, a barometer of wholesome expression of freedom in a society. I layered my new choreography *Silk Roads* with ancient postures and gestures from Pakistan adapted from its art, its street scenes, and even a priceless brief brush with authentic Kathak. I also created two new solos, *Dariush* and *Khaybet*, that to this day are mainstays of our company repertoire.

My dance, *Dariush*, is an homage to the great king of Persia, Dariush, who reigned from 548–486 BCE. The dance is a technical powerhouse of martial arts, acrobatic kicks, and leg extensions, layered with intricate gestures and postures gleaned from the artifacts of the Swat Museum, dating to a time when Pakistan was part of the expansive Persian Empire. Myriad gestures and postures come alive as if called up from a séance and finally recede into a sculptural pose.

Khaybet means *shadow* and my dance that is named this is my reference to the ancient Egyptian *Book of the Dead* in which it is written that at the moment of death the spirit leaves the corporal body, but the shadow lingers. *Khaybet* is a woman's first-person account of what it was to have worn a burka her whole life and her painful journey as a disempowered woman right up till death claimed her. The female soloist wears a long tunic and a veil with head covering, never revealing her face to the audience. In place of facial expressions, sharp angular movements express deep rage from having lived a life shrouded within a burka. At one point, the dancer places her hands on either side of her mouth and then reaches plaintively to the audience as if projecting a silent scream. Then, as if possessed, she is pulled and dragged through the space by unseen forces. The dancer fights against this unseen force, her gestures all pantomiming her resistance and self-protection against the abuse from the implied others and approaching death, until she finally succumbs; she turns away from the audience, lifts her veil, and solemnly walks off stage.

The lessons I learned by being the observer of dance there, in all its contexts, have fed me for more than twenty years. Due to fear for my safety—the possibility of my being kidnapped or worse—the US Embassy did not allow me to perform or teach in Pakistan. At the end of my trip, I had an insatiable hunger to dance unrestrained by sociopolitical barriers.

Heretofore dance had been many things to me, spiritual and physical, aesthetic. But from this point forward, dance would forever be for me, first and foremost, a representation of freedom. I now understood that dance is a basic human right that needs protection. Dance is synonymous with the fundamental right to be, to self-expression. This trip defined my thoughts about the repercussions of religious and governmental policies on the private as well as the professional field of dance and is the primary reason I speak out so fervently about the need for artistic freedom and the protection of human rights. Rights of expression cannot be taken for granted, even in a democracy, even in modern America. Dance as if your life depends upon being able to do so—because it does.

As a Korean American, I grew up hearing stories about the Korea my great-grandparents and grandparents were compelled to leave in 1903, a country they always described as a place of rolling rural hills and Ginkgo trees, a majestic palace like a precious jewel encircled in a setting of sacred temples. So, when a professor of modern dance from the Sejong University in Seoul asked me to teach for the month of June at the university in the summer of 2000, nearly a century after their forced exit, my heart leaped, and so did my feet. This was an extraordinary opportunity to experience Korea firsthand, to live and teach there for a time and to better understand my ancestry, absorb and integrate the cherished homeland that my grandparents had recounted so fondly with my contemporary identity.

I quickly found out that modern Korea is a very different place from the memories passed down to me for three generations. After twenty-three hours of flights and layovers and connections, I arrived at Incheon International Airport and made my way via bus to Seoul along six-lane highways surrounded by Fortune 500 brand-emblazoned office skyscrapers and towering residential high-rises. This, the capital of South Korea, was a city built of sheer grit and might after the Korean War, which had left Seoul with the ruins of 20,000 tall buildings and 55,000 individual homes.

I am a fourth-generation Korean American who hardly speaks any Korean, and I quickly realized that in this country I was perceived as more American than Korean. I tended to believe this interpretation to be a dismissal rejection of half of myself—a half as essential to me as my American identity. And this perception was the exact opposite of my experience in the United States, where I was "the other," more Korean than American. I would have to sort all of this out. As a dancer, I reflexively move with some fluidity, anticipating the next steps on my path and moving ahead in a coordinated graceful way. That training is internalized, and I even move this way on crowded streets. But here, *ajummas*—old women—curtly elbowed my ribs to ensure I would get out of their way. My gait revealed me as the foreigner who could not keep up with the pace of the city. Walking on sidewalks was a veering to and fro in a pack, hip-checked and jounced and jammed off-stride in passes that were the equivalent of a roller derby rink. Even in 2000, when mobile technology was still getting established, everyone seemed to have a cell phone that was smaller, faster, and smarter than mine. The quaint stories that I held in my mind about the Korea of old were quickly washed away by a super chic, urban youth culture that flew in the face of conservative Confucian values. I felt as if I had raced forward in time like a Victorian traveler in that science-fiction tale *The Time Machine* by H. G. Wells. My only solace came from insatiable devouring of familiar delectations at the prolific food kiosks. There I, too, learned and adapted the American hustle version of "outta my way," "I'm walkin' here," and "lemme in," to elbow my way toward bul kogi, kimchi, and yaksik.

I taught daily modern dance classes at Sejong University. I led thirty students, ages eighteen to twenty-three through modern dance warm-ups and combinations, in a twenty-five-hundred-square-foot dance studio with high ceilings and enormous windows through which poured abundant natural light. They all spoke some amount of English, but I still required an interpreter. Unlike in the United States, dance students here were predominantly male.

I began each class with the students all lying supine on the floor with their eyes closed. I talked them through checking in with their bodies. "Consciously relax your face, neck, and shoulders, your ribcage, the muscles along your spine, your hips, thighs, calves, and feet. Breathe deeply in and deeply out." I encouraged them to consider the neurological and energy pathways of their bodies that flowed from their spinal cord to their extremities. I asked them to accentuate the movement of an arm, a leg, a hand by sensing its origins along the spine. After a short interval I had the students open their eyes and continue to hold onto those sensations. I had them slowly stand and articulate their spines by rolling down and touching the floor and rolling up to standing again. They arched backward as far as they could and then returned to center. I had the students circle their shoulders and articulate their rib cages in small circular motions, then sway their hips side to side. After a series of tendus and dégagés, they swung their legs forward and back to warm up their hip joints. After being fully warmed up, we moved through the whole studio space with inverted handstands followed by rolls and traveling leaps across the floor. I ended these classes with movement combinations that stemmed from the center of the body outward through their limbs to the fingers and toes. Core initiations were emphasized: a subtle movement of the spine would create a ripple effect that propelled the legs and arms. It all moved smoothly; the interpreter communicated my instructions with great exactitude and intentionality.

The Korean male dancers were acrobatic wonders, lithe and with a nearly feline natural dynamic range. We focused on and built upon this quality. One day, I asked the students why it is that they train so tirelessly and dance with such passion. A dancer explained, "Military service is mandatory. In order to be exempt, to be discharged from serving, we are required to have won a major competition or award. If we don't receive a national or international award, our lives, our artistic careers are interrupted by a year-and-a-half of military service, and with that our careers are effectively over." In essence, prizes, acclaim, publicity, and near celebrity status were their only acceptable legitimization for devoting themselves to dance. And—crucially—it got them out of the bleak regimented life of a soldier. Talk about incentives. Their struggle to be accepted in a society that appreciates art but favors lucrative careers created turmoil in their minds and hearts. That said, it is notable that because of this governmental ultimatum, the athleticism and astonishing acrobatic technique was almost uniformly spectacular. And I noticed that a close-knit dancing community survived, which provided vital collective support for one another in the midst of a legendary, systematically imposed rivalry, and this support system was important for these dancers.

There was one element that proved elusive for the dancers, however.

The capacity for expressing nuance, suffusing gesture with subtlety, the ability to hint at the range of human frailties or the interplays of vulnerability was absent. Any sense of softness in the quality of movement was unnatural and difficult for them. Even the Korean Shamanistic dance traditions that Eleanor King had studied, and which were beginning to seep into contemporary Korean dance, were now void of nuance. Instead, these were acts of determination, extremes, of endurance, frenetic dancing that would continue for an hour or more without rest. References to *Shinawi*, the ritual music of the shaman, often accompanied these hybrid contemporary and traditional dances. Eleanor King would have been disappointed by the lack of subtlety. I believe this conspicuous and consistent lack of subtleties in shades of expression, of finesse in their dance language is due to Korea's struggle to be a successful country in the twenty-first century. Their national focus on becoming leaders in technological advancements in the global marketplace came with a price. Fair enough. But also unavoidably clear to me was that as a dancer and choreographer, I needed the capacity for expressing delicate distractions, fractional shading in movement. The ability to discern and express the ineffable is central to art, to dance. I simply could not practice my own art without that dimension, that *X* factor. Dancers have to bring that to the floor. It cannot be adhered, external like so much appliqué.

During one of my final days in Seoul, I stumbled upon an historic burial mound. This mound was near a subway exit. I had gotten lost and in desperation went up a hill to get a view that might restore my bearings. I quickly discovered that the entire hill was, in fact, a burial site. Cloistered between a highway and urban skyscrapers, I sat down next to a long worn gray slab stone, an entrance to a crypt about three feet by four feet across. I had the urge to thank my ancestors for their journey to America generations ago. I pondered my great-grandparents sorrow of not being able to maintain their family grave plots in North Korea and South Korea. Filial loyalty even after death was of great importance to them.

I often speak with other Asian American friends who express a deep pull to their motherlands, rendered always with melancholy disconnect.

A yearning, a mourning for something lost, just out of reach and inchoate. For the second-, third-, and fourth-generation American, the homeland is a "memory"—or more accurately a construction, a collage of stories heard and repeated, or edifice of photo albums and ephemera—of a physical place that has long ceased to exist. It is more an imagined place, a state of mind and heart, shared with strangers: of thrills and chills, careening up and down, heart-stopping bumper-car rides through crises, regimes, diseases, wars, amnesties, separations, empires, and eras. Collages quilted together of shreds worn thinner through time and distance. Stories told, stories repeated. Breaths held, knuckles white. Welcome to Ancestry Amusement Park.

On that hill, I got more than my physical bearings. The perspective permitted me to invite an internal dialogue and to gather my emotional equipoise. Was I the Korean outsider, understanding only large cultural concepts but never privy to cultural refinement? I seemed to be the transient visitor allotted entrance by blood passport, bearing the stigmatic stamp of a deserter. Koreans who were born and raised outside of Korea are often thought to somehow have lost touch with the motherland. They are called *Kyopo*. While I sat on this sacred mound against an urban backdrop, the word *Dongpo* suddenly came to mind. *Dongpo* describes a transnational link to Korea and means brethren. Perhaps the indelible markings of remembrance passed through the prodigal son, forcing his return. I deeply admired the skills, the techniques, and strengths of the dancers I met here. But I could not remain. I was not tempted to do so. I was not called from within to create and realize my own choreographic art, my dance visions with them. A crucial ineffable *X* factor of simpatico and inspiration was missing. I was grateful for the infusion I had received here of what was half of myself, my distant blood and genetic origins and identity in this nectar I had consumed. But this would never be home. I was not even sad. The trip had not been in any way a failure of any latent fantasy or wish or agenda. I looked out upon the city, through the eyes of a long-lost brother, but one who was unquestionably American. It was time for the monarch to migrate home once more.

eighteen **PERU** TERRORISM, TOE SHOES,
TEMPERS, TEMPO, AND TRACINGS

In 2004, I was thirty-six years old and had been living in Washington, DC, for fifteen years. I was burned out from years of nonstop dancing, choreographing, and teaching. I needed spiritual rejuvenation, the sort that I had taken for granted in the magical landscape and traditions that were my youth in Santa Fe. Up until this time I had always felt guided by signs from the universe. I summoned the benevolent twins, Serendipity and Synchronicity, and asked them for guidance.

That May I was sitting in my office when I received a call from a representative of the US State Department. He told me that Doug Sonntag, dance program director at the National Endowment for the Arts, had recommended me for a choreographic residency in Lima with the Ballet Nacional del Peru. Olga Shimazaki, a well-known Japanese Peruvian ballerina then in her fifties, had retired from stage and become director of Ballet Nacional del Peru. She wished to acquire contemporary dance works by an American choreographer. Well, hello!

Olga and I e-mailed. I sent her video samples of three of my repertory works. One was the sinuous group dance *Silk Roads*. The second was *Fractures*, a minimalist trio for two women and one man, about a woman who loses her love to a rival woman; the dance is set to *Spiegel im Spiegel*, a work for piano and a single violin composed by Arvo Pärt in 1978. The third piece I sent was the technically challenging solo *Dariush*. Olga called me soon thereafter to say that she very much liked my choreography for its "elegantly subtle Asian aesthetic." She asked me if I would set all three dances for her company, and she also commissioned me to produce a new group work for them. I eagerly agreed to her proposal.

Olga and I exchanged stories about our Asian backgrounds and our experiences as fellow "Chinitos," individuals who had grown up in Latino communities. Olga's parents, like my own, were both artists;

her father had been the conductor of an orchestra and her mother was a concert-level pianist. Her parents had met in Peru. The Japanese originally began immigrating to Peru as agricultural workers in 1899 much as had the Koreans who immigrated to Hawaii in the early 1900s. When she learned I was from Santa Fe she said, "The Japanese here share that city with you." She said that after Pearl Harbor, the fear of a "Yellow Peril" in both North and South America led to a pact between the US and Peruvian governments. In exchange for new military weaponry from the United States, the Peruvian government consented to track and then deport Japanese Peruvians to North American internment camps. A large number of these Japanese Peruvians ended up in the Santa Fe internment camp over which I grew up. This would be one of many strange connections I would have to Peru.

Olga invited me and a team of three of my dancers as assistants to come to Lima in early June for a little longer than four weeks. We would set a full evening of my choreography on the Ballet, including a new thirty-minute group work, all of which would be presented in the National Museum's auditorium. I had five weeks to prepare in Washington before we flew to Lima, where we would need to hit the ground running. For the new piece I chose several orchestral musical compositions by the twentieth-century Argentinian composer Alberto Evaristo Ginestera. The exact theme of the dance would have to wait until I met the cast and began choreographing. At this time the Ballet Nacional del Peru occupied the entire basement level of the National Museum. My choreographic commission would be supported by the US Embassy in Lima and the US State Department. Furthermore, I negotiated with the US State Department to have my full company join me and my team at the end of my residency with the Ballet Nacional del Peru for an additional week so we could perform my work *Tracings*, in the city of Trujillo at the Teatro Municipal de Trujillo.

On a sweltering day the second week of June, I boarded an American Airlines flight bound for Lima with my team: Tati Valle-Riestra, a limber and versatile dancer who had grown up in Lima; Leonardo Torres, a muscular dancer born in Colombia, trained in modern dance and gymnastics; and Sarah Craft. Eight hours later we entered Lima's

Aeropuerto Internacional Jorge Chávez. Armed guards held the leashes of drug-sniffing German Shepherds as they scanned the crowds. A group of women from the Peruvian highlands, dressed in traditional bright hand-woven wool skirts, shawls, and black bowler-style hats, approached the nearby escalator with trepidation. It was obvious that they had never been on one before. We spotted a sign with the scrawl "Señor BURGESS" and walked toward an embassy official, who expedited our luggage and passport clearance. We made our way outside to the awaiting official SUV and climbed in. It was winter in Lima, cold and wet. I struggled to shut a door made heavier for its layers of bulletproof hardware. The windows, unlike normal glass, were fascinating: the inch-thick windowpanes had an odd gelatinous overlay that could flex to hold shards of glass in place. I barely had time to absorb the significance of this feature when I saw outside my passenger-side window the outskirts of Lima.

The airport was a half-hour drive from the city through heavy traffic. I peered at gray cinder-block homes with window frames that held panes without glass. Curtains filthy from car exhaust blew in and out of the gaping panels. Stray dogs scavenged along dirty streets and sidewalks. We passed gas stations, 24-hour convenience marts, and food kiosks before coming to a neighborhood of casinos, flashing marquee lights and neon signs shaped in the universal symbols of dice, go-go dancers, and poker cards in a straight flush. The boulevards widened toward contemporary urban glass and stucco office and apartment buildings, with the occasional Baroque-style mansion refereeing the tight span between pairs of modern buildings. We finally arrived at upscale Miraflores, a downtown district where historic eighteenth- and nineteenth-century homes and Inca ruins from 1,500 years ago coexist with modern highrises. We pulled up and unloaded our gear at the La Paz Apart Hotel, on Avenida Alfredo Benavides, next to El Koryo Korean restaurant: I took that as a welcoming gustatory omen. Our rooms were simple, clean, and equipped with kitchenettes. Resting in my room I was overcome by a sixth sense of familiarity with Lima. Could it be because this city was the center of the Spanish empire in South America and that Santa Fe was Spain's farthest vestige of their empire?

The next day I went to the US Embassy for a briefing while my troupe explored. If the Embassy Compound appeared like a vault, the intimidating security briefing room with its thick steel doors and walls was like being inside a safe deposit box. Here I was informed about two dangerous groups: the Shining Path (Communist Party of Peru) and the Tupac Amaru Revolutionary Movement (a Marxist guerilla movement), named for the last monarch of the Neo-Inca State, and who was executed in bloody overthrow by his Spanish enemies in 1572. Both entities surged in terrorist activities in the 1980s and 1990s and by the early 2000s still had occasional resurgences.

The Shining Path had terrorized Peru with rural and urban bombings and murders. It was partially dismantled in 1992, when its leader, Abimael Guzmán, was arrested after having been found hiding in the apartment above a major modern dance studio in Lima. Guzmán and several of his cronies had been hidden and supported by a dancer, Maritza Garrido Lecca, who lived above her studio. The covert relationship between Guzmán and Lecca rocked the dance community of Lima for years. Dancers were paranoid of one another, and the government was distrustful of the artform and all its practitioners.

In 1996, the Tupac Amaru group took over the Japanese ambassador's home on the night of a party celebrating the Japanese Emperor Akahito's sixty-third birthday. Tupac Amaru revolutionaries laid siege to the residence and took these political dignitaries captive for 126 days.

In 2004, I was warned that both organizations, though on an apparent decline, still existed. In fact, I did see for myself, through the graffiti on abandoned buildings and construction sites, that they were still leaving their marks. Modern dance's proximities to Abimael Guzmán still posed an unanswered quandary to the US Embassy.

The embassy briefed me on safety so that my dancers and I could be prepared to work in the region. It was more in-depth than any other briefing I had ever undergone up until this time . . . and even to this day. The security team sat me down for a crash course in caution, in which I was to tutor my dancers. Here's a hint: Windows. When selecting hotel rooms, I was to choose only those above the second floor and in the back, away from the street—no big picture windows with views. Doing so will reduce injuries from car bomb blasts. And those small windows in the rear? They should be ajar, curtains always closed. The air pressure of any explosion can turn jagged glass shards into projectiles. Drawn drapes—*might*—help deflect the shards. Shoes should be at the bedside, as should a flashlight. Escape routes should be memorized and practiced in case of fire and blinding smoke. Be alert to people who crowd too close: purses and pockets are vulnerable to theft and taxicab–related kidnappings are not uncommon. I was informed that a device at our hotel would alert embassy security to our comings and goings. Frankly, I wasn't sure if this last was reassuring or threatening. I concluded that it was likely both. Nothing here would be as it initially seemed either. In finale and farewell, officers proudly led me to a line-up of mannequins clad in state-of-the-art gas masks and bulletproof vests and riot gear. After two hours I was told by the embassy's cultural staff, "We are so glad you are here, welcome to Peru, and your goal is to engage the dance community as far and as widely as possible." This postscript of welcome was accompanied by big smiles and handshakes.

I returned to my hotel from the protocol indoctrination with a deep sense of responsibility to ensure the safety of my dancers. I went to the front desk, called my dancers from the lobby, and changed all four of our rooms from the front to the back of the hotel on the second floor. Once in my new room, I opened the windows and pulled the curtains closed. In the dark I contemplated what lay ahead. While the dancers moved their luggage to their new rooms, I took a long restless walk that night toward the busy plaza of Miraflores. I passed artisan stalls filled with hand-tooled leather belts and bags, jewelry, ceramics, and carved gourds. I sat on a park bench and listened to a local band as people danced salsa around a rustic makeshift stage. I wandered past run-down gated mansions from the 1800s and abandoned lots with boarded-up hovels. Nocturnal animals howled in the cold temperature of a Lima winter night.

Walking this district, I was a child in Santa Fe again, strolling along Canyon Road, imbibing its heady mix of magic and mystery. As I returned to the hotel, a woman in traditional Andean clothing, approached and asked if I would buy a small *canopa*, a two-inch stone figure of a llama, a pre-Columbian votive figure. She spoke Quechua, the language of the Andean highlands, alternating with Spanish, but I understood her. I bought the smooth beige llama and placed it in my pocket, a good luck charm. I was at peace, I felt that I belonged, no one questioned if I was a foreigner. I understood this place, its logic and chaos, its mix of sanctity, superstition, and danger.

Back at the hotel, excited about the coming day—our first day of rehearsal—I left word for Leonardo, Tati, and Sarah to meet me in the lobby early in the morning and I retired to bed. I placed the little soapstone llama on my nightstand—much as I had when I was ten, with my little Lion Dog opium weight, and fell into the magical realism of dreams about the insides of ornate Spanish cathedrals, Incan ruins, and meanderings from childhood.

In the morning at breakfast, I went over plans with my dancers who would serve as my choreographic assistants. I called a secure cab, and we rode fifteen minutes through heavy traffic and thick exhaust fumes to arrive at the Museo de la Nación. The blocky six-story museum with dark-tinted windows has the look of a nouveau-Incan stone temple. Olga Shimazaki greeted us in the grand exhibition hall. "Welcome! Please call me 'Olgita,'" she said. Olgita was in her late fifties, about five feet tall, sparkling eyes, and olive complexion perfectly framed with a chestnut and burgundy bob. Her eyeliner was applied with a slight flare upward at the outer edges like a young Audrey Hepburn.

She led us down a flight of cement stairs to a maze of dance studios, storage spaces, locker rooms, and offices. In the largest dance studio, we sat on chairs set up for us along one wall. We watched her company take a ballet class taught by a tall thin Cuban instructor who demonstrated a quick series of foot and leg combinations. At barre, the dancers followed his lead. When the pianist played, they executed tendus en croix with sharp accuracy, stretching and pointing their feet along the floor and extending their legs with straight knees; forward, side, back, and side again. They repeated this combination a second time, twice as fast as the first. Next, they did dégagés, brushing their beautifully arched feet several inches off the floor at lightning speed.

Their frappés struck the floor, they flexed then pointed their feet, and finally, after a series of leg swings, they completed their barre with grands battements. They kicked faster than I had imagined humanly possible. Olgita pointed out to us each dancer's strengths and flaws, "She is too slow, she has incredible balance and flexibility, she needs to lose weight, he isn't musical." Sitting in on the class served to introduce us to the individual and collective potentials of the ensemble toward realizing our program. It was a review of the troops.

That said, it's not that easy to determine the performance abilities of a dancer until you see how they move across the floor. After barre, twenty-six sweat-soaked dancers walked to the center of the room poised for further instruction. Ballet's language is French at its core, but around the world its instruction is layered with other languages. In Lima it was "French-ish," a mixture of French and Spanish. The teacher said, "Pas de bourrée en tournant, paso, paso preparación y vuelta y vuelta." To the dancers this meant do a turning waltz, then take two steps, prepare, and turn, and turn again. From this simple dance phrase much could be determined about each dancer's performance ability; how they commanded space, how competitive they were, how they interpreted the music, whether they finished a phrase and commanded being seen, or if they walk away without finishing, perhaps prone to giving up.

It was soon obvious to me who were the best dancers, and I made my casting choices quickly. Gabriela, a muscular powerhouse with the unique capacity to express female elegance and masculine strength would dance *Dariush*; the long, flexible, and vulnerable-looking Mairette would dance the lead in *Fractures*; Misael, a handsome Cuban, would be the male lead; and Lesly, a fiery redhead, the other female lead. Nine additional dancers of a similar height who moved well together would be the cast of *Silk Roads*. I cast Gerardo and Carolina as the male and female leads of my new commissioned work *Acorralada*, "corralled" in English. The theme was the classic adaptation of Romeo and Juliet: a young couple whose love was not condoned by society at large. Gerardo stood out for his physical beauty and presence: black hair, probing eyes, lean, muscular, feline confidence. Carolina, limpid and graceful with buttermilk complexion and dark brown hair, possessed an unaffected repertoire of pantomimic gestures. This last announcement caused a stir among the other male dancers. Gerardo was new and had never had a lead role before. Unfair! I quashed the resentment by casting all ten of the tenured male members as the chorus. Carolina would be the sole female dancer. Rehearsals could begin.

In order to mount a full program, for the next month we worked four-hour days Monday through Saturday in three adjacent studios. Tati, Leonardo, and Sarah occupied two studios and taught my repertory pieces while I remained in the large studio with Gerardo and Carolina to work on a pas de deux centerpiece for *Acorralada* as well as to work with the chorus. These rehearsals corroborated my belief that a well-trained dancer can dance any style. I believe this is why I have been successful in choreographing for both modern and ballet dancers, because I see movement as all one art, regardless of technical style.

Dancers who have not moved together before in an intimate pas de deux require time to understand how each other's bodies work. It is a courtship of sorts. When partnering, two dancers have to locate each other's centers of gravity. A dancer's center of gravity is somewhere just above the pelvis and below the sternum. But when a dancer touches another dancer, they share a new center of gravity. It is now a point between the two. Partners become one organism that must bend and lengthen its knees at the same time, walk in unison, and figure out how to balance while holding on to each other. As Gerardo and Carolina came to understand how to move in tandem, I set a series of intertwining arabesque promenades and assisted pirouettes. They soon were moving as one.

At the end of our first four-hour rehearsal, we had the beginnings of a tender duet in which they held each other, stroked each other's bodies, and interlaced their limbs. I dismissed Gerardo and Carolina for the day and checked in on the other two studios. Gabriela was an incredibly fast learner and was already halfway through learning the vigorously acrobatic six-minute solo *Dariush*. *Silk Roads*, a work of twenty-minutes duration, was going much more slowly. They had only learned two minutes of the dance because this work relies on a sustained quality of movement that was not precisely in their training. Their Cuban ballet studies emphasized a frenetic quickness. The company was struggling to learn the steps, couched in a sinuous underwater quality. It would take the full four weeks to ready this work.

During the first six rehearsals of *Acorralada*, I decided that the group sections would represent societal pressures working against the young couple's intimate relationship. For the ten chorus dancers, I designed spatial patterns that crisscrossed the stage in military formations that suddenly shifted into concentric circles that surrounded and trapped the young couple. Dancers leapt across the stage and performed tours jetés, turning scissor movements, of the legs in the air; they turned with arms overhead and lunged menacingly forward in formation. They waltzed with contorted, angular positions of their torsos and arms and kicked their legs rapidly in order to suggest their disapproval of Gerardo and Carolina's union.

Also housed at the Museo de la Nación was the newly formed Orquesta Sinfónica Nacional Juvenil. This orchestra consisted of young instrumentalists in their late teens and early twenties. I asked Olgita if the director of the orchestra, Maestro Wilfredo Tarazona, might consider having his orchestra accompany *Accoralada* by playing the Alberto Evaristo Ginastera score live. She looked quite excited, "We have never collaborated before, but this might be the perfect reason to do so! Shall we go ask?" We walked upstairs to an auditorium on the first floor where the full forty-piece orchestra was seated onstage, rehearsing a Villa-Lobos score. Maestro Tarazona, with his back to us on his podium, dipped and swooped and jabbed his baton to indicate dynamic cues and tempi to his talented, young eager musicians.

At the end of the movement, Wilfredo waved his arms and shook his head, reprimanding each section. The abashed musicians remained in their seats as he stepped down from his platform. Wilfredo turned and saw us seated in the front row. He was in his early forties, disheveled, dour, brow furrowed in serious focus. He nodded as we approached. In front of the full orchestra, Olgita introduced us in polite, formal Spanish. She pitched the idea of a collaboration. I held my breath in hopes that Wilfredo would accept the challenge and consent to perform this piece by one of the most important twentieth-century classical composers of the Americas. After a long back and forth, Wilfredo said, "Sí." I was thrilled. For the first time in my career, I would have an actual live symphony orchestra to accompany my choreography. In the United States, this is most often simply not financially feasible.

After several choreographic rehearsals, I felt certain that *Acorralada* needed a visual arts component as well. I asked Olgita if she knew of any artists who might design some set pieces. She suggested Eduardo Tokeshi, a well-known Japanese Peruvian painter and sculptor. Eduardo blends colonial Peruvian art with an Asian aesthetic. From the sixteenth through the eighteenth centuries the Cusco School of painting evolved, a pairing of both indigenous and Spanish imagery that summed up the cultural dichotomy of Peru. Some of its recognizable elements include elaborate images of the Virgin Mary, Christ, archangels, and saints painted in yellow and red and earth tones, accented by intricate gold leafing. These paintings don't adhere to a traditional sense of perspective. Rather there is a deliberate flatness to the subjects. Eduardo expounded upon this concept and palette and combined them with subjects ranging from nineteenth-century prints by historic Japanese artist Hokusai, to current "Japanime" (Japanese Anime) characters.

One evening Tati—who grew up in Lima and is herself also a gifted painter—and I went together to confer with Eduardo at his home and art studio. He is a heavy-set man who exudes the warmth of Hotei, the smiling Japanese god of good fortune. I explained that I was hoping to add versatile set pieces that could be manipulated easily and to include platforms to walk on, tiers that could be stacked to reflect the changing mood of each scene through changing colors. I elaborated: "Bright colors would represent young love and charcoals tones would represent the menacing intrusions of a society bent against the couple's happiness." I shared with him my vision: "I have in mind the couple being elevated during certain parts of the dance, then progressively having less room on which to dance together as they were infringed upon, trapped by the chorus." He urged me to go on. "I want to show that as the group becomes more menacing, the couple becomes more isolated, having nowhere to run or hide. They are . . . corralled. . . ." My reverie trailed off. "A tall order," Eduardo said. He smiled. He said nothing more then but pulled out the chair from his drawing desk. He touched it with his muscular thick hands, turned it upside down and sideways, rubbed a spot of paint on it, inspected it, and finally said, "Tengo una idea, I have an idea."

At my rehearsal a week later, Eduardo showed up with ten set pieces. They were chair-like structures with jagged bright backs like oversized origami folds. They could be walked on, stacked, and even cleverly manipulated to dramatically change colors by pulling turquoise, red, and yellow Lycra covers off them, revealing flat charcoal and black forms underneath. In that mode, when pushed together and stacked, they conjured a desolate mountain range. Olgita and I were ecstatic. I thanked Eduardo profusely and immediately set out to incorporate these pieces.

I challenged each dancer to spontaneously incorporate a chair into the choreography. This improvisational exercise immediately abstracted the dance. It created a violent juxtaposition between the graceful young couple's love duet and the disapproving chorus. The chorus became a grotesque mob wielding lion tamers' chairs. One by one, each chorus member placed their respective chair on the stage—the ground—in front of Carolina. Gerardo assisted her step up so she could stand on the first seat; she stepped forward onto the next seat and the next, creating a path that snaked across the studio.

I asked the dancers to remove the colorful covers and to stack the chairs; Carolina and Gerardo then clambered higher and higher along an elevated serrated landscape until they stood eight feet off the ground, surrounded by a mob of ten fierce, convulsing dancers below. I asked the trapped Gerardo and Carolina to hold hands and jump into the crowd below on the final cymbal crash of the Ginastera score, "Estancia," which in South America, refers to a cattle ranch. The choreography for *Accoralada* was dramatic, telling a tale of a love that could not last under negative societal pressures. I was extremely pleased with how the seventeen-minute choreography had come together with its visual elements.

Our next challenge would be the live music rehearsals. The company had been rehearsing for weeks with recorded music. The penultimate and the final rehearsals for *Acorralada* were scheduled to be on the auditorium stage at the Museo de la Nación with the full pit orchestra. Live music adds another challenge to dance performance.

Music recorded in a controlled sound studio, tweaked to perfection artificially, does not sound the same when played live. Furthermore, the conductor must make absolutely sure that the tempi are as close as possible to what the dancers have been rehearsing. There is no margin for fluctuations. Having never worked with a symphony orchestra, I was extremely nervous about these two critical rehearsals. The dancers took their places on stage and the orchestra began to play, softly, slowly, and tentatively. They were not attacking the Ginastera score as needed. The dancers moved as if in quicksand, struggling with the slow tempi and straining even to hear their musical cues. Five minutes into the rehearsal, the dance collapsed. I said, "Please stop, Wilfredo. Can you speed the tempo and have the orchestra play louder?" My request enraged Wilfredo. He began to swing his baton at a deliberately—perversely—frenzied rate. The orchestra played faster and faster; no dancer could keep up. The musicians stopped and stared at Wilfredo, who persisted in his conducting gyrations for several minutes before he at last stopped. When he did, it was to storm out of the theater. Olgita darted out to calm him and speak sense into him. Fifteen minutes. Forty-five minutes. An hour. Then Olgita and Wilfredo returned arm-in-arm. The dancers reset and the adrenalin-fueled orchestra began to play. Now the tempo was correct, and the orchestra played with gusto.

Wilfredo's emotional outbreak had actually heightened everyone's performance. Gerardo and Carolina responded to the corrected music with their tender duet as the chorus surrounded them with ritualistic intensity. After a successful run through of *Acorralada*, the dancers seamlessly rehearsed *Silk Roads, Dariush*, and *Fractures*. After the final dress rehearsal, I profusely thanked Olgita, who had by now become a dear friend. Then I thanked Wilfredo and the orchestra, and I wished the ballet company good luck and bade wistful farewell. The National Ballet's performance was a success, and this evening of dances is still regularly performed. In 2018, the Ballet performed *Silk Roads* yet again to enthusiastic audiences, and in 2022–2023 *Acorralada* and *Fractures* return to the Ballet's performance season.

After watching the final dress rehearsal, Leo, Tati, Sarah, and I hopped in a cab and rushed to the airport to meet the seven other members of my beloved dance company, who had just arrived. My work at the Ballet now complete, the next phase of the project was a performance tour supported by the US Embassy. As the dancers embraced, I permitted myself to savor the tenderness, the buttons-bursting pride, and elation. This was a cohesive ensemble of individuals, sharing a rich identity and professional family name. I was exhausted but had to rally because the next morning we were scheduled to depart at 4 a.m. for our eight-hour bus ride to Trujillo in Northwestern Peru.

Our chartered private bus took us from Lima and drove through the relative wilderness, at last pulling up to a hotel on the busy outskirts of Trujillo. Somewhere between the bus and the hotel entrance, one of the company member's bags was stolen. If there was any silver lining, we concluded, it was that at least the pilfered suitcase did not contain any costumes or other performance essentials. We left this sketchy hotel in favor of a tiny one in the historic downtown of Trujillo. Architecture here is Spanish colonial, stucco haciendas of mustard, midnight blue, and vermillion. Large wooden doors give privacy to interior gardens and courtyards surrounded by living quarters. This necessary move in hotels would prove to be yet another silver lining, and we all turned in early.

On July 25, I awoke at 6 a.m. to see crowds gathering on sidewalks and streets. By 11 a.m. marching bands and folkloric musicians and dancers appeared. "What's going on?" I inquired of a man nearby. "This is La Fiesta de Santiago de Chuco," he said. "Each July we celebrate the Patrón of our province. Today the dance groups—the pallos, the quiayas, the Negritos, quadrilles, and the condor Quishpe—honor a warrior who was turned into a condor by a sorcerer, they honor Santiago de Chuco." Dancers in bright costumes—elaborate headdresses, masks, many adorned with large bells—stomped rhythms in sync with marching musicians. Here was the regional history of Incan Empire and Spanish conquest told in dance. Even the horses, the Peruvian Pasos, danced; the unique horse breed is trained to prance forward, sideways, backwards, and circle to the music in a range of complicated steps and gaits and caprioles. The silver lining had turned to pure gold. The festivities continued deep into the night, and I registered all of this jubilation, this dancing cavalcade, those equestrians and capering horses, in my mind's library as future choreographic inspiration.

The next morning, we rode our touring bus to the Teatro Municipal de Trujillo built in 1876. We parked outside the theater with its pink stucco façade and unloaded costumes and props. We explored the decaying theater, with its four hundred faded red velvet seats and 125-year-old raked stage. Traditionally, theatrical stages were angled downward so the audience, on a flat plane below, could see all aspects of the performance. Nowadays we build theaters exactly the opposite way, with a flat stage and raked audience seating. I had no advance notice of the angle of the stage and, standing on it, I felt like I had vertigo, that I might lose my balance and roll into the orchestra pit. That evening we would perform my hour-long dance *Tracings*. I asked the dancers to take to the stage so the technical lighting crew could set cues. The lights flickered and audibly buzzed due to the strain they were putting on the building's electrical capacity. The theater manager, a man in his seventies, wearing a frayed brown sweater with a black cat hand-embroidered on it, went by the appropriate nickname, "El Gato." I asked him if the lights were okay. "El Teatro tiene un duende en la casa," he said. Translation: the theater has a mischievous spirit. Oh boy. It would appear that we were at the mercy of that entity. Flashbacks to the ghosts of Halcyon House. Now, as then, I was sure the ghosts would be our invisible stagehands. We spent the day warming up, getting used to the stage rake, and watching the technical crew madly patch and repatch lights plugged into a vintage dimmer system that easily dated back to the 1950s.

The performance was to start at 7 p.m. and at 6:50 audience members began to enter the house. We delayed. We delayed a bit longer. By 7:30 p.m. the theater was three-quarters full. Mustering diplomacy, I asked the producer if we should start because it was already a half hour past curtain. He said, "No. *Here* we give the audience *time*." Well. Alrighty then. By 8 p.m. the house was occupied well beyond its capacity, and we were given the approval to begin.

I'm no fool. I realized we needed all the help we could get. I pulled an apple and a chocolate bar from my dance bag, and I left them both on my dressing room table and spoke aloud, "Look, you guys. I know you can hear me. This is for you, duende en la casa, please, I fervently beseech you, please allow our show to go well here . . . in *your* house." With that I darted to the wings to join the rest of the dancers. After all, you can take the boy out of Santa Fe, but you cannot take Santa Fe out of the boy.

The curtain opened. *Tracings* is an homage to three generations of my family. It is a bit like a séance. The main dancer acts as a thread throughout the piece, coming in and out and illustrating transitions. She invites the other dancers, costumed in all white, to enter stage like ghosts that emerge from the darkness and are gradually illuminated. The dancers ripple sequentially through their bodies, from their torsos outward to their hands and feet, as if sleepwalking or in a deeply focused moving meditation. The phrasing is ritualistic, each person partaking in Tai chi–style gestural phrases that toss unseen energy across the stage from one dancer to another. This is done with hypnotically sustained phrasing; the dancers move seamlessly like undulating waves of the Pacific Ocean. At one point they manipulate suitcases representing their arrival to Hawaii and line the stage with dozens of pineapple props until fields of a pineapple plantation unfold.

The middle point of *Tracings* is a duet for Tati and me. We sense each other's presence, reach out to each other from across stage, and in a controlled game of cat-and-mouse move next to each other and at last lovingly embrace. At this moment, the full cast of ten dancers, which include Tati and me, move as phantom wisps across stage as if enacting a movement meditation. The stage is engulfed in gentle waves of rippling arms and legs.

The dance ends with a prayerful processional, slow-motion unison gestures that are associated with the sequences in picking pineapple, and then a final exit. As we began this last processional the lights began to flicker. The effect was not only ghostly—and pleasing—but was as if their exit processional was lit by hundreds of tiny candles. As the dancers left stage, the lighting blew once and for all. It occurred to me, in droll relief, that for my prescient propitiation and bribery of the house spirit, back there in my dressing room, I really should have claimed the credit.

For our bows, the crew brought up the house lights since the stage lights weren't working. The audience went wild with appreciation and rose to their feet in a long and lusty standing ovation. I had been particularly worried that the agricultural immigration theme would be too foreign to Peruvian audiences and that it wouldn't resonate. However, the Japanese Peruvian history of being agricultural workers paralleled my family's experience so closely that people embraced the performance with simpatico and open arms. Audience members flooded backstage. One young audience member, a man who told us that he had driven three hours, "just to see the American modern dance company," then exclaimed, "*mágica, magical!*"

I entered my backstage changing room. I looked at my dressing table. My offerings to the duende en la casa of the apple and the chocolate were gone.

Mágica.

Back the next day to Lima, I took several days to wander Miraflores. I discovered what is now my favorite restaurant in Peru, Huaca Pucllana. It is named for—and literally built upon—the grounds of an Incan adobe temple complex that dates back to 200–700 CE. The original clay and adobe pyramid was built in honor of a protector deity. Today one can sit here on the earthy portal and look out on the ancient ruin illuminated at night.

It was here at Huaca Pucllana that a mysterious man with an Incan, Spanish, and Asian face smiled at me and I smiled back. Well over six feet tall, he gracefully walked over to my table. "My name is Johann," he said. "But call me 'Chino.'" I said, "I'm Dana, but people call ME 'Chino.'" We laughed and I invited him to sit. He had a gentle soft-spoken manner. We could have been brothers—so close were certain physical similarities—or he could have been my doppelgänger. When I listen intently to someone, I have a habit of tilting my head right and I slightly shift my left ear forward. I have since childhood in emulation of all those holy statuaries. I studied Johann's face; he tilted his head left and shifted his right ear forward. We moved as if mirror images. I gestured with my right hand as he gestured with his left. We spoke first about the spirit of the Huaca Pucllana—this sacred place in Quechua that had brought us together—then about the history of the Incas, the Conquistadors, colonial art, and finally dance.

Uncanny, *parecidos*, look-alikes. He was also a dancer. Moreover, he had danced minor roles at the Ballet Municipal de Lima. Three hours passed. The restaurant was closing. We departed Huaca Pucllana together, strolling then slowly through Miraflores feeling a seasonal chill that gave us an excuse to walk closer together, to gently bump arms. We walked to Larcomar, with its view of the Pacific Ocean. The Morro Solar cross, a giant illuminated landmark, glowed hauntingly across the bay. It was a mystical beacon over the clear sky and dark waters.

Johann took my hand as we looked out to the sea. Holding his hand felt like when I was a child in Santa Fe holding Bobbie Romero's hand in front of the San Miguel Chapel altar, feeling somehow safe and understood, a feeling of wellbeing and warmth. I felt that I had found safety with this man, that I had made my way back to the innocence and beginnings of love. Johann put his arm around me, and we kissed. Johann and I saw each other every night that week. He called me Chino, and I called him Chino. That's how I came to finally accept and love this nickname. What I thought might be a short situational fling, then maybe a fine transitory romance, became a sustaining and durable romantic love that we would nurture for several years, long distance. Johann would be a major reason why I would return to Peru over and over like a migrating monarch.

Right before returning to the United States in 2004 on that first trip, I was approached by two local dancers, Luis Valdivia Duran and Jorge Miranda, about teaching several master classes for Ballet San Marcos, a modern dance company based at the Universidad Nacional Mayor de San Marcos in Lima; chartered in 1551, it is the oldest university in South and North America. I stayed for an additional week after the company departed. I was fascinated by the draw of the historic location to be honest, and I would return to teach for longer periods in 2005 and 2007.

Ballet San Marcos functions out of La Casona, an old Jesuit novitiate built in 1605 and said to be haunted by a young priest who walks the halls that lead to his former quarters. La Casona is one of Lima's most important historic architectural sites. The perfectly restored Spanish colonial buildings in colors of mustard, orange, and deep blue are built around five interlocking courtyards, each with a spectacular garden of palm trees, local fauna, and a central fountain. The courtyards, or patios, are defined by brightly colored, two-story buildings with arched walkways on all four sides and ornate windows with dark wooden shutters. Ballet San Marcos is housed in El Patio de Los Jazmines (Jasmine plants). When I got out of my cab and stood in front of La Casona, I experienced déjà vu. With neither a guide nor directions, I walked past the guard, through the complex maze, directly to the dance studio, as if doing so were a habit.

The large dance studio was on the second floor. Skylights overlooked the jasmine garden. I climbed the stairs to the studio, entered, and met Vera Stastny, a British ex-patriate in her seventies who had been the director of Ballet San Marcos for almost three decades. She reminded me of Maida, crystal blue eyes, sharp aquiline features, and a defiant attitude. Vera and her husband, Francisco Stastny, an art historian, arrived in 1963 to Lima. He was originally from Prague but was a nationalized Peruvian.

Vera's company members and students were interested in all styles of modern dance from Graham to improvisation. But they had been trained in such a way that they all appeared rather stiff and held their bodies as if standing at permanent attention. To combat this, I taught a class that centers around exercises of visualizations of the musculature and bones of the body, in order to find and promote release.

Each day, for a week, I gently corrected students' postures in Spanish, guiding them through the correct stacking down of the cranium, rib cage, and pelvis over the legs and feet. Rolling down the spine, they placed their hands on the ground, and rolling back up they reached to the ceiling. I had them move across the studio, improvising level changes. The last combination of each day was an open movement free-for-all across the floor. It was inspiring to see the shift of their bodies from rigid and inelastic to easeful and free. At the end of class, the students thanked me, and Vera, in her cheery British accent, said, "Don't forget us here at La Casona. I came here for love, I can tell,

Lima calls you, too. If you want to come back and work with us, and I certainly hope that you do, I will get you a Fulbright." I was taken aback and at the same time was overwhelmed by the inescapable feelings of déjà vu at La Casona. I agreed to her offer on the spot. I would take a rejuvenating sabbatical from DC and return to Peru to heal from my burnout in 2005.

When I returned to Washington, DC, Vera and I stayed in touch via e-mail, and she approached the Fulbright Program Office in Lima. I returned in 2005 undertaking not one but two consecutive fellowships under their Senior Fulbright Program. The second would be in 2007. Vera was as good as her word. She endorsed me twice to teach and choreograph for the Ballet San Marcos. For both of those stints I lived in Miraflores for six weeks at a time at the La Paz Apart Hotel and worked at La Casona daily. I continued to experience a warm familiarity there, a welcoming that I have never felt anywhere else in the world. When I walked down the streets before and after rehearsals, I never felt disoriented, lost, or scared even though I had been warned many times about how dangerous the area was.

I felt I had been in Lima in a past life. Each new corner delivered me to yet another familiar street scene. In addition, I was fluidly moving between the time zones of the present and the epochal clock of the distant past. I experienced time as malleable. In the 1500s Santa Fe was the farthest reaches of the Spanish Empire, and Lima was the heart of the Spanish Viceroyalty in South America. I find it perhaps not just coincidence that the design of both is similar but on very different scales. Lima is built around grand fortified plazas; Santa Fe is also built around fortified plazas but on a miniaturized scale. I understood the historical connection between the two cities despite the difference in size. Vestiges of the 1500s were not anomalous to me; they were comforting, almost familiar.

I was often drawn to visit sacred sites, cathedrals, and convents. I would sit in regal Spanish cathedrals from the mid-1500s with looming ornate altars of silver and gold, mirrors, colonial paintings, and life-size figures of saints that sparkled in the light from votive candles and light filtered through stained glass windows. I was filled with awe and wonder, like when I was a child in Santa Fe visiting the San Miguel Chapel. I wandered the crypts of the Basilica y Convento de San Francisco de Lima, which were filled with the bones of more than twenty-five thousand people. I pinned milagros to the vestments of carved saints in the church above. At the Basilica y Convento de Santo Domingo where lay Saint Rosa and Saint Martin's remains, I learned about Santa Rosa's ability to heal the sick and San Martin de Porres's ability to levitate and his skills of bilocation. Representations of the miraculous and of the sacred body were everywhere; they were not so much extraordinary or exceptional as they were utterly normal, a natural and integrated aspect of daily life.

At lunch I ate with locals at *chifas*, Peruvian Chinese restaurants. I was never questioned, never made to feel I was an outsider. I belonged here. And here was the other thing: wherever I went, people called me Chino, as if they had known me since childhood. Here I no longer minded the nickname—I loved it, the familiarity of it, the conferral of belonging, fraternity, that it recognized. People's facial features were familiar in their mixture of Spanish, Incan, and Asian bloodlines.

I created a dance for the Ballet San Marcos to be performed in the main auditorium at the Universidad Nacional Mayor de San Marcos. *Retratos* (Portraits), a twenty-minute dance set to Spanish Baroque Peruvian music, premiered prior to the end of my first Fulbright. The dance was inspired by the Cusco School paintings that I saw at La Casona and in museums and cathedrals. I decided to choreograph a duet that included a series of static portrait-like postures of a man and woman, at times close and intimate and at other times uncomfortably formal and cold. These poses juxtaposed to expansive modern dance phrases that prefigured the many aspects of their love.

For *Retratos* I cast two talented company members from the Ballet San Marcos, Maria Elena Riera and Juan Salas, who were consistently taking my classes (and who are today senior lead dancers in the Ballet), because both were emotional, theatrical dancers who had also partnered many times. Juan's mix of Incan and Spanish features, a warm olive complexion, large eyes, and a prominent curving nose complemented Maria Elena's high cheekbones, narrow angular eyes, pale skin, and jet-black hair. Their features suggested credibly that they were stepping forth from paintings of today as well as five hundred years ago.

I began choreographing their duet by instructing Juan to lift Maria Elena over his shoulder as she did an expansive fan kick. When he slowly transported her down, she softly touched ground; I asked them to spin underneath themselves on their toes and slide to the ground. Then Maria Elena rolled on top of Juan at which point he placed his hands on her hips and assisted her back to standing. She helped him up to standing and they paused in a repose, side by side as if subjects in a formal portrait. Oh, how I was drawn to the concept of living portraits. I continued to interweave their phrases until they stopped once again in a held pose but this time awkwardly facing slightly away from each other. The pose suggested isolation trapped within the borders of a frame. And there it was again, my fascination with boundaries and the borders around a painting, and the stepping out of it. The outcome of the duet was a series of danced phrases imbued with images that unfurled the varying emotional states of their relationship.

Happily, in 2006, I was able to host the Ballet Nacional del Peru at the Kennedy Center. Olgita and four of her soloists flew to Washington where they presented six repertory works to a full capacity audience on the Millennium Stage, a small stage that presents free performances 365 days of the year. They performed duets, solos, a quartet by Peruvian choreographers, and my trio *Fractures* that were met with overwhelming enthusiasm by the audience, many of whom were Peruvian American. My creative relationship with the Peruvian dance community—the mutual giving and receiving, the reciprocal insights and influence, the collegiality of two different cultures—is the perfect example of optimal dance diplomacy. Such are enduring collegial friendships, deepened respect, and mutually enriched understandings and a knitting of sinews that only ripen and bloom with time. Audiences grow this way, too, for both constituencies.

When I returned in 2007, I continued to teach dance technique classes as well as choreography classes. I especially found profound inspiration in the depth of the dedication of the dancers of Ballet San

Marcos, as they to strove consistently to become mature artists of distinction. They have achieved their goal. Vera Stastny has since retired but her senior dancers, Maureen, Luis, Juan, and Maria Elena, continue to guide the company.

My dance company has toured throughout Peru six times over the years. We are set to return in our 2022–2023 season. My family of dancers and I continue to tour—India, Egypt, Mongolia, Mexico, Cambodia, Israel, the West Bank, Indonesia, Europe—every continent on that world atlas I used to spread out on my childhood bed in Santa Fe. We have a packed calendar of annual commissions and appearances.

Since that day, when I heard one word for the first time, and I asked my father what it meant, I have learned its deepest meaning for myself. Through art, through dance, I have experienced the entire range of emotions, intellectual, political, spiritual, and cultural exchange; I have been exposed to people of all different colors and sizes and abilities, paupers and royalties, saints and sinners: the Gamut. *The Gamut.*

Each of these experiences deepens my understanding of humanity, of our shared stories, and reinforces my belief that dance _is_ our universal language. The bronze Lion Dog my father gave me from our first excursion to that little curiosity shop still occupies a crèche on my nightstand. He is guardian of my childhood dreams of faraway places. He is my morning and bedtime reminder of how far I have traveled in my dance journey and in my interior journey, and how far I intend to still go, and to give and to receive. The Lion Dog sparked my wonder about faraway places. In the midst of my loneliness and feelings of displacement, I was emboldened to accept myself and a faith that there were places who would accept me as one of their own, if I just kept putting one foot in front of the other, taking risks, and exploring. I have traveled the longest journey of all and have come home: from being an outsider to one of being a global citizen, at last at ease, all around the world. Dancing all the way.

The First Dance Company Members, Washington, DC, 1992.
Private Collection of Dana Tai Soon Burgess.

Sarah Craft, Dana Tai Soon Burgess, *Helix* sculpture by John Dreyfuss, Washington, DC, 1998. Photo by Mary Noble Ours.

above Miyako Nitadori,
Susanne Bryant, *Vertebrae*
sculpture by John Dreyfuss,
Washington DC, 1998.
Photo by Steve Slaughter.

left Dana Tai Soon Burgess
in Mitchio Ito's *Pizzacati*,
Washington, DC, 1998.
Photo by Mary Noble Ours.

Sarah Halzack in Mitchio Ito's *Ave Maria*, Washington DC, 2009.
Photo by Jeff Watts.

Dana Tai Soon Burgess in the Swat Valley, Pakistan, 1999.
Photo by Sueraya Shaheen, Private Collection of Dana Tai Soon Burgess.

Connie Lin Fink in *Khaybet*, 2008, Washington, DC, 2008. Photo by Mary Noble Ours, Collection of Dana Tai Soon Burgess Dance Company.

Dana Tai Soon Burgess Dance Company, 2008, Cuzco, Peru. Photo by Connie Lin Fink.

top Dana Tai Soon Burgess, "Tati" Maria Del Carmen Valle-Riestra in *Images from the Embers*, Washington, DC, 2006. Photo by Mary Noble Ours, Collection of Dana Tai Soon Burgess Dance Company.

bottom Miyako Nitadori in Tracings, Washington, DC, 2002. Photo by Mary Noble Ours, Collection of Dana Tai Soon Burgess Dance Company

Kelly Moss Southall, Anna Kang Burgess, Christin Arthur in *Tracings*, National Portrait Gallery, Washington, DC, 2019. Photo by Jeff Malet, Collection of Dana Tai Soon Burgess Dance Company.

There is a mountain in Sri Lanka that is held sacred among Buddhists, Hindus, Muslims, and Christians alike. In the Sinhalese dialect of this area, it is known as *Samanala Kanda*. In English this translates as Butterfly Mountain. Every November, thousands upon thousands of *catopsilia pomona* begin to appear here in dense swirling clouds. Also known as "lemon emigrants" or "common emigrants" due to their migration pattern, they continue to arrive on Butterfly Mountain until the last full moon of April, which signals the start of the monsoon season that lasts through September. The butterflies churn in shimmering formations, dancing in the air, twirling and flirting their way up the mountain, where they will feed and breed. In the days after successful procreation, most will die. This trip represents the completion of a fleeting lifecycle that typically lasts but six weeks. Why here? This is a place of supreme sanctuary, a habitat of little pollution or threat. They are not dreaded or resented as pests. Far from being disturbed, here they are revered.

At the peak of *Samanala Kanda* stands a five-feet-eleven rock formation, on which there is a depression called the *Sri Pada*, or sacred footprint. Buddhists believe this indentation is the hallowed footprint of Lord Gautama Buddha, and Hindus believe it is Shiva's footprint from when he took the form of the divine dancer. It is a holy site, a universal pilgrimage destination scaled by thousands of visitors annually. During the dry months—December to early May—the number of pilgrims swell. As they ascend, the trekkers behold the butterflies beckoning. And under their feet, the sides of the mountain are covered with winged carcasses, thick as bright decaying leaves.

No matter which origin story one holds about *Samanala Kanda*, at the core is the evidence of the miracle of procreation and reincarnation.

The life of a fragile and yet deceptively mighty butterfly is emblematic in all cultures, of birth to death and birth again.

I learned about Butterfly Mountain as an adult. I was deeply moved by the connections the place held for me, to my childhood in Carmel and Santa Fe. There are many versions of Buddha. But Gautama Buddha was the one figured in my bedside talisman. Clouds of monarchs had swirled around me as I took my first tentative steps; they danced and circled me flirtatiously, inviting me to toddle, to walk, and finally to dance, to give chase. Like the butterflies, I am driven by some impulse that impels me to migrate, to approach art and life challenges, to create dances in an ongoing quest for individuation. Migrations of these butterflies to sacred spiritual sites are analogous to my own habitual pilgrimages to museums. Museums are my sanctuaries, to which I make humble pilgrimages, for inspiration, for sustenance. There is little, if any, separation between my creative "choreographer self" and my "daily real-life self." No matter how I might try to compartmentalize, life and art come together as one.

One of the great assets of being in the nation's capital is the variety and availability of art. In the Washington area, there is always something to nourish a seeker; Washington, DC, has more than seventy unique museums. Among the nineteen Smithsonian Institution's museums, galleries, and its National Zoological Park, ten are located within approximately a one-mile radius from Third to Fourteenth Streets. This is my haunt, my walks from the National Portrait Gallery to the National Air and Space Museum to the National Museum of African Art to the National Museum of Natural History and more. I study portraits of key figures from our American past, linking them to our present cultural conversations. I study artifacts associated with scientific discoveries and archeological digs. The Smithsonian's overall collection in 2022 houses more than 154.8 million objects. Over the years I have prowled through thousands of paintings, sculptures, installations, and Americana in search for answers to life's universal questions. But even with my near daily visits, I will only be able to view a fraction of this massive collection. It is a galaxy with several solar systems. I am its awestruck voyager.

The year 2000 marked the start of a restless twenty-year journey; my regular cross-pollination of choreography with private and public art became less episodic, more formalized. I accrued some metrics of my own, of performances, premieres, collaborations, audience following, and reviews. During these two decades I would build more than forty new dances: a thick portfolio and a reputation for doing the sort of deeply satisfying work that made me very proud. Commissions and collaborations brought me success, audiences, and recognition in this new hybrid space.

In this era I built and sustained warm relationships with gallery directors, curators, artists, and museums—contacts that were both brought to me and that I sought out. They came to see my works, in rehearsals and performances, too—dance works that were, after all, outgrowths of their own collections. These collaborations, we together discovered, added breadth and dimension and a novel new kind of dynamic art experience for their visitors. Everyone benefited.

One of my most formative migration stories of this period took me to Hamburg, Germany, in 2000; this journey helped me understand more deeply why I was so drawn to galleries and museums, both public and private. This trip also gave me the opportunity to explore and identify with my father's German ancestry, an unexplored recondite fraction of my hyphenated American identity. In Hamburg, I met the man who would become a role model, the renowned expat American ballet choreographer John Neumeier. He had built a museum around himself in which he could happily and creatively live and work. He would express his interior world into an exterior art collection, keenly designed as his incubus and fortress, to protect and inspire his creative process.

"Why don't you accompany Sarah and me to Hamburg this summer?" said Polly Craft, mother of my company dancer, Sarah. "We're going to attend John Neumeier's Nijinsky Gala and meet up with him as often as possible. We're going for two weeks. You and he really should meet." As a teenager, Polly, already a talented ballerina, danced in John's nascent works when he was barely in his twenties. This was back in Wisconsin, decades before he had moved to Germany and became an international choreographic superstar.

Polly said that Sarah and my friendship was akin to the one she shared with John. "Seeing all these important performances set by a choreographer at his prime, and being able to meet him, would allow you to see how he crafted his work and world," she said. "You would see firsthand how a vastly successful career in dance is sustained over decades. You'd see how one can actually balance prolific output with a rich life." Among the first things a dancer learns is the restraint and discipline needed to avoid stepping on a partner's toes. In the same way, coltish eagerness can make it hard not to step on another person's words. This was one of those times of necessary pause. I restrained myself with some difficulty until she had finished talking. I was ready to say, "I would love to!" before Polly could finish her question, "Can you clear your calendar? We depart in late June." I rescheduled all my teaching and rehearsals in that midsummer trough; this was not difficult to do in Washington, as locals escape the summer heat and the onslaught of the tourist season. Dance studios slow to a crawl in these steamy months and don't resume their normal buzz until after Labor Day. This was Serendipity, indeed.

Before locking the door to my 350-square-foot apartment, I took a last look at the futon on the floor and bare white walls. My eyes settled finally on one surface: a small black-and-white, twelve-inch-by-fourteen-inch poster, one of many that had originally advertised the premier performance of my dance company. With that, I headed to the airport with the same faded duffle bag I had originally used in my move from New Mexico to Washington. I was thirty-two years old.

This was my first trip to Germany. I knew so little about this side of my family. I had never met any of them. My great-grandparents on my father's side had emigrated from Bavaria and the Black Forest region to America in the mid-1800s to escape hunger and to own a piece of land where they could build a home. It was my hope that after this trip I would also even better understand my father.

This would be the twenty-sixth annual Nijinsky Gala, named after the legendary Polish dancer and choreographer Vaslav Nijinsky, who was a luminary of the Ballets Russes. The gala consists of a week of performances of John Neumeier's repertoire danced by his company,

Hamburg Ballet, as well as those by a select few invited international companies and choreographers. At the grand Hamburgische Staatsoper, the Hamburg State Opera House, with its almost 1,700 seats sold out night after night, we savored performances of John's *Othello, A Midsummer Night's Dream, A Cinderella Story*, and many others. Each of his ballets was masterful detailed storytelling, moving at times from a near motionless duet, focused and delicately shaded, to a sudden rush of epic full chorus in thematic movement variations that swooped across the stage.

In 2000, John had created his life's masterpiece, and the premiere of the eponymous ballet, *Nijinsky*, was the highlight of the Gala. It told the story of the iconic dancer's rise to stardom and eventual decline into schizophrenia and obscurity. The ballet begins with a representation of Nijinsky's final dance in public in 1919 and then moves through tender allusions to his signature choreography and dance roles in *Scheherazade, L'Apres-midi d'une faun*, and *Les Noces*. The audience rose to its feet after the premier of *Nijinsky*, clapping in unison, demanding multiple curtain calls.

John had trained his Hamburg Ballet dancers to move with fluidity and then to cunningly freeze in sustained poetic tableaux. This visual start-stop effect—as if the dancers turned to marble, then resume motion—is among John's signature pedagogical trademarks. The rush of a male chorus—the magical birds that live within Cinderella's tree in *A Cinderella Story*—that flock around the heroine, waving their arms as wings, suddenly settle to poetically present her with a pair of slippers. In *Othello* the chaos of a brutal battle scene is juxtaposed with a poignant, minimalist love duet between Othello and Desdemona; the couple tentatively take hands and circle each other in an exquisite slow-motion walk before finally embracing. This freeze-frame of sculpted poses accentuated narrative emotion, and none more potently than that of vulnerability. John knew how to focus audience attention on telling human details—barely discernible micromovements—too often lost in the momentum of dance, especially on a grand stage.

On our third night at the theater, we were invited backstage at intermission to meet John, an elegant man, fifty-nine years old. His white silk canton shirt collar peeked over the top of a trim black suit. John served us German sparkling wine, Sekt—delectable and refreshing—and gave us detailed assessments of how he felt the evening's performance of *Othello* was going. Too soon gentle bells signaled that intermission was coming to an end. As we thanked him and prepared to return to our seats, John said, "Why don't you stop by my apartment tomorrow at 4 p.m. for cocktails?" We eagerly accepted.

Polly declined to join us, wanting Sarah and me to meet John by ourselves. We walked from our bed and breakfast to John's apartment building, a grand Beaux-Arts foyer, warmly suffused with the indirect sparkling illumination of a large crystal chandelier. We walked up a curved marble set of stairs that led to a small landing with only four doors: two large doors for residents and two small doors for maid or cook service. Locating John's large front door with ornately painted gold molding, I pounded the bronze knocker twice. John answered the door himself, an open bottle of Piper-Heidsieck Rare Champagne in hand. I thought of the dancing and leaping reflections in that faceted foyer chandelier, so like the bubbles in a glass of Sekt or Champagne. We entered his apartment congratulating him again on the prior night's performance of *Othello* as well as *A Midsummer Night's Dream* from two nights prior. He answered in his quiet voice, "Oh yes, you liked them, then? I am so happy to know that. Now, forgive me, please, just look around . . . feel free to enjoy and wander about. I am speaking to a dance writer friend just now in the other room. Done soon." John retreated then to the dining room to join the writer. A maid in uniform approached and said gruffly, "Deine mantel [Your coat]." We each handed her our coat.

John held court in this sprawling apartment, a theatrical backdrop and stage. Every square inch of twelve-foot-high walls was covered floor to ceiling with priceless art and framed ephemera of great dancers and choreographers of the past three hundred years—programs, tickets, correspondence, photos—illuminated by the natural light that emanated from four large windows that overlooked the street. His home was, in fact, a museum. Turning around and around, ogling high and low all the art around me, I felt as if I were floating among myriad effervescent bubbles in a bottomless flute.

Two works in the foyer caught our eyes. The first was an original 1917c advertising poster designed by Pablo Picasso. It depicted one of Picasso's costume designs for the ballet, *Parade*, choreographed by Léonide Massine—a ballet in which Massine also danced the role of the Chinese Conjuror. Picasso's stylized design was of a dancer in a Chinese *cueue*—a long braid—shown in a vivid red-and-gold Chinese jacket with the words Théâtre du Champs-Élysées, 13–27 Décembre below its feet. Next to it was an original 1911 Ballets Russes poster designed by Jean Cocteau: a deco-style lithograph of Nijinsky, costumed and in mid-pose, on a rich green background. A gold text band above the image read: "Théâtre des Champs-Élysées; Direction Gabriel Astruc."

The maid returned to us with heavy crystal flutes of Piper-Heidsieck and motioned us forward. Each of the rooms lay before us to explore. Gold-leaf frames outlined autographs and personal documents of Vaslav Nijinsky, along with sketches he had done during his decline into mental illness. Here, too, was Léon Bakst's 1910 costume designs on paper for the Mikhail Fokine ballet *Scheherazade* steeped in an Orientalist perspective of billowing harem pants, turbans, and scimitars in the colors of deep blue, sienna, and gold still vivid.

And there were watercolors by modern Russian American painter Abraham Walkowitz of Isadora Duncan in motion, arms raised and feet afloat, defiant dances inspired by the ancient Greeks. Walkowitz had met Isadora Duncan in 1906 at Auguste Rodin's studio. Those reminded me of a line from her famous 1903 lecture in Berlin, "The Dance of the Future," which became a manifesto for modern dance. The line went like this: "I might make an example of each pose and gesture in the thousands of figures we have left to us on the Greek vases and bas-reliefs; there is not one which in its movement does not presuppose another movement." I had first read the lines of Duncan's lecture in my dance history course at the University of New Mexico almost two decades prior to this moment. The concept was so powerful that her words had always stayed with me. And now, here she was, her words animated in portraiture.

After a few minutes voices mingled in leave-taking, and the writer waddled toward the foyer, nodded in our direction, was reunited with his coat by the maid, and departed, and John soon joined us. Sarah and I expressed our awe at his home gallery. He was pleased and proud of his exhibits. "These days, I hire art scouts to scour auctions wherever they might be, worldwide; it has become my wish to acquire the best works of art and dance memorabilia, the better to round out my collection."

I was truly and utterly in awe, every icon I had learned about in Professor Bennahum's dance history classes at the University of New Mexico were here on these walls, as if they had leapt out of textbooks for my inspiration. I had been in galleries and established museums, but John's comprehensive personal curation of rare dance artifacts was revelatory for me. The potential of a residential space to provide focused, creative energy through the art and ephemera it showcased was a potent take-away. I loved museums but they were separate from my life and work as a choreographer. Yet here was a man whose passion, his life and work were so intertwined that he had to create his own museum, and he got to live in it, work in it, draw his inspiration from it, and to share it. "Prosit!" Cheers.

The phone rang and John was called away once again. Sarah and I migrated to a sitting room. There we perched in the corners of a cinnabar-hue velvet Victorian couch. Next to me was an étagère filled with bronze statuettes of Nijinsky, Baroque Meissen porcelains of dancing figures. I peered through the glass, feeling the same wonder I had as a child with my father in the Gamut. But this was a profound and discerning collection curated over a lifetime, the evidence of a sensibility steeped in key historical milestones of dance history.

Sarah and I peered out at the dining room, taking in the richly grained Biedermeier dining table for twelve from the 1840s. Atop it were an outsized silver Victorian vase filled with fresh flowers and a porcelain figurine of Anna Pavlova, the Russian prima ballerina of Ballets Russes whose portrayal of Mikhail Fokine's *The Dying Swan* is still the standard today. Beyond in a sitting nook at the windows facing the street stood a two-foot-tall bronze statue of Nijinsky in the role of *Harlequin* poised atop a four-foot-high green Connemara marble pedestal.

I had been let into the very wellspring of a museum collection. In fact, John had recently negotiated a tremendous deal with the city of Hamburg. John planned to build a museum that would not only house his collection but that would also be his residence—as resident master of his collection—until his passing. At that point, his collection would be bequeathed in perpetuity to the city of Hamburg.

I considered my practical and minimally appointed efficiency apartment back in Washington, my futon pressed in perilous adjacency to the mini eighteen-inch-wide gas stove. This was the same stove whose broiler served as my only warmth in the winter when the radiator was all too often cold. I lived in a single room; my decorations consisted of my little Buddha, the Lion Dog charm, my small company poster, and a dressing mirror. And my tiny closet? It was crammed with props and costumes. My flat was a place to crash and from which to dash to a dance studio. I had moved so often as a child that I was comfortable living as a nomad, with all my funds poured into my art. This was, after all, the life model my parents had presented.

What more was dormant inside me artistically that I was holding back? Had I defaulted on my potentials, occupying no more space than a mouse hole, a troglodyte urban cave dweller? Time spent in contemplation of John's domestic world, and how it fed his artistic one, changed my romanticized notion that artists should "struggle and starve," or that living in extreme asceticism, in poverty and hunger, somehow validated and elevated my art. Really, how did Vincent van Gogh's work improve by dint of his starvation?

I vaguely recalled then something I had once read from letters Vincent wrote to his brother, Theo. It was something like, "If only I might have a strong bowl of soup, I feel my work would be better." I was completely and eagerly willing to continue to make any and all sacrifices toward realizing my art. But at this point, thankfully, my living in such self-denial seemed unnecessary; in fact, I now realized, it was depleting of what I needed most to be and to do my best.

On this pilgrimage to meet John Neumeier, I came to embrace a new conviction: artists should be honored in society, as they are the keepers of humanity's legacies. I dream of a world in which "starving" is not the immediate synonym or crossword puzzle clue for "artist." Sarah must have tapped into my thoughts. She often did so. She said empathically, "I think my mom wanted you to see this place because she believes in you, she sees something similar in you and John. She wants you to succeed and expand your vision for what you can be. In fact, I think she sees us as a repeat of her youth somehow, her friendship with John when they were young."

John finally joined us, sat, quietly sipped his champagne, as we sipped ours, and then said to me, "Dana, I would like to invite you to teach a modern class in my school. And I would like for you to show my students your Michio Itō solo, *Pizzacatti*." Polly had obviously spoken to him about my teaching, choreography, and the Itō dances. Two days later I would teach a modern dance class. In those intervening two days, I studied and memorized my class lesson in German, to demonstrate to John how aware I was of this opportunity and my commitment to excelling in it and investing in his students' success.

My class took place at the Hamburg Ballett's Ballettzentrum—the ballet school—a five-story brick building designed by the late Fritz Schumacher, Hamburg's "building director" from 1909 to 1933. He opposed expressionism and embraced the *Neue Sachlichkeit*, or New Objectivity, utilitarian architecture. His imprint is still seen in the police stations and other bureaucratic headquarters. Originally a girls' high school, now this structure with nine enormous dance studios was Ballettzentrum Hamburg Balletts-John Neumeier.

In one of those large studios, I taught twenty students, all thirteen–sixteen years of age, as John sat and observed without ever interrupting me. They were responsive and quick; they loved my novel perspective because they had been training in the classical Martha Graham technique with Frau Schinckendantz and, as young people, were likely somewhat weary of her class format. John was especially interested to watch as I danced the Itō solo. After class he peppered me with questions, "Where did you grow up?" "How had you learned the

Itō repertoire?" and "Tell me about your work and the life of a young choreographer in the States."

He was fascinated by my Asian American sensibility and knowledge of Itō. I answered his barrage of questions; perhaps I was a curiosity of some kind, a connection to the dance scene in America from which he had defected decades earlier. John had been a Hamburg outsider who had created a world in which he could be the ultimate insider. He felt my hunger to do the same; I was the young artist he had once been. He quietly asked, "Dana, next week, would you like to sit in on my rehearsals?" I eagerly said, "Ja bitte, danke schoen!" In his warm smile, I imagined my father would have been pleased that Germany was embracing his son and that his son was embracing Germany.

John's company rehearsals took place in the largest studio at the Ballettzentrum. On this particular day, John would be choreographing a new duet for two hours and then separately, for an additional hour, he would check in on how a large ensemble section from his Nijinsky ballet was looking. He wanted to ensure that this chorus section wasn't losing its performance edge, its technical and emotional crispness, which can occur to choreography after being performed multiple times. Dancers can fatigue, and often need movement notes from the chore-ographer or a rehearsal director to maintain their clarity.

John's rehearsals only started when his full artistic team was com-pletely assembled. In the case of choreographing a new duet, this didn't just mean the two lead dancers chosen to dance the roles. This team included a secondary cast consisting of two additional understudies. Present also were two rehearsal directors, a videographer, a pianist, a sound technician to stop and start the stereo system, and a "choreolo-gist," a person who notates the choreography, the actual movements of the dancers. His choreologist was trained in Benesh notation, a system invented in Britain by Joan and Rudolf Benesh in the late 1940s. Benesh notation uses little stick lines that are sketched left to right on a five-line staff, to represent stances of the body, with vertical lines representing time. This notation is similar to modern staff music notation and can be placed next to a musical sheet so that the movement notation aligns with the musical accompaniment. We don't use this system much in

America. We use another standardized system developed by Rudolf von Laban called "Labanotation." It uses abstract symbols that are written on a vertical three-line staff, from up to down. I don't use either system, though. I have devised my own idiosyncratic system of stick figures with jointed articulations, little arrows that imply movement directions and sketches of spatial patterns as they would appear from a bird's eye view of the stage. This individuality of course defeats the purpose of others being able to decipher my notes, but I enjoy my peculiar shorthand notation, nonetheless. My system serves me and my own work far more naturally than were I to try to adapt either of the other conventional notations to my intention. I was really fascinated to sit next to the choreologist to see if there might be any correlation to the stick figures I draw in my notebooks in rehearsals and when I am inspired by a work of art that I see in a museum.

I was so engrossed by John's methods that I forfeited sightseeing with Polly and Sarah to instead observe John for the next week. This intense sojourn into John's artistic process marked a turning point in my own professional methodologies. For example, up until this point, I had run everything in my own rehearsals. I videotaped when needed, I pressed "play" and "stop" on the stereo system (such as it was), and I took all the notes, often while composing in real time. John was so much more focused, having long since delegated ancillary tasks to others. Going forward, I would not step into a rehearsal of my own without an assistant or two. But there was one big difference, likely a selfish one: I would not employ a choreologist. I adored the process of jotting down images in correspondence to movement. I loved it jealously, I craved it, far too much to ever surrender it. I wanted my hands on it.

I learned the dimensions of John's synchronization of his dancers and his accompanying music. For example, he would listen to a few counts of music, show the dancers where to move an arm or leg, and then he would back the phrase up so the music and discrete dance steps could be repeated. He would then continue forward by adding on four to eight more counts of movement and start again from the top of the phrase. This was different than many ballet and modern choreographers who in general set long 32- or 64-count phrases for the dancers or have the dancers improvise to curate and set movements developed out of their experimentation.

John's process resembled the game Twister. Out of this movement-by-movement game came clear choreography that wound into a knot, and then he would untie it movement by movement again. At the end of the two-hour rehearsal, an entire duet with unique interlacing movements perfectly melded with the music. Because it had been built so painstakingly and so closely with the counts of the music, it felt like a complete duet. The choreography didn't appear to need editing and the dancers didn't need additional coaching in musicality or quality of movement dynamics. John's was a process that could be used for not only ballet but adapted for any dance form, including modern dance, applicable to many scenarios. I was thrilled to consider how to build new duets and even trios and quartets in the future with this process.

After dismissing the four dancers, his artistic team remained awaiting a cast of more than twenty male chorus members. The double doors swung open and the young men poured in, placing their sweatshirts and dance bags on the floor along the back wall of the studio, and quickly assembled into uniform starting formations in silence and awaited instructions. Here I took note of something else about John's approach. John never raises his voice. His extremely polite manner, no emotionality, resembled my own. Taking note of his classroom demeanor made so clear to me that speaking softly commands more attention from dancers than does a raised voice.

The impact of this approach was unforgettable for me watching it play out during this rehearsal. The chorus was readied to rehearse a large section of his ballet *Nijinsky*, a section set to the music of Dmitri Shostakovich. This was thrilling because I had seen the work performed on stage and I was curious how it would look without costumes, theatrical lighting, and sets. This was the jewel of the gala, the namesake ballet that had premiered two nights prior, and would be performed again this evening as well as at the close of the gala. This particular section was the most complicated, an important arc in the ballet representing Nijinsky's decline into madness and his incarceration within a mental asylum. It demands unified chaos from the chorus, individual movements suddenly coming together in unison with a crazed passion and frenetic speed and accuracy. The music commenced over the stereo system and the dancers performed the ten-minute section.

At the end of the section's run-through John remained silent. The two dozen dancers waited for his notes—approval, direction, displeasure. John said not a word. He rose from the bench upon which he had been sitting. Then somewhat portentously, he stood on it, above the group. This established, among other things, that he would not be coming toward them. In a near whisper, he said, "Please come closer." The dancers took tentative steps forward. He repeated softly, "Please come closer." The dancers crowded around him. In a voice that soothed but at the same time suggested defeat, he said, "I don't believe that you are embodying my choreography. The energy is not right. How can I help you?" The dancers were shaken. They so respected John. Out of the ensuing prolonged hush, a male dancer said, "We are very sorry, Herr Neumeier. We can do better. Please, give us another chance?"

He stepped down from the bench, sat and pursed his lips—an implied, albeit skeptical consent—as the dancers scurried back to their starting places. John nodded to the man operating the sound equipment and the room filled with Shostakovich's searing and slicing score of death and life. Fear-spiked adrenalin had infused the dancers' energy as they matched their imperative to the score. The dance looked like completely different choreography, transformed by focus and momentum. At a crescendo in the music, the dancers stopped, remaining in place, nervous to move before John released them. John rose and said, "Now I do surely see and feel my choreography." The dancers relaxed. John whispered to himself, "Sehr gut, Ja, sehr gut," almost inaudibly. The message "very good, yes, very good" seemed to have escaped unbidden; when he realized I had heard him, John pursed his lips once again, turned to the dancers and said, "That will be all for today, you are dismissed. Vielen Dank." The dancers courteously bowed in respect to John and left the studio.

With each rehearsal I became more keenly aware of the symbiotic relationship between John's ambient dance imagery and his chore-ography. Gestures, torques of the body, poses of the torso in art and photographs he curated in his home had infused into his own work. For example, an extended section of Nijinsky was an adaptation of a series of portraits that John displayed in his apartment, done in 1912, of Nijinsky dancing *l'Après-midi d'un faune*. Nijinsky had choreographed and danced in this ballet set to the music of Claude Debussy. John had reanimated those memorialized signature movements, decades later. I wanted this symbiosis, too, this complete connection of home, to art and daily life.

Polly, Sarah, and I returned to Washington. I resumed my teaching and rehearsing schedule refreshed and inspired. I also continued to examine my one-room apartment, so devoid of art or proper furni-ture. A furniture store just across the street from my apartment was having a big going-out-of-business sale. The next week, I splurged on a contemporary three-foot-square glass dining table and a faux white-and-gold Louis XV chair, I slogged each piece back individually, and began to set up my nascent sanctuary. I assembled the table, and then squeezed it between my closet door and the front door. Here I could sit, focus, and spread my choreographic notes out on a proper surface. In a gold-colored frame I purchased up the street at Rite Aid, I tenderly tucked a black-and-white portrait of Michio Itō performing *Pizzacati*, taken by Japanese American photographer Tōyō Miyatake. Tōyō's family still had the original photographic plates from which they made this photo and all others; the Miyatake family had sent me this photo from their studio in California, which, in 1923, he had originally founded. I hung it on the sliver of white wall above the table. These small shifts in my space reflected a major shift in my consciousness.

At the end of this first visit, John made sure to invite me to return the following year for a month-long residency during which I would teach and set a choreography on the advanced students of his company. I did so and I stayed in the guest artist quarters at the Ballettzentrum. I set a new six-minute work titled *Shanti* on six students, an explo-ration of modern dance partnering techniques that expanded their vocabulary. But my fondest memory is that of guiding the students through the creation of a site-specific dance for—of all things—the Ballettzentrum's main stairwell.

Urging the young dancers—who were, after all, kids—to embrace the freedom of running up and down stairs, improvising, doing their favorite movements in an exploration of multiple vantage points, vertical ones as well as those that involved peering and poking and dangling around corners in a kind of dancers' equivalent of, say, cubism: this was the DNA of choreographic modernism. We were probing the partially visible, questioning and redefining traditional sightlines and reoccupying spaces in nonconforming ways. I got as much rejuvenation out of this project as they did, performing their choreographic study informally, for a class of twenty younger students, seven- to ten-years-old.

There was something in the electricity of that day that made me consider the personal freedoms that a ballet boarding school takes away within the guise of a strict curriculum. This rigidity of the daily focus and on the large conventional stage could no doubt build an excellent ballet technician, but perhaps it sacrificed and censored the best parts of childhood and the creative impulse. I thought about being a child in Santa Fe, wandering through the desert, studying plants and animals, feeling the wind in my hair and sun on my skin, how much this freedom to roam unhindered, to be sensate, had formulated my art. How a forfeiture of that natural unbound freedom would have cost a tremendous amount of creative impulse and outcomes. The fire within would not have sparked. The frisson of having to make mistakes and live in the hurly-burly tumbles of life—and not in a boarding school—was crucial to art creation. Strictures serve technical execution, perhaps, but they snuff out imagination. At the end of my residency, I thanked John and we spoke at length about how well the students responded to experimenting with choreography and improvisation. He seemed quite pleased because he was deciding upon changing the offerings at the school somewhat, updating and modernizing classes.

Upon returning to Washington, DC, my career took off. And in 2001, the Dana Tai Soon Burgess Dance Company opened the modern dance season for the Kennedy Center for the Performing Arts. I would be touring and working on new commissions now, which meant sacrificing a return residency in Germany. In 2004, I would reunite with John backstage at the Kennedy Center Opera House when Hamburg Ballet toured John's *Nijinsky* to the United States. John and I planned to see Polly and Sarah Craft at their home the day after that triumphant performance.

In the years following our Hamburg visit, Polly had become bed-ridden with a recurrence of long dormant cancer. She would soon be in hospice care. I picked John up from his hotel and we drove to Maryland, talking all the way about his ballets. He was very pleased with his company's performances but longed to return to Hamburg so he could continue work on a new ballet of the Hans Christian Andersen tale "The Little Mermaid." John would premiere his ballet in 2005 on the Royal Danish Ballet, a specially commissioned work to commemorate the two hundredth anniversary of Andersen's birth.

Upon our arrival Sarah greeted us and led us to Polly, who was reclined on the couch. John held her hand and they reminisced about dancing together over four decades earlier. They spoke about his new choreographies and his company's performances of *Nijinsky*—all conversation led there—and that dancer's end station of schizophrenia. Polly reflected, then, on her own hallucinatory terminus: "John, I had a dream that I was a beautiful black colt. I had leg muscles and I could push into the ground with my hooves, feel ground under my hooves as I galloped faster and faster. I jumped. I flew in the air as I used to in the studio with you when we were so young and starting out. Somewhere in this deteriorating body is dance, is a knowing of sensation that endures within."

John squeezed her hand in sustained acknowledgement that this was the last time he would ever see his friend and dance partner. Then the two entwined and caressed each other's arms, shoulders, tenderly and wordlessly. He then gently, weightlessly, curled over her, sheltering her beneath butterfly wings. What I took in there, mesmeric and unforgettable, was the ultimate rendering of his start-stop choreography: life in real-time was informing art. I was privy to the unplanned eloquence in this freeze-frame, a stationary ballet of life cycle, a real-life and wrenching, wordless, soft pas de deux of farewell.

We said our relatively banal group goodbyes—words were impotent, in fact, profane, compared to their final dance. I drove John back to the Kennedy Center stage door, where he slipped into the sanctuary of a dark theater. Polly passed away a few months later. Sarah retired from the company and from dancing in 2005. She has since moved to Ithaca, New York. I am the godfather to her daughter, Valentina, who studies musical theater. I will forever love and appreciate the Craft family for welcoming me into their lives, and for having such a meaningful and transformative impact upon my own—for dancing with me.

twenty NAM JUNE PAIK AND THE
ELECTRONIC SUPERHIGHWAY

In 2008, I went on one of my routine visits to the Smithsonian American Art Museum in search of choreographic inspiration. In the Lincoln Gallery, which houses contemporary sculpture and painting, I
heard the distant cacophony of a radio or television set. I followed the
sound, much as I had the day I discovered Carlisle Gymnasium at the
University of New Mexico. I came upon the installation I had been
looking for, *Electronic Superhighway: Continental U.S., Alaska, Hawaii,*
a piece by Korean-born video artist Nam June Paik. This forty-by-fif-
teen-foot media amalgamation is constructed from more than three
hundred video screens and flashing television sets, outlined in colorful
tubular neon lights in the shape of each of the fifty states. Within each
neon-outlined state, the TV monitors broadcast a loop associated with
that state. For example, images on monitors within the neon shape of
Alabama played news scenes from Martin Luther King Jr.'s Birmingham
Campaign. Nearby within the neon-outlined rectangle of Kansas, film
highlights from the *Wizard of Oz* played.

I felt an inherent confusion overload about America's identity, about
the identity of "the great experiment, the American union" as I experienced the sights and sounds emanating from fifty individual state identities. How was the viewer supposed to filter through all this material?
It seemed the image of America had become shaped by not only real
events but also created characters and images that have accrued and
infiltrated our consciousness. Then what of the individual identity? Of
a Korean, American, biracial, Santa Fean, gay choreographer? What did
people perceive of me when they looked at me? Conversely, how was I
filtering through images associated with each of my parts? Perhaps we
are all being culturally programmed to make assumptions about others,
a nonstop, pulsating barrage of media, historical events, and romanticized Hollywood versions of stereotypes that clog our porous minds.

Nam June Paik is an artist my father admired greatly and about whom he had spoken much to me growing up. Since then, I had wanted to view his work. Paik is called the "Father of Video Art." He had a complicated self-identity. Paik's father was called a *Chinilpa*, a derogatory Korean word for an ethnic Korean who collaborated with the Imperial Japanese. In 1905, the Korean Empire became a protectorate of Japan, and in 1910 Korea would be annexed by Japan, a rule that lasted until 1945. When Paik was eighteen, he and his family fled Korea in the midst of the Korean War, briefly moving to Hong Kong, then to Japan. He then studied in Munich with the Greek musicologist, pianist, and philosopher Thrasybulos Georgiades. In 1964 he left Germany for the United States and was introduced to "family car trips" on the original superhighways, the ones that offered everyone the freedom to, as one ubiquitous television jingle of the day exhorted, "See the USA in your Chevrolet!"

Paik fell in with an international band of alternative and avant-garde artists and friends in the 1960s and 1970s who lived in Europe and America and who called themselves Fluxus. Members believed that process and experimentation with no boundaries was more important than a "finished" material product. They aspired to art that required engagement and not passive viewing. Throughout his life until his death on January 29, 2006, Paik pushed audiences to ponder the place of technology in an ever-turbulent society.

Paik's story, his work that expressed his vantage point informed by personal experiences of displacement in both the East and West, resonated with me. When Paik passed away his artwork continued as his artistic voice, as if his thoughts had been downloaded to his sculptures as everlasting artificial intelligence. I was consumed by an idea to create a dance that would interact with his prodigious videos. I envisioned projections of his work on the backdrop of a grand stage while my choreography would be danced in the foreground.

I couldn't find any information for reaching Paik's estate in order to obtain permissions to incorporate his videos in a new dance work. One day I was discussing Paik's work and my predicament with my dear friend, Terry Hong. Terry is a Korean American activist and author. She works for the Smithsonian Asian Pacific American Center (APAC), a nonprofit national museum center that shares how the Asian Pacific American experience informs history, art, culture, and literature. Her blog, BookDragon, started in 2009 and showcases books and author-related profiles, the majority of which are by and about Asian and Asian Pacific Americans. Terry has an extensive arts network, and, lo-and-behold, Terry and the now executor and nephew of Paik, Ken Hakuta, were old friends. She gave me Ken's phone number.

Ken had made a name for himself with his syndicated television show, *Dr. Fad*, which ran from 1988 to 1994. I had read a profile of him and about his show in the *Washington Post*. The show was geared to six- to twelve-year-olds, and on this platform he showcased the scientific inventions of children.

"Hello, Mr. Hakuta? My name is Dana Tai Soon Burgess. I'm a choreographer. I have a dance company, Dana Tai Soon Burgess Dance Company. "I often create dance that relates directly to visual art. I go to a lot of museums looking for my next inspiration. I was just at the Smithsonian American Art Museum and was taken by the exhibit of Nam June Paik's *Electronic Superhighway: Continental U.S., Alaska, Hawaii*." I took a breath after that. "He was your uncle, yes?" I pushed ahead. "I'm inspired to compose a modern dance that interplays with his videos—I would be celebrating his art. So, you see, I am seeking your permission to access and incorporate some of Nam June Paik's film-based art into a new dance."

He said, "I know who you are! You're that Korean guy who choreographed *Tracings* at the Kennedy Center in 2003." We chatted warmly then, the ice now broken. "I made a donation to the Smithsonian Asian Pacific American Center and earmarked it to specifically support your dance." I was shocked. I clumsily thanked him profusely for having done so. Up until his spontaneous eruption, I'd had no idea that he had been the secret sponsor of *Tracings*. Those were precious and timely funds we received from the Smithsonian, to support dancers' salaries for the performances at the Kennedy Center. He was one of those financial angels who never drew attention to their gifts. I was utterly gob smacked. Had I not made this call, I might never have known.

Ken then continued, "By all means, do come by my place at five or so today. Can you? I love new ideas!" He spun out his address, which I quickly jotted down.

A few hours later I was in the Cleveland Park neighborhood of Washington, in his home, a red brick art deco–style mansion from the 1930s designed by architect Waldron Faulkner. This was the same renowned architect whose firm, Faulkner, Kingsbury & Stenhouse, had from 1964 to 1968 renovated the Old Patent Office (which had originally been built over a thirty-one-year span from 1836 to 1867). The building was renovated from 1964 to 1968 to become two museums, the National Portrait Gallery and the Smithsonian American Art Museum. I searched out information about Ken's home on the Internet following our initial meeting . . . and . . . Oh . . . my. It would seem that his home's architectural lineage, so embedded in Washington history, might also be related to the concept of home as museum, and museum as home.

I rang the doorbell on the imposing bluish-green patina double doors. A maid answered and ushered me into what I guessed to have been an almost 10,000-square-foot residence, into an open living room with Shaker chairs, lean contemporary couches, and walls that were a reverential exhibition hall of large-scale sketches, collages, and paintings by Paik.

At the very end of the long room, at a large wooden table with a view of the vast backyard garden sat Ken, who had positioned himself with some stagecraft. He was a slight man of about sixty, with jet-black hair and thick silver wire-framed glasses. Ken had made his fortune in the 1980s by buying the rights to a Japanese toy, the Tako, or Octopus, for $5,000 and rebranding it as the Wacky WallWalker. When flung against a wall, the sticky gummy-rubber toy with multiple octopus "legs" would adhere, and then, moved by gravity, appear to "walk" down. He reportedly sold more than 240 million of them worldwide before the fad declined; various media outlets at the time said that he had taken in about $80 million. Marketing was Ken's art, everything from herbal health supplements, bottled teas, and antiques. Ken conjured the childlike alchemy of an ever-upbeat Midas aiming his "What if I try THIS . . . ?" to turn the everyday into gold. His generous grin reminded me of Ebisu, the Japanese god of prosperity, always portrayed as a man carrying a fishing pole and red snapper under his arm. The grinning guy at the end of the table, in his bright tropical shirt and khakis, was the incarnation of this optimistic fisherman, making his own good luck, casting his hooks into the sea, and reeling in his prize catch projects.

Ken lost no time. "Please, have a seat. What's up with your idea for a dance?" he said. I pulled up a pine Shaker ladder-back chair with a woven fabric seat and joined him at the table. "First, thank you so much for meeting with me. So . . . here is my vision: I want to make a modern dance that addresses how we view our identities, and specifically hyphenated Asian American identities. And further, what does it actually feel like, to be inhabit that middle space, ever pulled between tradition and modernity? I want to somehow incorporate your uncle's art in that choreography."

By 2008 my troupe had consistent fall and spring seasons of mixed repertoire and one major premiere of a new dance each season. We moved between varying venues in Washington, including the Kennedy Center. Audiences were alerted to when and at which venue we would be performing through our electronic newsletter, advertisements in local newspapers, and pre-performance press stories. This particular fall season we would perform in late October at the 1,500-seat Lisner Auditorium downtown. I envisioned that this was where we would present the debut of this new work, and I told him so.

Ken's answer came readily. "My uncle loved dance and performance art, anything new and intriguing. So, sure! Why not?" He then gestured in the direction of his landline telephone, in the shape of a Mickey Mouse standing in big yellow shoes. On the base were push buttons for dialing; Mickey's white-gloved mitt was the cradle for the handset. "I'll call my guy who handles all those copyrights, archives permissions, and fair-use details, and so on, and give him thumbs up. Use whatever you like for the dance."

Thrilled, I still had some sliver of bandwidth to wonder: why would he not have more naturally pointed to his chest or back pocket—a mobile phone—to dramatize intent to set our deal in motion? Then the realization: doing that would have been too obvious and not fun for him—or for me, his guest. The artist's nephew was entertaining me with his own performance art. I loved this guy now even more. For Ken, this—our byplay—was a duet. I had asked him to dance with me, and he had accepted. The choreographer, me, was being choreographed by him, on his stage. Who was leading whom? I was having a ball.

That topic settled, he blurted: "So . . . mood rings. I'm thinking of bringing them back. Remember them from when you were a kid? Would you buy one now?" I stammered, then gamely answered my playful benefactor, "Yes, I had one as a kid. What's not to love, right?" He rose and I followed. "Hey, take a look at some of my uncle's work. Great, right? These collages of glued-on newspapers and crayon sketches. Hey, and this sculpture, too." I was struggling to keep up with his ebullience and joy at having a playmate.

The tour concluded, I thanked him profusely for his crucial and enthusiastic support as he saw me to the door. "Sure, sure, talk to you later," he said, drawn now by the impatient summoning rings of Mickey. By the time I got home, indeed Ken's "guy," curator of his uncle's trove, had already e-mailed me. I had access to the films!

Synergy asked Serendipity to dance.

Losing no time, the curator and I set about sifting through online archives. I narrowed the choices to three of Nam June Paik's earliest silent, black-and-white experimental shorts, each only two to four minutes in length: *Hand and Face* (1961), *Button Happening* (1965), and *Cinema Metaphysique* (1967–1972). These best depicted self-portraiture, discrete images of Paik's youthful face, torso, and gesturing hands. Each gave insight to a young Asian American artist's quandary: how might he fully accept his body, his own image, in the context of a Western society that often portrays Asians in fixed and oversimplified stereotypes, stigmatized or reductionist ways, and always marginalizes the Asian. To be sure, Asian women had always been reduced to tropes—an object for the taking, coy temptress, seductress, or schemer. But I was interested now in the particular Western stigmatization of Asian males, historically and perpetuated in present-day America. Indeed, beyond mere acceptance, how might the artist in fact peel those imposed Western projections and tainted, adulterated perceptions away, to locate, embrace, celebrate, and love the authentic, actual Asian self?

At the time that Paik made these films, living in Germany and America, he was somewhat a serial anomaly—Korean by birth, lived in Japan, moved to Germany and then to America. His was an identity of many hyphens. Did he consider himself Korean, American, European?

My own dilemma was in always feeling bifurcated. And my core question was this: does the hyphen connect or actually separate? As a Korean American I did not feel fully accepted by American culture even after generations of family members who had lived their entire lives on American soil. Was I placed within the confines of the cliché, "model minority" myth? This was one of a monolithic shorthand, the lumped together group of overachievers—like exaggerated cartoon versions of accomplishment—who excel in STEM, beneficiaries of the bounties of America, but who, nonetheless, were treated with suspicion and bias, relegated by American society as perpetual foreigners, others, and who rarely attained leadership roles in that society.

And what of a Korean American artist, a profession that didn't fit into this trap? Had my "outsider" profession in any ways saved me from this model minority categorization? Was I an anomaly like Paik? And if so, then what?

The complications of the hyphenated identity posed an artistic challenge on a multitude of levels including logistical. How, then, to integrate the choreography so that at no point would the video projections or the choreography overpower or subsume the other? This collaborative media and dance hybrid work itself was, arguably, a hyphenated beast, right? An artist—me—wrestling to create one unified piece of artistry from two "hyphenated" sources. That irony kind of thrilled me. In wrestling to achieve some equipoise between the two, my challenge would be deeply about a hyphenated new work, something I was using as more than a set or background. But it was also going to be about achieving a balance between portraiture in motion as well as movement.

After studying Paik's films, my first move was to convene my eleven company dancers, seven females and four males. I had always been sensitive to hiring culturally diverse dancers. Beyond their technical gifts, I had selected each member in my company for their continual struggles to be accepted in America. Virtually all my company members had stories of identity disjointedness, as immigrants and as the offspring of immigrants. Their artistic interpretations of my work, their collective abilities to connect emotionally with the choreography I create, steeped in images of otherness and to move audiences to deeper awareness and reliability, had always been integral to whatever successes I had enjoyed as a choreographer. It would be especially key to creating and pulling off this work.

So, this initial gathering to discuss the project came as no surprise to any of them. I asked each to share their personal immigrant experiences and their ancestors' stories. I asked, "How do you self-identify?" The answers: Japanese, Korean American, Taiwanese American, Cuban Ecuadorian American, Swiss living in America, Peruvian, Irish American, Korean adoptee, and "Heinz 57." I asked other questions such as, "How did you or your family come to America?" and "How old were you?" "What is your biggest struggle as a dancer in America?"

Katie's words capture a common thread, "I was born in Korea but was adopted at the age of one by my Caucasian parents who live in New Jersey. I feel as if people make a lot of assumptions when they look at me, preconceived ideas from ingrained images of the past, of 'how Asians look.' These images usually outweigh how I feel about myself: I am an American from New Jersey. People tell me all the time, 'You speak English so well!' I don't even speak Korean!"

Priceless stories, priceless material.

At home that evening I read through my copious notes and sketched out a choreographic plan. I envisioned battles in dance that adapted the martial arts katas—the highly organized and celebrated dance steps of conflict—I had learned twenty-five years ago as an identity-conflicted teenager in Santa Fe. This dance would depict the never-resolving identity and cultural struggles associated with displacement. It would, in fact, reflect my own point of view: identity struggles never really are resolved conclusively, satisfactorily. I scrawled across a page what would be the title of this dance: *Hyphen*.

When the dancers joined me in the studio for our first rehearsal, I had them work through a movement phrase I had constructed of arms and hands slicing, sharp leg kicks, and abrupt drops to the floor. I had the whole cast learn this initial martial arts–like phrase, and then I divided the cast into four couples and one trio. I assigned one person in each couple to perform the phrase in slow motion and instructed their partner to improvise, to trace the outline of the other's limbs with their hands as they slowly performed the phrase. Once this task was done, I told the duos that they could perform at any speed they liked, fast or slow.

Because these dance partners had an open choice in deciding how to trace the limbs, what evolved were four varying duets related to each other by the original common phrase but ultimately looking very different due to the dancer's tracing choices, speed, and even the dynamic range used to do so. For the trio I incorporated John Neumeier's meticulous process of building through the game paradigm of Twister, one movement added at a time. "Move your arm here, stop, now you extend a leg here, stop, now you press your hip against him here, now perform together. Good! Let's continue." This slow add-on component process created a completely different trio, one that didn't trace around limbs, but which instead interlaced bodies.

Over the next ten rehearsals I kept working on the duets and trio. They grew longer and more complicated, until at last I felt that I had enough coordinated movement material to consider spatial patterns. I directed the dancers through the space, intricate pathways, and patterns, at times zig-zagging the stage and at other moments orbiting one another like galactic planets and suns. This process created a nonstop flow throughout the studio, a constant interplay of attacking arms and legs investigating positive and negative space and of intricate interlocking limbs.

I wanted a sense of mayhem and confusion that would reflect the unsettled internal emotions of the dancers' stories. I layered the work over and over again with choreographed dance attacks and near misses. For example, at the instant a dancer appeared to be in line to receive a kick, that dancer dropped to the floor in bare aversion, then pushed up to resume standing, punched out with two hands, which in turn were averted by their opponent-partner.

Two Korean American dancers dueled: athletic Connie chopped her arm toward Katie, who ducked just in time for Connie's arm to sail by her head. Katie then turned and kicked at Connie, who dodged her leg by rolling to the floor. This attack and near-miss phrasing continued throughout each duet. I then linked the duets and trio with locomotive phrases—runs and premeditated walks and lunges; the studio came alive with narrowly avoided collisions. I added a new unison phrase, a circle of the head and neck, a backwards run, a spin into a lunge that led to a handed stand—legs sailing in the air until landing on the floor. This group unison phrase repeated several times during the dance, appearing suddenly. It was the representation of unison from chaos, adding unexpected order to the chaotic staging.

I next returned to Paik's films in search of gestures to layer over the movement phrases, to bring a connection from the stage background projection to the forefront. Paik's film *Hand and Face* portrayed him covering his facial features with his hands, obscuring the parts of his face—eyes, nose, and lips—clues to his cultural identity. There is an implied underlying shame in the way Paik masks and compartmentalizes his features. I loved how the viewer could infer from his simple gestures the turmoil his fragmented identity caused him. I added these gestures over the top of the dance phrases I had constructed and timed them with the video projection. In this way, the dancers synched-up with the video. They appeared to dance in unison with Paik.

After three months of rehearsing, three days a week, four hours each day, the dance began to crystalize. I could now begin to think about the inclusion of props. I added a television set on wheels that played Paik's films, assigning it to a dancer to wheel about stage in-between her movement phrases. This was my tribute to Paik's favored medium and also played with the idea of scale on stage, a huge projection in relation to a small moving image.

But with one month of rehearsals left before our premiere, I felt something was still lacking. It gnawed at me that I hadn't yet addressed Katie's unforgettable statement about how people made assumptions about her because of their preconceptions built upon historic images of Asians. I thought more about this battle between tradition and modernity. How do outdated images of Asia—or any culture defined by their facial features or their skin color—create the intractable struggle that hyphenated Americans deal with today? There was something I needed to add to *Hyphen's* staging to clarify this concept. I had Nam June Paik's modern videos; I even had a television set on stage! But I needed to juxtapose these to representations of antiquated "tradition" so that they might achieve their full collective impact. I sought a local resource for such props. And that source would prove to be easily within my reach. Literally.

In the eight years since first having met John Neumeier, sitting in his private museum, I had altogether changed my concept of "home" as a Spartan efficiency. Dance had been good to me. I had been able to save some as well as to keep investing in my company. I had purchased an efficiency at a real estate market low and during a real estate boom flipped it to purchase a large Beaux-Arts apartment that I fixed up, built equity, and sold in order to purchase a three-bedroom house in the Palisades neighborhood of DC. The art of moving had afforded me the space to collect antiques—not dance memorabilia—Asian antiques and Asian American memorabilia that reflected parts of my interior world. The art on the walls now included nineteenth-century Korean Shaman and Ancestor paintings and an original 1870s print of San Francisco's Chinatown. The floors and surfaces showcased an array of classic Asian vessels, ranging from multipurpose baskets to oversized iconic lacquer Thai Buddhist temple offering bowls.

I sat in my living room, which had become my sanctuary, pondering "tradition." I realized that I had the perfect stage props for *Hyphen* right in front of me, curated for a few years. Many of the items were oversized—perfect to be seen by audience members seated at a distance. I examined my inventory: what most captured "tradition?" Containers. Vessels that existed to be filled over the course of one's lifetime, with items to be carried from one place to another, a metaphor for the cultural histories that we each carry within us and for the immigrant trek. First, I chose a red, three-foot-tall round classic wedding basket from China, its three interlocking tiers held in place by a bamboo handle. Next, I chose a large table-serving steamer basket, designed to hold cha sui boa—steamed buns filled with sweet pork. I added to my props a three-and-a-half-foot-tall Burmese wood lacquer temple offering box, and then a vermillion oversized Thai rice bowl—two feet in diameter and eighteen inches high. Two scarlet bamboo baskets, both three feet high—one Chinese, the other Korean—rounded out my "prop shopping." I loaded these emblematic treasures into my car and took them to rehearsal.

They would serve their purpose, and they would add colorful antique contrasts to the frenetic contemporary choreography and Nam June's stark black-and-white images. I introduced the objects to the dancers, and I asked them to consider opportunities in which they might interrupt their phrases by manipulating the large props. It was time for them, in this piece, to interact—hands on—with art. To bring those artifacts to life through touch. Might they, say, use their hands to pretend to fill the vessels with unseen grains of rice, or portray bathing their faces with invisible water from within a given vessel? These intonations, incantations, created a collage of relationships to the past within the focal point of the present. The items were vestiges of an earlier time, symbolic repositories for cultural histories that loomed even in the midst of modernity.

Soon thereafter, I pondered: how will all this mesh now with music? Unusual for me, I had saved for last the decision of a musical component for this twenty-minute dance. I called my good friend Laura MacDonald for help. Laura, in her early forties, had been a gifted dancer for several modern dance companies in the United States before retiring from the stage to assume a successful career writing computer programming and overseeing websites at the NASA Goddard Space Flight Center in Maryland. She had helped me with music before. She was an aspiring composer and tech wizard who understood the connection between pulsating electronic music and the natural pulses of the human body, and she was keenly gifted at applying those insights in the portrayals of dance.

Laura came to rehearsal several times in order to parse carefully the structure and rhythms of *Hyphen* before we discussed my interest in a score that was not only contemporary and electronic in nature but that also could speak to the dancers' personal histories. A tall order to fill. All my disparate elements—silent films, props, choreography, and music—would have to be underpinned by her score.

Everything came together when two days later she returned with a concept. Laura proposed to incorporate the dancers' individual voices, telling their stories, in the composed score. Her concept recalled for me the ways that NASA astronaut voices, like Neil Armstrong's, for example, carried simple words home, to Earth, electronically, disembodied from across the vast unknowns of outer space, simple words of feelings and sights, meanings now deepened and made poignant because of the vast distance between "them"—others, speaking of experiences we could only imagine but not inhabit—and "us." Her concept was pitch perfect genius.

Laura pulled out a recorder and interviewed the cast, "As a hyphenated person, do you feel the hyphen connects or separates?" "Where are you from?" "Where do you fit in?" "How do you self-identify?" Over the next two weeks, Laura wove their answers into a sound score that contextualized the whole dance. To hear Miyako say, "I was born in Japan and now I live in America, but people don't think I am an American"; and Connie say, "My father is white and my mother is Korean, I'm something in between"; and Katie say, "I was born in Korea but grew up in New Jersey"; and Ricardo say, "I am Cuban Ecuadorian American" animated the theme of the work. Their voices added a personal relevance to the fraught cultural anxiety of *Hyphen*. Laura took these interviews and mixed them into a driving electronic score and delivered the final version a week later.

In the first musical rehearsal, everything clicked, all the refinements and polishing we needed to finalize *Hyphen* began to fall into place. Over the next six rehearsals we cleaned the dance; the dancers' confidence and their investment shone. *Hyphen* was complete in mid-October 2008, one week prior to its premiere when costume designer Judy Hansen delivered a set of streamlined, gray-toned costumes: charcoal jersey pantsuits that she had not only designed but had also personally constructed. This strategic unified color would make the dancers appear to have walked right out of Paik's projected black-and-white films.

My associate director, Kelly Southall, supervised the rental of a huge projector with a wide-angle lens that could project a giant fifty-by-twenty-foot image onto the cyclorama, and with that element secured, we headed to the theater. *Hyphen* had its premiere on October 24, 2008, at the Lisner Auditorium in downtown Washington, to almost one thousand audience members who had come to see our regularly scheduled fall season performances. The production had been supported by foundational and governmental grants as well as angel investors nurtured by my board of directors throughout the year.

Hyphen was completely different from the other works on the bill of my mixed repertoire. *Meditations* was serene, a dance for three couples, one I had originally set on the Ballet Memphis; another was the solo *Khaybet*, the solo I created about a woman's emotional journey portrayed from under a veil that I created when returning from Pakistan and the Afghan borderlands. I also programmed *Chino Latino*. This was an upbeat work based on stylized cumbias and salsa steps, set to Spanish music from Latin and South America. The work referenced the history of Asian communities living throughout the Americas. In its own way, *Chino Latino* also spoke to hyphenated, transplanted, and transfused identities, but with a percolating positive-accentuating take.

But the work that brought down the house was *Hyphen*. I had come upon a perfect way to close the dance, I thought, and tonight would either prove me right or wrong. After the twenty minutes from start to finish—as the dancers continued in movement struggles—the curtain is abruptly and purposefully closed vertically, a statement that the struggle for clarity of the hyphenated identity is never resolved. The crowd went wild wanting more and rose to their feet.

This turned out to be the last performance I would watch from backstage in the capacity of performer. As an encore, I danced a modern take on a tango with Tati Valle Riestra in *Chino Latino*, a duet that I had choreographed to Carlos Gardel's tango, *La Hija de Japonesita*. I had been reducing my stage performances for the past several years, as I had several male company members who were entirely capable of taking on those roles. From this time on, I would be backstage only as choreographer, rallying the troupe, overseeing technical details, and meeting with press and the VIPs who had helped to keep our company growing. I didn't mourn leaving stage. After more than twenty years of dancing on stage and juggling all the intricacies of choreographing, I now prepared to step into my next stage, as a full-time choreographer and company director.

But what a high note on which to mark that milestone transition in my career.

Hyphen toured to New York City in 2009 at the Jack H. Skirball Center for the Performing Arts as part of an evening of my work presented by the New York University Asian/Pacific/American Institute. In 2009, we also toured three cities in Mexico with the support of the US Department of State. In 2012, just days after returning from a tour of Jordan, we would perform *Hyphen* in the Kogod Courtyard as part of massive visual projection "happening" at the National Portrait Gallery in conjunction with an exhibit titled *The Kyopo Project* by Korean American photographer CYJO. The project explores identity and immigration through the lens of Korean ancestry. CYJO's portrait of me standing in a black t-shirt, jeans, and cowboy boots became part of the permanent collection of the National Portrait Gallery that same year along with a portrait of ubiquitous mainstream leading man and Korean American television and film actor Daniel Dae Kim.

I had met CYJO in 2007 when Terry Hong had made an introduction. Later that year I had received a query from CYJO to photograph me; I agreed and went to New York City for a photoshoot at her midtown loft studio. I had almost forgotten about the portrait until she informed me that it would appear on the walls of her exhibit next to that of Daniel Dae Kim. The critical success of her exhibition not only brought a deeper understanding of the Korean diaspora but also a new broader audience to my own work.

Hyphen is still relevant in 2022 as America struggles with making an inclusive place in its mainstream for diverse and hyphenated cultural identities and—if—and then, how—to build equity for all voices. For me, *Hyphen* is a milestone of a new movement and choreographic structure that answered a creative challenge, one that deepened the investigation of my own identity. It is a fulcrum of my hyphenated identity.

twenty-one CREATING OPPORTUNITIES, CREATING ART

The years 2008 to 2010 were an intense period of building the infrastructure of the Dana Tai Soon Burgess Dance Company. I used these years to reinforce its foundations and construct strong walls of support to ensure the longevity and wellbeing of my burgeoning ensemble and our repertoire. We were in a major artistic growth spurt, doing more and more performances, which was straining our scaffolding. In order to keep up with demands, we expanded from a six- to an eleven-member board of directors. The board now included individuals with specialties not only in dance but also in business development, public relations, marketing, law and contracts, visual arts, fundraising, and education. We also hired business consultants to assist us in assessing the strengths and weaknesses of the organization, and we created a new four-year strategic plan with clear action items and milestones. Of key importance were the guidance of arts-management guru Michael Kaiser; our dedicated executive director, Nicole Hollander; and our development director, Bianca DeLille.

During a board retreat, one discussion focused on my artistic goals for the next decade. I had an epiphany—a clear understanding of my migratory path. I had grown up surrounded by visual artists, and my most successful and gratifying choreographic works had all been directly related to visual art. Why not focus on placing my choreographic process and performances in those very venues where the best visual art is housed . . . museums? Gallery as stage, visitors as audience.

Historically modern dance has had forays into museums. These include Trisha Brown's historic *Walking on the Wall* (1971) at the Whitney Museum of American Art, in which her dancers utilized rigging and harnesses that actually allowed them to defy gravity and walk along the walls of the gallery, and Merce Cunningham's *Museum Event No. 1* (1964). This was performed at the Museum des 20. Jahrhunderts, in Vienna, Austria, a dance designed for alternative spaces outside of traditional theater settings. The dance was shorter than an hour, had no intermission, and fit into a specific museum space.

But these and others have been "one and done," performances that periodically made it into museums but did not create consistent ongoing relationships among choreographer, curator, and collection. Dance had still not sustained a place at the table, in part because previous choreographers' core visions were not aligned with the ongoing connection between visual art and dance, but also because the institutions themselves were not interested in creating a permanent place for dance within their fortress walls, walls that contained heavily insured world treasures and the mother tongue of "legalese," legal liability. This could be a dance on a mine field.

Although I understood and communicated with dance producers all the time, the world of museums was an enigma. Through introductions via my board, I spoke with several curators at public and private museums. But they did not oversee collections I sought to work with. Rather these were market-research conversations to better understand an industry that was alien to me. Curators and art historians were the keepers of these citadels. They seemed to view their museum spaces as sacred shrines of stasis and me as an intruder. I was asking for animating movement to be included routinely, in a place where relics had traditionally been stored undisturbed.

Furthermore, the connection between art as commodity and the relationship of the collector/donor to a museum held no parallel in the dance world. For example, a collector of Edvard Munch's paintings will experience an increase in monetary value of their collection when the market demand is higher than availability. Part of what drives this demand and valuation is the inclusion of Edvard Munch paintings in museum collections. Value goes up when an artist's work makes it inside a museum's sacred walls, because the brand receives a special institutional stamp of prestige as well as international tourism dollars. But here is where the dichotomy between dance and the visual arts becomes crystal clear. Dance cannot be sold at Sotheby's, it cannot be coveted in a private collection, or stationery, hung on a wall for a century in a museum. Thus, its market price cannot easily be quantified and manipulated into currency by the millions in the way a painted or sculptural work can. This makes dance the undervalued country cousin, an underdog of the art world.

When it came to the battering down of the doors of a museum, dance is akin to David in the biblical story of David and Goliath. But here was I, David, knocking on the door, politely. And what is more, I did not aim to knock down the gargantuan beast. I had come courting. Instead of a slingshot, I brought flowers. I wanted to dance with him. I wanted us to set up housekeeping together, in his house—his many houses—and to invite all sorts of our mutual friends and families.

I had the desire to invest in the convergence of visual arts and dance and had done my groundwork, and although the journey for long-term entrée to the museum community wouldn't be a simple one, my board and I decided that it was time to craft and implement a plan to topple the giant. I visited collections and identified a short list of art, artifacts, and eras that spoke to me artistically, that I found inspiring, and could lead to a dialogue with curators and historians through a residency situation. An invitation to the front rooms and a seat at the dinner table. I was not interested in just placing a dance in a museum; rather I was looking for a structure that would enrich and inform a dialogue about the art itself, thus leading to the creation of choreography that was an informed and thoughtful response to art, and which, I argued, would re-enliven that art and revive museum attendance among old and new constituencies. Static art as inspiration to create dynamic new and original art.

We systematically researched museum collections and drafted for each gallery a short list of what I thought might be compelling and smart, timely, and in keeping with the mood and setting for the works in discussion. These packages included the company's history, a statement about my personal interest in that collection, and a list of my previous choreographic works based on visual art and their critical reviews.

Only when fully prepared did we track down the identities of the appropriate curators and scholars. We then set about learning a bit about their predispositions and affinities and further individualized our packages, the better to position ideal dance projects and to establish the many ways they might see a stake in this for their institution. I did not want to do just any old project—this was always about a mutuality of energies, pitching dance projects that could augment upcoming as well as permanent exhibits. We framed my campaigns as invitations, to step with me into my vision, to imagine how an original dance could increase their attendance. How exciting it would be for a visitor to happen upon a rehearsal or view a performance in an exhibition hall. We e-mailed, sent letters of introduction, and called upon small private museums as well as large museums.

I reserved for myself the task of making the personal approach, and I opened conversations with a dozen DC museums and galleries. These conversations were uphill battles at first, as we knew they would be. I met resistance from museum curators and staff who felt they or their museums were not equipped to deal with public dance performances. Others demurred, saying much as they liked the idea, the potential for dancers moving in their galleries and accidentally damaging the art was just too high. They invoked liability, insurance riders, injury, security overtime, and all the "but what ifs?" disaster scenarios. They predicted bureaucratic resistance: even if they liked the idea, there was going to be pushback up the chain. "It's not me, mind you. It's all those other people." One curator gritted her teeth as she exclaimed in a Connecticut accent, "We couldn't possibly have dancers in the galleries. Not possible. Imagine, now, just imagine them with all their kicking and prancing, knocking over a priceless sculpture or crashing into a Renoir." I explained that dancers trained their whole lives to understand their bodies in relation to space and that they would be the safest individuals to have near artwork. In fact, they would be of less risk to the priceless properties than, say, the average student on a field trip or a too-curious adult. But my response fell on deaf ears. Another curator said, "We just don't have the budget to pay extra guards to be on duty for public performances in the exhibition halls." I proposed a remedy: "Perhaps a dance aficionado could make a donation to pay the guards' salaries." Her response, "If there is a private donor out there, I would undoubtedly recommend that those funds be dedicated to the upkeep of the facility and further acquisitions, before paying the guards to oversee some kind of visiting dance show. Besides we have a wonderful lecture series, where historians explain the significance of our collections."

But some I could tell didn't really believe or like what they were compelled to say. Most of these people were in the art world because they were people who cherished creative projects of all kinds. They wanted me to help them get to where they wanted to be. They were leaning in for the winning arguments. Bring on the bullet points. I got busy getting better at framing my pitches. I built up the incentives for them and I flicked away their straw men of resistance.

Overall, in the beginning, the curators and art historians seemed more interested in the security of their collections and insurance policies than how to accomplish onsite performance programming that thoughtfully aligned with and illuminated their exhibits. I had anticipated resistance, particularly in respect to the potential of art being damaged. But most museums evolved from a Victorian anthropological mandate and sensibility: viewing was a formal occasion; and a museum's mandate was to house safely and securely the "primary tangible," the artifact record of humankind. Dance was intangible, somehow transitory and lesser, not really real. Dance is not to be taken as seriously—"aesthetic" versus its marginalized country cousin, "kinesthetic."

But for me museums were my hangouts, my lairs, my treasure islands. The word *gallery* for me was a synonym for *clubhouse*. And they were also sanctuaries. And not just mine. They belonged to everyone. I had come to see their resistance as my challenge. And if not mine, then whose? I had to somehow convey to curators that I understood and upheld their missions, and that such a synergy of artistic forms could elevate the experience for visitors even further. When I felt deflated by my mission, I was like a Santa Fe outsider once again. But this time, I was an adult. I was experienced, I was equipped, and I had a conviction worth nourishing. And modesty was not going to serve this conviction. I had a track record of success. I had distinguished credentials of my own, and reviews, and was coming to them at least as a peer and colleague. And I was going to challenge the system. I tapped into my martial arts training for this purpose. In martial arts, one moves the opponent's energy and momentum back to them, refusing to receive it. One does not behave as if seeking to promote a battle—quite the opposite—that is why it is termed an art. The core tenet of all Japanese martial arts, and especially aikido, is something called *sen-no-sen*. In this framework, the martial artist comes prepared to initiate a response well in advance before the anticipated attack can gain traction. What better artistry to employ in my outreach to reluctant visual-art defenders at museums? My task would be to establish viability, to dismantle their trepidations by showing them that I understood their concerns and come prepared to provide solutions. And because I did, I think it helped me to win many over.

Of course, these overtures came in the midst of me running a company that had rehearsals and theater engagements. Like all of us, I still had to pay my bills and the dream-chasing had to tuck in as I could do so. Still, I did my daily appointments and outreach, pairing an upbeat tone of retail imperative with faith and patience. I knew in my heart that if we just kept contacting museums, stayed with the plan of introducing me and my work that I would get a break, that there must be someone inside one of these citadels that understood the cultural significance of dance. All I needed was one foothold. If destiny is one big crapshoot, then I was Sky Masterson in *Guys and Dolls*, betting his future on a fateful roll of the dice, praying as he tossed them. "Luck Be a Lady Tonight," and it turned out she was.

After months and months of conversations, out of all the no and never responses, there came a resounding yes!

In 2010, the Corcoran Gallery of Art was an independent institution, with a longstanding mission to celebrate and encourage "the American genius." The Gallery occupied a massive Beaux-Arts building across from the White House grounds at Seventeenth Street NW near Pennsylvania Avenue. Since 1869, it housed a distinguished collection that had grown to include works by Childe Hassam, Edward Hopper, John Singer Sargent, and scores of other artists from eighteenth-, nineteenth-, and twentieth-century America. This was the American terroir of venerable domestic art.

By this time, unfortunately, the Corcoran was best known for a controversy. In 1989, several corporate boards of trustees and US representatives put pressure on the director of the museum to cancel its planned exhibit, *Robert Mapplethorpe: A Perfect Moment*. They argued that the images of same-sex couples, consensual sexual bondage, and full nudity would horrify the public. The exhibit moved to a small display space run by the nonprofit Washington Project for the Arts. In fact, I viewed this exhibit in 1989 when I stumbled upon it in Chinatown on one of my weekly art excursions: black-and-white photos of flowers, nudes, and subculture sexuality. The Corcoran's decision to cancel this exhibit due to political censorship damaged the museum's future, put its board in chronic crisis management mode, and, ultimately, in 2014, George Washington University would purchase the building and break up and disperse its fine collection. Now it has been renamed and rebranded as George Washington University's Corcoran School of the Arts and Design.

But in September 2010, I received a call from Sarah Newman, the vivacious curator of contemporary art at the Corcoran who was familiar with my *Helix* dance from a decade earlier. She responded to an introductory call I had made in late 2009, pitching my work as well as a dance company rehearsal residency. Sarah is known in museum circles to be enthusiastic and innovative in pursuit of new ways to engage audiences and to be quite open to experimentation. They had a dazzling exhibition, she said, of the deciduous work of Spencer Finch, a Brooklyn-based artist. The exhibit, *My Business, with the Cloud*, had as its central piece a site-specific twenty-foot "cloud"—myriad shards of blue cellophane pinched together by clothespins—suspended aloft, fourteen feet above the floor, in the museum's second-floor gallery named the Rotunda. Natural light shown through the Rotunda's domed skylight, providing cloud-filtered indirect illumination. Finch intended for this "cloud" to reference a moment in 1863 when American poet Walt Whitman and President Abraham Lincoln crossed paths at that intersection. In fact, the poet and the president frequently did exactly that. Visitors walking underneath the work were invited to imagine the dispersed dappled light as it had likely appeared during Whitman and Lincoln's convergence.

After tantalizing me with the description of this central piece on display, she urged me to meet her there. "Dana, look, I want you to come see the cloud, to just pace around the Rotunda, stroll under it, experience it above you," said Sarah. "You just might be inspired to create a dance associated with Finch's installation, to be presented by us, in this space." She had taken my proposal and run with it, toward me. This was now also our intersection. I was walking on . . . clouds. And so I set off to join her at the Gallery. We ascended the Corcoran's grand white marble staircase, flanked by marble neoclassical statues, to the Rotunda. "I'm looking for someone who might take on the challenge to create a performance related to Finch's exhibit. You're actually the first person that came to my mind—a choreographer who might find Finch's work and this space of some shared narrative energy and interest," she said. "Don't you?"

Viewing the cloud, I was first struck by its impermanence. It was pieced together in such a tenuous way that it surely would not withstand the moment it would have to be uninstalled. Sarah was right. Boy was she right. There was a beauty in its intrinsic ephemeral identity that fascinated me. This was a chance to work with a sculpture that was not marble, not bronze or fiberglass but deliberately created for short-lived viewing.

There was another terrific element to this proposal as well: an element not overhead but, rather, underfoot. The Rotunda, approximately one hundred feet across, had a smooth wooden floor well suited for the bare feet of modern dancers. The modern dancer seeks out floors that will not grip or grab the toes or torque the ankles when the dancer swivels or turns. They need surfaces that, when the foot perspires, won't cause slipping but rather will work organically with damp-foot duet, supporting a stability of motions. I could practically feel my toes inside my socks and shoes, wriggling and urging me to take note of their ten unanimous votes in favor. The "ayes" had it.

The project posed three challenges. The first was how to create a dance in the round. The second, how to create a dance that implies and sustains a relationship with an installation that hangs well above the dancers' heads, out of their physical reach. And third, how to braid the first two challenges into a thematic connection to the year 1863. But those were merely considerations, and not at all reasons to decline.

"Yes, yes, I get it, I see it, I feel it. I accept!"

With that, we went forward. She did not need to consult others. Sarah and I mapped out a rehearsal schedule for the next two months. I told her that I would need to rehearse with my company regularly in the Rotunda. We agreed that at the end of that period, we would perform three public shows in the Rotunda in December. We shook on it, and hugged on it, in reciprocal congratulations and exhilaration.

For the next eight weeks, my studio was to be a round room void of my usual studio mirrors, with Finch's installation floating above. To prepare for rehearsals I began to research the American psyche of the 1860s, a time of deep conflict between the North and the South, locked in bloody battles over the abolition of slavery. Civil War fatalities reached over 618,000. Death touched every American's life in 1863. Washington was populated with wounded and maimed soldiers.

I listened to music composed in the 1850s and 1860s and decided upon a suite of songs by American composer Stephen Foster, considered by music historians to be the father of American songs. These were the same songs that I had often listened to as a child of four and five on my battery-operated record player. *Songs by Stephen Foster*, a compilation, recorded in the early 1970s, had been a Christmas gift from my father. I loved being lulled by and singing along with the soothing mezzo-soprano and baritone voices, the piano, and melodeon. Foster had written "Beautiful Dreamer," "Ah! May the Red Rose Live Always," "Linger in Blissful Repose," "Jeanie with the Light Brown Hair," "Wilt Thou Be Gone, Love?" and so many more. His were melodies that many generations knew by heart. They were sung on porches and in backyards and bedsides, easily harmonized by nonprofessionals, without instrumental accompaniment. In listening to them anew on my computer, most appropriate, I thought, were his lyrical, wistful, elegiac, and melancholic works. I settled on songs that referenced loss, death, and unrequited love, or love that would never be. Most important, these of course would have been tunes certainly well known by both the poet and the president.

With my score and emotional terrain set, in late September, I began to choreograph on nine of my company dancers, seven women and two men. Prior to my first rehearsal, I thought there would not be a specific narrative and that the dance would remain abstract. However, art dictates its own course. It is more about invitation to its elements rather than imposition upon them, and an artist simply cannot fight the imperative that expresses itself when all the elements come together.

Whatever I might dream of being able to accomplish as a choreographer in full confidence of being able to embark upon an ambitious dance vision and to then actually bring it into fullest realization depends upon having cultivated a ready and diversely talented ensemble. It is their assorted gifts and tools upon which I as the choreographer must depend. Having a stable company in which each member knows one another well—individual capacities, flexibilities, relative assets and insights, idiosyncrasies, too—permits the choreographer to pursue a vision. As a dance piece evolves, the individuals gel in ways that exponentially build toward something profound and consequential, a shared consciousness for performers and audience. When I got this commission, I was aware that I was in a superb professional position as I had a cohesive and enviable ensemble. This was our moment.

Sarah Halzack would dance as a young woman overcome by grief at the loss of her love, a Northern soldier, killed in Civil War battle. Gallery visitors would easily relate to grief of those at home, in any time of war including the ongoing wars in Iraq and Afghanistan. Sarah was an angelic lead dancer for this. Her high leg extensions, ease of turning, and natural adagio quality combined with her ability to tune bravely into a sorrowful emotional characterization undergirded a doleful character, wandering, seeking her lost beloved. And that soldier—or, rather, his inchoate spirit—would be danced by handsome Kelly Southall. Kelly had the gifts of deeply emoting through his liquid lyricism and natural musicality. He perfectly embodied the elusive spirit of her dead betrothed.

With these two anchoring roles installed, I was able to create phrases for them that emphasized dreamlike sustained movement sequences that wafted across stage. I was taken aback by how much the imagistic songs of Stephen Foster—like a séance—summoned my own formulization of a natural pervading melancholic theme of the period. An ill-fated wartime love story would provide the through line, channeled in the forty-minute dance. I built a love duet that was seemingly cut short, surrounded by a chorus of mourners. A tender duet, all its phrasing consisting of floating weightless, disembodied in appearance, restrained with adagio extensions of the legs that floated upward and downward, gentle assisted lifts of Sarah by Kelly as if unbound by the physical restraints of earthly gravity.

I set elegant waltzes to both "Linger in Blissful Repose" and "Jeanie with the Light Brown Hair," the tempi indicated by the score topped with longing heavenward gazes and reaches upward to the cloud; at the end of each song the dancers settled to the floor in a repose of death. Images of Civil War battlefields, foreboding moments that accentuated the instance that Kelly pulled from Sarah's arms, coaxed by the vocals to join the surrounding troops. From that point forward, tableaus of loss and grief ensued, a dancer echoing Sarah's sadness kneeling, gently touching a still, supine soldier or multiple bodies arrayed, eyes-closed innocents, men and women slain in towns, across the floor of the Rotunda in simulation of the human toll, the aftermath of hideous battle.

Sarah wandered through each scene in lilting phrases that succumbed in grief to the floor and rose again, executing unfolding leg and arm extensions before continuing her search for her beloved fiancé. The chorus would slowly rise from their deathly poses and reconfigure into another waltzing scene only to double over and crimp into the floor again, defeated in battle. In this way they suggested multitudes, and not specific continuing individuals. Sarah was the witness to unremittingly morbid scenes, all clues to the world of loss within which she was both trapped and propelled as she searched for Kelly. I positioned him always just out of her view, behind her and to her sides.

As I built these dance scenes in the Rotunda, I realized that I had to view them as the audience would, from all vantage points of the circular room. My process was to pace the circumference of each evolving section, searching out the best angles to optimize the appeal from multiple vantage points, moving the dancers closer and father apart in proximity to one another so as not to obstruct the viewing angles. When a phrase seemed too focused on a singular directionality, I would instruct the dancers to redirect to another facing. In my circling search for the best perspectives, I grasped that Kelly should mimic my path. I instructed him to walk the perimeter, to slowly, ever so slowly pace along the outer edge of each scene like an eternally beleaguered specter, one for whom there could be no rest.

My piece, titled *America's Cloud*, embodied the emotional state of 1863 in a multi-angulated suite of short dances sewn together by images of grief represented by a couple doomed to be eternally adrift, who could not return to each other's comforting arms. The imagery was further supported by our then permanent costume designer, Judy Hansen, who created an assortment of uniform-like shirts and trousers and dresses in shades of blue that related to the colors of Finch's cloud. I would finally perfect an image between Kelly, Sarah, and the cloud that signified the work was complete.

By early December the dance was set, the company prepared for the unveiling. Seventy or so VIP visual-art guests and museum members took up their sightlines, both seated and standing, along the circular periphery. The dancers appeared in the large doorway of the room, walked solemnly into the space, and then assumed their starting postures, as soldiers and mourners. The dance commenced together, footsteps cued by piano notes, their spiraling elegant arms rising and falling with the melodeon, their graceful turns and releases to the floor aligned with the vocals. And finally on the last note of "Ah! May the Red Rose Live Always," Sarah came face to face with Kelly, just as he slowly fell to the floor in a final repose of death. She lightly landed upon him as a butterfly might upon a dying rose. Sarah slowly reached from him and then upward with the same arm to the floating cloud, implying that she could see his spirit depart the earthly plane and ascend. A dissolving image of grief, a final sense of resolution and peace.

The transfixed audience, quiet until the end, audibly exhaled as if they too sensed Kelly's spirit ascend. After a minute transfixed, they broke their reverent silence with loud applause that echoed thrillingly through the Rotunda. Kelly rose and took Sarah's hand as they bowed.

The chorus joined them for several more bows as the audience sounded their approval. The dancers departed the room. Attendees, still mesmerized by the work, proceeded to a post-performance cocktail gathering in the adjacent gallery (this helped bring everyone back into the here and now), arriving with questions for me: "How did you construct the dance?" "How do you visualize movement in the round?" "How do you conceptualize movement in relation to an art installation?" These questions came from engaged visual-arts patrons and Corcoran subscribers who even after arriving early and standing through the whole performance were not fatigued. Quite the contrary: they were energized and intrigued by my choreographic process. They were building connections to—and an understanding of—the marriage of art and dance: a marriage in which each medium and the fresh setting had opened a rich tap of an art that was arguably more than the sum of its parts. They were now our earliest stakeholders in this hybrid, aroused by a new cross-pollination. We had hoped with this premiere to receive feedback that would lead to refinements and reveal blind spots toward future successes. However, this initial foray was received with complete positivity. The space, the floor, the concept, all our elements and painstakingly careful planning had come together ideally. In debriefing later, we concluded that this was largely because we all had been so very conscious of the stakes that we anticipated and avoided many potential issues. It became our earliest template and established our trustworthiness and viability.

Our next two performances cast a similar hypnotic spell, and Sarah Newman was electrified to not only see the work multiple times but also to hear how pleased the museum patrons were. She said, "A couple just told me how the performance actually made them think more about the installation than the artist talk they attended several weeks ago!" Material metrics, like growth in attendance, bore out our first impressions: that, like us, audiences were not only ready but restless for such collaborations and that site-specific collaborative arts were at home in a museum. We were giving viewers a multidimensional, dynamic experience of art, beyond just passively looking and moving on. We gave them a reason to linger, to contemplate, to ponder and feel.

My overwhelming take-away (which I already suspected would be the case) was that I loved creating in the unconventional non-proscenium space, in particular that of a museum, where I was surrounded by art and ideas, aesthetic tastes and stimulation that was nourishment for me and my work. The paradigm nourished my company members as well. I was enriched by conversations with new audiences who were not the typical dance-subscription buyer. Dance belongs where the people are. Dance belongs where people can find it. Where people can find me. And my company. The monarch had migrated to a whole new country.

twenty-two HONORING THE BALLETS RUSSES AT THE NATIONAL GALLERY OF ART

By 2012 the planning and hard work my board had put in motion over the last twenty-four months was yielding good results. In November I received an e-mail from Kay Casstevens, the deputy chief director of development for the National Gallery of Art. She had become quite familiar with my work, having attended several of our shows after my 2010 outreach to her. She asked if I might call her regarding a potential project. Kay was an avid dance supporter, a gifted tap dancer, and a tap dance teacher on the side. She was an ideal prospect for supporting my vision of more museum engagements. I called immediately

"Dana! So good of you to call me back so quickly." Kay lost no time in small talk. As in a rhythmic tap dance sequence, Kay's words were cheery and crisp, brightly time-stepped to her point. "We have an exciting exhibition about the Ballets Russes coming to the Gallery in a few months. We haven't formally presented dance at the museum—only small snippets here and there over the years—but we have an interest in trying something of import tied to this exhibit. Let's meet." Stomp, hop, step, flap. The following week I met Kay on the light-filled ground floor of the East Wing of the National Gallery of Art, a museum designed by Chinese American architectural visionary I. M. Pei, which opened to the public in 1978. This auspicious venue, designed by a fellow Asian American would provide a galvanizing synergy for me and also expose audiences to another Asian American artist. Could it be, I wondered, that my talisman the Lion Dog from the Gamut in Santa Fe was working some magic here? It certainly appeared so.

Kay was in her fifties, youthful and ebullient, with a waifish dancer's elegance and grace of movement that complemented her manner of speech. She explained her concept as I accompanied her up the stairs to the second-floor atrium. This was déjà vu, a reprise of what I had done with Sarah Newman when she and I ascended the stairs of the

Corcoran to the Rotunda. Suddenly I felt like I was some character in *The West Wing*, which so brilliantly captured the DC "walk and talk" way of doing business. I had to smile, in step next to her. This was the second time that such a career-transforming interaction took place for me because someone invited me on such a DC walk and talk. She might as well have beckoned, "Dance with me." My heart was pounding in just that kind of excitement. We were Fred and Ginger.

In those moments of our echoing footfalls, before she even spoke of her idea, I dared to entertain a revelatory question: was I now—this Korean American kid from Santa Fe, the one always the outsider, other, and observer—becoming somewhat of a "Washington Insider?" In between the sound of our soles on the stairs, I swear that I could actually hear the sounds of my own monarch chrysalis, cracking open.

"The National Gallery of Art is planning an exhibition to open in May 2013, based on the Ballets Russes," said Kay, "not only the troupe's groundbreaking dances, but also their collaborations with visual artists and music composers. We plan to call the show *Diaghilev and the Ballets Russes, 1909–1929: When Art Danced with Music.*" The Ballets Russes was founded by Russian impresario Sergei Diaghilev (1872–1929) in Paris in 1909. The company combined Russian and "Orientalist" aesthetics with Western traditions and modernism. "Orientalism" refers to Edward Wadie Said's book of the same title published in 1978. His book criticized postcolonialist appropriations of the cultures of the East that conflated exoticized images in order to support imperialist ambitions of the West. The Ballets Russes' repertoire included such ballet suites as *Scheherazade* and *Les Orientales*, a series of quasi-Asian dances inspired by appropriated images of the Middle and Far East. The choreographer, Mikhail Fokine, is said to have been inspired to choreograph his *Danse Siamoise*, with its hyperextended hand gestures, flexed feet, and golden costume, when he saw a performance in 1900 of the Thai Classical troupe, the Nai But Mahin Dance Company, in St. Petersburg, Russia. These ballets fed Western audiences' hunger for exotic images of the East that portrayed far-away cultures of mystery and myth.

The Ballets Russes was the most important dance company of the twentieth century because it was a grand-scale laboratory of artistic collaborations among dance, music, set, and costume design. As a world-class showman and promoter, Diaghilev was driven to create a cutting-edge dance spectacle as had never been seen on the great stages of Europe. He assembled immense talent, systematically commissioning teams of artists and composers. It was with the Ballets Russes that composer Igor Stravinsky, Vaslav Nijinsky, and painter Nicholas Roerich created *Le Sacre du printemps*; composer Claude Debussy, Vaslav Nijinsky, and painter Léon Bakst created *l'Après-midi d'un faune*; and choreographer Léonide Massine in tandem with Pablo Picasso, Jean Cocteau, and composer Erik Satie created the ballet *Parade*. These were astounding collaborative and ambitious productions that would elevate and challenge the art form of dance for decades to come.

The dancers of the Ballets Russes had become superstars whose personal lives had also become legendary. Diaghilev's lovers would include a line of breathtakingly beautiful male dancers and choreographers including Nijinsky, Léonide Massine, Serge Lifar, and Anton Dolin. Balletomanes—maniacal ballet fans—followed their sizzling affairs with a kind of Adonis worship. Balletomania made 1960s Beatlemania look like a meditation group.

Kay showed me a list of the items that would be on display: more than 130 original costumes, set designs, paintings, sculptures, prints and drawings, photographs, and posters by artists such as Léon Bakst, Natalia Goncharova, Pablo Picasso, Henri Matisse, Giorgio de Chirico, and others. These men and women brought the most important artistic developments of the early twentieth century—including futurism, cubism, and surrealism—to the ballet stage. But the one component not curated yet in relation to this exhibition about dance was—"you guessed it," said Kay—actual live dance. Absent was the actual artform that had once tethered all these artifacts.

My thoughts flashed to John Neumeier's obsession with the Ballets Russes that had taken over his life and had become his very livelihood. John had become a channeler and I was open to following in his metaphysical footsteps, to create from inspirations of the past. Kay and I had a long conversation about the significance of each work on her list of items to arrive at the museum, all on loan from around the world. Kay said, "If you can see yourself creating a new work, based on a theme mined from the works in the exhibit, and which can be performed in the atrium, then I think we can move forward with commissioning from you an original dance work that will premiere in August 2013." She had me at "If."

The atrium was on the second floor, a seventy-by-forty-foot area where a special dance floor would be laid. Adjacent to it, would be ample audience seating of up to two hundred chairs, supplemented by standing room along a third-floor balcony that overlooked the dance area. I asked Kay when I could actually see the works in the exhibit so that I could make crucial artistic choices. It was agreed that I would have access to the exhibit before it opened to the public. Furthermore, the National Gallery of Art would take care of the dance flooring, the technical crew, publicity, and ticketing. Yes, there would be a sound system and minimal theatrical lighting. I would have three months from the first time I viewed the exhibit to the premiere date, just enough time to create and finish the work. Rehearsal time would be limited to only the day of the performance. This constraint was outweighed by the opportunity to create a new dance to be performed especially for this extraordinary exhibit and in this museum.

Kay and I shook on it. I thanked her and left—not really walking but practically dancing out of the gallery.

At the end of April 2013, just as the exhibition was being mounted, I was given access to the galleries. Notebook in hand, I jotted ideas for the themes and dashed off images. I began studying each artifact, even as exhibition handlers made last minute adjustments to objects. Being the lone visitor with each item created intimacy and luxuriant ease. I was free to have dialogues with each piece for as long as we had things to share, and to move between works as if at my ideal endless convivial cocktail party, some familiar faces stippled with other unfamiliar ones across the room to whom I would introduce myself.

I stopped in front of the lush mauve, emerald, and blue velvet fabrics of Vaslav Nijinsky's original 1911 costume for *Le Dieu bleu*, designed by Léon Bakst. This was a ballet in which he had his entire muscled body painted blue to portray the blue Hindu deity of love, Lord Krishna. The costume still shone with opulent gold-threaded braids, his elaborate Cambodian inspired golden crown, still ready for the stage. This was the costume Nijinsky wore for his first lead role with the Ballets Russes. This costume epitomized turn-of-the-century European lust for exoticized images from the East. Those representations had been incorporated into art nouveau design and were inspiring the direction of art that would penetrate the art deco period. I considered each artifact in my thoughtful search for inspiration.

I continued past three mannequins each displaying costumes by Nicholas Roerich for Nijinsky's 1913 ballet *Le Sacre du Printemps* (The Rite of Spring). The avant-garde ballet, with its stomping steps and flexed feet, caused the audience, used to pointe shoes and ethereal Romantic ballets, to unravel into catcalling in disapproval and the pure mayhem of a riot. But these events were too well known, *Le Sacre du Printemps* had been overused as a theme of inspiration for decades, from renown choreographers such as Pina Bausch to even the smallest regional ballet and modern dance companies.

After several hours of turning different possibilities in my mind, I at last came upon the exhibit that would be my selection. My choice this time was not based on a painting but rather on my interest in set designs and costumes with symbols as clues to an artist's interior motivations. And when the decision came to me, it rushed with undeniable power. The concept of love and attraction, of aging and memory.

Set up in the last galleries of exhibition were Giorgio de Chirico's original costumes and his set designs for George Balanchine's 1929 ballet *Le Bal*, one of the last dances the Ballets Russes would perform before Diaghilev's death, the end of the company's twenty-year run. In this russet-painted gallery stood four mannequins on a platform of faux marble building blocks. One mannequin was wearing a white tulle dress with sylph wings with a black swirl painted on the bodice. And there were three male costumes, suits that all contained varying hues of blue, rose, black, and white, all with different architectural motifs painted on them—Roman pillars and arches, building blocks and bricks. These were allusions to his own cultural background, his

Sicilian father and Greek mother. On the walls hung his painted set designs depicting a marble Greek nymph, an arched marble doorway, and a white horse.

Here I read about how de Chirico founded the *scuola metafisica*—the metaphysical school of art—which profoundly influenced the surrealists with its illogical perspectives, imposing shadows, mannequins, statues, and images of Roman architecture. In a 1909 manuscript, de Chirico wrote of the "host of strange, unknown and solitary things that can be translated into painting . . . What is required above all is a pronounced sensitivity." Among de Chirico's most frequent motifs were arcades, "The Roman arcade is fate . . . its voice speaks in riddles which are filled with a peculiarly Roman poetry." His costume and set designs reflected his own identity symbols. I sketched them into my notebook, all the while trying to channel and decipher his interior world, clues to his hyphenated cultural background and perhaps even his thoughts about love and aging. Perhaps all artists build intricate languages of symbols in order to express concepts too emotionally complicated to put into words alone. Perhaps an artist's interior world stores such strong traumas and fears that soliloquies are turned into painted symbols or into choreographed steps as forms of self-preservation.

I read the synopsis of Balanchine's obscure ballet. At a costume ball, a young man dressed in a military attire is attracted to a masked, young woman. When she removes her mask, she is revealed to be in fact an old woman. At the end of the ball the woman removes yet a second mask. She is a beautiful young woman after all. This odd double-reveal leaves the young man to question his own attraction to beauty versus substance and his repulsion to old age.

This cautionary tale confronted me with my own grappling with aging; I was forty-four, just considering what it means to grow old . . . and at the same time I was building the architecture for my romantic love relationship. My then fiancé (now my husband) Jameson and I have a sizeable age difference: I'm sixteen years his senior. Perhaps Balanchine's character, confronted with and repulsed by age, triggered my own insecurities? Was the costume ball a metaphor for the characters we encounter throughout our life? Were the "masks" ways in which we attempt to cover up our true emotions and neurosis associated with love and aging? This was an opportunity to pull off the "masks" I wore or had ever held in holstered readiness, and to confront unsettling feelings about youth, love, and aging.

I still had a few weeks to consider the theme and build a narrative, as well as the logistics of purchasing props and costumes before I started on three months of rehearsals. Our costume designer, Judy, met me at the exhibit, studied the de Chirico designs and costumes for style and colors, and spoke with me about my emerging characters for the dance. I pictured a memory maze of sorts in which a middle-aged woman "of a certain age," somewhat ostracized by society, reflects on her faded youth and realizes that her lover is no longer attracted to her aging body. The setting would be a metaphoric ballroom in which she is confronted by her inner dialogue.

Once the forty-by-thirty dance floor was set up in the atrium, the actual stage space would be fairly small, so I decided not to cast the full company (which was at the time eleven dancers), and instead I cast nine—five women and four men. I set to work searching the Internet for music that would support three typical dances from European courts of the past: the Pavane, the Tarantella, and the Galliard. These are all formal, distant, mannered, and measured steps. These dances could be effectively juxtaposed to quiet works from the later Romantic era, with its music that so often evokes melancholia and wistfulness, memory and elegiac reflection. Claude Debussy's familiar reverie *Clair de Lune* naturally came to mind. I had the idea that if I could set up two distinct worlds, one of formality and one of emotionality on stage, then I could build a moving dance narrative tension.

I began rehearsing my nine dancers three times a week for four hours each session in an offsite dance studio located at the Georgetown Day School in upper Northwest Washington. This was a new state-of-the-art studio with fourteen-foot ceilings, sprung wood dance floors, and mirrors. One of our board members, Jan Tievsky, was an original founder of their dance program, and she had negotiated a brilliant company-in-residence relationship that allowed us to further build the dance program through curricular development, teaching, and lecture demonstrations. As time went on this collegial relationship allowed for our dancers to teach our technical style of modern dance from lower to high school students and allotted us rehearsal space. A win-win situation.

I choreographed my own renditions of court dances for the three couples who now moved in uniformed, geometric patterns with quick footwork. They now would have an extra layer of modern torso movement and intricate hand gestures. I cast dancer Tati Valle-Riestra, who was in her forties, as the lead dancer. Sarah Halzack would be Tati's young self, and Kelly Southall the man losing interest in Tati as she succumbed to age.

For the young lovers, I choreographed a series of intricate barefoot duets, suggestive of nuanced and complex emotional conversations that hinted at magnetic attraction mitigated by tentative retreats and passionate embraces. Sarah flirted with Kelly as he circled her. She turned in *arabesques*, swirling with arms held defiantly overhead; he traced a series of circular hand patterns, palms facing up—signifying earnest pledges of his love—over and over, atop syncopated steps and a jig with an Irish-dance quickness while he held his hands to his heart.

Sarah and Kelly's movement was out of sorts from the six-member core who I had maintain distance from their respective partners, only touching and bowing in curtsy-like moves performed with restraint and composure. In this way the formality of the chorus was a backdrop permitting Sarah and Kelly's interplay to stand out as all the more dynamic. Sarah's phrasing countered Kelly's projection of passionate youthful desire. For the pair, it was an intricate fixated courtship.

Tati's character was the only dancer without a partner. She mimicked Sarah's dance steps from afar but with a contrasting dynamic, one depleted, drained of energy, one of melancholy inflected by age. I placed Kelly and Sarah's duets in the midst of ball scenes so that when the chorus momentarily froze in unison mid-step, the continuing exuberance of their duet shone. Tati stood and stared at Kelly and Sarah from a distance, as if studying a moment in time that she could not recapture, when her relationship was passionate, and she was young. In Sarah and Kelly's final duet, Tati replaces Sarah mid-step and Kelly unknowingly embraces Tati, but upon realizing she has aged, Kelly abruptly stops his rhythmic footwork and pushes away; he turns and begins slowly to walk away without looking back, his departure leaving her quite alone, irrelevant to her lover, solitary on the dance floor with the chorus as onlookers.

Tati reaches to Sarah, but she slowly rotates to face upstage, leaving Tati to view Kelly's long exit. At this moment in the staging, I asked Tati to gently shudder, to subtly fold forward as if her gut ached from the remembrance of her lost youth, to cover her eyes and mouth in a silent tearful weeping. This image of reflection, a haunting of one's past beauty and love, inspired me to title the dance *Revenant Elegy*.

After dozens of productive rehearsals, we were nearing completion and ready for one last layer, the costumes. I nervously awaited their arrival. I had signed off on Judy's design sketches two months prior. Two weeks before the premiere, she delivered the costumes for *Revenant Elegy*. Not only had she designed them, but she had also sewn each one. For Sarah and Tati, Judy created flowing gowns in variations of rose with crinoline slips layered underneath. Sarah's vibrant rose leaning into fuchsia, alive to bursting, was underpinned with expansive crinolines. Tati's was a dusty rose version layered over a single flattened crinoline slip. The costumes signaled clearly that the two dancers were, in fact, representing the same individual, separated in time by at least two decades. Kelly wore a rich fuchsia corseted vest and leggings in shades similar to Sarah's. The male core members were outfitted in black velvet corseted vests and leggings, and the women in black bustiers and long flowing black skirts. The story line crystalized when the company performed the dance in the studio wearing Judy's costumes. The colors and designs of the costumes enhanced the story line by providing clear visual definitions.

At noon on August 11, 2013, two hours before the two o'clock premiere, ticketed patrons streamed in, to stake out the best sight lines among the unassigned seats. The museum's sound engineer and I did a final sound check of the recorded musical montage with the dancers readied for their single allotted dress rehearsal. They took the stage and danced, taking crucial note of spatial adjustments needed in the unfamiliar space.

Above me on the third-floor mezzanine, I could see people pressed tightly against the glass rails, angling for a clear view of the stage below. In that moment, I remembered some of the other unique tiered environments for which I had tailored and performed—or had set dancers to perform—and that were decidedly not formal, intentional stages. My mind went back to the youthful performance I gave at the UN General Assembly Hall, akin to Cirque du Soleil aerial feat.

I thought about the sort of literal and figurative climbing I had been doing in satisfaction of this art, this career that had identified me, had selected me at such a young age. Dance and I belonged to each other. I had never attempted to rebuff it as a suitor. I recognized it as the love of my life, and I welcomed its every ravishing. I thought about *Revenant Elegy*, then, too. Unlike my poor Tati character, the aging and regretful midlife dancer, dance had actually embraced me throughout all these years. I was willing and eager to make full use of any available surfaces and spaces—no matter how unconventional and arguably contrarian. And unlike Tati in the dance I had written, there was no rebuff or lack of accommodation that was so daunting that I would not persist beyond its impediments in continually wooing, in winning. A staircase? Sure. Want my company or me to dance on a ladder? Can do. And in fact, . . . done it. DONE IT. Bring it on.

The questions of my life had not been IF I could make something work. They had only been about HOW to make something work. I had spent my entire life making—perceiving—every space as a dance space. Such places were thrilling challenges, opportunities. Constraints make for the greatest art: what else are the formal strictures of, say, a sonnet, or haiku? The artist must find liberation in the limits. And so Dana Tai Soon Burgess Dance Company premiered *Revenant Elegy*, on the second floor, in the glass-enclosed atrium of the National Gallery of Art, in view of the entrance to the featured special exhibit, *Diaghilev and the Ballets Russes, 1909–1929: When Art Danced with Music.*

By the time the dance was about to commence, every single one of the two hundred chairs was filled and standing room encompassed the whole second-floor atrium and stretched across the third-floor balconies. People were still pushing up the escalator and stairs in hopes of catching a glimpse of the show. The crowds had responded to the museum's advertising campaign in the *Washington Post* as well as to their social media posts and ads on Facebook.

With more than five hundred audience members and a line out the museum door, Kay Casstevens asked if we might be able to perform a second show in order to accommodate the large and demanding crowds. Images of the raucous riotous audiences of the Ballets Russes filled my head. I agreed—yes, we would do so—and the company was ecstatic as well. Kay made the announcement of a second performance to take place immediately after the conclusion of the first, and the crowd calmed to a silence. I said just a few words about the inspiration for *Revenant Elegy* and the dancers took their places.

Their measured entrance permitted the crowd to focus fully on the dancers as they moved across the stage in courtly, deliberate fashion. Sarah and Kelly performed their intricate duets while Tati gently mirrored Sarah's defiant movements from afar until Tati gently shuddered in grief-filled despair as Kelly moved away from her and in so doing, brought the dance to a close.

The audience's thorough approval echoed with thrilling loud acoustical bounce throughout all those hard surfaces of the great exhibition halls. The dancers left the stage at the last moments of a protracted ovation of easily more than a minute, savoring this palpable connection with those in attendance. They had just enough time to hurriedly prepare for their next performance, which was in just a half hour, as the hall cleared of this one, making way for the hundreds of new patrons who filled a reluctantly vacated seating area that was still humming, alive with departing audience energy. I ran to our makeshift backstage, a storage area just off the atrium and made sure the dancers had water and that they touched up their makeup and hair, and then I dashed back to the front of the house in time for Kay to ask me to say a few words about dance and art.

The company's second performance was received with even more appreciation—if that were even possible. After the performance Kay found me, gave me a long hug. "Thank you so very much. That was absolutely gorgeous and showed how an exhibition on dance can inspire a new dance!" I was thrilled to receive her words. The success of these two performances stirred a buzz across all the museums on the National Mall—especially among those who had initially demurred or declined my approaches—about this concept of adding dance to their exhibits. Kay's extraordinary leadership example marked a crucial tipping point. Now when we knocked on doors, we would not only be invited in, we would be warmly welcomed and "what took you so long?" And what is more, *Revenant Elegy* would stay in our repertoire for many years, by popular demand, even becoming a featured work among our 2015 performances at the Kennedy Center for the Performing Arts.

As important as *Revenant Elegy* was in my professional life, the work I did on this project helped me to explore and to understand and then to more peacefully calm my fears of aging and relax into my own love relationship. My spectral memories and second-guessing, my worries about the future or growing old alone turned to warm thoughts of looking forward to growing old with Jameson. I had no intention of living a life of regret or imagining what might have been.

Art had taught me how to live; it had now also taught me how to love and be loved.

twenty-three THE KREEGER MUSEUM

A JEWEL BOX IN THE CENTER OF DC

In September 2014 I received a call from Judy Greenberg, the founding director of the private Kreeger Museum, located on five acres in the exclusive, upscale Washington neighborhood of Foxhall. I was familiar with the museum and had often wandered through its sculpture garden. Judy asked me to meet her at the museum, hinting at the possibility of an artist residency—one this time not earmarked for a visual artist and that was sweetened with the outcome of a commissioned original dance.

This was not a behemoth public art cathedral; it was a small, dense, and priceless jewel box. This was a closely curated accrual of works, overseen by a streamlined staff. The museum is named after David Lloyd Kreeger, who served as CEO and then a member of the board of directors of the Government Employees Insurance Company (Geico) in the 1970s. David (1909–1990) and his wife Carmen (1909–2003), were avid art collectors who lived in a home for which they had commissioned the design by architect Philip Johnson. Built from more than nine hundred tons of travertine, the home was conceived as a family live-in base that would also showcase their extensive collection of art from impressionist to contemporary, African to Asian. They amassed works by Claude Monet, Pablo Picasso, Pierre-Auguste Renoir, Paul Cézanne, Marc Chagall, Joan Míro, and Frank Stella; sculptures by Auguste Rodin, Constantin Brancusi, Lucien Wercollier, and Henry Moore; and traditional African masks and Asian sculptures.

The Kreeger Museum also has soaring thirty-foot-high ceilings, walls of glass, and uninterrupted sparkling hardwood floors throughout. Be still my heart and heels. Those floors! For a choreographer, that's the deal-sealer. I was a goner.

For the last three years, I was not making decisions for my company without the exploratory input and final backing of my board. My company was now a mature entity, with a trusted close cabinet, that worked with me as sounding boards and backstops and to make decisions that would insure the long-term best interests and stability of this company.

The board chair of DTSBDC was then Bonnie Kogod. Bonnie is an arts patron who had already led a long and productive career in arts administration and spent many years with the Los Angeles Arts Council, serving as a project coordinator, moving on to director, and finally executive director of the council. Bonnie and I first met at a small dinner party thrown by Jimi Yui, the designer of top chef kitchens, including those of Thomas Keller and José Andres. Bonnie and I were seated next to each other and felt an immediate connection. We talked all night about Greece, from where she had recently moved back to the States, to past lives and to making art. Bonnie's taste in art was impeccable and she had known the Kreegers well, personally. When the time came, it was natural that Bonnie would join me for my meeting with Judy at the Kreeger Museum the following week.

As we entered the museum foyer, a guard eyeballed my notebook and Bonnie's chocolate brown Bottega Veneta handbag, no doubt making sure neither was large enough for us to make off with a masterpiece. Also standing guard next to the front desk was a second-century CE stone Bodhisattva from the Gandhara region, three-and-a-half feet tall and two feet wide, atop a large wooden pedestal. This was my own Buddha talisman, I thought, and so much more welcoming than imposing, this gigantic version of my cherished charm. How auspicious!

Having checked in, we were free to wander into the main gallery, a 1,500-square-foot room with a towering three-story ceiling and glass walls on either end. This room was filled with Monet seascapes and landscapes from the 1880s and '90s. We slowly made our way to the end of a long wall hung with expressionist paintings and together lingered at two side-by-side Van Goghs, both from 1886 and depicting vases of cut flowers. As we walked into a side room, Bonnie informed me that this had been the Kreeger family dining room, and it was where the Monets had formerly hung. Today here hung nine impressive Picasso paintings marking the artist's evolution. They ranged from an early timid portrayal of a woman seated at a café, *At the Café de la Rotonde*

(1901), painted at age twenty, to a self-assured late abstract, *L'homme au casque d'or après Rembrandt* (1969), which he painted when he was eighty-eight.

There was no protective glass. It was an intimate and personal meeting between the art and us: no mediation, no scrim, and no barrier. No signs telling us what we could or could not do, or a hushed timbre above which we could not speak together. I could closely study the master's brushstrokes. This was a relationship with the artist's work and the artist, the likes of which I had always dreamed. I shared my thoughts with Bonnie, sputtering, words tumbling, "I feel as if through these visible brushstrokes, I can feel the physicality of Picasso's being. When I draw a deep breath, I can almost smell the paint. And will you look at the abandon he had in his eighties—nearly ninety he was—and the contemplative care he painted with when he was in his thirties, and over here—look at this 1914 Cubist period, *Nature morte avec fruit, verre, et journal*. All his thoughts, emotions, and movement are here, right here, inches away, in front of us." Bonnie's answer, "Fantastic, so fantastic!"

Picasso and I could dance.

Just then another private security guard approached and informed us that Judy would see us now. He pointed toward a hall at the end of which we would find a large, closed door. As we walked in that direction, we noted that the walls on either side were paneled with paintings by Joan Miró. I knocked reverently on the carved solid cherry wood door. "Come in, it's open!" Judy, in her mid-sixties, was dressed in a stunning tailored emerald tweed wool suit that set off her reddish-brown hair. She was seated at her large midcentury modern desk, flanked by a bookshelf of coffee table–sized books on art and collections from around the world, stacked to the high ceiling. Seated across from her was Helen Chason, the head of public relations and membership, a vivacious brunette in her forties. Helen was wearing an olive-green velvet 1930s-style dress. They both rose and offered for Bonnie and me to sit on the other side of Judy's spacious office, on a long green chenille couch. As we took the couch, Judy and Helen moved to sit on matching adjacent chairs. The palette of their coordinated attire, combined with the green couch and chairs and the pastoral view of the lawn through the wall of glass, coalesced, creating the look and feel of our being in a painting that had come to life.

Judy opened the conversation by telling us about the history of the collection, how David Kreeger had been a self-taught collector who bought what caught his eye. She shared how his collection had even saved Geico during a major economic downturn in the 1970s, when he sold thirty of his paintings. The garnered cash from those sales he then invested in Geico and revived the company. I told Judy that I had visited the museum's sculpture garden many times. Judy said, "I am so very aware of your work. I know that you create dance works inspired by works you discover in museum collections. Might you consider doing the same for the Kreeger Museum?"

I nodded enthusiastically, and I immediately blurted out the vision that had already been formulating in my mind for the past fifteen minutes, "*Picasso Dances*. I already see the project." Judy laughed and said, "Well, I certainly understand that! But maybe we should give you a chance to see the whole collection first before you come to a final decision. Shall we?" We all stood, and Judy and Helen gave us a personal tour of the museum. They walked us to four works, one by Georges Braque, a Marc Chagall, and two paintings by Peter Paul Rubens. Then we headed downstairs to an impressive collection of African masks by the Puna, Fang, and the Ashanti people as well as Washington Color School paintings by Sam Gilliam.

But I had fallen in love with the Picassos and nothing else would suffice. At the end of the tour, Judy said, "Now tell me what do you think? What interests you?" My answer, "The Picassos." Judy and Helen smiled in warm approval. Helen explained that they are often approached by entities and individuals seeking to lend various kinds of support or engagement. The Spanish ambassador to the United States had recently asked them to keep the embassy in mind if there was a project with a Spanish tie-in. If there ever were a project that he could support, this would surely be the one.

If we could come up with a really terrific concept, Helen said, the ambassador would certainly find it reasonable to absorb the costs.

"Ideally, I would wish this project to be something of substance, that would honor Spanish culture," a project that the ambassador could literally walk across the street from his home to the museum and enjoy. (The ambassador's private residence was literally across the street from the museum.) Helen asked, "Exactly what might a dance residency entail?"

I suggested choreographing the dance in the main gallery of the Kreeger Museum, in an allotted twenty by twenty-five square foot area, defined by a temporary outline of black tape on the floor. "Audiences take note of tape on the floor as a boundary and honor it nearly as much as physical stanchions," I explained. "In this way we would keep the view of the gallery open. They could watch us work, in real time, watch me rehearse the dancers."

The vision thrilled them, and it thrilled Bonnie and me. Judy then asked if we might like the Picassos moved into the main gallery, "to be with you." I thought that so very generous. Had I actually heard her correctly? It was something that would not have occurred to me to even request. This would allow us to work in the space on the beautiful wooden floor surrounded by the inspiration for the work. "Yes, of course. And that way the public can make immediate connections between the choreographic process and the paintings," she said. "Watching you work on the dance with those paintings, well that's an extra value added to their visit, too," said Helen. She was already ahead of us, framing her press release.

I would do my research in advance, speak with the directors about their insights to the paintings, and build a framework for the dance off-site. Then the new thirty-minute dance would be incubated at the museum, during four-hour rehearsals every Saturday over three months, January through March 2015. And at the end of those months, we would present two performances, one for museum members and the other for the general public. Judy and Helen loved the idea. Bonnie loved the idea as well, but doing her job as board president, she relieved me now of the more detailed agreements about logistics, the commissioning fee, liability insurance, press, and numerous mutual expectations. After an hour of Judy, Helen, and Bonnie hammering out the details, while

I stared at those Picassos, Judy said, "Dana, we have a deal! I will get you a contract next week that outlines everything we have agreed upon. *Picasso Dances* will be a reality!"

When we were wrapping things up, shaking hands, and saying farewells, Bonnie remarked: "It's so nice to be back at the house." Judy looked at her quizzically. Bonnie, such a seasoned Washington insider, seamlessly said, "I dated the Kreeger's son, Peter, when I was in high school fifty years ago. I remember having dinner here many times in the old dining room with the Kreegers, surrounded by their Monets." I let it sink in, the Kreegers were indeed a family, and they ate their meals—they hung out—in a dining room surrounded by their acquisitions, and those priceless pieces happened to be by some of art history's most thrilling and original artists. They had their home designed with far-sighted specifications, to house their art collection, and upon their deaths their home shifted naturally from a private residence to a museum. Today Peter Kreeger serves as one of the directors of the museum's board. Her comment was a lovely coda.

I returned to the Kreeger Museum several times during the next two weeks to narrow down my final choices among the Picasso paintings. I stood studying each, my face only inches away from pigments that formed lines and images on the canvases. I found myself at a familiar vantage point, one of investigation, that was formulated the first time I stared at my father's canvases propped on a wooden easel, trying to decipher symbols and anagrams formed by his brushstrokes, believing them to be clues to his internal life. Perhaps this formative childhood memory is what has driven me to prowl museums in search of inspiration, my first yearnings for fatherly acceptance had become a habit and my life's great propulsion.

I narrowed the Picasso paintings down to four, *Nature morte avec fruit, verre, et journal*—Still Life with Fruit, Glass, and Newspaper, 1914; *Tête de femme*—Head of a Woman, 1921; *Nu assis appueyé sur des coussins*—Seated Nude Leaning on Pillows, 1964; and *L'Homme au casque d'or après Rembrandt*—Man with the Golden Helmet, After Rembrandt, 1969. I chose these because the styles of painting corresponded with Picasso's life and revealed the process of his artistic maturation.

This was going to be a different dance process for me, one that I hoped would reveal my own maturation of process. This new work would be derived from a deep dive into a great artist's life through my own close interpretations of paintings done by a single artist over a span of decades—not a singular moment in time. In fact, *Picasso Dances* would rather be a suite of dances based on milestones from youth to old age. This would not be a narrative like *Revenant Elegy*, but a deciphering of images from Picasso's aesthetics that had moved from his blue period through cubism and finally arrived at the very beginnings of neo-expressionism.

The colors of the dancers' costumes would be key for this dance suite. I called Judy Hansen and asked her to meet me at the museum. With a color guide and fabric material swatches, Judy and I matched the colors of the four paintings to the colors and textures of fabrics. Each material was also chosen for the way it could move and accentuate movement, contributing its own natural fluidity as well as shape to the body. There was diaphanous white silk for *Nu assis appueyé sur des coussins*; heavy crêpe in red and sapphire for *Tête de femme*; red, black, and Prussian blue organza for *L'Homme au casque d'or après Rembrandt*; and green jersey for *Nature morte avec fruit, verre, et journal*.

For the music I chose six short chamber pieces by Manuel de Falla, a Spanish composer and contemporary of Picasso. My suite would be a reunion of artists who had memorably collaborated before. Picasso had designed the sets and costumes and Manuel de Falla had written the musical score for a Léonide Massine ballet for the Ballets Russes, titled *El sombrero de tres picos*, or The Three-Cornered Hat, which premiered in 1919. Manuel de Falla's passionate, poetic compositions are said to speak to the heart of Spanish culture, and he, like his countryman Picasso, defined and distinguished Spanish culture in the twentieth century. The suite of piano compositions came to thirty minutes in duration, varying from the dark ascetic piece, *Pour le tombeau de Paul Dukas* to the fervent *Aragonesa*.

And so, each Saturday from the museum's opening at 10 a.m. until 2 p.m., I met with seven of my dancers, five men and two women, in the main exhibition hall. And sure enough, Judy Greenberg had arranged for the gallery to move the four Picassos, hanging them to the left and right of our allotted rehearsal space. This was also the busiest time for the museum, which insured that as many visitors as possible saw the dancers at work. Two security guards stood in the gallery, one on either end. They watched over our dancing space, gently instructing visitors not to get too close to the black-tape borders.

The dancers were ebullient to be so close to the paintings, to be associated with Picasso and these masterpieces. This proximity added enormously to our sense of purpose and our collective adrenalized energies.

We were treated with respect. We were treated by both staff and visitors the same way they treated cherished art. We were the artists, and we were the art. The support was mind-blowing. All the while I was communing with Picasso. Picasso—if this is not clear already—is my favorite painter. His father, Don José Ruiz y Blasco, was a painter as well. Picasso was prolific, unafraid of experimentation, unafraid in art and fearless in his often-complicated joie de vivre, his love interests, his muses. And he believed in his calling as an artist and that his art was worth acknowledgment and of support from the highest levels. He would approve of the way we dancers were being treated in this home.

I admired his brazen self-confidence, the "take THAT!" brush-strokes in his old age. These works hung so close I was able to study them mere inches away whenever I craved further close inspection of his forms and the direction of his brushstrokes. No sketchbook needed. I could feel the immediacy of Picasso's works. And having them together this way allowed me to determine what I loved about each painting and to see how they related to one another—their shapes and geometric planes of vibrant red and blue, yellow, green, white, and black, brushed on with playful abandon. Here were the inherent motions of Picasso himself, his body energy and movements, captured on canvas. His brushstrokes danced beside us.

With the De Falla piano compositions playing in our gallery, I for-mulated a clear alignment of the music with the images in the four can-vases. The suite of dances would have an opening movement—a caval-cade of the whole ensemble of dancers followed by four movements.

First, a men's trio, three impassioned matadors inspired by *L'Homme au casque d'or après Rembrandt*, an abstract portrait of a soldier in a horned cabasset, who with his forward thrusting arms seemed poised to jump out of the frame and into our midst. Was he more man—or minotaur? Second, a playful, flirtatious female solo inspired by *Nu assis appueyé sur des coussins*, an abstract portrait of his second wife and muse, Jacqueline Roque. Next, a duet for a man and woman, an emotionally turbulent duet inspired by *Tête de femme*, a cubist image of a woman's face depicting a psychological dark and light side—the duality of her emotional states played out with the man she loved. Then a trio for two men and one woman, based on *Nature morte avec fruit, verre, et journal*, an early cubist still study of the forms of fruit, a glass, and a newspaper on a table. The final movement of the suite would be a reprise, a coda danced by the full cast. Each dancer would be dressed in colors from the paintings and that their movement phrases would be built from my interpretations of the paintings' images, implied emotions, shapes, and brushstrokes. I wanted the dancers to seem as if they had walked right out of the canvases.

With limited rehearsal time, this structure would allow me to work quickly. We had eleven rehearsals: one or two devoted to choreographing each movement of the suite and the remaining three allocated to cleaning and rehearsing the finished dance.

First, I dove into the male matador trio. The three dancers I cast were all swashbucklers: Alvaro Palau, a dancer from Colombia formerly of the Washington Ballet, with features that reminded me of an Egyptian Coptic portrait—pale skin, wide-set dark eyes, full lips, and hair in ringlets; Ian Ceccarelli, an Italian American, with features and a physique akin to a classical Roman statue who was deeply musical (having grown up with a mother who was an opera singer); and Felipe Oyarzun Moltedo, an emotive dancer from Chile with classic Spanish features like an El Greco and a background in the Marinera—that graceful courtship dance that is a mix of Spanish contradanza and Andean folkdance.

I structured their rehearsal as a series of competitions: who could pirouette the most times, to jump and kick the highest, to essentially outdo one another with each dance phrase I assigned. The rehearsal became a playful contest between the dancers, challenging one another's physical limits to such a point that losing balance, one would falter. At these moments, the other two men would rush to support the third. When Felipe kicked so high that he teetered on the edge of crashing to the floor, Ian and Alvaro rushed to catch him; when Alvaro did four pirouettes and struggled to complete a fifth, Felipe and Ian would grab hold of him, right him on his leg and assist him in taking his final turn.

Atop this whirlwind celebration of macho energy, I added the postures and gestures of matadors in an arena, deep lunges with arms spoking outward, index and middle fingers pointing like banderillas,' the decorated wooden sticks used in the arena to stab the vanquished bull. I intertwined Alvaro, Ian, and Felipe's spatial patterns so that they constantly wove among their competitors. The outcome was a testosterone tour de force, puffed-up chests, and challenging glares like stalking peacocks.

The next Saturday I choreographed a solo for Sarah Halzack. I asked Sarah to start off reclining on the floor as if on an imaginary cushion, in the same repose as the painting *Nu assis appueyé sur des coussins*. Then I had her rise to standing, mimicking the pathways of brushstrokes on the canvas. For example, I asked her to move left to right, up to down, and across on long, extenuated diagonals, all the time accentuated by an exuberant flow of extending arms, flexible leg kicks and chainés, tiny chains of close footed turns. A swirl of paint of the canvas became a triple pirouette, a drawn-out line emerged as the slow developé of a leg. Picasso's brush play was embodied by Sarah's coltish movements until she at last returned to her beginning spot where she resumed her reclining repose.

I set the male and female duet on Felipe and Katia Nori. Katia has a photographic memory for movement. I have not met another dancer who could study a complete 64-count dance phrase once and recall it—execute it—as perfectly as Katia could. This duet was wholly different in approach from the other dances. This was a duet that I built out from the psychological imagery of *Tête de femme*, a painting depicting a woman's face as two profiles: one angry, in red, and the other serene, in white and blue. I wanted Katia to embrace moments of tenderness and at other times in anger to accentuate her dual states. For example, I had Katia embrace Felipe and then, as he embraced her, sharply pull away. I had Felipe gently outline the form of Katia's limbs with his hands only to have her writhe in annoyance. At times I had Felipe partner Katia, ecstatically lifting her into the air, only to have her push him to the ground—after which she continued in defiant steps, reclaiming her space and control over him. I choreographed highs and lows in manic conflict with Felipe's constancy and enduring caresses. I coached Katia's movements to veer between sharp and erratic initiations to sudden adagio, her phrasing always confounding and eluding predictable outcomes.

The trio was cast on Kelly Southall, Sarah Halzack, and Ben Sanders. Ben was a tall blonde who resembled a young Erick Hawkins (the first man to dance in the Martha Graham Company). This trio was perhaps the easiest to choreograph because *Nature morte avec fruit, verre, et journal* permitted the dance to be built of shapes and forms, objects depicted in the painting. In their first rehearsal, I had the trio intently study the painting and mimic each of the forms they saw, through their bodies, often instinctively working together to accomplish their respective visions. A cubist newspaper seemingly fractured in three became Kelly supporting Sarah on Ben's back. Then, Sarah's rounded arm next to Kelly's rounded back as he leaned on Ben's downward sloping shoulder became a drinking glass with a rippled surface and Ben's cupped hands suggested slices of a pear. The building process became a game: how many images could they make into associated movements? Once the shapes were decided, I strung them together as morphing stop-start depictions that made their way across the floor. What we now had was effectively a cubist canvas on the move.

The introduction and the coda were both choreographed over two rehearsals. For these rehearsals I asked them to wear their now-completed costumes. This allowed me to track each dancer, each referenced painting. I now had all the movement motifs needed to choreograph the short ingress and egress. For the introductory cavalcade, set to De Falla's *Cortejo de Gnomos*, I asked each dancer to choose a series of what they considered signature moves from their choreography. The matadors chose aggressive prideful stances, Sarah wispy directional poses, the duet an array of ambivalent embraces and withdrawals, and the trio, their favorite interconnected shapes. I combined these sequences and placed unison walks and poses in-between, implying a giant mural of the combined paintings, a shifting and reshaping collage. For the coda, set to De Falla's *Cancion*, I had the entire cast reenter and assigned different short phrases from the four movements and finally developed one long unison phrase that united the entire cast before having them freeze in sculpted poses at the end of the musical composition. The result was a colorful mural made up of abstracted lines and forms of the Picasso paintings. In their bright costumes, the cast resembled kinetic painted forms now returning to stasis.

These Saturday rehearsals not only proved fruitful choreographically but also they gave me insights about how to work day to day within a museum. As a chrysalis is to the monarch, so was a museum to me, the choreographer. I had intuited this already, but now I was absolutely certain of it. It was not just as metaphor. It was a fact of my identity, my art, my humanity, and my being. I lived inside art, and it lived within me. And in this working model, where visitors could observe our creative processes and even interact with us, the museum was not just a studio but a think-tank, a real-time, beta workshop. We could overhear visitors' remarks to one another, not just about the paintings but also about us; I began to imagine, and to actually feel, that this was how a painting or a sculpture experienced being viewed and discussed by human beings. I remembered, too, that a group of butterflies is rarely called a roost or swarm. The official designation is actually "kaleidoscope." True. And in our Pablo Picasso pageantry and movement, we were certainly that.

An audience member's approval or disapproval—or lack of engagement—comes in nuances as subtle as brush strokes or dance steps themselves. And the audience is never wrong. Approval can be as subtle as a child's smile upon seeing three dancers hit an unusual shape. It can come as a patron points out to a companion, as they make a new and closer investigation of a painting, stretching their own powers of observation, to make a connection between the dancers' steps and an abstract painting. It can come even as our trial-and-error motions lean more closely into error. Who doesn't relate to that?

During one water break, an elderly woman asked me, "That female solo, it's this painting, yes?" and pointed to *Nu assis appueyé sur des coussins*. "Yes, it is!" I responded gaily. "I could tell right away, the way it starts in the same reclining pose as the painting and how the dancer expresses such youth, fancifully and freely. Picasso must have truly loved his muses as much as you do." Does engagement with one's audience get any better than that?

And then there were the moments after we had worked through a section, a tentative partial performance in progress, that the gallery goers would spontaneously clap in approval or stay strangely quiet, not stirring. I could tell what was working and what was not by their responses. I could read this stillness too.

This truly was one of my happiest choreographic experiences: communing with Picasso's paintings, pondering his artistic intensions, and studying the maturation of his brushstrokes. I was maturing as well. I had graduated to working closely with art at the highest levels, I had seen genius up close, and through the study of four paintings I had thought further about the life cycle, the hand of a young artist in relation to a midcareer artist and a mature, arguably end-of-life-cycle artist. Now at midcareer I suddenly felt a sense of relief, I had arrived with confidence, my craft and I were hitting our stride and I was gaining clarity about my own identity. I felt like I was doing good work, satisfying and meaningful work. And I was feeling a connection between my two halves, one Asian and one Caucasian. My identities were all etched in the mottled design and stained-glass filigree of monarch wings. I was not one thing, or half-things. I was many things, and I was all things.

The Picasso paintings, like a Rorschach test, a mirror to my interior, brought up many thoughts, especially about my father. I wondered what Picasso's relationship was with his own father, the painter. And now after decoding in my fashion these Picassos, might I now have the skills to read the histories held within my beloved father's brushstrokes? Had this inquiry provided the underpinning of my *Picasso*

Dances imperative all along, somewhere underneath the surface? Isn't everything, in the end, about our own origin stories and coming of age ... and our parents? And aren't all our migrations, no matter how far we travel, all about making our way back home?

It was during this period that I got a rare call from my father. We hadn't spoken at length by phone for several years due to his failing hearing. Instead, we wrote each other via e-mail. I was just beginning my rehearsal process for the new dance. "How are you and those Picassos getting on?" "What do you perceive as Picasso's relationship to dance?" I filled him in. He listened encouragingly and warmly. He suddenly said, "Dana, ... I'm painting again!" He had pulled his easel, brushes, and paints back out of the garage, he said, and had completed three canvases. We talked then about primitivism and cubism. A week later I received an e-mail from him citing this 1907 quote, from remarks Picasso made after a visit to the Musée d'Ethnographie du Trocadéro (Trocadero Museum of Ethnography):

> A smell of mold and neglect caught me by the throat. I was so depressed that I would have chosen to leave immediately. But I forced myself to stay, to examine these masks, all these objects that people had created with a sacred, magical purpose, to serve as intermediaries between them and the unknown, hostile forces surrounding them, attempting in that way to overcome their fears by giving them color and form. And then I understood what painting really meant. It's not an aesthetic process; it's a form of magic that interposes itself between us and the hostile universe, a means of seizing power by imposing a form on our terrors as well as on our desires. The day I understood that, I had found my path.

How does the child of a painter reconcile his or her own artistic life with that of their parent? The eyes of our fathers are behind our own. They are how we first learn to see form, to recognize beauty and acknowledge its power. This project aroused me to fully experience this intergenerational connection, its eternality.

With that phone call and e-mail, Dad had accepted my hand once again, as when I was ten years old, to cross over the threshold that led to magic, the gamut. And the space of just a few more days I would come to understand that something enormous had shifted. Now it was he who was reaching to me, his adult son, asking my support and presence as he crossed his own next threshold, alone.

Picasso Dances premiered at the Kreeger Museum on March 26, 2015, to an intimate audience of 120 invited guests who sat in the main exhibition hall. At the post-performance question-and-answer session, this largely visual arts–oriented audience was intrigued by the choreographic process, by the intersection of dance and art. "How was each section pieced together?" "What does a choreographer see when looking at a painting?" I answered, "Images from an illustrious life filled with movement. To my eyes they dance." The following two performances, on March 26 and 27, elicited questions from comparably inquisitive attendees unfolded with museum patrons and members. This was the sort of audience give and take I savored.

Our performances received wonderful reviews from Rebecca Wren at the *Washington Post* and elsewhere. I took in the exhilaration and deep satisfaction of my company dancers. I took stock. By 2015 I had amassed a twenty-year deep portfolio of original performed dance works. I had toured my company around the world from India to Mongolia, Egypt to Jordan, Mexico to Venezuela. My work had been presented at major theaters in New York City and Washington, DC, the Asia Society, the Kennedy Center, the Smithsonian Institution, the Skirball Center for the Performing Arts, New York's Lincoln Center Out-of-Doors. And DTSBDC had even performed at the White House.

I had paid a lot of dues, on a wide range of "stages," honed my craft through decades of passionately making do, adapting to surfaces that were anything but stages, too. This included makeshift outdoor sand stages in Aman, a theater in Chennai with lights hung on bamboo batons, a crumbling burned-out opera house in Quito, a music festival riser in the jungles of Surinam, sucking in breaths at an oxygen-thin elevation of 11,152 feet in Cusco, on a thick felt floor used by tumbling Mongolian acrobats in Ulaanbaatar, and even inside something as pedestrian as a shopping mall in Toronto. These bare feet had endured every kind of fineness and coarseness, every sort of dirt, sand, splintering wood, pitted brick, and cool slate. Yet each step had led to a better circumstance and to my learning more about how to create and present my work. I was ready for a major career leap.

What I had learned from all these performances was that I often did not need what I might have once thought I needed. I didn't fundamentally need a formal stage, what I craved was an ongoing relationship to the visual arts and to audiences. I needed . . . family. I needed a continued familial connection, to be aloft, invisibly held steady on the kite of childhood memories of my parents' artmaking, to conversations about the creative process and performing for new audiences as family. I also thought about the responsibility I carried to not only fulfill my dreams but to those unrequited ones of my parents' as well—to be represented in major collections, next to the best artworks in the world.

At midlife, I felt that I was at a tipping point of self-actualization. I had achieved much; I had built a name for myself, created a repertoire of dances, and built a wholesome business structure to support and house them. I had cultivated a family of dancers who trusted my compass. People that I respected and loved and upon whom I depended, to realize my own dreams, had come to trust my instincts, and they trusted my care for each of them. Yet I felt that my next migration was about to occur. I could again feel transformation, the flight instinct, within my whole being. I rode the lift under my wings upward to the National Portrait Gallery, and it was there that I next touched down.

twenty-four ALIGHTING AT THE NATIONAL PORTRAIT GALLERY BECOMING THE FIRST CHOREOGRAPHER-IN-RESIDENCE

In late November 2016, after conversations and negotiations with Kim Sajet, director of the National Portrait Gallery and the Board of Directors of the Dana Tai Soon Burgess Dance Company, I was named the first-ever choreographer-in-residence for the Smithsonian Institution. After more than a year of vetting, my official Memo of Understanding was signed by the secretary of the Smithsonian, Dr. David J. Skorton, and me.

I am headquartered at the National Portrait Gallery where for the last six years I have created dances that illuminate American diversity, and which animate the depth and breadth of the American experience. My mandate is to enliven and interpret their permanent collection as well as their rotating, short-term exhibitions, through dance, thereby allowing audiences a direct experience of how the visual arts can inspire new art and give birth to original, fresh, and dynamic interpretations. This inclusion of a dance component, in an ongoing and coordinated expression of commitment, facilitates the visitors' deeper and more meaningful interactions with, connections to, and experiences of these collections. My work as a choreographer animates static forms on canvas and those frozen in bronze and clay and all other media.

As choreographer-in-residence, I create two major works a year, one in the spring and one in the fall, scheduled in concert with the gallery administration. I also design lectures and demonstrations about the history of modern dance and have worked with the Smithsonian's Center for Learning and Digital Access on video programs about my choreographic process. The company rehearses and performs throughout several spaces in the National Portrait Gallery, from the Nan Tucker McEvoy Auditorium (a 346-seat theater) to the Kogod Courtyard, to the many exhibition halls.

My work at the Smithsonian reminds me of the 2006 film by director Shawn Levy, *A Night at the Museum*. The ghosts of each art-filled exhibit hall speak to me as I wander, contemplating masterful portraits and sculptures. I visit the collections, catching a serendipitous inspiration with my sketchpad in hand, often stopping to work out a movement phrase in front of a portrait that has captured my attention, and continue on. The collection comes alive; rich imagery, historical contexts, and personal stories enliven new dance phrases, new alphabets of movement—new dialects using those alphabets.

One might say—and they would be absolutely right—that I have realized my dream of being surrounded by art, and, in fact, the vast Smithsonian Institution has become that home for me. It has the enormity of its breadth and collections to keep me ever turning new corners. It feeds the child within me, the drive to satisfy my curiosities about the world, about human beings, about the nature of art and artmaking itself as individual self-expression as well as of community.

In preparation for my programs, I meet with our nation's top curators and art historians learning the backstories of featured artists and their masterpieces. I ask about the provenance of paintings and photographs and probe the sociopolitical contexts that surrounded these artworks. I find out what events impacted an artist's life and how these factors manifested in their art. I study portraits in search of symbolism and hidden clues; I read memoirs, journals, and biographies voraciously, in search of personal stories and anecdotes about the passions that inform their subjects, the taproot of their fervor. All these inquiries infuse my dances with their fervor. I seek to connect with visual artists not only of the past but also of the present, to let them know that I witness their lives, their influences, their desires to communicate their messages and connect with generations who follow. I want each dance to be a vehicle by which a viewer can contemplate history and portraiture anew. I seek to represent our nation's people and stories through the art of dance.

I am often asked how I became the Smithsonian Institution's first choreographer-in-residence. And how did such an official position come into being? While it seemed to be one of those "overnight" news-making events, a headline of sorts in the arts world, in fact, it had been years . . . decades . . . in the making.

My Smithsonian residency had its real jumpstart while I was engaged in projects such as those at the Kreeger Museum and the National Gallery of Art. Between those two projects, in July 2013, I received a momentous phone call from Amy Henderson, an art historian at the Smithsonian's National Portrait Gallery. The National Portrait Gallery was authorized and founded by Congress in 1962 with the mission to acquire and display portraits of "men and women who have made significant contributions to the history, development, and culture of the people of the United States." Today, the Smithsonian's National Portrait Gallery continues to narrate the multifaceted and ever-changing story of America through the portraits of diverse individuals who have shaped its unique rich culture.

Amy spoke to me about her upcoming exhibition, *Dancing the Dream*, the first Smithsonian exhibition about the history of American dance. It would be a comprehensive story, she said, told through paintings, sculptures, prints, videos, and photographs, including images from all periods, genres, and styles, from Isadora Duncan to Misty Copeland, from Fred Astaire to Gregory Hines, from Rita Moreno to Paula Abdul. For this exhibit, Amy was looking to provide museum visitors with an actual dancing dimension.

She asked if I might come down to the gallery that week and explore some ideas with her related to that upcoming exhibition. Amy is a world-class historian specializing in the lively arts—particularly media-generated celebrity culture. Her books and exhibitions range in spectrum from the pioneers in early broadcasting to Elvis Presley, Katharine Hepburn, and Katharine Graham. A few days later I met Amy at the G Street entrance of the gallery. This was an entrance that when first moving to the area I stepped through each Sunday to view the collection and jot down notes of choreographic inspiration. My life was coming full circle in this moment of déjà vu.

Despite the fact that our circles might very well have intersected, we had not actually formally met before that day. I told her how aware I was of her work, the respect I had for her impact there. She responded with equal warmth, telling me that she was familiar with my reputation, my touring. The international performances had fascinated her, but so, too, domestic performances. She had spoken to several other museum curators and knew that my company and I had worked with great success over many years in a wide range of museum settings, and with a diverse range of presenters and sponsors. She had always read the reviews of my performances, she said, too, and congratulated me on a recent one, in which I was identified as "not only a Washington prize, but a national dance treasure." It was gratifying to be in her company, in this place. We shared our mutual acquaintanceships with other living artists. We joked a bit, too, about how media loves titles, like "DC's Diplomat of Dance," and "poet laureate of Washington Dance." We got each other, in warm simpatico, right away.

And here we were, on one of those delicious Washington, DC "walk and talks"; "Come with me, won't you?" she said, and I felt myself to be dancing with her on air as we bounded through the gallery. "I want to show you something." That "something" was unbeknown to me until that moment: she had chosen to highlight in the exhibit a twenty-by-thirty-inch, black-and-white portrait of me, taken in 1998 by Mary Noble Ours. In it, I was dancing *Helix* in tandem with the sculpture by John Dreyfuss. She wanted to begin our visit by showing me where it would be hung.

I was thrilled because the National Portrait Gallery had meant so very much to the development of my work when I first moved to DC, providing comfort and solace and a life force like sunlight in my early twenties. And now, hearing that there was to be a photo of me, dancing, in the same exhibit as my dance idols, left me overcome. I stammered with sentiment because this was well beyond my ability to even take in.

I would need all my professional discipline to move out of that reverie and prepare to take in what came next. Amy then came to the reason for her having called. She asked if there was anything I could add to the exhibit in the way of actual dancing: "This exhibit is about dance, and it can't go up without actual dancing!" Amy was willing to push the potentials of the museum experience. That day we conspired to turn an exhibition room, one among several rooms dedicated to this exhibit, into an actual dance studio, a living laboratory for the public to experience in real time how a dance is created. We even talked about live-video-streaming the rehearsals to tens of thousands of viewers via the Smithsonian's streaming channel.

We outlined a plan for open rehearsals that would take place weekly during the exhibition's long run—October 2013 through July 2014—with the outcome of the rehearsals to be not one work but, in fact, a pair of "new major dance works" to premiere in the museum's Kogod Courtyard. This enclosed space, with its elegant glass canopy of wavy glass and steel appears to float over the 28,000-square-foot courtyard and lets in natural light. It is considered one of Washington's largest and most magnificent event spaces. Here the museum would set up seating for audience members, turning the courtyard into an elegant theater.

In October 2013 my company began open rehearsals inside the National Portrait Gallery's *Dancing the Dream* exhibition. We were, in fact, a living installation. We were a new example of the cross-pollination of portraiture and dance. Not only were we to interface with patrons—we were not to be "other" or with a "do not disturb, work in progress" isolation—but we were also going to live stream via a special camera installed in our new first-floor-gallery studio, aimed to best capture us on our new dance floor!

Here in the exhibit I began rehearsing my dance company, in order to choreograph a new thirty-minute dance, an homage, based on the portraits of my own dance heroes and heroines, dancers and dance-makers of stage and screen, from Loie Fuller, Ted Shawn, and Michio Itō to Bob Fosse. The contractions and releases of Martha Graham, the tap steps of James Cagney, the high kicks of Rita Moreno, and the disco *Saturday Night Fever* moves of John Travolta.

In wandering the exhibit, it dawned on me: why not have the musical score include the actual voices of these silent portraits? Why not include interviews of past choreographers and entertainers and their associated best-loved musical scores? I wanted audiences to actually hear about, and from, these innovators of creative processes, to savor their passionate personal stories. Online, I found many resources: a recording of Liza Minnelli talking about how dance enlivened her world and allowed her to express the love she felt for her audiences; Shirley MacLaine—a Santa Fe resident—speaking about her past life connection to dance; Ted Shawn contemplating growing old but still feeling connected to the artform; and Bob Fosse talking about his obsessive choreographic idiosyncrasies. The voices of dance artists would be appropriately interlinked with references to the music from films across the eras of Hollywood: *Sweet Charity*, *Saturday Night Fever*, Jimmy Cagney's *Yankee Doodle Dandy*, and even Shirley Temple and George Murphy's *Little Miss Broadway*.

In the gallery, surrounded by the portraits of dance legends, I began to mold the new dance that I titled *Homage* on ten of my dancers, five men and five women. At first, I was worried that I would be distracted by visitors to the museum who would come upon us working. But their presence, in fact, made me focus all the more on the choreography. I became hyperaware of the dance phrasing as I tuned out passersby who stopped to watch us work. There were no barriers, no tape on the floor or stanchions. There were also moments that I actually loved when a family sat along a wall and stayed to watch our rehearsal for an hour or two, or when a gaggle of teenagers drawn by the sound of our music would happen upon a rehearsal and take camera-phone selfies and still photos or, even short videos featuring the dancers in motion.

I built *Homage* from a collaging, layering like decoupage of dance references. I would make a movement phrase, choose a moment or milestone in dance history, and manipulate the phrase so that it looked like it was from that period. The way dancers train has changed over time, and these changes, combined with the social mores of each period, have modified the look of dancers' bodies and how they approach movement. The way people danced in the 1930s is different than the way they danced in the 1970s or even the way people dance today; dance reflects societal norms, customs, and attitudes toward sexuality (acceptance versus inhibition and restraint, overt expressions, or coy innuendo). It is increasingly free of gender specificity. I would make a dance phrase and then have the dancers perform the phrase rigidly filled with Martha Graham's contraction and release technique, for example, or with the abandon of the disco dance the "hustle." For me this exercise was freeing, and for the dancers it was such a fun challenge. It was an investigation, a poignant, elegiac homage to American dance history and its greatest icons. I formulated intricate duets, quartets, and group sections that referenced many historic dance artists so that audiences would better understand the evolution of American dance.

I also had immediate feedback in a way I had not before from viewers, and this was because of their access and real-time curiosities being so piqued and welcomed. During dance breaks, people who had been viewing a rehearsal would seek to share what they thought they were seeing. "I had no idea dancemaking took this much work." "I think I recognized some of the gestures. Are they from those portraits over there?" And then there were e-mails from fans who were following the creation of the dance on the Smithsonian streaming channel. "I'm a dance student in South Carolina and I've been watching your rehearsals for three weeks now. I take tap, jazz, and contemporary dance and can see how all my training comes together in the dance." We were reaching and having dialogues with audiences of all demographics, and in a whole new way.

One day in October, Amy Henderson stopped in to observe. At the end of rehearsal she said, "May I just say, that as a historian who loves dance and musical theater, you are nailing it. I get all the references to my exhibit! I love it! But more important, you know, I can feel and see how stirring this is for our art constituency." Her approbation anticipated how enthusiastically the audience received the work when it formally premiered in the Kogod Courtyard in November 2013.

An hour before the late afternoon show, several hundred audience members had already gathered, filling all the two hundred seats and now also standing on the far perimeters of the fifty-by-forty-foot dance floor we had installed. By the time the dancers entered the space we had four hundred people eagerly awaiting the show.

A dance performed in the courtyard, under its expansive glass canopy with sun shining through, and the same dance performed in a darkened theater differ in experience for both the performers and the audience. In a dark enclosed theater, the performer dances to a wall of darkness, knowing the audience is out there but never seeing their individual faces. Whereas, here in the courtyard, the dancers had clear view of the individuals in the crowd. An intimate relationship between performer and audience member quickly evolves.

The music montage started and *Homage* began. The dancers wore an array of costumes by Judy Hansen that referenced dance luminaries. In a tight spandex shirt and bell bottom jazz pants à la late 1960s, Kelly brilliantly mimicked the postures and gestures of Broadway choreographer Bob Fosse, his head tilted back at an angle, weight sitting in one hip, mimicking holding a cigarette with one hand, the other hand on his hip. He was accompanied by a recorded audio interview in which Fosse talked about his rehearsal process as a Broadway choreographer. In a 1970s dazzling purple sequin pantsuit, Katia entered and danced jazz steps in the persona of Liza Minnelli, as dancers swirled in a circle surrounding her.

Then there was a quickstep duet by Alvaro and our new company member Christin Arthur. Christin is half Korean and half American and her path included sojourns with Ballet West in Utah as well as the Universal Ballet in Seoul. They danced to the voices of Shirley Temple and George Murphy singing "We Should be Together." Christin was in a short black-and-white baby doll dress reminiscent of the child actress's most recognizable attire and Alvaro danced in a formal white shirt and black dress pants.

But perhaps the most poignant moment occurred at the end of *Homage* when the five couples scattered, gently danced with one another, and lovingly embraced, to an excerpt of Shirley MacLaine's 1969 rendition of "It's a Nice Face," a simple song from the soundtrack of *Sweet Charity*, her voice shaky with tearful tenderness. The simple ending image reinforced that love, the longing to connect with others, through dance and music, visual art and film, is perhaps at the heart of why we all dance.

The dancers took their bows. Their applause echoed through the Kogod Courtyard. The National Portrait Gallery had accepted not just portraits of dancers as part of its collection but now dance itself.

It got better.

The director of the National Portrait Gallery, Kim Sajet, an elegant tall blonde woman in her forties approached me and said in an Australian accent, "I loved that!"

And this brings us back now to when Kim inked my contract to be the first-ever Choreographer-in-Residence at the Smithsonian in 2016.

Kim is Dutch, raised in Australia, and before moving to America she was a curator and a museum director. Upon moving to America, she became the president and CEO of the Historical Society of Pennsylvania, after that, the vice president and deputy director of the Pennsylvania Academy of the Fine Arts. Subsequently she was the director of corporate relations at the Philadelphia Museum of Art. At last, she assumed her role at the National Portrait Gallery. Kim is also the first woman to direct the museum. She had a forward-thinking vision to transform the traditional staid museum environment by energizing each through unique collaborations and interdisciplinary projects. Aside from furthering the vision of the museum, Kim is in charge of all the curators, the historians, programming, and fundraising. Our vision and goals were aligned like kindred spirits, and Kim had the power to make historic changes, a new paradigm for how dance and a stolid major museum could be official collaborators in the spirit of long-term capacity.

Three weeks after the premiere of *Homage*, I started my second commissioned work for the Portrait Gallery, as discussed with Amy Henderson, based on *Dancing the Dream*. I had come to know the museum so well over the past few months. I needed to create a work that was not in any way redundant. I paced the galleries restlessly until my gaze settled upon a silver gelatin photograph of Doris Humphrey taken by Barbara Morgan in 1939, titled *With My Red Fires ("Matriarch")*. This photograph portrays modern dance pioneer Doris Humphrey in the role of "Matriarch" from her dance *With My Red Fires*, which focused on romantic love. Humphrey, underneath a long billowing dress that resembled the type worn by Puritans in the 1600s, is portrayed in a deep leg bend, her body in partial darkness, her stern face illuminated.

Did her intense expression suggest that she was emerging from or receding into the undertow of a deep psychologic stage? Was she pondering the struggle between the psychological "light" and "shadow" selves, between desire and resistance? This question was the start of my choreographic parsing.

Prior to our first rehearsal, I listened to dozens of musical scores online until I settled on a work composed by Ernest Bloch, *Suite Hébraïque* (1951), arranged for piano and violin. This soulful work references traditional Jewish music and simulates the deep, lonely tones of a shofar.

On our first rehearsal back at the Portrait Gallery, in our dance studio in the exhibit, I instructed the full company cast of ten, six men and four women, to move close to one another, to clump into uncomfortable sculptured standing shapes with their focus cast downward. I asked them to constantly morph their poses atop small sustained slow walks, to add gestures of wringing hands and contorted arms suggestive of being within a thick mire, slowly moving as if through a bog. Here were the dark "shadows" of Barbara Morgan's photo of Doris Humphrey.

The next rehearsal, I played the Bloch score over our sound system and demonstrated how movements and dance phrasing could interplay with the music: piano notes as dancers' steps and the rise and fall of the bow of the violin as the rise and fall of the arms and legs. When this concept was clear for everyone, I began to create duets on pairs of dancers. In these duets the dancers made direct eye contact with each other and performed interplays of lifts and cantilevered balances. I choreographed several short duets, each couple in sequence would leave the group, and when finished, would return to the group. Finally, I asked Sarah and Kelly, now seasoned dance partners, to rush from the group as if making some great escape, a flight for freedom. On them I set a long duet of complicated lifts in which Kelly placed Sarah on his thighs and shoulders from which she reached her arms and limbs outward and upward. This duet would become the centerpiece of the dance. Here was the "light" from Morgan's photograph.

Museumgoers sat and stood in the room with us, causing me to hyperfocus and concentrate on the dance. The crowds had grown since *Homage*, drawn by a continued press campaign about the exhibit that included reprints of reviews in the *Washington Post* and the *New York Times*. Rehearsing in the same exhibit gallery with visitors triggered my thoughts on the human inclination to divide into affinity groups. The dancers as a tribe with shared movement traits versus the audience as another. Even though we occupied the same space, our intentions were not the same, the visitor's intention was voyeuristic while the dancer's was to learn a dance. In a way, the dancers and I were steeped in a shared consciousness that deepened, as did our will to focus, the latter sharpened when visitors entered the room. Their comings and goings only heightened the dancers' connections to one another and forced them to concentrate even more closely to my direction. Sure, this was all a little existential. But working in this shared reality with spectators lends itself to such rich contemplations.

Over the next several rehearsals I began to shape spatial patterns on stage and choreograph the exits and re-entrances of the duets from and to the group formation and I sharpened the timings of each duet. I added a spiral path for the group to move slowly, ploddingly across stage and then back again. Finally, I choreographed a tableau. I had Ben and Katia pull away from the group as if to dance a duet, but this time no duet occurred. In its place I instructed Ben to gently fall to the floor at which point Katia knelt next to him and tentatively touched his shoulder on the last note of the musical score.

In viewing the completed twenty-minute dance, I decided to call it *Confluence*, as for me the title implied a juncture of movement phrases, a meeting place of both light and shadow.

Judy Hansen came to study the Barbara Morgan portrait and to view the dance and meet with me about costuming. We spoke about the theme of light and dark, of magnetism and repulsion. For the men she designed formal black jackets with low V-neck lines that accentuated their pectoral muscles and pairs of fitted long black pants. For the women she designed long streamlined black dresses of a stretch net fabric under which was an additional layer, in white, that added dimension to the dancers' movements and heightened the theme of light and shadow.

On April 19, 2014, at 2 p.m., in the Kogod Courtyard at the National

Portrait Gallery, before an audience of six hundred museum patrons, Dana Tai Soon Burgess Dance Company premiered *Confluence.* The images of separation and attraction, of group "hive mind" versus individual desires was now amplified by the great expanse of the space. The courtyard allowed for better sightlines for the drama of each movement and spatial pattern. Flourishes of the black-and-white costumes were now outlined by a pristine charcoal-colored dance floor and the courtyard's stone walls and shown like sumi ink strokes on rice paper. Each musical leg kick and twirl came to life and then everything was still, except for Katie's hand moving downward in slow motion, finally gently resting upon the shoulder of Ben, lying on the ground at the last piano note of the Bloch's Sonata No. 1, Molto quieto for piano and violin. Katie lowered her head in the last audible lingering of the piano note and the tableau between the two of them crystalized.

In that final image of *Confluence,* I suddenly felt an uneasy foreboding as I studied Ben, the supine dancer dressed in black, on the ground. Was this actually an image of death? Was Katia's gentle touch on Ben's shoulder as if wings of a butterfly coming to a final resting place?

The audience let out an audible sigh as if they had been holding their breath in reverence of Ben and Katia. The rousing applause freed me from any creative trepidation. I joined the standing audience that by then was clapping loudly; their enthusiasm encouraged the dancers to take several bows, after which Sarah ran out of the bow line and beckoned, Judy Hansen, and our rehearsal director Anne Sidney, who cleans the dance movements and coaches the dancers for dramatic intention, and me to come to stage. We took one last group bow all together. Success!

There are few choreographies that take my breath away. *Confluence* is such a dance. From Barbara Morgan's photograph of Doris Humphrey emerged a nonlinear, abstract dance that is my ever-moving Rorschach inkblot test that speaks to me from a deep emotional reservoir. Dance speaks where words cannot.

Reading a review by dance writer George Jackson in *Danceview Times,* I sifted through my thoughts about whether the ending tableau was indeed an awakening or was it a demise? Is death within the cycle of life an ending point or actually a point marking renewal? The question would taunt me for several months, as I had been worried about my father's health. He had recently turned ninety and was experiencing an as-yet undiagnosed health problem; he would be taken over by chills, then go unconscious for minutes at a time, before at last regaining consciousness. My mother would stretch him on the floor and hold him until he revived, and she could help him up. Ten years earlier he had successfully recovered from lymphoma, but there was always the lingering concern of metastasis, and it hovered around this domestic tableau just like the final piano note in the Bloch Sonata Molto quieto. Mom and Dad were like Katia and Ben. *Confluence* was also my own inkblot test. My parents decided (as they always had) that they would handle this issue themselves, and their decision was to not seek a protracted process of diagnosis and treatment at his advanced age. They knew in their hearts that his cancer had come back in full force to now devour his frail body. My father's situation lingered in my thoughts and the dreams I recorded in my dream journals, but I pressed on . . . as did he.

After the premiere of *Confluence*, Kim Sajet, Bonnie, and I sat down for a long debrief exploring how we could build upon the successes of the residency, how we would expand this model long-term for me to create more dances that were inspired by their exhibits and permanent collection, and how we could continue to attract and to engage visitors in real-time.

Kim's initial openness to inviting me into the museum had well aligned with her plan to change the face of our nation's Portrait Gallery, making it a living museum that reflects the evolving American story, as told through its diverse populations. Prior to Kim Sajet's leadership the gallery was—to be sure—distinguished and venerable. However, it had been limited in its approach to collecting works of and about and by diverse Americans who make up its citizens. Her vision was perfectly aligned with my own. She wanted to shake up the staid and stolid image of an institution and to animate and energize it, to make it a place to regularly BE and not just to occasionally GO. To integrate it in visitors' lives and to make its collections relatable, deeply felt, ever relevant, and essential.

We both wanted a museum to be a sanctuary—not just for us, who had devoted ourselves to art, but for everyone. A place that felt as much like home as did one's own residence. Where art was not something separate, external, but where art was alive and as kindred as one's own kin.

Kim said, "When I got here our collection was predominantly filled with images of and about dead white men. I intend to change the canon of this museum's collection to be inclusive and contemporary, reflective of Americans today, and I can see your work as part of that process." And so, in 2014, we moved forward with a plan, Kim would create the position of Choreographer in Residence. This proposal, an outline for a new official position within the institution, would move slowly through committees and up the Smithsonian ladder, and finally be ratified in 2016. I had moved from the periphery to the center of a cultural conversation. I was no longer an outsider. My career of exploration of boundaries and identities was paying off for me, and arguably for many others. Dance was officially part of the national conversation. This felt so clean, so good, so deeply satisfying.

I wrote an e-mail to my father, telling him the exciting news. He wrote back quickly: "This is no small feat, an artist's life is not easy, it is a journey of sheer will and you have willed yourself into being seen and acknowledged alongside many other great artists and without a paintbrush, a lump of clay or a camera, but rather with your own two bare feet."

How I loved that.

My artmaking—an aesthetic that he had such a crucial influence in developing—my dances—had made it safely into museums. Dad was proud of me, and I was thankful to him.

The paperwork slow danced, picking daisies on its desultory way through institutional hierarchies for more than a year before its pages fluttered back and landed as a butterfly in the form of an official signed Memo of Understanding. But Dad would not ultimately see the memo.

And so it happened, the ending tableau of *Confluence* infiltrated my real life—life imitating art. On Wednesday, October 22, 2014, I was in my studio in the middle of rehearsal when my mobile phone rang.

The familiar New Mexico area code (505) flashed across the screen followed by a number I didn't recognize. I knew that something was gravely wrong when I answered and it was my mom's best friend, Tanis. "Dana. Oh, Dana. You need to come home to Santa Fe as quickly as possible. Your dad is in an ambulance heading to Saint Vincent Hospital, and your mom is riding with him. I'm going to meet her there now." I'm sure I stammered something, and I hung up, mumbled some words to the company, walked out, jumped in my car for home, and quickly packed. My husband Jameson—still then my fiancé—booked an airline ticket and connections for me and drove me to the airport at 3 a.m. for a 4:30 a.m. flight.

During the nine-hour trip to Santa Fe—two plane flights, one layover, and a car rental—I had plenty of time to ponder all the missed conversations with my father and unanswered questions about his life. Would there now be time to have those conversations? What had he dreamed of doing when he was thirty, forty, fifty years old? Were his dreams the same as mine? Did he have a favorite work of art? What were his regrets? Why had he so suddenly begun painting again this year—this very year—after all these years of dormancy? And this: did my work at museums somehow fulfill for him his own dreams, too . . . not just mine? Had I somehow completed his migratory route, like those monarchs?

Memories, they all spooled before me in those dark transitional hours.

At last, I arrived at Saint Vincent Hospital on the outskirts of Santa Fe. I found my father's cramped room, and I crumpled into a crackled faux leather upholstered chair at my father's bedside. He was sleeping.

Dad's pinkish beige sterile room was devoid of art—not even some cheap, mass-produced, generic pastoral scene. The view out the stingy, narrow, vertical-slit window was of a sliver of sky and an adjacent adobe-color medical building. Below, a gray gravel rock garden framed a single two-foot-tall squat and determined yucca plant defiantly surviving its arid solitary confinement.

My mother had gone home to nap a few hours and await the arrival of my brother, Ian, soon to land from Taiwan where he was working.

My vigil began in front of the window as I watched a splinter of the vivid Santa Fe sunset perform its lurid fan dance, moving progressively from orange to pink and finally purple before slashing toward total darkness. His sedatives wearing off, my father finally woke around 7:30 p.m., in a delirium that would become a night-long rant. During this soliloquy he relived navy intelligence stories from the 1940s. "We need to save the ensign, or he will be shot." "Quickly move out and gather the others before they arrive, or they will kill everyone inside." "They removed the mole, but they will come for you." In between his urgent commands, he asked me for ice chips for his parched lips. Throughout the night, I fed crushed ice slivers to Dad, with a small plastic spoon. By early morning, my exhausted father was put under, into a deep morphine-induced sleep. Mom and Ian arrived and after a brief family scrum with dad's doctor, it was decided that he would go home for hospice care.

The French *Danse Macabre*, or The Dance of Death, is an allegory born from famines and the Black Plague of the Middle Ages. It depicted a dancing skeleton leading the religious man, the rich man, the pauper, and the artist to their graves as equals. All succumb to the dance of death and, so, now would my father. His own process of dying would be the last views of his life—his life as the ultimate artmaking—to which I would be privy. Once again, I was that kid snooping around in the garage, when he was not aware, studying him. Observing. Absorbing. And loving him. How I loved him.

Mom had arranged for the delivery of a hospital bed in the living room. A social worker—a retired ballet dancer from nothing less than the American Ballet Theatre (what were the odds?)—was to aid us all in this transition. She said, "He will float into a peaceful fog of memories." I placed large headsets over my father's ears and played his favorite recordings of Johannes Brahms and piano works by Frederic Chopin as he lay there in his bed, I have to believe—I want to believe—comfortably. I intermittently removed the headsets to whisper words of support, ones that I hoped would ease him to leave his failing body to let his spirit fly, "It's OK to go, Dad. Your mother, father, and grandparents, they will lead the way."

For seven days and nights we held vigil until Halloween night his breathing rattled, faltered, and failed. Dad died at 12:01 a.m. on November 1, 2014, at the age of ninety; a painting he had done just a month prior of grays, purples, and black hung over his bed. I gently placed my hand on his shoulder . . . as light as a butterfly . . . as had Katie touched Ben at the end of *Confluence* . . . the death of a monarch.

My family decided to loosely follow Confucian practices; we opened a sliding glass door to release his spirit, burned incense and candles, and placed at his feet a tray of food and drink for his journey to the afterworld. Halloween was always my father's favorite holiday. He loved the costumes, the taunting interplay with images of the dead. Each Halloween he hung two cardboard decorations from the 1920s that he had since childhood—a pumpkin with Betty Boop eyes and hair in a bob, and a witch in silhouette flying on her broomstick past the moon. It was fitting that he sensed the importance of this holiday to his own life cycle, his preordained day to die.

The first of November is *Día de los Muertos*, the Spanish Day of the Dead. In Mexico the day's celebrations are inundated with images of monarch butterflies because they are said to carry the spirits of the departed. The first monarchs arrive in Mexico for the winter at the end of October and the beginning of November, coinciding with *Día de los Muertos*. This is when the portal between the living and the dead is said to be most permeable. That day families visit graveyards, setting up picnics over the graves of deceased family members to share a meal with the spirits of their ancestors. It is when ofrendas, or altars, are set up in homes, inviting the dead to visit and rest along their extended journey home. Photos of deceased loved ones are carefully placed on ofrendas among marigolds, sweet bread, and water, illuminated by candles and surrounded by *papel picados*, brightly colored paper cutout flags, and the smoke from copal incense. On *Día de los Muertos* the living and the dead commune freely.

Together my brother and I bathed my father's body and then dressed him in his favorite Hawaiian Aloha print shirt, khaki pants, and maroon leather loafers. The funeral home employees arrived within the hour to remove his physical body. Dad was cremated a day later with two items: his worn copy of the *I-Ching*, or as it is called in English, the Book of Changes—ancient Chinese texts of Divination—and his beloved badger hair paintbrush.

At home, his paintings—evidence of his life—occupied several walls of the house: abstract works done sporadically over sixty-five years, including the one he had recently completed. These paintings were all anagrams, clues to major events in his life, brief breakthroughs from the artist block that bullied him. It was his gallery of masks, his attendant companions in the end of life, as Tim Wengerd had his mask collection. I had no Enigma machine to decipher their coded messages. His paintings would, however, become mirrors facing toward my own psyche. Perhaps a canvas is meant to capture once-interior dialogues through images made from brush strokes. We study paintings to understand others as well as ourselves.

Mom was numb and my brother exhausted and distant. The following night I sat outside under the New Mexico sky staring at the stars and struggled to make sense of the connection between my father's creativity—his life—and mine. Like those next generations of butterflies, I inherited part of his consciousness and his art. Here, with no scrim of urban light pollution, the sky brilliantly shown the constellations, and Orion's Belt presided above me; I recalled my friend, Mary Motah, a Comanche medicine woman, and her telling me that her people originated from the stars. "They came from the blue star, Sirius, and returned to it again upon death" were her words. Perhaps my father was out there somewhere, among the vast cosmos carried along by a monarch, a glowing kaleidoscopic, swirling, dancing galaxy.

In the silence, I reflected on memories, back even to my first visit to the Gamut with dad. I thought of my many tours to faraway places and the full-circle migration, of my being back, here, to him, to my family, to see again the beginnings of the formulation of my life's intentions. Perhaps my quest for a place to belong was not in any one physical location any longer but rather within my layers of reconciliations—and my embracing—of growing up in Santa Fe with all its challenges, its rich heritage, its influences and its, well, confluences, and its lasting impressions. And at this moment I sensed my consciousness shift into full adulthood, welcoming a flood of thoughts of the new responsibilities I had toward my family as well as to my dance family, and to the field of dance. It became apparent that, like generations of other choreographers before me, I too was a monarch whose internalized destiny would someday be passed on.

Dance lulls us into a false sense of never aging. It is the "Water of Life" as referenced in the Alexander Romance—a tale written shortly after Alexander the Great's death in 323 BCE by an unknown author that has through the millennia become more fantastical and that describes Alexander the Great's journey across a region of darkness in pursuit of the mythical fountain of youth. Yet as Geoffrey Chaucer wrote, "Time and tide wait for no man," and this includes the dancer, the choreographer. With an unexpected urgency, having been confronted with my new position as the full "adult" versus "the child," I was changed, my way of thinking about dance-making shifted, fed my creativity, and pushed me to consider how to best serve our next generation of artists.

It was upon the death of my father, and my processing of all that this meant for me, that at forty-six, I became a man. And I was determined to be the best man and artist that I could ever be . . . and there was a lot of work to do.

It is no accident that *Confluence* is a stronghold of our repertoire, performed at the Kennedy Center several times to date and that is taken on international tour regularly.

We even took it to my home turf of New Mexico, in 2017, to both the University of New Mexico's Elizabeth Waters Center for Dance Theatre—in what had been the Carlisle Gymnasium—and to the National Dance Center in Santa Fe, located in the neighborhood where I grew up in the 1970s and early 1980s. My old high school friend and now internationally renowned costume designer Patricia Michaels was there for the event with her parents, and they sat with my mother.

Confluence proved to be a deep homecoming, and as George Jackson queried, "Is an awakening Burgess's intent?" The piece does capture the dualities, of endings and beginnings . . . and the answer is affirmative for me as a choreographer, an artist that had moved from being an outsider to an insider, the child who had once danced barefoot on the desert dirt and staved off bullies, had triumphantly come full circle . . . I had awakened.

Prior to the Santa Fe performance I received notice of a Mayoral Proclamation officially declaring March 18, 2017, "Dana Tai Soon Burgess Day." The proclamation was formally announced by Santa Fe council member Renee Villarreal at a pre-performance reception. I had to laugh, but with no bitterness. The Chino and Mariposa who had once been an outsider in his hometown was now officially designated its favorite son.

Since my formal Smithsonian appointment in 2016, I have choreographed ten major dances and eight dance videos, each inspired by the National Portrait Gallery's collection. I have artistic freedom to choose the exhibits and works that I set to dance, I experiment and create works that then move from incubation into the company's season and that include performances at the museum and also at regional, national, and international theaters.

In the 2020 season, the National Portrait Gallery's special exhibit *One Life: Marian Anderson* traced the life of the legendary American opera singer and icon of social justice activism who died in 1993; paintings, portraits, photos, and personal artifacts from Anderson's childhood to the pinnacles of her career and her civil rights work put her accomplishments on display. She was an extraordinary contralto with a three-octave vocal range and the first African American soloist to perform at the Metropolitan Opera House in New York City and also the first to perform at the White House. She integrated opera, paving a path for other African Americans in this art. In February 2020, just before the outbreak of Covid-19, in conjunction with that exhibit and in celebration of Black History Month, Dana Tai Soon Burgess Dance Company premiered *A Tribute to Marian Anderson*, a dance that incorporated a live performance by soprano Millicent Scarlett who sang with piano accompaniment, featuring songs from Marian Anderson's repertoire.

This was the launch of our season dedicated to social justice icons: our way of engaging BIPOC (Black, Indigenous, People of Color) voices, bringing stories from diverse communities to the forefront through dance.

A global pandemic would shape the next two years of our dance company. At first, we adapted, respecting masking and social distancing protocols even in our on-again, off-again rehearsals. Our schedule varied with each Covid-19 variant. Our finger-touches would have to be connected by invisible and imaginary threads, six feet apart. So be it. A creative challenge, sure, but not a defeat; we were a seasoned touring company with plenty of experience in making adjustments to the unforeseen. Defying all odds was as reflexive for us as defying all gravity. Lockdowns and quarantines then spun forward. Weeks became months and then two years. During all of these phases, we continued to dance together. All company classes were conducted via Zoom. We commenced solo and duet rehearsals and once we had our health protocols figured out, added group rehearsals.

The Arts Club of Washington, the oldest arts nonprofit in the District of Columbia and the former home of President Monroe, would prove to be one of our saviors. Right before the Covid-19 outbreak, this historic site had installed a medical grade air filtration HVAC system. What were the odds? When we began meeting in person, they offered us their space for rehearsals. The Arts Club of Washington was one of the few spaces open and willing to have us. In general, dance studios, theaters, and museums were either closed entirely during periods of strictest quarantine, or open only on an extremely limited basis.

By fall 2020, wearing matching masks and costumes, DTSBDC was able to perform a tribute program for a socially distanced mask-wearing audience of first responders, at an outdoor venue outside the Kennedy Center called The Reach. This would be our first in-person performance in more than seven months. The audience sat on a lawn six feet away from one another and forty feet from the front of the performance area. There were perhaps twenty-five audience members. This would represent the new base line from which, over the next year and a half, as vaccinations slowly rolled out, we would have to rebuild our audiences with consideration for their safety and that of the dancers.

What evolved for the dance company were two performance platforms. One we designed for the presentation of dances exclusively available online that we filmed out of doors and in large socially distanced spaces, and another set of works that we created for a scant few in-person venues.

During this period, we used the relatively dormant and confining periods of no travel as an asset. We innovated some new products. In response to the critical conversation about diversity, equity, and inclusion of all kinds in America and around the world, we premiered a series of dances on film. We distributed these unique films through our company website, social media, and community partners, as well as the Portrait Gallery's electronic platforms. These dances are inspired by the museum's portraits of social justice leaders including Charlayne Hunter Gault, Cesar Chavez, Dolores Huerta, Earl Warren, Rosamond Johnson, and George Takei. The timeless films have since penetrated a wide range of cultural and educational institutions.

I recently had the deep pleasure of meeting with actor and activist George Takei, who portrayed the original fictional character Hikaru Sulu from the *Star Trek* media franchise. We discussed his life, specifically his family internment as Japanese Americans and his thoughts on the actual history of Asian Americans. This conversation ultimately inspired the choreography for the DTSBDC dance video based on his official portrait that hangs in the National Portrait Gallery's *Struggle for Justice* exhibit.

In the wake of Covid-19, anti-Asian violence escalated. In 2021 incidents of assault against anyone in America whose lineage was Asian increased. To combat this I established a podcast, Slant Podcast (slantpodcast.com). Through a half-hour, one-on-one interview format, I converse with Asian American guests in the fields of art, literature, and stage. These interviews are designed to illuminate the diverse experiences and perspectives of Asian Americans as a means to build understanding and empathy for the community. With the assistance of producer Fengxue Zhang, who records and edits the podcast, our first season of fourteen podcasts, including David Henry

Hwang, playwright; Ping Chong, choreographer; and Adi Shankar, film producer and actor, among others, was made available on all listening platforms and we are currently deep into season two.

On March 20, the first day of spring in 2022, life begins to flow again for human beings as well as flowers, as vaccinations and masking have stemmed the epidemic. Dance facilitates communal healing and celebrates our literal abilities to physically connect and gather together once more. So many of my peers left the dance field over the last two years. But for me this was never an option.

Venues are beginning to open again around the nation and the world; our plans for touring are in full negotiations and our domestic performance season is underway. In May 2022 we performed a dance about immigration at our southern border titled *El Muro* / The Wall. It included live music by Martin Zarzar, formerly of the band *Pink Martini,* and an interactive set that exemplifies the concepts of physical, political, as well as emotional barriers. Fourteen hundred audience members attended our performances. In my role as choreographer-in-residence I make certain always that my work represents America's ever-changing voices, providing a platform for dialogue, diversity of all kinds, and global understanding through the art of dance.

In November 2022, my choreography will also celebrate Maya Lin, the Chinese American architect who designed the Vietnam Veterans Memorial, erected in 1982 in the National Mall of Washington, DC. The work will be inspired by Lin's unique Asian American architectural aesthetic and focus on minimalist shapes and lines that the dancers' bodies make as they move across stage—dancers as architecture.

And I will continue to spread the stories of our diverse and hyphenated America through lectures like the one I delivered about the history of Asian American dance pioneer Michio Itō in October 2021 at the annual Fulbright conference, in my capacity as the 2021 Selma Jeanne Cohen Dance Fulbright Lecturer.

And as if this rich career were not enough—oh, so much more than enough—for this migrating man, this Chino, this Mariposa from Santa Fe. The Smithsonian maintains a dedicated Butterfly Pavilion just across the National Mall at the Natural History Museum. Here in the heart of the cement city is a soft sanctuary for moths and caterpillars to make cocoons, to move through a chrysalis and safely emerge, spreading their wings to dance in the air, to take flight. And to ensure that those diverse butterflies will always find a home in this country. The Smithsonian has also given them center stage in its official Pollinator Garden: 11,000 square feet of plantings and habitats to showcase and nurture the butterfly life cycle. It is right smack dab on the National Mall and open twenty-four hours a day. Take a walk and visit them. Or better yet, do a little happy dance with them.

This Mariposa, this monarch is indeed home.

twenty-five DANCING FOR A PRESIDENTIAL ADMINISTRATION

I celebrate the thirtieth anniversary of the Dana Tai Soon Burgess Dance Company in 2022–2023. During the past decades I've been on a mission to be a bridge to other countries and cultures, to represent America as one who is enabled here to make a living as an artist, to take risks, and to grow and to thrive in a free and democratic society. To be a symbol, if you will, of its diversity and the opportunities that exist for people of all colors. I've done this by being an envoy of the United States Department of State, working in a semi-official capacity as a dance ambassador. My government has felt that my art is an asset in bridge building in other countries. And in this book, I've made observations based upon the firsthand experiences I have had while working to represent the United States around the world.

For all those reasons, I can't end this book without noting one of my most honored moments as a DC "insider": dancing at the White House by invitation of the Obama-Biden administration. Insofar as I have given my own life and art over to the belief in the power of art and dance as a bridge in the many states of this nation, as well as between nations of the world, I am a stakeholder in the health of our country's diplomacy. So, to be able to dance for the president and guests was a dream come true as I believe President Obama's two terms in office were empowering for Washington, DC, the country, and the arts.

The two terms of the Obama and Biden administration have afforded me the invitations and privileges to be present, up close to the power of presidential leadership to propagate good works. One of those opportunities included a reception Thursday evening, October 15, 2009. Vice President Joe Biden and his wife, Dr. Jill Biden, hosted an evening reception "to meet and to honor Leaders in the Arts, of the District of Columbia."

A week prior to the event, I received and accepted an e-mail invitation addressed to "Dana Tai Soon Burgess, Director of Dana Tai Soon Burgess Dance Co." In order to attend, I would need to comply with security protocols and thorough background vetting—something with which I was already pretty familiar, from my work with the State Department. There was a no-nonsense form attached to the fancy e-invitation. I filled out my name, birthdate, social security number, some other background particulars; I formally accepted the invitation, hit "send," and waited for word of final approval.

Within a day my security background approval was complete, and I received a second e-mail stipulating that I should bring standard identification, a license or passport, with me to the event destination: the official vice-presidential home located on the grounds of the United States Naval Observatory (USNO). The evening of the event, I entered through the security gates on Massachusetts Avenue NW and moved through a secondary security line outside the front door of the white nineteenth-century mansion at Number One Observatory Circle. This has been the official vice-presidential residence since the tenancy of Vice President and Mrs. Walter Mondale from 1977 to 1981. My name was ceremoniously checked off on the list of invitees.

I entered the residence. A young woman greeted me and ushered me in. "Please feel free to look around the first floor." The interior walls of the residence were then painted in a colonial naval blue that resembled the deepest blue-black ocean waters. Polished antique silver candle sticks were lined up along the length of a colonial-era antique walnut dining table. A stately framed silver mirror, straddled by mounted sconces completed the formal dining room. The overall effect was cinematic, a Disney *Beauty and the Beast* set. As a choreographer, looking over this august setting, I noted every item seemed potent, likely anthropomorphic, poised on a cue to any moment commence a waltz joined by animate cups and teapots, utensils, and silver service, I was certainly eager to dance with any one of them.

The cast of unusual characters had already made their appearances. Here were directors of the DC major museums, of theater companies, the Washington Ballet, and prominent local arts officials. In the course of the conversational waltz, I said hello to Lisa Gold, then director of the Washington Project for the Arts, now director of the Asian American Arts Alliance in NYC; Dorothy Pierce McSweeney, chair emeritus of the DC Commission on the Arts and Humanities; and Julian Raby, the director of both the Freer Gallery of Art and Arthur M. Sackler Gallery of the overarching powerful Smithsonian Institution. His scholarship is formidable, centered around Asian art. The occasion afforded us all the chance to cross-pollinate, too; many of us had not intersected in our careers, and we were now able to network and share goals in a way that was not a structured professional conference, with all those trappings and format, but instead, to mix and approach one another, share our missions, and make pivotal connections that informed our own goals.

Vice President and Dr. Biden entered the room and graciously welcomed the approximately forty guests. Dr. Biden then spoke to us about the importance of art and culture to America and to education, assuring our gathering that the administration acknowledged and appreciated art as a prominent and vital participant in the American conversation.

As the staff passed drinks and hors d'oeuvres among mingling guests, a social secretary asked if I might like to have an official photo of myself with the Bidens. Yes, I certainly would, thank you. I was ushered into an intimate side library that had been appropriated as receiving room where I sat with two other guests. A door opened, and I was asked my full name and then escorted into a room with one curved wall, painted in a mustard shade; the three windows were flanked by matching dupioni silk curtains. And there stood the Bidens. The vice president wore a formal black suit with an American flag lapel pin. He stretched out his hand and smiled warmly as he asked my name. "My name is Dana Tai Soon Burgess. It is an honor to meet you, sir."

"It's nice to have you here!" he said, following up with warm words of approbation for my work in DC and around the world, to teach and perform dance. I was impressed that he had taken the time to know so many facets about my work. Sure, he had been well briefed, but clearly he also had firsthand knowledge. I thanked him for his words and for having assembled such a warm and convivial gathering. The reception had struck just the right balance of formality and informality. He smiled broadly and then he then introduced me to Dr. Biden, who wore a black dress with diaphanous sleeves and three long rows of pearls. They placed me between the two of them and the camera flashed. I thanked them for their hospitality, and I took an extra moment to add, "Dr. Biden, I wish to thank you for your dedication to teaching." At the time Dr. Biden was teaching at a community college while she performed her official duties as SLOTUS, "Second Lady." She smiled and said, "Thank you for all you do for dance and dance education." A feeling that an American renaissance was being ushered in was in the air.

In early May 2013, during President Obama's second term in office, I got a call from Gautam Raghavan, then the associate director of public engagement for the White House. We had met in 2012, at an unveiling of several new acquisitions of Korean art at the Freer Gallery of Art of the Smithsonian Museum. He had since attended several of my dance company's performances.

Gautam and I shared some friendly back-and-forth. Soon he stated the purpose of his call. "Dana, might you come to the White House on May 28, to cap off the month of celebration of Asian American and Pacific Islander Heritage Month? We have in mind a themed program, 'AAPIs in the Arts.' Knowing your story and having seen your work on stage, I thought it would be great for you to speak about your artistic journey, and, if you would, to have a dance program—of your choice—as well and using members of your company." I was blown away. Deeply honored, I accepted, and bade him to go on with more logistical details as I pondered my best programmatic options.

He continued, "The event will be in the White House, in the early evening, in the East Room of the Executive Residence." There would be a small stage fifteen feet by twelve feet. There would be approximately one hundred guests, including high ranking military officials, diplomats, and arts luminaries from Los Angeles to New York and, of course, President Obama.

What an opportunity to connect dance with diplomacy! And I would bring a focus to the cultural contribution of people like me.

Gautam continued, "I must instruct you not to talk about this event." This was one of those "need to know basis" things you see in the espionage and political movies. Wow. Exciting. I learned something else in this call. Gautam read my mind, "The White House schedules events deliberately with very short lead times, for security reasons; all details are tightly held in secret, shared only with guests and presenters." Therefore, I would only have a short runway—about two weeks—to prepare my speech and to select and to rehearse a dance. Now THAT bit was unnerving. The call came to a convivial end.

OK. Well, I already knew which dance I would offer. I chose the short solo dance *Dariush*. I would cast Katia Norri. Her acute performance abilities would no doubt allow her to take a solo made for a large stage and reconfigure it to successfully work on a small stage. While I typically cast it with a male dancer, because *Dariush* is the name and story of a real male figure, this is a solo not bound by gender but by the ability to dance the story with a seasoned precision and attack.

That settled, I grappled with how to express in words—not dance— the deep connection I feel between my dance and my Korean American identity. I would have to prepare it well—no extemporizing—and to send a copy to Ellen Bernstein, the White House social secretary at the time.

On event day, Katia and I arrived early at the White House, around noon, to allow time for her to rehearse on stage. We moved through three security checks into halls flanked by more security, who stood guard representing each branch of the military. We were escorted down a long marble hall and up a marble staircase to the Executive Mansion and the East Room. While the elevated stage itself is necessarily small for this program, the East Room is the largest room in the White House. Most performances and the presentations of medals and honors occur here. This is also the room where both President Abraham Lincoln and President John F. Kennedy had lain in state after their assassinations, their deaths to be mourned by their public and loved ones. We wondered at the high ceilings lit by two huge crystal chandeliers. Large floor-to-ceiling windows surrounded by golden dupioni curtains amplify the natural light to the room.

Katia's stage was set in front of a large fireplace, in the magnificent heart of America's history. A White House residence butler entered and welcomed us with freshly baked chocolate chip cookies, milk, and coffee. We were too nervous to eat or drink at that moment. But this sensitive homey welcome put us at ease, fortifying our poise. Katia began a walk-through of the solo in silence on stage.

Bo, the First Family's Portuguese water dog, suddenly tore through the residence. A White House staff member went in pursuit, calling after Bo, who was having great fun ... and so it seemed, was the staffer. This appeared to be a regular dance. The staff member called out a breathless—and needless—and wonderful apology for the interruption as she continued to give call and chase. Katia and I broke into laughter, which calmed our jitters. The White House felt like a house filled with memories, love, vitality, and energy. And we would be making and leaving memories of our own here.

After about an hour, we were joined by Chinese American journalist and actress Lucy Ling, our emcee for the evening. Slim and tall in her sky-high heels, skirt, and streamlined matching beige blouse, she added to the luminous glow of the room. We introduced ourselves. Having seen Katia practicing her solo, she said, "Well you look very ready but I'm a little nervous; let's figure out how this evening is going to run." She walked away to coordinate with the White House technical crew, just then entering with audio and video equipment, cameras, lights, and a teleprompter. The sight of the teleprompter was a reminder to me that two days prior, the White House had asked for my speech so that they could read it, vet it, and load it into the viewer.

Soon best-selling novelist of the *Joy Luck Club* and a child of Chinese immigrants, Amy Tan, entered, her black bob shining and perfect. She and I were the evening's invited speakers. I had to pinch myself to believe that this was my life. I took in the setting and our hub of simultaneous preparations, blinking back tears of wonder, of awareness, of gratitude, of infinite appreciation of the occasion. Oh, how I thought about that little boy in Santa Fe, with his otherness and fears of the world. Now his people's contributions to the world of American arts and letters would be celebrated: an event to celebrate that former otherness as something now as oneness. I was enthralled. I was humbled. I was ready to share and to speak, to listen and to hear, my brothers and sisters, in this, the Peoples' House, the White House.

The sound man interrupted my reverie; he came up from behind and asked, smiling, "Do you want music? To run the dance with music? It's all set up." I eagerly said, "Oh, yes, wonderful! Thank you so much!" Katia, who had been figuring out the new blocking, then took her place on stage for her dress rehearsal. She danced *Dariush*, and when she completed the aerobic, gymnastic solo, she wasn't even out of breath. Something about the air and energy in that space gave her lift and extraordinary shaping.

Next, I rehearsed reading my speech on the teleprompter. President Obama's ties to Hawaii, and my own ties to that state, gave me an entrée to presume to speak directly to that shared deep family and personal connection. My remarks would open by sharing that with those gathered here with the president, to speak about my family's experiences in Hawaii and the relationship of immigrant family histories to artmaking. The president's brother-in-law, Konrad Ng, would be there as the director of the APA (Asian-Pacific American) Institute of the Smithsonian. So would Tina Tchen, the chief of staff to First Lady Michelle Obama. There would be numerous members of the House and Senate, as well. This was such an opportunity to demonstrate and express what the Asian American experience was for me, and to take in the sharing of others.

I had to get this right, and I had to cope with that teleprompter.

At first the words whizzed by on the screen at a harrowing speed. A solicitous technician said, "Oops, too fast? Try this." The speech was reloaded, the speed slowed until I was finally comfortable. My nerves and Katia's were now calmed. It was time to enjoy this moment in our lives. The stage was set and none too soon, the guests began to arrive!

Katia and I went to the Green Room (this was, in fact, a literal as well as artistic "green room"). Just then, President Obama himself entered! And why not? This was his house. He graciously introduced himself to each of us with the broadest smile and with individual focus. What a handsome grace he embodied, but also what humanity. President

Obama joked with Katia as she did sit-ups and stretches, feigning that he could never keep up with her in a contest. The banter, empathetic, spontaneous, and self-deprecating, loosened her and warmed her. The banter was so authentic. He knew how intimidating this setting could be, especially for performers, and he set us both at ease.

Gautam entered and ushered the president and the presenters to the Blue Room to prepare for official state photos. Amy Tan and I were talking when a staffer came up to me and said, "Since your husband is here, might we invite him to be in the photo?" I eagerly said, "Yes! I would like that so much, thank you." The staffer left and quickly ushered in Jameson who had been mingling with the other guests in the lobby outside the East Room. And here was that "need to know basis" discretion again: the staff had a security photo of each guest and the reason for their attendance. They recognized him without me having described him. He was escorted into the Blue Room and together we were ushered into yet another room. And there we would see President Obama. The president maneuvered us familiarly, placing one of us on either side of him. He hugged our shoulders with undisputable mirth and authentic warmth as we posed for the official photo. Jameson and I beamed. In the moments that followed, we each thanked him for all he was doing for the country and for the arts. Our photo with President Obama sits on an antique Korean trunk in our dining room that is topped by family photos. How much it means to us to have our marriage acknowledged, welcomed, and supported at the highest levels of this country.

We left President Obama and found our seats in the front row. Soon Lucy Ling introduced me. I spoke about the diversity of our American cultural tapestry, specifically how "art reflects our country's rich cultural mix and histories and interlaces with our family stories and personal identities. American stories can be the inspiration for the great art that moves us." I spoke about my Korean family's immigration to Hawaii and how my ancestors' lives and stories still inspire. I spoke of dance as a universal language, one that bridges across borders, that invites and creates friendships. Dance is hands and arms and hearts, all uniquely suited to reach outward and toward other people.

I then introduced Katia in the solo *Dariush*. Katia took the stage and performed flawlessly. Jameson, her husband Diego Norri, and I had watched Katia dance beautifully from the same row as the president of the United States. When she was done, we all applauded loudly. Following her bows and the evening's program, Katia and Diego also posed for a photo with President Obama. Diego is originally from Argentina and had just become a US citizen. Perhaps Diego and Katia encapsulate the ongoing East-West dialogue. Recently they expanded their family with the arrival of their daughter Emma who is, as we would say in Santa Fe, China Latina. After the event, I called my mom to relay the good news. Protocols had prevented me from doing so in advance. She was ecstatic and said, "I'm proud to be an American."

In such indelible memories, and such transformative encounters and moments, I see a glimmer of renewed hope for America, and I truly hope Emma grows up in an egalitarian America that embraces diversity and open borders and bridges.

I like to think that Emma, like me, is the next generation of the monarch butterfly.

"Tati" Maria Del Carmen Valle Riestra and company members in *Hyphen*, Washington, DC, 2008. Photo by Mary Noble Ours, Collection of Dana Tai Soon Burgess Dance Company.

Dana Tai Soon Burgess Dance Company in *Hyphen*, stage projection by Nam June Paik, Washington, DC, 2009. Photo by Mary Noble Ours, Collection of Dana Tai Soon Burgess Dance Company.

Dana Tai Soon Burgess Dance Company rehearsing *America's Cloud* at the Corcoran Gallery of Art, sculpture by Spencer Finch, Washington, DC, 2010. Private Collection of Dana Tai Soon Burgess.

Kelly Moss Southall, Ricardo Alvarez, Miyako Nitadori in *Charlie Chan and the Mystery of Love*, Dance Place, Washington, DC, 2010. Photo by Lawrence Luk, Collection of the Dana Tai Soon Burgess Dance Company.

Kelly Moss Southall, Sarah Halzack in *Revenant Elegy* for the National Gallery of Art, Washington, DC, 2013. Photo by Jeff Watts, Collection of Dana Tai Soon Burgess Dance Company.

Kelly Moss Southall, Sarah Halzack, Ben Sanders rehearsing
Picasso Dances at the Kreeger Museum, Washington. DC, 2015.
Photo by Laura MacDonald.

Christin Arthur, Dana Tai Soon Burgess Dance Company in company class at
the National Portrait Gallery, Washington, DC, 2017. Photo by Matailong Du/
Duma, Private Collection of Dana Tai Soon Burgess.

Christin Arthur, Dana Tai Soon Burgess, Ryan Carlough, Kelly Moss Southall, Christine Doyle in company rehearsal, Washington, DC, 2017. Photo by Matailong Du/Duma, Private Collection of Dana Tai Soon Burgess.

right Dana Tai Soon Burgess Dance Company in *The Foster Suite: The Remains of Loss and Longing*, The Smithsonian's National Portrait Gallery, Washington, DC, 2016. Photo by Jeff Malet, Collection of Dana Tai Soon Burgess Dance Company.

below Dana Tai Soon Burgess Dance Company in *The Foster Suite: The Remains of Loss and Longing*, The Smithsonian's National Portrait Gallery, Washington, DC, 2016. Photo by Jeff Malet, Collection of Dana Tai Soon Burgess Dance Company Collection of Dana Tai Soon Burgess Dance Company.

Christine Doyle, Dana Tai Soon Burgess Dance Company in *Margin*, The Smithsonian's National Portrait Gallery, Washington, DC, 2016. Photo by Jeff Malet, Collection of Dana Tai Soon Burgess Dance Company.

Christin Arthur, Alvaro Palau in *Confluence*, Washington, DC, 2014.
Photo by Jeff Watts, Collection of Dana Tai Soon Burgess Dance Company.

Ryan Carlough, Kelly Moss Southall, Felipe Oyarzun Moltedo in *After 1001 Nights*, Washington, DC, 2017. Photo by Jeff Watts, Collection of Dana Tai Soon Burgess Dance Company.

Ryan Carlough, Kelly Moss Southall, Felipe Oyarzun Moltedo, Dana Tai Soon Burgess Dance Company in *After 1001 Nights*, Washington, DC, 2017. Photo by Jeff Malet, Collection of Dana Tai Soon Burgess Dance Company.

Ben Sanders, Sidney Hampton in *Silhouettes*, The Smithsonian's National Portrait Gallery, Washington, DC, 2018. Photo by Jeff Malet, Collection of Dana Tai Soon Burgess Dance Company.

Christin Arthur, Joan Ayap, Christine Doyle in *Silhouettes*, McEvoy Auditorium at The Smithsonian's National Portrait Gallery, Washington, DC, 2018. Photo by Jeff Malet, Collection of Dana Tai Soon Burgess Dance Company.

Dana Tai Soon Burgess Dance Company in *El Muro / The Wall*, The Smithsonian's National Portrait Gallery, Washington, DC, 2022. Photo by Jeff Malet.

Dana Tai Soon Burgess Dance Company in *I am Vertical*, Washington, DC, 2017. Photo by Jeff Malet, Collection of Dana Tai Soon Burgess Dance Company.

Sidney Hampton, Jaya Bond, Christin Arthur in *A Tribute to Marian Anderson*, McEvoy Auditorium at The Smithsonian's National Portrait Gallery, Washington, DC, 2019. Photo by Jeff Malet, Collection of Dana Tai Soon Burgess Dance Company.

Felipe Oyarzun Moltedo, Joan Ayap in *I am Vertical*,
Washington, DC, 2017. Photo by Jeff Malet, Collection
of Dana Tai Soon Burgess Dance Company.

Joan Ayap, Felipe Oyarzun Moltedo in *A Tribute to Marian Anderson*,
McEvoy Auditorium at The Smithsonian's National Portrait Gallery,
Washington, DC, 2019. Photo by Jeff Malet, Collection of Dana Tai Soon
Burgess Dance Company.

Dana Tai Soon Burgess, President Barack Obama, Jameson Freeman at the White House, 2013, official White House photograph.

Dana Tai Soon Burgess, Anna Kang Burgess, Jameson Freeman, Santa Fe, NM, 2018. Private collection of Dana Tai Soon Burgess.

epilogue I STILL WAIT FOR BUTTERFLIES

A solo dancer can be a sliver of lightening, a streaking comet, the smoldering slow collapsing unto itself of pure energy, an embodiment of the formation of a star. Duets can be radiant suns, encircling each other. Ensembles are entire galaxies. Dance is forward propulsive: it inherently embodies optimism and potential. It toys with gravity. It moves toward connection. Connection is love.

After decades of being the solo dancer in my own private life, I at last found a permanent duet partner.

I am married to Jameson Freeman. We met on a sidewalk outside a restaurant in Washington, DC, on February 12, 2012. I was heading off to celebrate the birthday of a dear friend and dancer, Connie Fink. I dropped off Connie and her festive crew at the front doors of a restaurant, found a parking space, and walked back to rejoin them. I noticed a man standing nearby. He seemed to have a halo, a nimbus reflecting off his golden blonde hair, his warm eyes shone a pale jade. This is what Kindness looks like, I thought. We were drawn together inevitably as heavenly particles spinning in the universe. I motioned to my friends, "You go on, I'll be there shortly." We introduced ourselves, exchanged phone numbers, and within two days were on our first date—February 14, Valentine's Day. We married three years later.

Jameson writes plays, produces art projects, and is a longtime yogi, who once lived on an ashram in India. In addition to his writing, he conducts healing sound baths for private clients. These are guided meditations that focus on aligning the body's energies through the absorption of sound waves he produces by playing antique "sound bowls" and bells from Tibet. The bowls are instruments made specifically for this holistic practice.

On our first date, Jameson told me that from the age of nine through thirteen, he had been a dancer at the prestigious Connecticut-based Nutmeg Ballet Academy. He shared recollections of dancing the role of Fritz in their *Nutcracker* productions. We found that we shared many

of the same acquaintances, friends, and experiences. We had been circling each other like butterflies for years but had never met. We quickly
became exclusive and devoted to each other. His wholesomeness—a
rare quality—and empathetic soulfulness have nurtured a home for
me in the world.

In 2011, we traveled together to Southeast Asia, Cambodia, and
Thailand when I was invited to speak at a US Patent Agency meeting about trademarking. I addressed traditional dancers and artisans
about strategies for maintaining an artist economy in the midst of
encroaching cheaper, lower quality products imported from China.
Chinese business investors were pouring wealth into the city of Siem
Reap, where Angkor Wat is located. Here, tourist-focused businesses,
including major hotels and shops were suddenly under new Chinese
management and under relentless pressures to assimilate. They were
being pressured to let go of local crafts and traditional dance and music
entertainment in favor of less expensive, inauthentic Chinese appropriations. This incursion was displacing centuries' old traditions and
threatened the livelihoods of self-sufficient Cambodian artists.

After my talk, I led strategy sessions with community artists, moder-
ating their eager discussions about how best to educate tourists about
the value of their authentic goods and performance arts. I worked with
them toward developing their own inroads in the trademarking and
protection of traditional art forms.

The day after the conference concluded, Jameson and I toured the
murky Mekong River by boat. We disembarked our sojourn to visit the
Preah Norodom Sihanouk-Angkor Museum. Here mammoth stone
Buddhas from the Khmer Empire (802–1431 CE) are on display. The
next morning we saw the sunrise at 5 a.m. over Angkor Wat. We held
hands, connected, in love, reverence, and wonder as we explored.

At 11:00 a.m., at the very top of the main tower of Angkor Wat,
Jameson squeezed my hand, drew my attention, and asked me to marry
him. In front of us a giant Khmer Buddha—a huge version of the
miniature Buddha I had next to my bedside for decades—beamed in
approval and blessing. Having grown up in a time when gay marriage
and equal rights for gay people did not exist, the prospect of our being

legally married was profoundly meaningful. I openly wept with tears of joy.

Jameson and I were married on September 23, 2015, at 2:22 p.m., at the county clerk's office in Santa Fe just off the Plaza on Grant Avenue. Serendipity officiated: the clerk who stamped our certificate of marriage was a former karate student with whom I had studied at Makio's dojo decades prior. Jameson and I enjoyed a postnuptial party at the local Spanish Colonial Museum attended by family, friends, and even my University of New Mexico dance professors.

Jameson is supportive, kind, communicative, and, best of all, he understands my anxieties. As I move closer to showtime I'm always pensive and he understands that. Our home is a secure place for me to dream, like the Gamut. I have a husband who unconditionally embraces my history and my artmaking, and our future.

Time passes, and it is June 2021. Jameson and I have flown to Santa Fe and are visiting my ninety-year-old mother. Mom lives in a small adobe home on the outskirts of the city.

Whenever we are there, Jameson and I sit with her for long daily stretches on her sun-bleached *banco* (wooden bench) on the patio. On her lap is Dashi, her shih tzu. They are inseparable. Jameson and I gave her Dashi on the first Christmas after my father passed away. He was a rescue, who at the age of three, had been abandoned by a family living in Albuquerque. Jameson and I named him Dashi or "great virtue" in Mandarin. Both Mom and Dashi had been traumatized by their recent abandonments; they have moved together into their present peace of mutual healing. Dashi leans into my mom, she hugs him tightly, and she says, "Dashi has wise eyes like your father's." She repeats this to us tenderly on each visit and believes Dashi was sent to her by my father as her guardian. Dashi looks like the animated, life-size version of the little bronze Lion Dog my father gave me as a child from the Gamut.

There is just enough space for all four of us on the banco. Drenched in sunshine, we await the arrival of butterflies. We have an unencumbered view of the stage, mom's garden: sturdy stalks of beaming sunflowers, brazen hollyhocks, and numerous intoxicating fragrant bushes of wild rose. We catch our breath as the first spellbinding performer makes its entrance. A bright orange-and-black butterfly flutters over the adobe garden walls, a dazzling flash of apricot outlined in black against a terracotta backdrop. The monarch commences its spectacular circling, flirting and greeting, skipping from flower to flower. It clearly loves being exactly who it is. The dance of the monarch reminds me once more to enjoy the beauty of life. And then, answering to a cue we cannot hear, it flies spectacularly high above us, hovers a moment, as if to bow, and eventually floats out of sight.

Flanked by my past and future, memories dart in accompaniment to this performer: images of being a toddler covered with demonstrative monarchs in Carmel Valley, of my mother weaving at her loom, of my father delivering me to my first karate class, of my secretly watching modern dance classes at the University of New Mexico, the stages upon which I've danced from Cairo to Cusco, works I have choreographed, and the dancers I have met around the world.

The journey has been so satisfying and yet there is so much more on the horizon. New collaborations, new inspirations, and even new museum residencies. I reach over to stroke Dashi on the head, including Dad in my reveries.

I recently read that the wings of certain butterflies are actually clear and that the colors we see are the effects of light as it reflects on the tiny scales covering the translucent surfaces. These reflections of light register each of our unique vantage points and visions, projections of individual beauty.

The verb *esperar* in Spanish means both to wait and to hope. Dance has allowed me to externalize my internal world, to clarify and form my identity. Dance has swept me along an odyssey to kinesthetically interpret and express my reactions to the stages of life, to find peace and joy within myself as a bullied outsider, a gay Korean American choreographer from Santa Fe, New Mexico. I embrace the mystery of what is to come toward me artistically in the next decades. "*Yo espero*"— I hope—as I make the next dances and dive into new projects, I fervently hope to assist the upcoming generations of dance artists to believe in their own footsteps. I intend to urge them all along the way to stop and behold the wisdom of butterflies.